Amateur film

MANCHESTER 1824
Manchester University Press

STUDIES IN POPULAR CULTURE

General editor: Professor Jeffrey Richards

Already published in this series

Christmas in nineteenth-century England   Neil Armstrong

Healthy living in the Alps: the origins of winter tourism in Switzerland, 1860–1914   Susan Barton

Working-class organisations and popular tourism, 1840–1970   Susan Barton

Leisure, citizenship and working-class men in Britain, 1850–1945   Brad Beaven

The British Consumer Co-operative Movement and film, 1890s–1960s   Alan George Burton

British railway enthusiasm   Ian Carter

Railways and culture in Britain   Ian Carter

Darts in England, 1900–39: a social history   Patrick Chaplin

Relocating Britishness   Stephen Caunce, Ewa Mazierska, Susan Sydney-Smith and John Walton (eds)

Holiday camps in twentieth-century Britain: packaging pleasure
Sandra Trudgen Dawson

History on British television: constructing nation, nationality and collective memory   Robert Dillon

The food companions: cinema and consumption in wartime Britain, 1939–45
Richard Farmer

Songs of protest, songs of love: popular ballads in eighteenth-century Britain   Robin Ganev

The BBC and national identity in Britain, 1922–53   Thomas Hajkowski

From silent screen to multi-screen: a history of cinema exhibition in Britain since 1896   Stuart Hanson

Smoking in British popular culture, 1800–2000   Matthew Hilton

Juke box Britain: Americanisation and youth culture, 1945–60   Adrian Horn

Popular culture in London, c. 1890–1918: the transformation of entertainment   Andrew Horrall

Horseracing and the British, 1919–39   Mike Huggins

Popular culture and working-class taste in Britain, 1930–39: a round of cheap diversions?   Robert James

Amateur operatics: a social and cultural history   John Lowerson

Scotland and the music hall, 1850–1914   Paul Maloney

Films and British national identity: from Dickens to *Dad's Army*
Jeffrey Richards

Cinema and radio in Britain and America, 1920–1960   Jeffrey Richards

Looking North: Northern England and the national imagination
Dave Russell

The British seaside holiday: holidays and resorts in the twentieth century   John K. Walton

Amateur film
Meaning and practice, 1927–1977

HEATHER NORRIS NICHOLSON

Manchester University Press
Manchester and New York

distributed exclusively in the USA by Palgrave Macmillan

Copyright © Heather Norris Nicholson 2012

The right of Heather Norris Nicholson to be identified as the author of this work has been asserted by her in accordance with the Copyright, Designs and Patents Act 1988.

Published by Manchester University Press
Oxford Road, Manchester M13 9NR, UK
and Room 400, 175 Fifth Avenue, New York, NY 10010, USA
www.manchesteruniversitypress.co.uk

Distributed exclusively in the USA by
Palgrave Macmillan, 175 Fifth Avenue, New York,
NY 10010, USA

Distributed exclusively in Canada by
UBC Press, University of British Columbia, 2029 West Mall,
Vancouver, BC, Canada V6T 1Z2

British Library Cataloguing-in-Publication Data
A catalogue record for this book is available from the British Library

Library of Congress Cataloging-in-Publication Data applied for

ISBN 978 0 7190 7773 9 hardback

First published 2012

The publisher has no responsibility for the persistence or accuracy of URLs for any external or third-party internet websites referred to in this book, and does not guarantee that any content on such websites is, or will remain, accurate or appropriate.

Typeset in Adobe Garamond with Gill Sans display by
Koinonia, Manchester
Printed in Great Britain
by CPI Antony Rowe Ltd, Chippenham, Wiltshire

STUDIES IN POPULAR CULTURE

There has in recent years been an explosion of interest in culture and cultural studies. The impetus has come from two directions and out of two different traditions. On the one hand, cultural history has grown out of social history to become a distinct and identifiable school of historical investigation. On the other hand, cultural studies has grown out of English literature and has concerned itself to a large extent with contemporary issues. Nevertheless, there is a shared project, its aim, to elucidate the meanings and values implicit and explicit in the art, literature, learning, institutions and everyday behaviour within a given society. Both the cultural historian and the cultural studies scholar seek to explore the ways in which a culture is imagined, represented and received; how it interacts with social processes; how it contributes to individual and collective identities and world views, to stability and change, to social, political and economic activities and programmes. This series aims to provide an arena for the cross-fertilisation of the discipline, so that the work of the cultural historian can take advantage of the most useful and illuminating of the theoretical developments and the cultural studies scholars can extend the purely historical underpinnings of their investigations. The ultimate objective of the series is to provide a range of books which will explain in a readable and accessible way where we are now socially and culturally and how we got to where we are. This should enable people to be better informed, promote an interdisciplinary approach to cultural issues and encourage deeper thought about the issues, attitudes and institutions of popular culture.

Jeffrey Richards

Contents

	List of illustrations	*page* viii
	General editor's foreword	ix
	Preface and acknowledgements	xi
	List of abbreviations	xiv
	Film title conventions	xv
1	Making space for a neglected visual history	1
2	The amateur club scene	28
3	The rise of a hobby press	62
4	Family life as fact and fiction	92
5	Local lives and communities	118
6	Gazing at other people working	143
7	An indispensable travel accessory	175
8	Socially engaged filmmaking	208
9	Moving pictures, moving on	238
	Bibliography	251
	Index	273

List of illustrations

1 *Flag Day Fancy* (Dir. Mid-Cheshire Amateur Cinematography Society, c.1937) — 41
2 *Club Trophies, Southport Movie Makers, 1951–2010* — 47
3 [*Sykes Family Holiday in The Lakes*] (Dir. Peter Sykes, 1949) — 96
4 *Street Games We Used to Play* (Dir. Sam Hanna, *1957–59) — 100
5 [*Trains, Carnival and Dog Show*] (Dir. Harold and Sidney Preston, 1934) — 125
6 *The Burnley School of Nursing* (Dir. Sam Hanna, 1960–63) — 167
7 *Tour in the USSR, Part 2* (Dir. Horace Wilfred Taylor, 1932) — 196
8 *The Changing Face of Salford. Part 1, Life in the Slums* (Dir. Michael Goodger, 1968–69) — 218
9 [*Ban the Bomb*] (Dir. Tony Iddon, 1964) — 222

General editor's foreword

The philosopher George Santayana said of England that 'it is the paradise of individualists, eccentrics, heresy, anomalies, hobbies and humours'. This series has already published volumes devoted to two long-standing and cherished hobbies: steam railway enthusiasm and amateur operatics. Heather Norris Nicholson adds to that literature with this exhaustively researched and judiciously analysed study of amateur filmmaking.

Alongside the flourishing commercial cinema, there has been a long and honourable tradition of amateur filmmaking in Britain. Thanks to this hobby, a rich store of visual imagery exists to add a vivid extra dimension to our understanding of recent history: the people, the buildings, the public and private events, the ways of life and work. We can still see in these films a vanished world of cotton mills, coal mines, steam railways, air shows, funfairs, speedway, Whit Walks, Rose Queen coronations, May Day celebrations and Armistice Day commemorations, the world of the day before yesterday.

Drawing on the films themselves, interviews with the filmmakers and analysis of club records and specialist publications, Heather Norris Nicholson explores with insight, sympathy and skill almost every aspect of the hobby. She explains the significance of the local cine clubs, charts the rise of the specialist hobby press, analyses the ways in which family, community, working life, travel and holidays were constructed and depicted. She assesses the films devoted to social issues of the past and looks to the future of amateur filmmaking in the era of new technology. Several continuing themes run through the book, among them the question of how and why people got involved in the hobby, the relationship between amateur and professional filmmaking, the responses to changes in technology, the role of women both before and behind the camera.

She is fully aware of and engages with issues of construction, selection, perception and mediation which surround all kinds of filmmaking. But what shines through this book on page after page is the dedication, passion, ingenuity and creativity of the amateur filmmakers. This volume stands as a deserved tribute to them all.

Jeffrey Richards

Preface and acknowledgements

Until the later 1990s, academic interest in amateur film in Britain was scattered across disciplines, and mainly outside the core areas of film history scholarship. By contrast, many film archivists knew their collections held significant amounts of fascinating amateur footage and broadcasters were also long-established users of amateur material in different kinds of popular history programming. Archival staff supported researchers who travelled and talked about their film holdings, just as changing public funding regimes and agenda were intensifying the demands to make archival collections more visible and more accessible to ever more diverse audiences. Amateur film as a serious topic of study, primarily as a source of evidential visual history, thus attracted a small following of enthusiasts who supported each other's fledging events and projects. Similar strategies based on a combination of pragmatism and passion created close liaison within the archival community. The present status of amateur film studies is undeniably a product in part of the determined advocacy and commitment that brings archival and academic circles into a distinctive mutually strengthening relationship, enhanced by those who inhabit both academic and archivists' roles.

Who could have anticipated the international explosion of interest and scholarship in amateur film? Conferences at national and international level have proliferated in the past five years, in turn attracting younger researchers to read once there were some published titles on reading lists, to tackle research projects and to bring their own expertise and training into different settings in and beyond academia. Both established and emerging filmmakers have found fresh creative opportunities in working with found footage as well as material of direct personal significance. The interdisciplinary appeal of cine imagery has been significant in the breadth of interest and applied contexts into which archive amateur footage has reached out to different audiences and offered new approaches and insights. So too has been the frequently captivating nature of the material itself, as varied audiences experience the visual magic of watching fragments of past actions captured unofficially on cine-camera. Encounters with senior filmmakers, involved in the development of amateur activity either independently or as long-time members of the amateur club scene, have added compelling human detail, quirky recollections and collectively the weight of individual perspectives about past practices. An attempt at pulling different strands of interest together was now needed.

A regional setting made intellectual and practical sense. Film holdings at the North West Film Archive offered variety and regional distinctiveness as well as an excellent basis for broader comparisons. Some of Britain's earliest amateur practitioners had been active in the region, there was scope to tap into a still vibrant culture of filmmaking, and many historical details were available about different kinds of amateur cine practice. A fifty-year survey using the North West as its core without limiting the opportunities to explore further afield seemed an ideal mix. The year 1927 emerged as an obvious starting date, as shown by evidence discussed in later chapters for specific regional productions, film publications and club foundation, whilst also being important for cine activity more broadly. The year 1977 was more indicative of changing circumstances, and attention extends beyond both dates to set amateur practice within a wider understanding of social and cultural change.

Tapping into the riches of amateur footage, listening to the voices of its practitioners and those of their predecessors recorded in the hobby press, and encountering those whose daily work with archival collections safeguards amateur material have underpinned the writing of this text. Its pages testify to the hidden archive work of preservation and repairing, shot-listing, cataloguing and making accessible that characterises daily routines as at the North West Film Archive where past and present staff have given me their time and knowledge unstintingly. Such activities depend upon the often thankless grind of administration, and prodigious thanks are therefore due to Marion Hewitt, for her patience and support, as well as making staff time and resources available. Thanks are also due to other archivists in the UK for their help with queries; inestimable encouragement has come from archivists in North America too. I thank them all for their inspirational dedication, professional insights and energy.

Significant conferences and workshops have been key moments in furthering critical scholarship and discussion. Thanks are due to the organisers for their breath of vision and the creative dialogues fostered by genuine interdisciplinarity, as well as to those who have accommodated amateur film within imaginative programming of numerous smaller multidisciplinary events.

Generous co-operation has come from within today's amateur filmmaking circles and also from second- and third-generation descendants of former filmmakers. I express sincere thanks to all those who have contributed memories, loaned films and other recordings, articles, photographs, and answered questions via emails, letters, telephone, and during interviews.

Conversations with numerous scholars and creative practitioners, near and far, have prompted my thinking in different ways. Invitations, assistance with funding, feedback and the sense of being in and able to look beyond the 'home movies bubble' have been a source of strength. So too has been the championing of this activity by former work colleagues, particularly Melanie Tebbutt. Others in North America, mainland Europe and closer to home have shared critical thinking too. I apologise for omissions that are unintentional but perhaps inevitable given this book's genesis and the occasional serendipitous nature of encounters. I also acknowledge having had the privilege to share enthusiasms and good company with now departed influential film archivists, Marianne Gomes, Michelle Morisset, Sam Kula and William Farrell, and I also pay tribute to the research on home movie-making by the late Alan Katelle.

Discussion and questioning with students, past and present, at Manchester Metropolitan University and elsewhere have been refreshingly candid. Handling scepticism and doubt has assisted with rigour, clarity and readability. Staff at Manchester University Press too have been wonderfully patient as this work evolved. Thanks are owed to my readers for their close scrutiny and comments.

Above all, I offer thanks to my family, in particular to my mother for her questioning, proof-reading and encouragement, to my husband Steve, and to our daughters, Katya and Vikka, for their forbearance and coping strategies during my times of absence and adventuring in distant places. Finally, I thank the many named and anonymous people captured on or responsible for the films discussed in this book.

Heather Norris Nicholson,
February 2012

List of abbreviations

ACA	Amateur Cinematographers' Association
ACW	*Amateur Cine World*
AF	*Amateur Films*
APC	*Amateur Photographer and Cinematographer*
APP	*Amateur Photographer and Photography*
ARP	Air Raid Precaution
BACA	British Amateur Cinematographers' Association
BFI	British Film Institute
CCTV	Closed circuit television
CND	Campaign for Nuclear Disarmament
DHTA	Dartington Hall Trust Archives
EAFA	East Anglian Film Archive
FCS	Federation of Cinematograph Societies
GPO	General Post Office
HMHT	*Home Movies and Home Talkies*
IAC	Institute of Amateur Cinematographers
MM	*Movie Maker*
MO	Mass Observation
NBTS	National Blood Transfusion Service
NWFA	North West Film Archive
SAFF	Scottish Amateur Film Festival
UNICA	Union internationale du cinéma d'amateur
VHS	Video Home System
YFA	Yorkshire Film Archive

Film title conventions

Title details observe archival practice in cataloguing, as set out by FIAF (International Federation of Film Archives). [ ] indicate an attributed title for cataloguing purposes, where there is no evidence of a prior existing title; * or hyphenated dates indicates the approximate date of the filmstock, and may represent a date earlier than when the film was made.

Making space for a neglected visual history

'I've always felt that the amateur enthusiast has been an important figure in the cinematic history of this country. He has helped in the appreciation of the unusual film – film societies and cine clubs were the first to encourage British documentaries – and has always striven to raise standards and improve taste.'[1] In May 1955, *Amateur Cine World* (*ACW*) celebrated twenty-one years of amateur filmmaking in Britain. Directors, critics, actors and other film professionals praised how the amateur film movement had contributed to the development of national cinema. 'Amateur filmmakers are a stimulus to the professional film industry, and provide a growing audience for whatever we endeavour to do that is mature, imaginative and experimental', enthused John and Roy Boulting, the prolific twin-brother director-producer team and founders of Charter Films (1937).[2] Others acknowledged the close association between amateur and professional activity even as their very language hinted at difficulties within that same relationship: Sir Laurence Olivier observed that 'The professional cinema has good cause to be grateful to its amateur cousins, who do so much to stimulate and keep alive technical and artistic interest in the craft of filmmaking'.[3]

Paul Rotha, then Head of Documentaries at the BBC, spoke of his respect for amateur activity and acknowledged the 'number of distinguished filmmakers today who began with their own 16mm equipment'. Rotha foresaw the popular broadcast potential of amateur footage: 'And now television has come along to widen the chance of showing such films.'[4] Dilys Powell, then film critic for *The Sunday Times*, highlighted wider benefits of amateur interest: 'Not only have some remarkable professional talents emerged from the amateur movement; the amateurs contribute also a truly appreciative, because truly critical, audience for the commercial cinema.'[5] It would have been editorial suicide for *ACW* not to publish this fulsome praise. Such endorsement was splendid material for marketing the monthly magazine in a fast expanding and increasingly competitive area of specialist literature. These comments were also a welcome boost to the hobby's reputation in a rapidly changing postwar society.

During 2007, Britain's amateur film movement celebrated another anniversary, this time the seventy-fifth birthday of the Institute of Amateur Cinematographers (IAC).[6] Founded in 1932, this umbrella organisation supported the fledgling societies and clubs that were being set up by and for amateur enthusiasts.[7] The IAC has weathered profound social, cultural and technical changes, including the advent of hitherto unimaginable ways of being able to make, edit and circulate self-made ('user-generated' in contemporary terms) imagery. The organisation's survival is testimony to the initial fervour and continuing dedication to practical production work outside professional circles as shown by the celebratory and forward-looking events during 2007.[8]

Arguably, the fifty-two years spanned by these two anniversaries and their founding dates chart the main phases of growth and change within Britain's amateur cinema. They span the periods of pioneering interest and activity by enthusiasts with sufficient time and money to indulge a costly hobby; the postwar democratisation of cine photography as film and equipment became more available; and then, the evolutionary adjustment to successive innovations. Technological and societal shifts deterred some hobbyists but attracted the involvement of others. Innovations moved the most dedicated cinephiles into new areas of visualisation using videos, camcorders and a succession of changing opportunities for home-editing, presentation, distribution and storage. The IAC's celebratory year attested to how the spirit of amateur cinema lives on, despite the impact of new visual technologies and means to digitise and rework media for personal consumption. Indeed, non-professional interest in visual moving technologies, notwithstanding the change to different formats and the name change from film to video evident among many organised societies, is as vibrant as it ever was, even if the basic paraphernalia has changed beyond recognition.

The public celebration of IAC's continuing dynamism parallels more widespread persistence of the personal desire to produce and share moving imagery. Changing technologies, patterns of consumption and the increasing ubiquity of mimetic processes seem to intensify the visual aspects of memory-shaping and self-identification. Today's children grow up literally on camera. CCTV equipment documents their public presence. They exchange pictures via mobile phones and social networks. Family camera-users record childhood moments and rites of passage at home, school and elsewhere that construct visual life-stories and memories from birth onwards.[9] Today's unprecedented familiarity with being 'on camera' in voluntary and involuntary ways links to private uses of portable recording equipment that stretch back to home videos and the cine-cameras of the past.[10]

This attempt to examine people's fascination with sharing visual stories about themselves and others sets amateur film history alongside the diverse histories of cinema, media, social change and modernity. The evolutionary twists and turns, from early hand-cranked camera equipment and portable screen to current visualisation processes are a remarkable expression of sustained interest over time. Undoubtedly, amateur film played a key role in the journey towards 'life as representation' and our current consumption of moving pictures. This book explores five key decades of that journey from the rise of interest, first among Britain's wealthy, and then, as a more widespread leisure activity, to its retrenchment in the 1970s under the impact of video cameras.

A hobby takes shape

Notwithstanding the anniversary tributes, cited earlier, the origins of amateur cinema may be traced back to the very earliest experimentation in moving imagery.[11] Rival photographic companies in Europe and the United States developed products suitable for the home market from the late nineteenth century onwards.[12] Some early attempts were promoted as novelty toys before 1910 although more sophisticated equipment and published manuals were also aimed at adult audiences.[13] Advertising targeted people who wished to watch commercially produced films at home as well as those who were interested in screening their own motion pictures. Manufacturers brought out a succession of innovations that each sought to reduce the overall costs of camera, projector and film. Birt Acre's Birtac camera, dating from c.1898, was one of several devices that used 17.5mm rather than 35mm film and combined a camera with a projector.[14] The availability of cellulose-based 'safety' film from Pathé and Eastman Kodak in c.1911 helped to replace unstable nitrate-based products and boosted the appeal of home-based moving image shows.[15] As companies continued to explore ways of improving the safety and performance of products aimed at the amateur, a number of motion picture cameras had short-lived success before 1920.[16]

The early 1920s saw the real breakthrough in marketing equipment that appealed to the early enthusiast who was interested in making as well as showing commercially made films at home. Pathé brought out an amateur gauge 35mm film in 1922, and the following year Eastman Kodak launched a 16mm film gauge plus a lightweight, handheld Cine-Kodak camera and the Kodascope projector. Bell & Howell, among other companies, followed Kodak in making available equipment for 16mm, but manufacturers companies recognised that the profitable expansion of the home-based market could really come only through reducing costs, particularly the cost of film. Pathé introduced its first 9.5mm film and its Pathé Baby projector in time for Christmas in 1922, and its immediate success resulted in the Pathé Baby camera becoming available some months later. Efficient, safe, easy-to-use products had finally arrived in a form that would attract sizeable interest among the leisured classes.[17]

Further adaptations still had to occur if the new hobby was to achieve greater popularity and wider marketability, during times of company retrenchment and limited disposable income. Companies saw that the nascent amateur market might boost revenue during the Depression but only if purchasers could afford their hobby.[18] The launch of Standard 8 film involved 16mm film being run through the camera twice, exposing half of the film each time and offered the amateur user a fourfold reduction in operating costs. After processing, the film was then split and joined to make one new length, 8mm wide. The Cine Kodak Eight camera using 8mm film dates to 1932, and rival products included the Filmo Straight Eight by Bell & Howell in which an 8mm film gauge ran through the camera only once. Perhaps early amateur enthusiasts were less ready to purchase new cameras or more affected by broader economic conditions than manufacturers anticipated, and, even though the trade press responded quite positively to the new gauge, many of Britain's amateurs continued to use 16mm until after the Second World War.

This rapid succession of early amateur cine products may be traced through the exuberant advertising of the pioneer specialist press and trade magazines. Enticknap[19] charts early cinematic technologies while Wade's concise guide offers a well-illustrated overview.[20] Katelle's in-depth study of home movie origins in the United States includes many references to European developments too.[21] The strength of US commercial interest in promoting amateur home movie-making is seen by Zimmermann to have been central to the development of non-professional activity in North America.[22] Undoubtedly, advertising benefited sales elsewhere but, as this book explores, amateur film practice in Britain should be seen as being more than the result of commercial persuasion alone. Intellectual, social, cultural, aesthetic and other influences also helped to attract a variety of enthusiasts to the new hobby.

The complex interplay between amateur interests and commercial cinema went far beyond the nurturing of a lucrative domestic market that offered the means to show films at home and to emulate film industry professionals.[23] As Rachael Low points out in her classic studies of British filmmaking during the 1930s,[24] and as indicated by some of the opening quotations, early professionals were amateurs in all but how they earned a living when they started. Indeed, Katelle instances the framed image of Auguste Lumière with his wife and baby daughter having breakfast as a still from possibly one of the earliest home movies![25] Many early amateur and professional filmmakers shared interests in exploring cine technologies' capabilities and, regardless of their occupational status, home movies permitted opportunities for personal filmmaking untrammelled by worries about censorship or box office success.[26]

Amateur cinematography was an expensive hobby, particularly in the interwar years, and affordable mainly to people from wealthier backgrounds. The critical discourses that accompanied its first fifteen years of development (see Chapter 3) suggest that the hobby's appeal and widening social involvement were not due purely to advertising. Less tangible cultural and psychological links between visual memory-making and societal change were significant too. Amateur emulation of professional cinema was unlikely to have been the sole motivator either, and strident criticism of 'would be screen aspirants' was probably directed as much to those being filmed as those in charge of the camera.[27]

Developments elsewhere in cinema and newsreel encouraged public interest in home cinemas and encouraged both watching and film production.[28] Film rental companies and lending libraries grew, and trade publications circulated details of new films on formats available for home and cine society audiences. During the early 1930s, advice on how to set up and run a cinema at home borrowed its vocabulary from commercial venues, as did discussion of how newly formed amateur cine societies might attract women members to help in the box office or projection room or with serving refreshments.[29] The possibility that nascent cine societies might produce filmmakers whose home-grown talent could boost a flagging British cinema also helped to raise the profile of early amateur activity.[30] A film-watching audience, more critically informed about film interpretation through familiarisation with cinematic developments elsewhere in Europe and practical first-hand experience of making and showing their own material could, some enthusiasts claimed, could help to sustain and enhance a British cinema industry.[31] Class attitudes underline such assumptions that amateur cinephiles could potentially help to protect members of the cinemagoing public from the excesses of imported North American films.[32] Such debates echo the moralising rhetoric uttered by some commentators and sections of the establishment about the damaging threat of other popular cultural forms upon the general public, in particular, Britain's working classes.[33]

Just as the nascent corporate film industry extended existing professional and commercial interests into photography, exhibition and entertainment, the early decades of amateur film activity (c.1910–35) saw non-professional and professional interests intermesh with wider processes of cinematic development, commercial realisation and developing production practices.[34] But gradually a rather different kind of amateur interest began to occur both in Britain and elsewhere. These new amateurs were financially independent of the film industry taking shape around them.[35] They made films for pleasure and were, for the most part, separate from economically based professional enterprise, even though there are clear indications of shared aesthetic influences and overlapping interests. They functioned outside commercial imperatives: they were free to be spontaneous, whimsical, subjective and quite personal in decisions about how to develop their hobby.[36] They were pioneers of a fast-growing new branch of photography that came to be known variously as cine photography, home movie-making and amateur cinematography. While some filmmakers sought to be professional in all but how they financed their hobby, others inevitably never proceeded very far.

Typically, Britain's early hobby enthusiasts were affluent, white, middle-class and male, although exceptions as discussed later exist and some women's early participation centred on fiction films. Organised activity may be traced with certainty to 1923, when university students at Cambridge formed an amateur cine society (see Chapter 2). Given that Kodak and Pathé launched their own products for the amateur market within the same twelve-month period, the timing is indicative perhaps of the cine-camera's initial novelty appeal and desirability. Other pioneer users who functioned independently of any organisation predate the Cambridge group, but its formation may be taken as an indicative starting point for Britain's amateurs.[37] Importantly, there were numerous amateurs who used their cameras for personal reasons who remained outside formal networks of like-minded enthusiasts.

From its socially restricted use by middle- and upper-class groups in the 1920s and early 1930s, amateur film production developed into a small but flourishing middle-class leisure activity. As a distinctive offshoot of still photography, it soon spawned a supporting network of clubs and societies.

The recreational interest in amateur cinema coincided with a fervent adoption of film as a critical art form and a tool for communication by organisations on the British Left. As Hogenkamp points out, the costs of early filmmaking meant that the film camera was taken up by Labour sympathisers rather than by workers themselves although trade unions and workers' groups were inspired by film's propagandist role in the Soviet Union to set up their own film units.[38] For instance, *Liverpool – Gateway of Empire* (1933) was made by Merseyside Workers' Film Society on 16mm.[39] Elsewhere in the North West, companies made their own productions although surviving material is predominantly concerned with promotion rather than politics.[40] Shooting scenes of working practices as part of self-marketing (see Chapter 5) readily appealed to amateur cine users within the region's managerial and professional classes. If as Burton suggests, use of film by the co-operative movement for promotion and publicity both in and beyond its regional roots in Lancashire contributes to a fuller understanding of British workers' cinema and use of film on the Left, amateur practice affirms that bourgeois interests in filming people working were also flourishing.[41]

This book charts a more liberal interest that remains distinctively different from the filmic activities undertaken by and on behalf of the British Left. Its ideological messages may be less apparent but the footage still discloses contemporary concerns, attitudes and often the perspectives of the person behind the camera. Amateur fiction and non-fictional material exude prevailing understanding and sensibilities. Their subjects range from identity (personal, family and civic to national level), to contemporary issues (from animals in zoos and anti-war protests to urban development). Their geographical scale extends from the micro-politics of children playing or a family reunion to migration, travel, living or working overseas and Cold War politics. The cine-camera became a new form of personal expression, something through which people could make visual statements that, in different hands and on different occasions, could inspire, educate, entertain and, at times, be shocking. Almost in anticipation of Reithian principles of public broadcasting, some amateurs saw how their motion pictures could have considerable impact upon family members, friends and others who became their audiences at home and elsewhere. Cine equipment offered a new democratic means of participating in everyday life as amateur filmmakers found themselves in the role of commentators, journalists, record-makers and chroniclers at local and civic level.[42]

Unsurprisingly, there are echoes of the middle-class social engagement found among members of Britain's documentary film movement during the

1930s.[43] Amateurs shot local interest films as well as footage of relief work undertaken by Britain's Quakers during the Spanish Civil War.[44] Missionaries, teachers, government representatives, military personnel, and others filmed overseas too.[45] For some cine users, being there, witnessing and personal filmmaking was an antidote to the tide of visual factual and fictive narratives now washing through many people's lives and localities. For others, trying their hand at fictional story-telling brought pleasure and companionship. Yet the value of film in society still divided opinion even at the highest level.[46] For the Burnley cabinet-maker who became a woodwork teacher and filmmaker (see Chapter 6), the struggle to convince his local education department as to film's classroom benefits reveals that the British establishment was still far from unanimous in acknowledging film's potential as visual information.

Notwithstanding ideological differences, amateur enthusiasts increased in number during the 1930s as cameras became easier and more efficient to use. Technical improvements included experiments with synchronising sound and film production. Standard 8mm colour film appeared in 1932. Different sound projectors were commercially available in Britain by 1933 for showing films on 16mm at home, while in 1937 Pathé launched its Pathé Vox, a sound projector system for 9.5mm film. Eastman Kodak continued to adapt professional design features for the amateur market: technical developments included variable shutter speed, reflex viewing, wide angle and telephoto lens facilities, and a detachable film magazine that enabled easier loading and reloading of longer film lengths.[47] Cameras gained built-in light meters, and moved from being hand-cranked and clockwork-operated to being electric-driven. The widening choice of camera and projector equipment influenced how usage and practice evolved. There are instances of filmmakers who started in c.1925 using 9.5mm and within four years had changed to using 16mm.[48] Many enthusiasts did not simply replace equipment as new products appeared, despite the wishes of the manufacturers, and, from early on, people became accustomed to working with specific types of film gauge and camera. A minority of early amateurs also used 35mm film but the equipment's bulkiness limited filming to within the grounds of the family home.[49] Practical rather than financial reasons may account for these instances of a novelty hobby being discontinued within a few years, judging by the amount of high-quality footage that sometimes depicts a few garden parties, people playing tennis and other domestic scenes.

Another major innovation was the introduction of colour film for 16 and 9.5mm equipment by the mid-1930s. Colour film had been available earlier but the new potential for obtaining rich and natural colours was profoundly exciting for amateur filmmakers. In contrast to its more widespread adoption in the United States, use of colour film by British amateurs remained fairly limited until the early 1950s, and during the Second World War it disappeared almost completely. Surviving colour footage from the later 1930s probably reflects the income level of early hobbyists. Some footage of families at home and on holiday combined monotone with colour, perhaps indicating variations in availability (see Chapter 7). As wartime approached and stocks dwindled, filmmakers saved colour for particular moments, for instance a child's christening or first birthday or a specific scenic stretch of a touring holiday. Captured in bright colour, these moments seem to have had particular significance in an era when newsreel and commercial footage were still predominantly in black and white. At times the shifts between colour and monotone seem to have no obvious reason other than film being loaded in a hurry or at random. Through the 1940s, the amateur use of black and white footage predominated. One exception, a headteacher's eleven-minute film of his primary school made using black and white as well as colour during 1942, is discussed elsewhere.[50] Rationing, as evidenced by the survival of amateurs' correspondence and ration slips, also limited postwar colour film availability. Many filmmakers continued to use black and white filmstock or to combine small amounts of colour with monotone in the late 1940s much as they had done a decade earlier.

Retrenchment and resurgence

Amateur activity did not stop entirely during wartime, either among those left at home or among those on active service. Archival records from the Imperial War Museum and other collections attest to instances of military personnel who took their cameras with them but the amount of material is generally less than from among American and some Commonwealth units that saw active service.[51] Costs and the still socially restricted availability of cine equipment probably account for this difference, and surviving examples of cine footage tend to derive from military personnel in higher-ranking positions.[52] Footage filmed at home during the war years likewise offers a representation of society and self through predominantly middle-class eyes. Gender, class, status, generation and place affected who was available to record images at home or with their local cine club. Some wartime amateur footage derives from particular circumstances, for instance filmstock being available to a filmmaker ostensibly for other purposes including the making of training films, or a filmmaker not seeing active service for personal or occupational-related reasons.

Cine-cameras remained in use in some homes throughout the Second World War. Holidays, outings, birthdays, weddings and other family events were important occasions to document, perhaps the cinematic memory gaining new significance as a record of events being missed by absent family members. Sports days, camping trips and more routine aspects of school life likewise remained popular material to film. Activities associated with wartime attracted attention, including drill and training practice by home guard, scout groups and other local volunteers who assumed auxiliary wartime roles. Cine groups made instructional films on topics that included local emergency planning, disaster management and road safety. National and civic events attracted individual filmmakers' attention, so records survive of War Weapon Week in Bolton,[53] community commemorative events, royal visits, parades and wreath-laying. As with any photographic image taken after or at the start of a period of absence, the apparent jauntiness of soldiers being filmed during return visits home on leave or departing for service carries weightier undertones amidst the general air of jollity that pervades much of the surviving wartime family footage.[54]

After the war, the amateur scene changed greatly (see Chapter 2). Although some cine clubs had suspended their activities by the end of 1939, regular meetings resumed after 1946 and new societies arose as interests grew. Sometimes new or revitalised clubs emerged from just two or three like-minded enthusiasts joining together after years of restricted activity. Technical improvements in strategic and professional camera design gained commercial application and, as the relative costs diminished, amateur cine photography attracted a wider following. Recreational filmmaking reasserted itself as a more broadly based leisure activity and, where personal details are known, it is clear that between the late 1940s and mid-1950s more films were produced by white collar and public or commercial service sector workers, including teachers, civil servants and office staff.

Hobby filmmaking documented a new phase of domesticity postwar. Its novelty combined with the desire to establish or return to family life. Its focus and escapism also distracted from the destabilising effects of death, injury, separation and other problems of readjustment. While permitting familial focus, nascent club structures offered peacetime scope for legitimate male non-sporting activity and companionship outside the home. Among the broadening managerial, commercial, public service and professional middle classes of postwar Britain, cine-cameras became an affordable accessory to record and memorialise early years of national peace and social and economic reconstruction. Renewed production of prewar models, sometimes with little more than a name change or minor change in design, occurred in the immediate aftermath of war. Sales swelled as first-time camera users were able to purchase from a profusion of new and improved products. They filmed offspring born into the postwar baby boom and charted each progression from cot to walking, pedalling their first tricycle and sitting on swings in the local park. Cameras monitored other shifts in family and economic status, including the move to a new house, buying a car and the first (and subsequent) holiday abroad.

National events including the Festival of Britain, the Coronation and diverse centennial civic anniversaries provided additional impetus for new cinephiles.[55] Improvements to the smaller film gauges and simpler camera design attracted new users, while the launch of more affordable amateur colour film that no longer included a processing charge within the selling price led to competitive rates among different companies. Standard 8mm filmstock gained wider use in Britain during the 1950s, gradually moving into the 9.5mm market that persisted well into the later 1960s but, unlike in France, never regained its prewar popularity. Meanwhile 16mm became the preserve of the more serious non-professional and remained important across Britain for some club productions.

Amateur cinema, boosted by cheaper materials, better colour filmstock and a stream of publications, thus ceased to be a minority leisure activity and was taken up increasingly by men, some couples and, more rarely, single women during the later 1950s and 1960s. Kodak's launch in 1965 of the Super 8, shortly to be followed by Fuji's Single 8 version of an equivalent cassette-loading system, widened cine photography's appeal further. The positioning of the sprocket holes on the film made splicing and home editing easier and the resultant projected picture larger. Trimly designed cine-cameras, largely made from plastic and which operated with an easily loaded cartridge system that allowed the film to run through the camera, attracted fresh interest. Making and showing home movies no longer required specialist knowledge and people could point and shoot with their lightweight camera just as they could take multiple holiday snaps in colour. Enthusiasts claimed that democratisation of amateur cinematography had been achieved in just over forty years. People could take their cameras on honeymoons, package holidays, days out, into their local school, place of work and elsewhere. They could replicate the quirkiness of such broadcast successes as *Candid Camera* (presented by Bob Monkhouse on British television, 1960–67), relive special occasions or enhance their own importance through showing films about themselves and others in their living rooms to family and friends. In some families, 'the man with the camera' was dad, granddad or an uncle with an interest in recording family life. Some couples became seriously involved in filmmaking as a shared hobby, and sometimes became actively involved with a local cine society too. While regional news coverage gradually spread from its introduction to television in 1957,[56] amateur cinema enabled ordinary people, with no previous expertise in using a camera, to be able to tell their own stories about how, where and with whom they lived.

In one sense amateur film passed from being a specialist leisure activity to being an adjunct of modern living.[57] Prices continued to restrict use and availability. Passing around snapshots from a still camera remained cheaper and easier than showing films even on the living room wall. Social changes perhaps meant that family gatherings – the typical audience for many home movies – happened less frequently than in the past. The cost of four-minute films, together with their processing and postage meant that they did not reach everyone. Film was used sparingly even by many who did take up the hobby, attracted by the availability of second-hand equipment and cheaper models. Even from the later 1960s, certain sections of Britain's population remain underrepresented within the visual historical record of amateur film footage that has so far reached Britain's regional film archives. Amateur films depicting family life within Britain's Black and Asian communities remain very rare, although it seems possible that some material may still not have come to the attention of public archives. Exceptions exist, as in the personal films of Raj Malhotra, whose filmmaking included personal footage shot at and close to his home in Coventry as well as extensive coverage of public events, including marches, concerts and demonstrations where he filmed his friends and associates within the Indian Workers' Association.[58]

Widening ethnic diversity found within the medical and other professions during the 1970s also means that family footage of life at home and with friends as well as overseas holidays may be found within regional archival collections, as shown by footage of the Misty and Kapur families made in the North West and during holidays in India (see Chapter 7). The adoption of children of mixed parentage or other backgrounds into cine-wielding white families occasionally offers glimpses too of households that sought to defy prejudices in postwar Britain.[59] Younger filmmakers, of varied backgrounds, attracted by the cine-camera's potential as a tool for visual expression and documentary, also helped to diversify the contexts in which cine footage was made. Experimental films, perhaps unconsciously exploring issues of identity and belonging, made by Jem Norris on Super 8 in the early 1970s used Victorian funerary art and family-owned antique toy lead soldiers. Menelik Shabazz, already emerging as a figure within what Cameron Bailey has described as the 'cinema of duty' socially engaged strand of 1970s Black British filmmaking, used a cine-camera to produce uncompromising imagery of crowd restraint and police violence during the 1976 Notting Hill Carnival.[60] Alongside the use of personal and found footage already popular in avant-garde artistic circles on both sides of the Atlantic and well-suited for reworking into new productions,[61] cine equipment acquired fresh status for its facility in producing documentary realist and eye-witness material. Cine-cameras had also become cheap enough for Britain's growing numbers of university students to receive as a birthday present or to purchase after a summer vacation working.

Amateur film never attracted the mass appeal sought by its early exponents, but by the mid- to later 1960s, it attracted enthusiasts who varied in gender, age, background and occupation. Changes in family life, leisure time and, above all, the introduction of the video camera and its rapidly developed compatibility with television for home screening, from the later 1970s precipitated the gradual decline of popular interest in cine film. It seems ironic that the very time when cine equipment reached its lowest price relative to other consumer goods, and when membership levels in many cine societies were at their peak, video technologies began to undermine amateur practice.[62] While some societies accepted video users within their midst and adapted their names to accommodate changing practice and preferences among some of their members, the new technology's arrival was more contentious among other parts of the formal network. Its cassette-loading format, different ways of being edited and then playback via a television seemed far removed from the painstaking techniques of working with small-gauge film and a projector. In common with the history of Britain's organised recreational activity during the 1970s and 1980s, cine clubs witnessed falling membership and regular attendance at meetings dropped (see Chapter 2). Across the regions, nonetheless, many enthusiasts and cine societies continue to make films. Indeed some groups still remain active, often with small numbers of dedicated and sometimes now quite elderly members. Many of today's amateurs are also already retired or close to retirement. Chapter 2 taps into the determination and enthusiasm that typifies Britain's amateur filmmaking scene during the past half century. This, in essence, is the British amateur film movement that this book seeks to explore through reference to its societies, filmmakers, specialist literature and, in particular, the films produced between the mid-1920s and c.1977.

The focus is primarily upon documentary-style material that has a broadly social content, whether filmed in or away from home, as in travel and holidays, or in amateur topicals and other forms of reportage. Elsewhere scholarship charts some of the distinctive strands within Britain's amateur cinema that engaged with fiction, animation or work that may be called avant-garde.[63] It would be misleading, however, not to recognise that some filmmakers explored different styles. Others started and stayed with making with family and holiday films. Animation attracted some filmmakers, particularly those who could draw and also set aside space at home where materials might be left undisturbed.[64] Others animated only titles and other short sequences while some enthusiasts preferred story films or developed camera skills suited to interests in transport history, natural history or flora. Similarly, while some filmmakers were closely involved with their societies, taking part in club productions, competitions and officer roles at local, regional and national level, others pursued their interest independently of formal structures. Examples of these different practitioners and their practices are discussed in later chapters.

One key area omitted here, however, is the amateur work that derived from various Left-wing related organisations including trade union and other workplace-related filmmaking groups. Arguably, this ideologically underpinned practice has received more attention than the middle-class male recreational activity identified in this book. Not surprisingly, interest in films associated with Britain's labour movement draws upon two very well-established historiographic traditions, namely working-class experience in and away from the workplace and also diverse interests in the classic formative years of Soviet Russian cinema. It would be misleading to suggest any close connections but aspects of the parallel nature of interests in film by different social groups seems worthy of comment. First, the wide-ranging nature of the earliest periodicals aimed at the amateur reader defined film so broadly that critical essays on the innovatory styles of continental directors including Pabst and Eisenstein featured alongside news on amateur groups and reports from local urban watch committees.[65] Second, the socially engaged films of Britain's documentary movement during the 1930s were produced overwhelmingly on behalf of rather than by the working classes. As shown later, social awareness prompted at least some middle-class amateur filmmaking activity even if the tone now seems patronising in its wishes to liberate others from social, economic, environmental or physical disadvantage. Sometimes the decision to make a film about aspects of local life and community history involved meeting people and shooting in places that were not directly familiar to the predominantly middle-class hobbyists who still formed the 'hard core' of numerous northern amateur societies.

This introductory historical overview provides a foundation for subsequent chapters that explore more detailed aspects of amateur activity. These opening remarks are substantiated by supporting evidence, whether drawn from specific footage, interviews and correspondence with filmmakers and cine society members or from supplementary printed or unpublished archival materials. Readers are also directed to key texts that have helped to set this interpretation of amateur practices within relevant social, cultural, economic, aesthetic, ideological and other twentieth-century contexts.

Finding frameworks

Almost since its earliest beginnings, film has been the focus of study, analysis and theory. The recognition of amateur filmmaking as a discernible and influential component within broader cinematic developments at a national and international level first occurred largely outside conventional academic areas of film and media studies. Rather, social historians, historical geographers and film archivists began to draw more attention to the significance of amateur footage as cultural memory. The media historian, Patricia Zimmermann made a pioneering historical study that charted home-movie making in the United States from its inception to the 1960s.[66] Katelle, as already mentioned, has greatly expanded understanding of practice and technological developments in North America and Europe.[67] Chalfren's interpretative frameworks have been influential on both sides of the Atlantic.[68] Other writers, both in and beyond the United States (see for example European work gathered by Kapstein),[69] including Schneider,[70] Stone and Streible,[71] Szczelkun[72] and Rhu,[73] meanwhile have sought to build upon and diverge from Zimmermann's seminal work. Aasman's studies of Dutch home-movie cultures provide comparative insights into domesticity, gender and family relations.[74] De Klerk[75] explores Dutch cine practice within late colonial settings that may be set alongside other kinds of overseas expatriate visual encounter.[76] Roepke has produced significant work on amateur activity in Germany.[77] Odin has contributed to the theoretical interpretation of home movies in and beyond metropolitan France,[78] and exploratory work in Finland draws attention to the stories told on camera by young people.[79] Cuevas's anthology brings together, for a Spanish readership, issues of reworking home movies in contemporary documentary, avantgarde and other creative practice.[80] Shand's work evidences interests emerging from a younger generation of British scholars from film studies who approach amateur film in multidisciplinary ways.[81] Howe draws upon visual aesthetic history in her own incisive work in Australia.[82] Craven, too, moves beyond an established background in feature film to draw upon sociology in his discussion of amateur practice.[83]

Meanwhile, international, national and regional television networks find archival footage an appealing, relatively cheap and accessible source of material to screen, less bound by copyright constraints than much professionally produced material. Some amateur film societies find that their club productions, which may span back over almost eighty years, are now marketable to television companies in search of material with local and regional human interest. Independent visual artists and experimental filmmakers, including Richard Fung,[84] Péter Forgács,[85] Terence Davies[86] and Jonas Mekas,[87] have long engaged with archive imagery. Reworking amateur footage of personal and wider significance continues among emerging filmmakers internationally. Projects span from the informal happenings and bus tours of the 1960s to contemporary large-scale collaborations.[88] Whether Reich and Korot's use of Bikini Atoll and Hindenburg disaster footage in a video opera or 2010 Turner Prize nominees the Otolith group's incorporation of archive material within their futuristic trilogy, evidence points to the creative versatility prompted by moving image, as do other imaginative institutional, multi-media and cross-disciplinary projects using footage in exhibitions, performances and forms of public intervention from local to international level.[89]

Archivists contribute to discursive practice, sharing their knowledge of unique collections and also helping to develop frameworks in which theories, policies, interpretation and ethics may be furthered. Work by Schwartz and Cook,[90] albeit informed by still image interpretation, helps to further understanding of the archival context in which much moving image now resides. Thill, Kmec, de Klerk and others working in European film archives and elsewhere[91] also sustain debate on the significance of moving imagery through publications and organising events.[92] While numerous archivists across Britain, mainland Europe, Canada and the United States passionately defend and publicise their amateur repositories and link their expertise with scholarship and artistic endeavour,[93] elsewhere amateur film, as in India,[94] may still be championed largely by individuals working independently. For all this disparate interest in non-professional cinema, there has been no systematic critical study that yet deals with the emergence of amateur film practice in Britain, although Craven's edited collection highlights some of the diversity now emerging in studies on amateur cinema, as do various landmark international gatherings on amateur film.[95] Research is also valuably helping to build up detailed analysis of work within different production and regional settings.

Themes and approaches

Against this dynamic background, this book combines empirical detail with theoretical perspectives. The technological development of cine equipment is comprehensively covered elsewhere[96] but socio-historical positioning of regional amateur cine practices within broader trends of British society and culture has not been previously attempted. This book traces the development of amateur interest as well as the rise of supportive, organised formal networks of special-interest clubs and societies, and the attendant growth of a widely circulated and influential hobby press. Through considering these associated contextual communities, amateur cine practice emerges as a dynamic, self-critical and diverse body of activity that co-existed and interconnected with more charted aspects of British cinema history, photography and leisure activity. A seemingly peripheral aspect of visual history emerges as an integral and highly nuanced component of how, as in Denzin's phrase, a 'cinematic age came to know itself'.[97] For a more inclusive understanding of cinematic practice, it seems appropriate to reclaim amateur activity from its once rather marginalised position as clichéd, substandard and of little interest, and to now conceptualise the promotion, production and consumption of amateur activities within this broader framework.

The book forms a series of linked discussions each focused upon a different aspect of amateur cinematic practice. Chapter 2 explores the growing network of clubs and societies, plus their associated regional activities and patterns of membership over approximately fifty years. Personal testimony gathered through contact with amateur filmmakers, together with reference to regional club records, informs this exploration of the supportive settings that underpinned much amateur activity. Chapter 3 discusses how a new specialist hobby literature accompanied the rise of amateur cinema. The perspectives of contemporary commentators thus inform past activity. Subsequent chapters examine regional filmic practice in relation to the making and showing of amateur films on the family (Chapter 4) and local lives and communities (Chapter 5). Discussion of films concerning working experiences (Chapter 6) is followed by a focus on travel-related cine footage made mainly by filmmakers with links to Lancashire or Yorkshire (Chapter 7). Socially engaged cine activity refers to material from further afield so that a wide range of issues are included (Chapter 8). The final chapter points to directions that further trans-disciplinary work on amateur film might take, particularly given the impact of digital technologies, the growth of interest in memory studies and the recent surge of interest in personal use and user-generated moving image for which amateur cinema may seem a direct ancestor.

This introduction raises issues that thread through subsequent chapters. Accordingly, references to key literary sources are mainly set within the relevant chapters. Here broad areas of interest are identified so that readers gain a sense of different intellectual perspectives and biases that inform the overall project. The relationship of amateur to professional film weaves through details of the club scene and the hobby press in the following two chapters but, throughout the book, amateur activity is related to broader changing cultural and visual practices. Links with professional interests are discussed as is the claim that amateur activity might revitalise national cinema. Audiences often remain elusive in cinema history studies but the advisory material provided by the hobby press offers clues to viewers' responses as well as contemporary thoughts on filmic content, production and amateur aesthetics.

Reading amateur footage through twenty-first-century eyes requires a critical engagement with diverse forms of source material that balances searches for meaning with critical rigour, sensitivity and integrity. Understanding cine footage requires bringing under scrutiny archive material that is often far removed from where it was originally made and watched. This search to unlock past motives and meanings remains tentative and reliant upon close contextualisation and historical contingency. Photographic and cinematic histories offer comparative insights although inherent differences exist too.[98] Sociological and historical settings disclose the material conditions and consumption of amateur visual practice and locate filmmakers and their audiences in specific domestic, local, regional and national contexts. Amateur activities neither emerged nor evolved in a visual, socio-spatial or temporal vacuum. Filmmakers' private and personal statements about self, status and society were bound up with where and how they lived, worked and made sense of themselves, their surroundings and the times they lived through. Their self-expression using available picture-making techniques mediated wider processes of identity formation, memory-shaping and social transformation. The sensitivities of handling visual memories, whether in photographic form or as a flickering projected image highlight concerns about materiality and culture, as explored by Edwards and Hart, and in Kuhn's work on family photographs.[99] The oral testimonies of elderly filmmakers contribute complementary perspectives.[100] Their individual commentaries and films of home, family, community and being elsewhere connect local knowledge to broader events.[101] Similarly, these filmic forays into documentary, fiction, civic story-telling, natural history and campaigning provide windows upon wider contemporary concerns and interests.

Amateur films juxtapose personal and collective memories and entwine private and public histories. They memorialise unofficial versions of official commemorative moments and actions. The selective process of recording for subsequent shared recollection creates particular versions of events. Each person in charge of a camera frames the view, choosing to include and exclude others on very specific terms. The resultant material is not only riddled with issues of race, gender and authority that are specific to time and place. Amateur film productions, whether made by one person, a couple or a group of enthusiasts, disclose what might be called the situatedness of knowledge production.[102] Many film enthusiasts were self-taught and they learned from each other, encountering tips and warnings as they pursued their hobby. The meanings found in their films offer personal variations upon more widely mediated notions of people, place and experience and they may be understood differently over time.

If amateur film reclaims past experiences and settings that may have since disappeared, does it replicate understandings known through other sources? Admittedly, for much of its history, cine films were largely made by and for those in positions of influence. Their social equivalents were the most likely to be able to leave their mark historically in written and other forms too. In their use of film, England's middle classes found a new accessible medium though which ideas and experiences could be shared and passed on.[103] For all that the filmmaker's gaze usually denotes broader power relations, exceptions exist as revealed by the work of women hobbyists and other enthusiasts who came from outside the core of middle-class white male followers. Amateur imagery also captured visual details and meanings that supplement, challenge and at times compensate for other evidential gaps and silences. Many filmmakers crossed social space in search of visual difference and the colonial gaze prompted distinctive forms of ethnographic curiosity and visual trophy seeking that disclose attitudes and behaviour and encounters elsewhere.[104] Filmmaking in some marginalised communities may provide visual testimony to forebears and cultural practice known otherwise only through oral records.[105] Films of traditions and work practices that no longer survive likewise form connecting tissue between past and present. The final chapter returns to these issues and briefly considers the scope for research-related projects and visual repatriation.

Approaching amateur film involves questions of knowledge formation, memory gathering, story-telling and self-reflexivity. Interpreting other people's filmic memories requires caution: neither the evidence on cine reels nor the memory is simply an archival deposit. Just as an upsurge of research helps to remap our understanding of the memory, reels of cine film are not merely unmediated captured moments in time.[106] If visual interpretation is informed by recent research on the dynamic slips, gaps, elisions and alternative ways of remembering, understanding imagery as past visual evidence attracts its own critical reappraisal. Image analysis may involve reading projected scenes as depictions of historically verifiable occasions, corroborated by other evidence, yet, valuable though such approaches might be, there are limitations.[107] Rather than only reading amateur film as visual evidence and clues that 'tell it like it is' (or was), some cine practice may be understood as intentional memory-making that, in psychological terms, also involves 'telling it as it might be'.[108] This catapults image interpretation from the chronicling of seemingly happy families, communities and national well-being into psychically more unsettling worlds of imaginary construct, fictive belonging and uncertainty. The suspensions of disbelief when making or watching seemingly happy family home movies are, as Citron reminds us, 'necessary fictions' that help us through life whether assisted by the framed photograph or the image projected on to the living room wall.[109] It is no mere act of complicity or denial in recognition of the presented ideal. There can perhaps be unspoken or shared wish-fulfilment that tacitly acknowledges how real and reel children, families, picnics, localities, holidays and weather differ. Grasping the mimetic scope of a cine-camera as a device for projecting desires or dealing with trauma relocates amateur cinema as open and active, with meanings that are provisional and fluid, capable of being told and retold differently. As Zimmermann urges, amateur material is not 'nostalgic images of a past shrouded in longing, desire and quaintness'.[110]

Archival contexts

The journeys undertaken by films between filmmaker and their present archival home are relevant to this search for visual meanings.[111] Long-neglected amateur films continue to be retrieved and received into archives everywhere. However donated or reclaimed from attics, cupboards, buildings and skips, their survival reflects their growing recognition as sources for understanding past experience. It is now axiomatic for many people that archive footage confers significance and historical authenticity. It has become recognised as historical source material in its own right. Tracing the journeys made by once discarded visual memories into their current archival settings connects with ontological and epistemological shifts in historical enquiry and attitudes towards popular culture, social history and heritage. Entrusted by family members or complete strangers, material once made for private screening now enters the public domain and becomes eligible for online streaming, broadcasting, academic or other uses.

Watching such films raises ethical issues in relation to the public use of material that sometimes was intended only for the intimacy of family and friends. These mediated private lives from the past have no control over their own image and are vulnerable to misrepresentation or misunderstandings that fail to reflect the diversity, complexity and sensitivities of different experiences. Just as the films themselves are artefacts, made, remade and sometimes still in their raw unedited state, the archives they reach are also cultural goods shaped by decisions, policies and objectives. Both archived film and the archive repository are made in and over time: their existence, their survival and their meanings are the consequence of power, authority and the actions of others.[112]

An appraisal of amateur film practice opens new ways of understanding personal and collective unofficial visual versions of the past and helps to vindicate the various struggles to set up and sustain public film archives.[113] Titles, labels, shot-lists, categories and other details frame how archive amateur footage have been catalogued, accessed and understood. As film enters an archive, it undergoes acts of relocation and reallocation. As its former personal significance changes, it acquires different meanings that reflect societal change and archival interventions as well as more philosophical and theoretical concerns. Empirical detail, informed by critical approaches flexible enough for others to make their own assessments, has a rightful place in exploring changing meanings and the reshaping of historical visual narratives.[114]

As more visual data becomes available without details of context and provenance via YouTube and other hosting systems, the importance of understanding the respective challenges of working with and without metadata require urgent attention.[115] Access via online streaming, downloadable content and dynamic archival ways of generating and accessing metadata brings unprecedented data abundance, fosters creative cross-disciplinary approaches and confers new international significance upon visual heritage.[116] Enhanced visibility and access enhance the status of amateur moving imagery within visual culture, but they carry their own risks too. Nor simply for the beleaguered archival community that could, arguably, face its own demise and reduction to data handlers and storage providers, with scant regard for the inherent expertise and knowledge built up over time about individual collections. Unless users retain the capacity to situate imagery within relevant interpretative contexts, amateur cine practices will become harder to research.

Recent archiving initiatives in putting associated materials online are to be welcomed. Crowd-sourcing and tagging initiatives that supplement catalogue data offer innovative models of authorship, expertise and context-building. Seemingly unimportant details acquire significance during specific investigations: how, for instance, films were edited, ordered, labelled within a filmmaker's collection. Similarly, ephemera and specific objects, jottings or memorabilia may illuminate a particular filmmaker's interests and cine projects. Visual forensics combine with the rigours of media archaeology, and archival historiography in probing into and beyond the digitised collection, conservation, storage and cataloguing of data.

Paradoxically, digital access may distance some potential users even as it makes certain types of material more accessible. Unless all footage gains equal treatment, and publicly funded repositories are in no position to attempt wholesale digitisation, it also risks adding layers that select, shape and affect a user's ultimate understanding of footage. Conversely, an online presence, if only to consolidate physically dispersed holdings, as in Northern Ireland, is a significant step towards redressing past geo-politically determined inequities in cultural heritage provision. Digital access via online clips, metadata or live streaming is qualitatively different from directly encountering the materiality, serendipity and humanity of visiting an archive. Just as the digital era benefits the humanities, it is timely to remember that perspectives from the humanities also inform our understanding of digital potential. Too many insights, ideas and juxtapositions would be lost as illustrated through the following chapters. The interpretation of amateur cinema would be the poorer. Perspectives and connections between different aspects of moving-making practices would disappear even as they are gaining better understanding in more inclusive understanding of past cinematic cultures. The visual stories, made and shared by amateur filmmakers, as considered in this book, are part of a more broadly conceived understanding of Britain's cinematic past. Let us now shift focus and consider how those amateurs became attracted and sometimes addicted to their hobby, sometimes for decades.

Notes

1. Harry Watt (documentary filmmaker), quoted in G. Malthouse, '21 years of amateur movies'.
2. *Ibid.*, p. 38.
3. *Ibid.*, p. 37.
4. *Ibid.*, p. 38.
5. *Ibid.*, p. 37.
6. *Film and Video Maker – 75th Year Commemorative Issue, IAC 1932–2007* (May–June 2007) pp. 1–35.
7. M. and J. Coad, *The IAC*, p. 7.
8. See *Film and Video Maker* for numerous reports on members' and public events during 2007 and early 2008.
9. B. Cross, 'Mimeses and the spatial economy of children's play'; see also D. Buckingham, *After the Death of Childhood*.
10. H. Norris Nicholson, 'Amateur film culture and practices'.
11. J. Fullerton and A. Söderbergh Widding (eds), *Moving Images: From Edison to the Webcam*; see also A. D. Katelle, *Home Movies*, pp. 1–69.
12. Katelle, *Home Movies*, pp. 1–69; see also L. Enticknap, *Moving Image Technology*.
13. L. Donaldson, *Cinematography for Amateurs*, p. 7.
14. Katelle, *Home Movies*, p. 53.
15. See, for example, one of the earliest self-help manuals: F. A. Talbot, *Practical Cinematography and Its Applications*: 'written with the express purpose of assisting the amateur – the term is used in its broadest sense as a distinction from the salaried, attached professional worker – who is attracted towards cinematography. It is not a technical treatise, but is written in such a manner as to enable the tyro to grasp the fundamental principles of the art, and the apparatus employed in its many varied applications' (Preface).
16. See note 12.
17. See, for example, G. McKee, *Half Century of Film Collecting*; *The Home Cinema: Classic Home Movie Projectors, 1922–1940*.
18. See for instance, B. Winston, *Technologies of Seeing*.
19. Enticknap, *Moving Image Technology*.
20. J. Wade, *Cine Cameras*.
21. A. D. Katelle, 'The Amateur Cinema League and its films'.
22. P. Zimmermann, *Reel Families*.
23. See Chapter 3. Practical manuals featured in general interest hobby series too: for example, E. W. Hobbs, *Cinematography for Amateurs*, was part of a series designed 'for the handyman, the expert and the Amateur, practical manuals with many helpful illustrations dealing with almost every subject of interest to the man who does things himself'.
24. R. Low, *History of British Film: Films of Comment and Persuasion of the 1930s*.
25. Katelle, *Home Movies*, p. 51 (Figure 83).
26. M. A. Lovell Burgess, *A Popular Account of the Amateur Cine Movement*, p. 4.
27. G. H. Sewell, 'On the set'.

28 L. McKernan, *Yesterday's News*.
29 A. J. Bromley, 'Sitting room cinema'.
30 Lovell Burgess, *A Popular Account of the Amateur Cine Movement*, p. 8.
31 K. Macpherson, *Close Up*; see also J. Donald, A. Friedberg and L. Marcus (eds), *Close Up, 1927–1933*; L. Marcus *The Tenth Muse*.
32 Lovell Burgess, *A Popular Account of the Amateur Cine Movement*, p. 26.
33 S. Nicholson, *The Censorship of British Theatre*, p. 5.
34 J. Barnes, *The Beginnings of the Cinema in England*; see also V. Toulmin, P. Russell and S. Popple, *The Lost World of Mitchell and Kenyon*.
35 Lovell Burgess, *A Popular Account of the Amateur Cine Movement*, p. 4.
36 T. Langlands, *Popular Cinematography*, pp. 8–9; G. H. Sewell, *Commercial Cinematography*.
37 See also Coad, *The IAC*, p. 7.
38 B. Hogenkamp, *Deadly Parallels*, p. 9.
39 The *Merseyside Workers' Film Society* (1930), started by a group of socialist teachers in Birkenhead, followed the establishment of the *Federation of Workers' Film Society* a year earlier, and sought to encourage the making and screening of high-quality films to working-class audiences: www.screenonline.org.uk/film/id/1305751/, accessed on 5 May 2010.
40 The North West Film Archive (hereafter NWFA) catalogue identifies 31 such films shot between 1926 and 1958 including Metropolitan Vickers Electrical Company Limited (?), c.1927: [*A Visit to the Factory*], NWFA Film. no. 962 (b/w, silent, 1 min. 24 sec.); *1927/28: [*Crucible Melting*] NWFA Film no. 973 (b/w, silent, 4 min. 10 sec.); 1928: *Summer School for Professors and Lecturers in Engineering* NWFA Film no. 961 (b/w, silent, 1 min. 7 sec.); Carborundum Co *1929: *The Jewels of Industry*, NWFA Film no. 83 (b/w, silent, 15 min. 54 sec.); *1932: *In the Firelight*. NWFA Film no. 87 (b/w, silent, 9 min. 37 sec.); Lever Brothers, *1931: [*Port Sunlight*], NWFA Film no. 323 (b/w, silent, 23 min. 25 sec.).
41 A. Burton (ed.), *The British Co-operative Movement Film Catalogue*, pp. xiii–xxxvi.
42 H. Norris Nicholson, 'Cinemas of catastrophe'.
43 H. Norris Nicholson, 'Purposeful pleasures'; see also League of Nations Child Welfare Committee, *Recreational Aspects of Cinematography*; and M. Winter and N. F. Spurr, *Filmmaking on a Low Budget*.
44 H. Norris Nicholson, 'Shooting the Mediterranean'.
45 H. Norris Nicholson, *Screening Culture*, pp. 94–9.
46 Commission on Educational and Cultural Films (CEC Films), *The Film in National Life*; see also BFI, *The Film in National Life. Conference Proceedings*.
47 Katelle, *Home Movies*, pp. 98–9.
48 Gerald Mee (Stoke Cine and Video Society), Personal communications with author, June–August 2007.
49 See, for example, films made by the Birtwhistle family at their home Billinge Scar and elsewhere during the 1920s and 1930s: NWFA Film nos 237–240 and 273.
50 Arthur Hulme, 1942: *School Life in Wartime*, NWFA Film no. 911 (b/w and colour, silent, 11 min. 1 sec.).
51 See for example, Captain Rowsell (USAAF pilot), 1945: [*Captain Rowsell's Norwich*,

EAFA Cat. 1292 (colour, silent, 8 min.). Information kindly supplied by Jane Alvey, EAFA, 7 June 2011.
52 A. Motrescu, A. 'Uncensored politics in British home-movies'.
53 J. E. Hallam, 1940: *Lord Derby Visits Farnworth*, NWFA Film no. 883 (b/w, silent, 13 min. 0 sec.).
54 E. Hart, 1940–42: *Norma's Birthday Party and Family Get-together*, NWFA Film no. RR788/4 (b/w and colour, silent, 9 min. 32 sec.).
55 See, for instance, 'Provincial', 'Postscript to a festival visit'; G. Malthouse, 'Leader strip'.
56 J. Burleigh, 'BBC celebrates 50 years of television news reporting'.
57 The postwar spread of cine use fulfilled some of the early expectations about the rise of home cinema and projection as shown by one author's preface: 'The ordinary gramophone is out of date, radio is almost commonplace, and television is somewhere in the future. The home talking picture might well fill the gap', in B. Brown, *Amateur Talking Pictures and Recording*.
58 R. Malhotra and N. Puwar, 'Selections from Raj Malhotra's (Indian Workers Association) cine collection'; see also N. Puwar, 'Social cinema scenes', p. 259 and note 3.
59 See, for instance, recently located 8mm colour silent footage produced by the Clarke family, in Manchester during the early 1960s: NWFA Film no. 1592/3.
60 C. Bailey, 'Cinema of duty'; see also S. Malik, 'Beyond the cinema of duty?'
61 C. Russell, *Experimental Ethnography*.
62 Coad, *The IAC*, p. 160. See also J. M. Moran, *There's No Place Like Home Video*.
63 See, for example, M. Roepke, 'Analysing acts of acting in amateur films', and G. Edmonds, '"Remember, remember …"'.
64 Conversations with amateur filmmakers during *A Day to Remember. The 75th Anniversary IAC Film and Video Institute*, National Media Museum, Bradford, 30 June 2007.
65 Macpherson, *Close Up*; see also Donald, Friedberg and Marcus, *Close Up, 1927–1933*.
66 Zimmermann, *Reel Families*.
67 Katelle, *Home Movies*.
68 R. Chalfren, *Snapshot Versions of Life*.
69 N. Kapstein (ed.), *Jubilee Book. Essays on Amateur Film*.
70 A. Schneider, 'Home movie-making and the Swiss expatriate identities'.
71 M. Stone and D. Streible, 'Introduction: small gauge and amateur film'.
72 S. Szczelkun, 'The value of home movies'.
73 L. F. Rhu, 'Home movies and personal documentaries'.
74 S. Aasman, 'Home movies, a new technology, a new duty, a new cultural practice'; see also S. Aasman, *Ritueel van huiselijk geluk [Rituals of Domestic Happiness]*.
75 W. L. Titus, 'Extended family films from the Dutch East Indies'; see also D. Hertogs and N. de Klerk, *Uncharted Territory*.
76 For Arctic missionary settings, see P. G. Geller, 'Into the glorious dawn'; for postcolonial insights see also A. Motrescu, 'British colonial identity in amateur films', and 'Private Australia'.

77 M. Roepke, *Privat-Vorstellung. Heimkino in Deutschland vor 1945* [*Private Screening: Home Cinema in Germany before 1945*].
78 R. Odin, R. (ed.), *Le Film de famille*.
79 S. Tenkanen, 'Children as amateur filmmakers'.
80 E. Cuevas (ed.), *La casa abierta*.
81 R. Shand, 'Amateur film re-located'.
82 M. Howe, '"The photographic hangover": reconsidering the aesthetics of the 8mm home movie'.
83 I. Craven, 'Introduction. *A Very Fishy Tale*'.
84 R. Fung, 'Remaking home movies'.
85 E. van Alphen, *Towards a New Historiography: Péter Forgács and the Aesthetics of Temporality*; see also B. Nichols, *The Memory of Loss: Péter Forgács's Saga of Family Life and Social Hell – in Dialogue with Péter Forgács*.
86 See, for instance, *Of Time and the City*, (Dir. Terence Davies, 2008) for its extensive use of archive newsreel footage.
87 D. E. James (ed.), *To Free the Cinema: Jonas Mekas and the New York Underground*.
88 Mark Neuman (Northern Arizona University), Conversation with author, 17 September 2010.
89 Steve Reich and Beryl Korot, *Three Tales*; see also the Otolith Group; see the introductory essays, poetic musings and self-reflections in the exhibition catalogue by Y. Dorme, *Images cachées – Hidden Images*.
90 J. M. Schwartz and T. Cook, 'Archives, records and power. The making of modern memory'; J. M. Schwartz and T. Cook, 'Archives, records and power. From (post-modernism) theory to archival performance'.
91 P. van Wijk (ed.), *You Can't See What You Don't Know*.
92 S. Kmec and V. Thill (eds), *Private Eyes and the Public Gaze*, pp. 7–11.
93 In 2010, Cor Draijer, the owner of a Dutch film transfer company, loaded five thousand home movies on to the Internet Archive: www.archive.org/details/collectie_filmcollectief.
94 A. Abraham, 'Deteriorating memories'.
95 Craven, *Movies on Home Ground*.
96 Katelle, *Home Movies*; see also Enticknap, *Moving Image Technology*.
97 N. K. Denzin, *The Cinematic Society: The Voyeur's Gaze*.
98 P. Bourdieu (with L. Boltanski, R. Castel, D. Schnapper and J.-C. Chamboredon), *Photography: A Middle-Brow Art*; J. M. Schwartz and J. R. Ryan (eds), *Picturing Place*; A. Kuhn and K. Emiko McAllister, 'Locating memory – photographic acts – an introduction', p. 1.
99 E. Edwards and J. Hart (eds), *Photographs Objects Histories*; A. Kuhn, *Family Secrets*.
100 R. C. Smith, 'Analytic strategies for oral history interviews'.
101 R. J. Grele, 'Oral history as evidence'.
102 See discussion of development since Donna Haraway's important introduction of the concept 'situated knowledges', in D. Haraway, *Simians, Cyborgs, and Women*, pp. 183–202); see also E. Engelstad and S. Gerrard, 'Introduction. Challenging situatedness'.
103 See also I. Craven, 'Neither fanatical nor lukewarm'.

104 See my work on travel-related amateur footage in bibliography. See also Hertogs and de Klerk, *Uncharted Territory*; D. Macdougall, 'Anthropology and the cinematic imagination'; J. L. Peterson, *Making the World Exotic*; Motrescu, 'British colonial identities'.
105 H. Norris Nicholson, 'In amateur hands'; *Screening Culture*, pp. 98–9.
106 An overview is offered by B. L. Craig, 'Selected themes in the literature on memory and their pertinence to archives'. See also J. M. Law. 'Introduction: cultural memory'. See also P. Ricoeur, *Memory, History, Forgetting*.
107 R. Shand, 'Theorising amateur cinema'.
108 M. Gergen, 'Life stories: pieces of a dream'.
109 M. Citron (ed.), *Home Movies and Other Necessary Fictions*.
110 P. R. Zimmermann, 'Speculations on home movies'.
111 P. Houston, *Keepers of the Frame*.
112 Schwartz and Cook, 'Archives, records and power. The making of modern memory'; R. C. Jimerson, 'Embracing the power of archives'.
113 Museums, Libraries and Archives Council, *Hidden Treasures*; Film Archive Forum, *The Moving Image Archive Framework*.
114 C. Steedman, *Dust*.
115 H. Norris Nicholson, 'Virtuous or virtual histories?'
116 See for instance the aims of the Internet Archive, San Francisco (set up in 1996), and available at www.archive.org/about/about.php, accessed on 14 May 2010.

2

The amateur club scene

Linking up with like-minded people was the next step for some new cine enthusiasts, once family and friends had been tried out as both subject and audience. Many converts trace their own discovery of amateur filmmaking to attending a meeting where amateur films were being shown and talked about. The impetus varied: a local advertisement spotted by chance, an invitation to accompany someone else to a club or attending an amateur film show. Many cine users operated away from formal support networks, but some soon connected with other pioneers eager to share cinematographic interests. In a broadcast made in 1986 to mark Warrington Cine Society's fiftieth anniversary, Percy Hughes reminisced about his club's origins.[1] Another founder member, John Langdale, who had first used a 9.5mm camera at school, read a newspaper notice about setting up a local group. He was 'very enthusiastic, very knowledgeable and seemed to have plenty of time – as public school boy – which I [Percy Hughes] hadn't got.' These embryonic cine clubs attracted enthusiasts whose interests overrode differences in education, background and class. Links developed across the increasingly heterogonous middling classes of interwar Britain and nurtured a minority interest against a background of worsening social, economic and political problems at home and abroad. From these fledging groups emerged specialist organisations that developed a sophisticated range of social, technical and educational activities over the years.

This chapter outlines the historical development of club formation. Regional and national outreach offered by the Federation of Cinematograph Societies (FCS) and the Institute of Amateur Cinematographers (IAC) is identified too, as is the part played by amateur film competitions. Similarities emerge when comparing how clubs began and evolved in response to technological changes and the broader societal and cultural shifts that affected people's involvement in formal or organised leisure pursuits. Yet, generalisations cannot mask the distinctive contributions of many individuals. Without such dedication, sometimes sustained over decades, such a buoyant component of cultural visual practice would never have taken root. This chapter draws upon the testimony of filmmakers who were willing and able to comment about regional club activities and their own involvement.

Banding together

According to the veteran filmmaker and private collector Angus Tilston from Merseyside, the setting up of Croydon Cine Club in 1899 was the first British instance of any organised amateur activity.[2] If verifiable, this would be a remarkable development in the history of cinematic development as a whole, let alone amateur activity, given its closeness to cinematic experimentation and public exhibition by the Lumière brothers, whose photographer had visited Liverpool two years earlier.[3] Evidence of organised activity may be traced with more certainty, however, to the years following the British launch of Kodak and Pathé's cine equipment during the early 1920s. The Cambridge University Kinema Club, founded by Peter Le Neve Foster and Cedric Belfrage in 1923, and one year earlier than its equivalent at Oxford, was described in the hobby press as the first amateur movie club in the world.[4] Le Neve Foster later founded the Manchester Film Society, remained active in making films and contributed to amateur cine literature for many years.[5]

During the mid-1920s, interest in cine film grew rapidly. Reporting in *Amateur Photographer and Photography* (*APP*) after an inaugural dinner in July 1927, the first secretary of the Amateur Cinematographers' Association (ACA) wrote of 'the ever-increasing numbers taking up cinematography as a hobby'.[6] There would be, he enthused, 'branches ... established all over the country' where members could show and comment on each other's films, share outdoor gatherings for filmmaking and establish a 'circulating library' of members' own films. The same magazine's next issue bore the expanded title, *Amateur Photographer and Cinematographer* (*APC*) in recognition of the 'considerable amount of space' devoted to cine film over the previous three years and an acceptance that 'amateur cinematography has come to stay'.[7] A later editorial in *Amateur Films* (*AF*) commented upon 'the formation of new clubs to foster the hobby all over the country'.[8] Stockport Cine Society, Manchester Film Society and Newcastle Amateur Cine Club came into existence in 1927.[9] The last was founded by James Cameron primarily 'to make story films following the example of the early commercial filmmakers', and the club's archive includes still photographs taken during outings of young women and men posing behind cine tripods.[10] The club claims to be one of the oldest surviving groups anywhere. Accordingly, 1927 seemed to be appropriate as the starting date for this fifty-year survey of cine practice.

Working together enabled enthusiasts to share equipment and expertise and use each other in acting roles, and guaranteed an audience. Club membership conferred self- and collective identity and many groups rapidly acquired secretaries, minute books, subscriptions and other hallmarks of many civic, amenity and occupational or professional organisations. Clubs inculcated a common culture and practice, based on the sharing of ideas and activities, as identified in Craven's discussion of amateurism.[11] Perhaps group membership helped to validate cine use too and to deflect some of the criticism that the new hobby attracted. Ridicule came from commercial cinema, from a rather ambivalent still photography establishment and also from others who satirised home-movie making (see Chapter 3). As one editorial claimed in late 1927, it was 'a sign of the times that amateur cinematographers are already banding themselves together'.[12]

During the 1930s, despite economic recession and escalating political tensions at home and abroad, new societies proliferated across the regions. The Royal Photographic Society's acceptance of a specialist kinematograph section was mirrored at provincial level. In Merseyside, the earliest organised cine club activity was held under the wider umbrella of Liverpool Amateur Photography Association.[13] On the Wirral, Wallasey Amateur Cine Club attracted twenty-two members during its first six months of independent existence, and within five years completed an impressive ten films as well as acquiring its own cinema with sixty seats.[14] Elsewhere, interest in motion picture making prompted photographic societies and other local amenity societies to set up sub-groups, as at Preston, while at Hebden Bridge a cine section formed within the Literary and Scientific Society. Clubs were often less than ten miles apart, reflecting the geographical scale of people's social worlds when car ownership was still a rarity outside affluent circles. Within and beyond the region, small informal groups as in Dewsbury, Huddersfield, Bradford, Wakefield and Barnsley announced their existence in the expanding news columns of the newly founded *Amateur Cine World* (*ACW*).

By 1934, some clubs had ambitious production schedules. After receiving encouragement for *At Face Value*, Bolton Amateur Cine Association began work in 16mm to document the 'evils of slum life' as understood through children's eyes.[15] Accuracy was emphasised and local council input would ensure the authenticity of 'any built up sets'. No one seemed to doubt the ability of adults to represent children's perspectives. In Manchester, fantasy prevailed and filming at Belle Vue Pleasure Gardens included 'free passes and placing two elephants, a sea-lion, a camel and a tame wolf at the director's disposal'.[16] Another ambitious co-production by Peter Le Neve Foster and Roy Clayton used trick photography and multiple exposures plus 'a 20 ton plaster world model, a medieval throne, a cardinal's study and Greek sculptor's study'. Casting involved 'a Neolithic child played by Ingelisa Holst, the daughter of the violinist'.[17] Not far away, the newly formed Hyde Cine Society planned 'a film of the Walt Disney variety' that might become, according to club publicity, 'the first cartoon film produced by any amateur society'.[18]

Further south, Stoke on Trent Amateur Cine Club (now Stoke Cine and Video Society) was founded in April 1935 in Hanley by John Martin, a pharmacist or photographic chemist as he was then known.[19] Martin bought Baby Pathé 9.5mm equipment in 1923 for about £6, and his earliest footage depicted family friends and their young children. He became inspirational for many local filmmakers and he was soon joined by a husband and wife, Laurie and Stuart Day, who were to both make many award winning films and remain active members for many decades.[20] Martin became the first president of the northern section of the Federation of Cinematograph Societies, and the organisation became particularly active in the late 1930s.[21]

Warrington Cine Society (now Warrington Cine and Video Society) began in October 1936 when, according to the club's surviving first Minutes Book, 'six men met at George Kirkham's'.[22] This brief entry skims over the circumstances that led to the club's formation, involving a friendship and passion for motorbikes shared by another founder member, Percy Hughes, mentioned earlier, and the entertainer George Formby, the latter becoming the society's first president. Following two biking accidents, and involvement with a locally made film of Prince Edward of Wales's visit to Warrington in 1928, Hughes tried to set up a cine section at the local camera club. Told that 'moving pictures would never replace [photo-plate lantern] slides', Hughes teamed up with Kirkham, a furniture sales assistant working in Manchester and running a tiny 9.5mm film hire company from his mother's house. By 1935, Kirkham owned a 9.5 mm camera and ran a small mail-order cine business. He notified recent customers by post of his wish to form a club. Thus started a society that has continued, apart from brief closure during the early 1940s, to function regularly through to the present.[23]

Meetings with purpose

Surviving records, members' reminiscences and regular contributions about club activities and members' productions to *ACW* and other specialist publications reveal the 'semi-formal' character of these early groups.[24] Many defined themselves separately from film appreciation societies as their focus was on practical production and critical response, rather than watching professionally made hired films. Early on, the label 'film society' was sometimes used, as at Manchester, where members combined practical interests with watching newly available productions, particularly those not readily shown in commercial cinemas. The early hobby literature shows that a broader awareness of professional cinema informed how club members sometimes tackled their own productions.[25] More experienced cine users readily advised newcomers about how to set up or run a club too. In his article 'The Ideal Cine Club', G. H. Sewell distinguished between 'serious amateurs' and those that 'play Hollywood'.[26] He suggested that clubs should adopt a constitution and have a reference library. They should aim to 'to bring interested people together, encourage the art and science of cinematography, and also foster and develop study, research and experimental work in all branches of cinematography'. For years, reference to the 'serious amateur' remained a standard feature of news reports on clubs and camera innovation.[27]

Men and women both took part in early club activities. As shown by the repertoire of early award-winning productions built up within some clubs, some women made films although more attended to watch material or take part in social events. Amateur fictional work often required women willing to display what Aldgate has called 'melodramatic emotionality' at a time when, even in mainstream cinema, male portrayal of 'emotion' and 'sentiment' was problematic.[28] Opportunities existed for female directors and scriptwriters in the earliest clubs in London, Manchester, Newcastle and elsewhere. One of Manchester Film Society's spectacular filmic denouements in 1929 included villainous attempts to lure the heroine Miss Scholfield to the top of the Fireworks Grand Stand at Belle Vue, before her lucky escape.[29] Frances Lascot, an early member of London Amateur Cine Association, was hailed as the nation's first woman director. As 'the maker of the first All Ladies Film',[30] she commended her knowledgeable camerawomen's 'nimble fingers' as they 'ruthlessly' cut, spliced and discarded during the editing process.[31] Women's ability to display strong feelings gained praise too in an early club contest that required each competitor to demonstrate 'a series of emotions'.[32] Given women members' early directorial prominence, their gradual concentration mainly into non-filmmaking aspects of club life in later decades parallels what happened to their professional counterparts. For aspiring female cinephiles, it is also indicative of how new duties of childcare and domesticity reshaped wider mid-century female participation in hobby activities. Those women filmmakers who established themselves within amateur cinema's formal structures – or remained outside it – often enjoyed leisure time that was uncompromised by family responsibilities (see Chapter 4).

Cine clubs developed differently, and reflected members' interests and time availability. Friends met in each other's homes, unless local contacts offered other venues. More clubs sought larger premises as membership rose in the postwar years. Individual filmmaking activities often predate the founding of specific clubs: George Higginson's remarkable films of Manchester's School of Art, made between 1929 and 1932, precede his years with Bolton Cine Society.[33] Clubs nurtured individual interests and encouraged group productions through regular weekly or fortnightly meetings. Apart from watching each other's films and those brought by visitors from other cine groups, practical sessions offered shared access to club-purchased equipment. More experienced members provided in-house instruction and a growing body of outside expertise soon developed through regional and national networks.

Club sessions ranged from specialist advice on choosing and using the latest commercially available products to demonstrations of improvised gadgetry. Some technically minded enthusiasts gained reputation on the club circuit – or through print – for particular skills in filming, processing, editing or projection. Club announcements testify to the hobby's intended wide-ranging appeal: 'cameramen, electricians, producers, actors, carpenters – all are welcome ... but sleeping beauties are not required', claimed Salford Cine Society in an appeal for new 9.5mm and 16mm users.[34] Changing technology's influence upon the hobby and club recruitment may be traced through announcements of club meetings on aspects of equipment design, gauge quality and projection specifications as well as on the subtleties of splicing, sprocket, lighting meter and sound systems. The technical focus within amateur activity drew praise from Alexander Korda and other establishment figures.[35] As with the critical response to feature films, such comments enhanced the hobby's overall reputation and helped to align it with professional practice. Other commentators cautioned that the hobby would not gain wider popular appeal unless simpler camera and projector equipment became available, as indeed ultimately happened with cine's replacement by alternative video media technologies.[36]

The transfer of technical knowledge became highly organised at Warrington Cine Society. From early 1938, each month included weekly meetings devoted to screening material from other clubs, indoor production, a film show of members' films, a lecture and trade demonstration slot and, where a fifth Monday occurred, any other business.[37] Inevitably, members' involvement influenced the approach, direction and long-term survival of clubs. Group dynamics affected a club's operation and internal tensions over equipment, finance, programming and the emphasis of production work. Despite the continuing flow of published and informal advice on club organisation, some groups lasted only for a couple of years or even less. External pressures led some clubs to close, during the war years. Low membership enhanced a club's cohesion but made it more vulnerable as people left for wartime service. Subscriptions were waived for members on active service, as at Hyde, but their names remained on circulation lists.[38] At Warrington, for instance, numbers had reached seventeen by the start of 1939 but by July average attendance had dropped to six. A decision to suspend further meetings until peace returned was overturned when nine people attended a special meeting in 1940 to discuss news of the Scottish Amateur Film Festival (SAFF). Although filmmaking did not resume until 1945, the club decided to run film shows, including screenings for US personnel based at Burtonwood Airbase, and occasional monthly meetings.[39]

Social activities consolidated club identity and strengthened friendships. They fostered a broader sense of belonging to an emerging movement that transcended the particularities of individual club programmes. In his 1986 television interview, Percy Hughes (Warrington Cine Society) recalled that shooting *Fishy Business* involved members having a club picnic before returning home.[40] Manchester's amateurs planned 'a week's camping trip to the Yorkshire moors to make a burlesque motor bandit film', and also undertook a three-day barge holiday together.[41] George Wain, filmmaker and writer, reported how twenty members from Hyde Cine Society visited a club in Stockport where 'informal suppers, dancing, table tennis or cards' followed the film show.[42] 'These [Stockport] members now are mostly level headed and sensible people and modern in outlook ... The flappers and others who joined up at first, thinking that they would be made into film stars right away have dropped out and ... filmmaking is being tackled in a serious way.' His comments and tone attest to the processes of self-regulation and internal validation that affected a club's reputation.

Widening networks

By 1939, much of Britain's club network benefited from affiliation to larger bodies. The FCS already offered loose association to numerous groups within southern England.[43] The wish for better understanding of activity nationwide, as well as some concern that northern club cine activity was rather eclipsed by activities in London and the southern counties, prompted societies from across Yorkshire, Lancashire and adjacent regions to form a northern section. Early officers included John Martin (Leek) as president and George Wain (Hyde) as secretary. Malthouse welcomed the northern initiative as 'not a house divided but rather a block of flats the tenants of which have not bothered to get introduced'.[44] Calls for cohesion became another expression of wartime unity: 'The cine societies are giving a lead to the movement. And the FSC is giving a lead to the clubs.'[45] An inaugural afternoon film show in Manchester, re-scheduled to avoid blackout conditions, attracted over one hundred people to watch films supplied from nine northern clubs. Other regionally based film shows arranged by the FCS for 'companionship' followed as part of the national war effort.[46] Wartime exigency thus reinforced centralising processes that had occurred within aspects of provincial middle-class life during the interwar years.[47] Yet, if mainstream cinema, the BBC and a London-dominated national press are sometimes seen as metropolitan influences extending their geographical range into provincial England, the co-ordinating structures within amateur cinema, also point to a strong sense of regionalism.[48]

Outreach by another umbrella organisation based in the South East influenced amateur activity profoundly. The IAC was founded in 1932.[49] Initially splitting from and then replacing the fledging British Amateur Cinematographers' Association (BACA), it also operated separately from the ACA, which championed local club development from c.1927. Club affiliation brought responsibilities and imposed the need for officers. Some groups preferred more informal arrangements and stayed outside the IAC's emerging national network. Early lists of regulations and permitted film locations, largely derived from codes of practice drawn up by official bodies with professional filmmakers in mind, reveal an early southern geographical bias. IAC membership offered technical and legal advice on sound or entertainment tax associated with public screenings as well as practical tips on using cameras at home, customs duty and travelling abroad. Other services included an equipment insurance scheme and maintenance checks by accredited and registered dealers who displayed an enamel IAC logo.[50] IAC affiliation conferred prestige and recognition, and also helped to raise the status and skills of many filmmakers but also differentiated between different kinds of cine user and amateurism.

Unashamedly, the IAC positioned itself at the forefront of Britain's amateur cinematography, with its own monthly members' *IAC Bulletin* and links to *Home Movies and Home Talkies* (*HMHT*) also launched in 1932. 'The Institute is built for service on lines hitherto unknown in the British Empire', publicity claimed, and various initiatives highlight early strategic thinking.[51] Titled patrons brought social distinction and publicity. Other known names drawn from commercial cinema and television attracted professional interest too. Membership savoured of privileged access to innovative visual practice and acquired social capital. Over three hundred people attended the IAC's first banquet, at the May Fair Hotel in London on 10 November 1933.

From its outset, the IAC's professional connections affected how Britain's amateur film movement developed, as in late 1933, when the organisation bestowed its own awards on members of the film industry.[52] Alexander Korda received the IAC's first annual Gold Medal of Merit for *The Private Life of Henry VIII* ('the finest talking picture made in Britain') while Hitchcock's *The Man Who Knew Too Much* received the IAC Gold Medal in 1934.[53] Such award-giving ensured a critical space for expressing opinion publicly on visual matters and obliged cinema professionals to participate within IAC activities. Media coverage was guaranteed. This close association between amateur filmmakers and the cinema industry as manifest through the advisory press is discussed further in Chapter 3. The IAC also sought professional involvement in the first national amateur 'movie-making competition' in November 1932 and at subsequent events. Medals, trophies and cash prizes for different categories of film attracted media coverage, and most of the male judges were drawn from within the cinema industry or film critics with national newspapers.

Film competitions

Competitions at club, inter-club and wider level attracted considerable amateur interest and expanded during the 1930s. Long-established within other branches of photography and a familiar feature of organised recreation, film competitions with awards for the best-made entry within each category could be organised within a single club or between neighbouring groups. Members and invited guests helped to judge and some local newspapers offered sponsorship as well as publicity. Competitions provided a framework within which cine users could produce a collaborative or individual film, according to certain parameters such as style, subject matter, camera type, film length or format. Competitions exposed films to wider critical viewers and offered more opportunities to show material. While some amateurs never became involved in competitions even at local level, for others taking part in national and regional events provided incentive and opportunity. Occupation, income, background, age and mobility influenced amateur involvement not only at club level but also within the growing networks that enabled amateur filmmakers to enhance their reputation and strengthen their skills. Award-winning films were discussed in the specialist press and available for screening, so non-competitive filmmakers were also exposed to high-quality amateur work.

SAFF had its origins in a competition that was organised for cine enthusiasts by the Meteor Film Producing Society and held in Glasgow in 1933.[54] The following year it was readvertised as an annual competition that by 1936 had been taken over by the newly formed Scottish Film Council (set up in 1934). SAFF then took place regularly until 1978, apart from during the Second World War when festival activities were suspended until 1948. As one of the oldest film festivals in the world, SAFF had considerable influence on amateur filmmaking, along with events organised by the IAC, as mentioned above and by *ACW* (see Chapter 3). Trade papers and the popular press promoted and sponsored club contests. Smaller events came to punctuate England's club calendar at local and regional level, also attracting a variety of sponsors offering cash prizes, medals and trophies. The amateur sphere was small enough for notable individuals within the movement to confer value at local level, as when Le Neve Foster judged Stockport and District Cine Club's film competition in 1934.[55] Such involvement echoed the participation of eminent professional filmmakers in the larger competitions during the interwar and early postwar years.

Clubs flourished as competition categories expanded, according to age, experience and gender, although appeals for more entries from women filmmakers recurred in the early 1950s.[56] Clubs benefited from screening the winning entries, running advisory sessions for aspiring filmmakers and the associated press coverage. Fears that competitive filmmaking would 'fetter' the free expression of the camera man' never disappeared completely but lessened as the benefits to amateur activity gained recognition.[57] Other hobbies saw opportunities for tapping into competitive fervour too: '*The Autocar*, to encourage the taking of photographs during motoring trips, is offering prizes weekly', announced *APC* in July 1927.[58] 'More motorists than ever carry cameras as part of their regular equipment, particularly when on holiday trips' the prose continued. The competition was later extended to readers of *The Motor Cycle*, a 'sister paper' produced for the hobby market by the same publishing house. It was symptomatic of the commercial ties within interwar Britain's emerging niche publishing on recreation.[59]

Reaching to readers in and beyond the club network, *ACW* announced its sponsorship of two trophies for the IAC and its own first competition on the theme of 'Weekend' in August 1934.[60] Entries required a seven-minute film on 16mm, 9.5mm or Standard 8mm, and novices had their own category. This event evolved into the *ACW*'s 'Ten Best' competition; carried on by its successor *Movie Maker* (*MM*), it became one of the most prestigious and long-lasting competitions in the history of Britain's amateur cinema. The postwar renaissance of cine clubs and amateur interests owed much of its impetus to hobby press coverage of competition-related activity and critical comment by professional filmmakers. Clubs in the North West also sustained the vibrant northern section of the North versus South competition: it was long championed by John Wright, a popular *MM* columnist, but instigated, according to some sources, by others in the northern amateur club scene. Conceived on the basis of friendly inter-regional rivalries, it opened new filmmaking opportunities and attracted loyal adherents. Strong regional affiliations emerged in positioning a dividing line through Staffordshire with members in Stoke on Trent, already well-established as an award winning club within IAC circles, firmly opting to belong north of the line.[61]

Overseas connections

During the 1930s, international amateur film interests rarely impinged directly on club activity within the North West, and awareness of overseas activity came mainly through the hobby press. While this might be viewed retrospectively as provincialism, it seems that language skills, economics, geography and the realities of many working lives constrained patterns of contact and attitudes. In the North West and elsewhere, filmmakers on the Left and for broader humanitarian reasons had links with Soviet Russia and with Spain during the Civil War.[62] However, most of the region's cine users functioned independently of the developing networks promoted by UNICA, the Union internationale du cinéma d'amateur, an international non-governmental organisation formed in 1931 from a 'Belgium federation of cine clubs'. UNICA first challenged clubs from Britain, France, the Netherlands and Austria to a film contest and evolved rapidly to organise a film competition in France with seventeen nations taking part under presidency of Louis Lumière two years later. Britain's membership was under the jurisdiction of BACA – 'a loosely knit consortium of amateur and commercial cine interests'. Amateur groups were only indirectly represented through the IAC, which suspended its membership of UNICA altogether between the late 1950s and the later 1960s. The lack of evidence for formal northern club links with UNICA marginalises its background presence within any regional history of amateur cinema. Further study of regional practice may disclose different patterns of relationship. Undoubtedly, structures for sharing interests overseas spread during the early and mid-1930s, and represented a spirit of popular internationalism that ran counter to the worsening political climate. As Washbrook observes, SAFF 'embraced and championed the theme of international camaraderie'.[63] The League of Nations invited amateur filmmakers to produce documentaries on aspects of their international work.[64] Bringing together people with interests in cine and travel was also suggested, although no evidence remains for such a group being set up.[65] Arguably, for filmmakers in the North West, there was so much going on at local level that involvement with organisations further afield was unnecessary, even though some affluent filmmakers regularly travelled abroad with their cine-cameras (see Chapter 7). Elsewhere, practice possibly differed, particularly in and around London where, occasionally, clubs reported on visits by amateurs from abroad. *ACW* welcomed entries to its 'Ten Best' from abroad and printed news of clubs formed overseas, including those sometimes founded by club members who emigrated and established groups within other English-speaking countries.

Amateur fiction

While much club activity sought to explore the cine-camera's potential to convey realism and documented diverse aspects of local interest, some filmmakers were interested in animation[66] and story film or fiction.[67] For such enthusiasts, the appeal seemed to lie in the cine-camera's capacity for creativity and the imagination, even if narratives sometimes brimmed with lifelike realism. Initially amateur fictional cinema attracted less research than material that now has historical interest, yet non-realist camerawork, narrative form and performative character embody wider changes in professional theatre and cinema. Club members often took on varied acting, script-writing or production roles. Collaboration between amateur drama groups and local cine clubs sometimes flourished as film crew and performers developed experience in working together. As in early commercial silent cinema, highly visual, melodramatic acting styles recurred. Inte-titling varied from pitchy punchlines to lengthier narrative links. Local theatre group members often welcomed the new opportunities for script-writing, directing, acting in front of the camera, costumes, set design and make-up. Lighting, composition, continuity and focal length as well as trying to add sound provided aesthetic and technical challenges too. Film offered a sense of permanence and enabled performers to see themselves acting.

Arthur Bromley, a key member of Manchester's Film Society, became a major influence in the setting up of Stockport Amateur Cine Players' Club.[68] Between 1928 and 1933, the club produced a historical fantasy as well as melodramas and mysteries centred on murder, robbery, kidnapping or other unexpected events.[69] Although some shooting scripts required only two or three characters and a single indoor or outdoor location with straightforward intertitling, plots were often elaborate. Filming required initiative, time and resources as two films were over thirty-five minutes long. *Bon Adventure*, the first 'feature film' produced by Newcastle Amateur Cine Association, made in the late 1920s, included rooftop chases, a biplane taking off, tracking dramatic long-distance pursuits over fields and a simulated fall from the top of a building and spread-eagled landing far below.[70]

Dream sequences provided opportunities for visual trickery and experimentation although detailed scenes shot on location often feature too. *Easy Come* (1933) made by members of Salford Cine Society on silent 16mm black and white filmstock focused on a mother who dreams that the family have won a competition.[71] A disastrous day at Blackpool ensues and the film ends with the mother waking to find that she did not win. Plotting and visual techniques – use of camera angles, fades, wipes, montage effects or different focal lengths – reflected filmmakers' competence and familiarity with other cinematic or dramatic forms. They are illustrative of evolving visual filmic vocabularies and the development of an amateur aesthetic that was nurtured by and yet sought to define itself differently from mainstream commercial cinema.

Just as the regional rise of plusher cinemas attracted middle-class audiences during the 1930s,[72] amateur fiction filmmaking seems an expression of cinematic form gaining greater acceptance as a respectable realm of activity beyond its popularist, Leftist and avant-garde circles. Productions often involved family and friends, as in the Mid-Cheshire Amateur Cinematography Society where the script-writer's wife acted in the films.[73] One such production was a ten-minute, silent, black and white film called *Double Strength*.[74] Trick photography duplicates objects and people as a wife tries every available

Flag Day Fancy (Dir. Mid-Cheshire Amateur Cinematography Society, c.1937). Image supplied by courtesy of North West Film Archive at Manchester Metropolitan University, film no. 4328 (b/w, silent, 15 min. 5 sec.).

remedy to cure her husband of chronic indigestion, before a dream reveals that each dose has double strength for her unfortunate spouse.

Double Strength contrasts with a short, silent club production called *Flag Day Fancy* made two years earlier (Figure 1).[75] Its moral tone and detail merit comment. On the way home from his local library, a man engrossed in his book on secret societies pushes into a woman collecting for charity. Thinking no more about the incident, he later accompanies his family on a picnic near a local castle but continues to read while his family enjoy themselves. At length, he notices and follows a Ku Klux Klan member along a path towards the castle where he is attacked and taken to a Klan gathering in a cave. The charity collector reappears and orders him to be thrown from a cliff, and, as he is hurled into the void, the man wakes to discover that he had dozed off while reading after the picnic. The film ends with the severely shaken father making a large charity donation, as if to compensate both for his self-absorption at the expense of charitable or parental duties. Notwithstanding the British bourgeoisie's well-known leanings towards the far Right, does the film offer more than mere exaggerated self-mocking finger-wagging at paternal behaviour on family outings? Britain's media coverage of atrocities carried out by the white supremacist group Ku Klux Klan was less frequent during the

1930s than in the previous decade but this club production may have been prompted by news coverage of Hugo's controversial nomination by Roosevelt to the US Supreme Court in 1937.[76] The horror lurking within a happy family outing to a local beauty spot parallels the reality of continuing Black oppression within the American Dream. For all that the makers use a visual motif associated with persecution elsewhere, and embed it within the familiarity of family and place, original artistic intentions are now lost. Visual striking imagery may have been selected arbitrarily to goad a flagging public generosity already stretched during the Depression years. Such interpretative ambiguities illustrate the need for further research on amateur fiction and highlight how embedded cultural values, ideologies and visual practices weave through this distinctive genre of club activity.

Local interests

Many individual filmmakers and cine clubs avoided fictional complexities and focused attention on where they lived. Varied subject matter was readily available; outside shooting did not rely upon additional lighting, and films about community events or the local area usually ensured a public audience. The earliest productions from many clubs across the North West were often documentary in style or simply edited reportage of royal visits and other civic or special occasions.[77] Just as factory gate footage projected at the start of film shows had attracted enthusiastic Edwardian audiences eager to watch themselves on screen as famously exploited by Blackburn's photographic entrepreneurs, Mitchell and Kenyon[78] and seen also in the localised making and showing of very early newsreels,[79] some amateur cine clubs saw films of local events as potential crowd pullers too. Members from other clubs sometimes joined in with productions if they lived nearby. Familiarity with local streets and buildings, as well as local contacts, often ensured that amateur enthusiasts accessed vantage points that were often equal to or better than those used by the official newsreel camera crews sent to film an event.[80]

Some cine clubs nurtured local interests by hosting public film shows about familiar people and places that also contributed towards financing better society equipment and premises. Local recognition of amateur film as a source of informative entertainment boosted a club's reputation and attracted new members too. Footage of local street scenes and celebrations associated with the coronation of George VI was so well received at Warrington town hall that the council offered to help the society.[81] By the end of 1937, five productions were completed, including *Processions and Celebrations* and *We Saw It Happen* on 9.5mm and *Grass-track Racing* on 16mm. *Warrington Walking Day* also attracted particular interest, and three public screenings were booked in February 1938 with tickets prices low enough – 6d (2.5p) and 1s (5p) – to avoid entertainment tax. The venue was not licensed for recorded sound or music, so a live commentary accompanied each screening. Subsequent films sustained public interest and included a royal visit and a war memorial dedication shot and screened eight days later. The club made *ARP* to inform viewers about air raid precaution, and civil defence if Warrington were to be bombed.[82] *ARP* was a response to public anxiety about gas attacks, some twelve months before the outbreak of war, and it combined drama documentary reconstructions and sequences shot in familiar places.

Amateurs and war

Film shortage, restrictions on using cameras, limits on evening activities and military call-up reduced cine club activity between 1939 and the later 1940s. One regional exception was in North Staffordshire. Stoke Cine Society's activities ceased but two of its younger members then attending Leek High School were instrumental in forming Leek Amateur Cine Society.[83] Gerald Mee (born 1926) recalls that a geography teacher, who supported the two boys' initiative in organising after-school film shows, helped them to organise three film shows in support of The British Red Cross, the Aid to Russia Fund and the Spitfire Fund. Youthful and technical inventiveness combined with wartime necessity. 'It was at this stage that I was given a portable HMV wireless set ... modified to take an input from ... my wind-up gramophone', recalled Gerald Mee in his mid eighties. 'I used to sit behind the translucent screen, suitably masked off by black curtains, and play 78rpm records and change them at appropriate points in the films, which I could see (in reverse) through the white screen material.' Mee left school in 1942, and, after university and National Service, returned to the relaunched Stoke Cine Society in c. 1950.[84]

Although some clubs suspended all activities during wartime, and stopped subscription charges for called-up members, amateur practice continued where circumstances permitted.[85] The hobby press regarded club activity on the home front as a contribution to national morale and public information. Recording wartime experiences was also recognised as having future personal and wider significance.[86] Cine footage made during active service seems infrequent as the War Office forbade filming in locations that might have even indirect strategic significance.[87] Surviving wartime scenes shot from a ship's bridge or of military personnel relaxing were usually filmed by higher-ranking officers during off-duty moments.[88]

Apart from one of Warrington Cine Society's founder members, John Langdale, who apparently filmed while serving in the Middle East, no regional evidence of club members using their cine-cameras during active service has surfaced during this study.[89] However, some cine club members maintained still photography while overseas, including Mee, whose improvised dark room in Malta survived as a shed decades later.[90]

In contrast, cine enthusiasts young enough to be eligible for National Service through until 1963 had a slightly better chance of being able to take their cine-cameras with them. Arthur Smith, an early member of Sale Cine Club in Cheshire, joined a photographic unit that served in Germany and Suez but high film costs meant that he did not use his own camera.

Boom years

Cine clubs boomed in the early postwar years, with suggested numbers doubling to between approximately 250 and 300 clubs between 1946 and 1957.[91] Some groups were relaunched through publicity, while new fledging clubs established themselves.[92] Despite petrol rationing, Warrington Cine Society resumed regular meetings in May 1947, with a mix of existing and new members.[93] Meetings were held at members' homes and the club quickly adopted membership cards, printed stationery and subscription rates at 21s (£1.05) for men, and 'half price for ladies and juniors'. Members soon made their first postwar film and resumed the prewar pattern of practical meetings, screenings and demonstration nights. The club became proud of its business-like administration and bookkeeping, as well as its high-quality output of award-winning films. Not all clubs within the region witnessed such speedy consolidation and focus.

Arthur Smith recalls his own early filmmaking activities, after joining Sale Cine Club in about 1951; it had a good reputation and a number of award-winning club productions.[94] 'It was largely a kind of social club but also made films ... fairly well-to-do people who would make 16mm colour films which were ruinously expensive of holidays and scenic areas of Wales and [the occasional] silent comedy or drama [that] were very good and polished. They used to take a lot of time about it.' Smith, with a couple of other younger members, feeling somewhat marginalised, formed Solo Films and they began to make their own films. An early production, *Doppelganger*, received praise and first prize in *ACW*'s Ten Best competition.[95] Success reinforced the young filmmakers' career ambitions and two of Solo Films' founding members went on to work professionally. Smith was still active as an independent filmmaker in 2007. His interests in cinema began at the age of eleven when he sold his train set to buy his first 9.5mm camera and started to make films, inspired by his father's love of films. Early projects included Stretford Pageant, a school visit to the Festival of Britain in 1951, and other school excursions. Through hiring films which he charged young friends to watch in the family garage, Smith became familiar with many cinematic styles that came to influence his own films. He insists that the high praise for *Doppelganger*'s aesthetic quality and imaginative portrayal of the Lake District setting did not purely derive from his early exposure to film noir and art-house material.[96] Smith recalls that he and his friends ran out of money, used cheap wartime filmstock, and only after processing discovered the fogging effects that so appealed to the judges.

The competition structure appealed to Solo Films' aspiring filmmakers and they made other award-winning films. Smith combined professional opportunities for working with a Manchester-based production unit on industrial films and newsreel with his recreational filmmaking. His experience and competence grew rapidly and, as he bought better equipment, productions with Solo Films became more ambitious, including a wining entry to a national road safety competition. Contact with other clubs, particularly Altrincham Cine Society, led to collaborations that cemented friendships able to withstand the interruptions caused by National Service and work-related moves.[97] From Solo Films, Arthur Smith, Alan Howden and Philip Jenkinson all subsequently joined the BBC and, many years later, Alan Coulter, another pioneer from the Altrincham Cine Society, also joined after a career in quantity surveying.[98] Contacts, an expertise derived from amateur involvement and determination characterise these club members' movement between professional and hobby-related film work.

Was it coincidence or a combination of circumstances in postwar North West England that enabled these amateurs to go professional? Certainly, the early vision of amateur activity as a nursery bed for nurturing professional talents persisted in the amateur press and elsewhere during the 1950s (see Chapter 3). While some filmmakers successfully moved between amateur and professional spheres, there were many others who hoped that they might become professional eventually.[99] Charles Chislett from Rotherham believed that his travelogues could help to promote postwar British tourism overseas.[100] Smith acknowledges that he was lucky on numerous occasions to be given the responsibilities and opportunities that enabled his hobby to become a career. Manchester's size, role and postwar economy were significant too in attracting regional independent television and then the formation of a regional BBC presence that offered employment opportunities in media outside London. A long history of commercial cinematic activity, evidenced by the film hire companies, regionally based production companies including Mancunian Films[101] and cinema networks[102] may also have been formative in attracting both young and older members to an expanding circuit of cine groups right across the region.

Social mobility

Undoubtedly, Solo Films was unusual in the career route of its teenager founders but not unique at either a regional or a national level.[103] The professionalism brought to club and individual productions remained independent of members' paid work, even if their activities connected with other professional interests. Until the 1960s, much club membership still involved people who after leaving school did not go to university but started to work in local government or a variety of expanding public, technical and communications services within in their home area. Newer cine users came also from within commercial backgrounds as well as from varied professions. Hobbies pursued either at home or, as for club members, within the company of fellow enthusiasts were still an established part of postwar culture.

The Coronation boosted both television and camera sales in 1953.[104] At Warrington, George Kirkham lucratively combined television rental and sales with cine film and equipment hire.[105] As elsewhere, 8mm, 9.5mm and 16mm formats became more cheaply available and, for the first time, club members made films on all gauges. Membership outgrew house meetings and people travelled by public transport or car to meetings in hired rooms. Larger venues were used for public film shows and, as clubs expanded, members found their own particular niche for involvement in production, social and administrative activities. Scope existed for launching initiatives as individuals seized opportunities to set up something new.

The recollection of Ashby Ball (born 1927) of how Southport Movie Makers originated is another striking example of youthful innovation in the postwar years.[106] As a child he had owned a hand-cranked toy film projector and a loop of 35mm film that showed a man juggling with a top hat. Family interest led to the purchase of a 9.5mm projector to show hired films and to Ball's own growing familiarity with cinematography. He had already traded in a 9.5mm camera for 16mm equipment when he joined a newly set up local amateur drama group. During the summer of 1949, Ball financed the group's first film. A subsequent fund-raising film show combined group productions with hired material and attracted the group's first commission, *Calling to You* (see Chapter 8).[107] Southport Movie Makers (as the club subsequently came to be called) thus began a commitment to making documentaries that continued over the next six decades.[108] Commissioned films on cultural and environmental themes, as well as dramas and comedies, have attracted awards consistently, although contemporary club details emphasise that they remain amateurs who approach their filmmaking with professionalism (Figure 2).

Youthful zeal started Hoylake Cine and Video Club on the Wirral in the 1950s too.[109] Keith Maxwell recalls saving, at the age of fourteen, for his first camera, a second-hand 9.5mm Pathé H model, after watching someone else filming on holiday. Seeing films regularly and attending the local photography club furthered his own interests, although there was no amateur activity nearby. His family bought him a hand-cranked projector, although his mother was reluctant to be filmed, and after leaving school Maxwell combined filmmaking with market gardening whenever opportunities arose. Through 'tagging along' on overseas school journeys he produced travel films with a former teacher who provided sound commentaries. The travelogues were popular locally, even

Club trophies, Southport Movie Makers, 1951–2010.
Image supplied by courtesy of Ashby Ball and Southport Movie Makers.

though screening rarely achieved perfect synchronisation. Maxwell started a cine section within Hoylake Photographic Society in c.1958 and, like many other enthusiasts, replaced his 9.5mm first with 16mm and then with Super 8mm. Using 16mm enabled simple animation, Maxwell recalls, as it was easy to add to his holiday films 'using the backwind facility to do dissolves and move letters around' while his own digital transfers now connect younger family members to his early films.

As membership grew, the club became independent and organised its own competitions. Several of Maxwell's holiday films won prizes during the early 1960s, although his main audiences were friends and family. As sound cine equipment grew bulkier, Maxwell decided to convert a stable on his own land into a thirteen-seater projection studio for the club (by now known at Hoylake Movie Makers). A purpose-built 'shed with seats in' with seating for twenty-six people later replaced the stable and became the club's home for meetings and social events, supported (in mid 2007) by a core of ten regulars who still attend charity nights using films of past horse races. Hoylake Movie Makers remains a distinctive group that reflects its founder's interests but illustrates the widening social reach of amateur activity.

Gaining confidence

In contrast, Bury Cine Society in Greater Manchester was a collective endeavour from the outset.[110] The club traces its unbroken history from 1959, although the first attempt at launching Bury Amateur Film Society in January 1955 prompted headlines in the *Bury Times*, 'Cine filming not a rich man's hobby'.[111] Despite the flurry of subsequent activity, a membership that swelled rapidly to at least thirty-four, and contact with other regional cine groups, the club lasted less than three years. Within weeks of its relaunch in 1959, members planned to film local life in Bury. It was a decision that was to have far-reaching consequences for the society and its relationship to the town, and discussion of raising funds by 'working as a film unit' quickly followed. *Our Town* was shown to over eight hundred people on its opening three nights, and later had a public showing in Angoulême, Bury's twin town. It attracted many subsequent private and public bookings across the region.[112]

Another club production, *Portrait of Wednesday*, began. As a 'study of contrasts', the town's story unfolded through different experiences 'not dwell[ing] on these characters but they become as familiar faces in a crowd'. This 'attempt to create a true impression of local life', took over a year to complete. Over twelve hundred people attended the opening screenings and again it attracted private bookings, as well as additional film work. Unlike its shorter predecessor, its screenings were ultimately limited by concerns about damaging the film as the society could not afford to copy it.[113] The problem was partially resolved by video transfer over thirty years later although the original filmstock has yet to be conserved.

These early successes prompted much pride but also concerns about their cost and time-consuming nature. The club subsequently stopped making films for local businesses and produced newsreels about Whitsun Walks, and other local events. Footage features opening or founding ceremonies for several buildings that have became civic landmarks, and a veterans' parade, on the fiftieth anniversary of the Lancashire regiments' landing in the ill-fated Gallipoli campaign. Members filmed the then Prime Minister Harold Wilson during a civic visit and allowed a late-arriving television crew to film using the club's lighting rig. The club subsequently received a gift of additional lights from the Labour Party.[114] Patronage, of varying forms, enhanced the activities at a number of clubs over the years, whether by chance or by more strategic networking at local level and beyond.

Some club members were unhappy to be known as 'the people who make the big documentaries' and preferred working with animation and comedies. Screening award-winning films at other clubs and in public venues benefited membership levels and club finances. The club established its own trophies to promote holiday filmmaking and deliberately sought younger members. Within five years, Bury was a key regional player and had achieved successes at national and international level. Proximity to other urban centres sustained social activity and networking that consolidated its local prominence. Its varied output and its meetings reflected members' interests. Promotional and demonstration gadget evenings kept members abreast of technological developments and made new purchases easier. Lectures by club members and visiting speakers disseminated innovative practice and expertise. Screenings remained popular, as did visits to other clubs within the region and further afield. Over half of the membership was over fifty, but younger members were very enthusiastic and programming accommodated generational differences. Programming for January 1966 included a film show about the Salford artist L. S. Lowry, and a screening of *Frankenstein's Experiment'* and *I Was a Teenage Birdman* plus other films made by a group of young filmmakers who called themselves the Delta Science Fiction Group of Manchester.[115] Such eclecticism helped clubs to withstand and embrace change.

By now, the North West amateur club scene had entered its most vibrant period. Memberships reached fifty at Bury Cine Society (1964) and sixty-five at Warrington Cine Society (1966–67) and new clubs had set up during the previous decade including Swan Cine Club (1955; now Swan Movie Makers)[116] and also Pendle Film Society in Nelson (now Pendle Movie Makers) in c.1960.[117] Preston and District Cine Society was set up initially in 1949 but closed by 1955 owing to the untimely death of its founder member, Jack Dempsey. It was launched as Preston Cine Club by Mrs Barrett, the owner of a local independent photographic shop, but her early death cut short her own attempts to foster local cine interest beyond merely selling cine equipment.[118] The club broadened beyond its initial remit to assist inexperienced new cine owners, and soon acquired the familiar range of club activities and film productions.

During the 1960s, various changes, however, began to affect both the newer and the long-established groups. Older founding members were beginning to retire or pass away and younger recruits were more likely to use Standard 8 colour film. Sound had become easier to add and the inventiveness of the early club pioneers was being replaced by an ever-increasing array of commercially available products designed for every stage of shooting, editing and presenting amateur material.[119] The middle decades of the last century were an important transitional period as club membership and interests gradually changed.

Arthur Bickerstaffe's description of his own club at Pendle as 'very much a middle-class, middle-aged society' with 'at most, a couple of under twenties' and 'a maximum of about thirty people involved, mostly men' probably fits many other clubs at the start of the 1960s.[120] Yet there were differences too. Pendle Film Society's early members included Tom Sparks (born 1927), a mill worker, although he also worked as a local cinema projectionist.[121] A career wish, born of a childhood love of animation and his own skills in drawing, and denied through family circumstances and attitudes, became an enduring hobby via the amateur movement. Sparks saw a press notice announcing the club's first meeting and thus began his own involvement. He made many animations and even more documentaries on birdlife during a twenty-year filmmaking partnership with Jack Spencer, a local headteacher 'with a good speaking voice'. Sparks recalls how 'they were all amateurs and they pooled knowledge' and shared cars on visits to other clubs to 'see what each other did'. He recalls that 'one or two wives came but left filming to the men'.

Other founder members included Peter Copestake and his wife Dee who both went on to win numerous local and regional competitions.[122] Peter

Copestake (born 1932) was a vet who traced his self-taught skills to a fascination for Britain's documentary movement. Copestake also acknowledges how his social circle widened as he visited other clubs and worked on projects commissioned by different organisations. Arthur Bickerstaffe, then employed at the local camera shop, recalls the club's annual dinners and picnics. The programme 'reflected the typical hobbyist's fascination with the latest equipment and gadgets' for whom 'the quality of the screened image was more important than the subject matter.' As in most organisations, there were dedicated key individuals. 'While most members were happy to attend weekly meetings and be informed and entertained, there was the inevitable clique who "ran things", and also, to be fair, produced most of the films which were different to family holiday movies.' From the newly formed club's decision, to enter the BBC's *Vanishing Britain* competition, through to the fiftieth anniversary celebrations, commitment has characterised club activity.[123]

The regional cine scene thrived during the 1960s. High membership enabled many groups to average several club productions per year, films often achieving commendation at regional and national level. Early material gained historical value in public film shows. As regional urban redevelopment and modernisation schemes transformed built form and social fabric, films about past local life attracted large paying audiences. Invitations to document local events and issues came to filmmakers in and outside the club circuit. Some members cautioned against damaging a club's reputation by tackling projects better suited to professional outfits. Altrincham Cine Society joined the club scene in 1967 and attracted attention by winning £200 in cash with its first club production, *Child's Eye View*, in the national Royal Society for Prevention of Accidents (ROSPA) road safety film competition the following year.[124] Successive award-winning productions assisted requests for council support for funded premises, and within a few years the club had free access to a sixty-seater cinema and club room that could also be hired out for community events. Financially buoyant and highly regarded, the club's recruits from Solo Films brought connections, either to independent filmmaking or within the BBC. Alan Coulter, a quantity surveyor who changed careers to become a sound recordist, initially with the BBC but later as a freelance, attributes his second career to the professionalism achieved through amateur activity. Arthur Smith, also mentioned earlier, had much involvement too with this club.[125] Both men emphasise that their amateur involvement did not overlap in practical ways with their professional work.

Changing times

The 1970s marks an important transitional period during which clubs repositioned themselves in relation to internal and wider changes. Older members were passing away and the greying of club attendance prompted, for the first time, subscription rates for retired people at Warrington and elsewhere.[126] Displeasure grew over manufacturers' apparent complicity in eclipsing earlier filmmaking technologies through withdrawing components and raising prices as new products were launched. Continuing concern mixed with pragmatism over commercially driven changes that seemed to favour cine users as relatively cheaper equipment became more widely available by the end of the decade. Trends in film format and camera design prompted renewal of the so-called 'gauge war' over earlier film types. Sound film gradually replaced silent filmstock, rendering another phase of innovative lip-synchronisation techniques superfluous to modern cine users. While the simplicity of operating Standard and Super 8 film gauges attracted some new recruits, other individuals left filmmaking altogether rather than adapt to modern formats. Clubs specialised, focused, merged and folded under the pressures as members negotiated their ways through a changing landscape of technical possibilities and cinematic expectations. On Merseyside, Wallasey Cine Group and Wirral Movie Makers evolved from Double Run Cine Group that, in turn, could trace its own origins to an earlier regrouping.[127]

Cine club membership levels remained stable but more recruits were coming from the over fifty-five age group rather than the under-twenty-fives although patterns of recruitment and retention differed greatly. Chorlton Cine Club, in Manchester, although formed only in 1960, limited itself to a membership of forty in the early 1970s.[128] Liver Cine Group, based on Merseyside, reported in 1971 that members exceeded one hundred.[129] Commentators spoke increasingly of falling numbers.[130] Although the picture remains patchy, the overall downward trend was unmistakable. Club activity relied upon more than simple numbers, and both interviewees in my research and the specialist press emphasise that club vitality over many years was often sustained by a much smaller inner band of dedicated individuals than individual club membership figures might suggest.[131]

Widening opportunities to further and higher education affected club recruitment in opposing ways. Old-established and newer campus-based groups generated term-time amateur activity independently of established club circuits. In Manchester, student productions ranged from aesthetic and esoteric experimentation to socially engaged reportage on current political issues or the noisy spectacle of fund-raising during Rag Week. Student filmmakers often gained access to locations and situations that might otherwise have been omitted from other visual records. Inevitably, student amateur filmmaking contributed to the loss of young recruits to amateur groups in their home areas even though it may have fostered a new generation of media-savvy teachers in schools from the later 1960s.

Campus activity did not radically change the gender imbalance within amateur practice. Student club productions, at least in the North West, usually involved more men than women, as did the wider club scene. Admittedly, the numbers of single women filmmakers had increased slightly during the 1960s even though, for one woman filmmaker in Preston, smoke-filled meetings symbolised the still predominantly male culture of club life. Numbers of women holding official committee positions remained small, particularly outside social and secretarial roles. More couples became jointly involved in club productions although instances of shared filmmaking interests also occur much earlier. Childcare duties prevented both parents' club attendance and domestic responsibilities still determined many women's involvement in formal cine activity.

Other societal changes were affecting club life and leisure trends. More homes had television, including colour television, and people began to watch and manipulate moving imagery in new ways. Clubs and commentators struggled to keep up with the aesthetic and commercial implications of fast-changing camera technologies.[132] The brave words of *MM*'s columnist, Ivan Watson, for instance, were undermined by video equipment's commercial availability – albeit at a price – within a decade: 'I can't see film disappearing for a heck of a long time.' He doubted 'that somebody should produce a really compact VTR device no bigger than a cine-camera, powered by penlight batteries, *capable of recording pictures in colour* – and costing less than £100. Technically, I don't think this is feasible at the moment or in the foreseeable future.'[133]

Clubs responded differently to developments in sound and tape-slide production. Some critics saw the latter, which involved projecting slides with accompanying music or spoken commentary, as a hybrid visual distraction from film production, even though it gained its own dedicated competition in 1970.[134] Negotiations between the British Amateur Cinematographers' Central Council and Mechanical Copyright Protection Society brought about changes in sound licensing for amateur filmmakers that indicated the increasing use of recorded copyright music to accompany film projection or as an integral part of soundtracks in film production. An additional licensing arrangement in 1973 to cover those aged seventeen or still at school may be seen as another endeavour to foster younger people's involvement.[135]

Clubs now coincided with the emergence of Britain's first generation of healthier retired people who had benefited from over two decades of public health care. Materially better housed and with more disposable income and personal mobility than in the past, people in active retirement boosted memberships for many local societies during the 1970s.[136] Although members were not primarily part of the age-group that was fast abandoning commercial cinemas,[137] demographically they were part of society targeted by expanding adult education, as mentioned by Chalke in her historical overview of the Grasshopper Group's decline.[138] Other clubs also noted a reduction of interest in animation although fictional and documentary output remained vibrant among many groups' productions.[139]

Political and economic influences affected the club scene too. In 1972, power cuts during the miners' strike restricted club meetings. Local authority energy-saving and early closing schemes disrupted clubs that held their evening meetings in council buildings. Continuing fuel shortages prompted the government to introduce a three-day working week and strained industrial relations affected life generally. Amongst other disputes, the national postal strike, as well as Kodak's own strike, slowed down film processing, which delayed club production and competition programming during 1973–74. Rising costs of rented club rooms and other overheads, equipment and film were variously ascribed to devaluation and decimalisation.[140] In the middle of the decade, cultural budgets were affected by public spending cuts and reduced the BFI's financial support for screening the Ten Best.[141]

Meanwhile festival activity thrived, as shown by twenty northern clubs supporting the Chorlton Film Festival held in Wilmslow, Cheshire. As festival-going practices took root within different kinds of leisure activities, the first British international amateur film festival was held successfully in 1975.[142] Organised overseas cine-making visits proliferated too, indicative of greater disposable incomes, increased leisure time and changes in international tourism. Long-haul destinations included Expo 70 in Osaka, via stops in Soviet cities, and varied shorter filmmaking opportunities set up by wide-ranging holiday organisations, as well as by individual cine clubs and the IAC, flourished in Britain and mainland Europe.[143]

Any assessment of amateur cinema during the 1970s, as in previous decades, involves considering the interplay of internal and external influences upon organised activities. By 1977, the club scene mirrored wider patterns of continuity and change that underlay the preceding fifty years of cine film activity. Cine usage had changed profoundly; it had matured from its initial nationwide scatter of independent and youthful enthusiasts, headed up by self-selecting zealous pioneers whose beliefs in creating an alternative to mainstream commercial cinema combined self-righteous confidence and optimism. Along with the unshakeable convictions of amateur innovators whose dedication established a vision of activity broadly acceptable to many within emerging cine circles, those early users of small-gauge film – often professional in all but how they earned their living – set up organisational structures and the basis for an enduring collective identity. Fifty years on, another generation of enthusiasts had assumed leadership roles amidst an increasingly complex social milieu.

If, in the aftermaths of two world wars, recovery, renewal and the return to peacetime normality embraced enormous societal gulfs between optimism, disillusionment, rebellion and complacency, during the later 1960s and 1970s, nostalgia and conservatism were also strong undercurrents in the nation's political and cultural consciousness. In the 1920s, modernity had been unsettling for some but for others a liberating blast of fresh air through lingering Edwardian conventions, class structures and attitudes. Early amateur creative fervour to form clubs, tackle group productions and self-advocate through print occurred largely outside Britain's avant-garde circles. Fifty years on, despite the persistent myth of 1960s Britain being a time of optimism and innovation, fresh fears about 'the corrosive effects of modernity' existed.[144] New tensions reflected changes in the nation's social, economic and ethnic make-up. They manifested themselves in a renewed retreat into domestic space where home improvements, gardening and television consumption of such popular series as the remarkably successful *Dad's Army* helped to offset unsettling challenges to identity and belonging.[145] As in the past, hobby club companionship maintained familiar routines too and even helped to insulate against broader changes, whilst perhaps unwittingly distancing itself from the very lifeblood needed for survival.[146] In the winter of 1977, the BBC's thirteen-part series *Caught in Time*, used home movies gathered by national appeal 'to provide a glimpse of fashion, family and political life as seen by the ordinary men and women' of the 1920s and 1930s.[147] Perhaps rather oversimplifying its aim 'to recreate a social history rather than a nostalgic scrapbook of the period', its commissioning fitted in well with contemporary historians' championing of 'history from below'.[148] Its appearance was timely too in acknowledging the wider interest and significance of amateur material. Implicitly, it was also a boost for practising cine philes.

Writing off the 1970s solely as a time of declining club activity would be disingenuous to amateur cinema. Undeniably, membership numbers had declined by 1977, but precise figures are unknown, as clubs records currently remain too geographically scattered for an overview. Furthermore, as clubs across the regions celebrate major anniversaries, the adaptive vitality of past amateur visual practice remains apparent. The amateur's picture-making impulse, whether for self-documentation or for creative collaborative effect, connects the origins of early cinema with the latest capabilities of digital media. How amateur passions not only sustained networked communities of club members but also generated their own hobby press is the focus of Chapter 3.

Notes

1 G. Malthouse, '21 years of amateur movies. *ACW* celebrates its majority', *Amateur Cine World*, 19:1 (1955), 37–8.
2 Angus Tilson (Swan Movie Makers), Correspondence with the author, 12 June 2007.
3 Scenes across Liverpool were filmed in 1896 by Alexandre Promio for the Lumière Brothers, who released footage in 1897.
4 Cited in *Amateur Cine World*, 5:3 (1949), 849. The BFI's *Catalogue of the National Film Library* (1936) lists *The Witch's Fiddle* (Dir. P. Le Neve Foster, 1924) as the first film produced by Cambridge University Film Society (aka Kinema Club). *Amateur Films* 1:7 (1929) also mentions *Big Dog* (Dir. Rudolph Messel) and comments: 'one of the original Oxford amateur cinematographers in 1924'. No further information about early activity at Oxford has surfaced in my research although Messel contributed to early film criticism, including *This Film Business*. Belfrage also established his reputation as a journalist and film critic.
5 (Anon.), 'Personalities. – No II. "Foster of Manchester"'.
6 C. J. Wilson, cited in F. J. Mortimer, 'Spirit of the times'.
7 F. J. Mortimer, 'The coming boom in amateur cinematography'.
8 G. H. Sewell, 'Talks to the tyro – I. What is it all about?', 252.
9 Name changes complicate tracing early clubs. For instance, *Wide Angle* (Newsletter of the North West region of the IAC) reported that Harry Secombe sent congratulations to Manchester Cine Society on its thirtieth anniversary (*Wide Angle* (Spring 1963), 12) although Peter Le Neve Foster cites his own founding of Manchester Film Society in 1927, in 'Every cine enthusiast must aim at originality'.
10 Tony Cox, '*History of Newcastle ACA*', Correspondence with the author, 13 June 2007. See also Michael Gough (Newcastle ACA Film and Video Makers), ... *And Still We Meet on Tuesdays. Celebrating 75 Years of Amateur Filmmaking* (Club production, 2002), kindly loaned by Doug Collender, June 2007.
11 See, for example, reference to Robert Stebbins's work on the sociology of leisure in I. Craven (ed.), *Movies on Home Ground*, pp. 6–13.
12 F. J. Mortimer, 'Spirit of the times', 455.

13 Angus Tilson (Swan Movie Makers), Correspondence with the author, 12 June 2007.
14 (Anon.), 'Club news', *Amateur Cine World*, 6:4 (1939), 185.
15 (Anon.), 'Club news', *Amateur Cine World*, 1:3 (1934), 77.
16 *Ibid.*
17 *Ibid.*
18 J. S. Fitton, 'Hyde Cine Society'.
19 Gerald Mee (Stoke Cine and Video Society), *Amateur Film Memories – The First 30 Years!* Draft publication and email correspondence with author, June 2007.
20 *Ibid.*
21 *Ibid.* See also *Amateur Cine World*'s editorial comments and club reports repeatedly during 1939.
22 Rob Evans (Warrington Cine and Video Society), Correspondence with author, June 2007.
23 *Ibid.*
24 Robert Stebbins's term 'semi-formal' is used while discussing amateur social worlds in I. Craven (ed.), *Movies on Home Ground*, p. 9.
25 See discussion of film criticism within *Close Up* in L. Marcus, *The Tenth Muse*, pp. 319–403. See also Chapter 3.
26 G. H. Sewell, 'The ideal cine club'.
27 See for instance, (Anon.), 'Movies for the home', and (Anon.), 'Making films in the home'; See also R. Stebbins, *Serious Leisure*, pp. 1–37.
28 T. Aldgate, 'Loose ends, hidden gems and the moment of "melodramatic emotionality"'.
29 G. H. Sewell, 'Our cover picture'.
30 (Anon.), 'Personalities. – No. V. "Frances Lascot"'.
31 F. Lascot, 'My very first film'.
32 (Anon.), 'News from the societies'.
33 S. Hawley, 'The outsider: the films of George Higginson'.
34 Salford Cine Society, 'All are welcome'.
35 A. Korda, 'Readers' thoughts'.
36 D. Arnold, 'How television could yet bring a home movie boom'.
37 Rob Evans (Warrington Cine and Video Society), Correspondence with author, June 2007.
38 (Anon.), 'What the societies are doing', *Amateur Cine World*, 6:8 (1939), 371; (Anon.), 'Letters'.
39 See note 37.
40 'Percy Hughes in conversation …'. Kindly loaned by Rob Evans, July 2007.
41 P. Le Neve Foster, 'Manchester Film Society news'.
42 *Ibid.* Wain, 'Hyde Cine Society'.
43 (Anon.), 'Note on Federation of Cinematograph Societies'.
44 G. Malthouse, 'Joy through strength'.
45 G. Malthouse, 'Markets for your films'.
46 *Ibid.*, 345; see also P. W. Harris, 'What about Christmas?'.
47 R. Trainor, 'Neither metropolitan nor provincial'; see also D.L. LeMahieu, *A Culture for Democracy*.

48 Richards, 'Cinema-going in Worktown'.
49 Coad, *The IAC*, p. 7.
50 Coad, *The IAC*, pp. 10–12; Institute of Amateur Cinematography (IAC), *International Itinerary, 1934*.
51 Coad, *The IAC*, p.15.
52 *Ibid.*, pp. 18–21.
53 *Ibid.*, p. 25.
54 J. McBain, 'And the winner is'.
55 (Anon.), 'What the societies are doing', *Amateur Cine World*, 1:7 (1934), 325.
56 See, for example, L. Wood, 'At your cinema: wanted – cine suffragettes': see also H. Norris Nicholson, 'Women and amateur filmmaking'.
57 G. H. Sewell, Untitled note, *Amateur Cine World*, 1:6 (1934), 245.
58 See note 7.
59 See, for example, the range of publications, including *Home Movies*, owned or controlled by George Newnes and their penetration into the domestic popular market, (Anon.), 'George Newnes'.
60 (Anon.), 'Weekend'.
61 *Altrincham Video Society. Some of Its History*, www.communigate.co.uk/chesh/altrinchamvideosociety/page1.phtml, accessed on 15 May 2007; *IAC North versus South – Introduction & Origin*, www.fvi.org.uk/events/festivals/northvsouth/north-vsouth-introduction.html, accessed on 11 March 2010.
62 See, for example, H. Norris Nicholson, 'Journeys into seeing'; 'Shooting the Mediterranean'; see also I. Aitkin, *Film and Reform*, pp. 182–3; R. Low, *History of British Film: Films of Comment and Persuasion*, p. 164.
63 R. Washbrook, 'Innovation on a shoe string'.
64 (Anon.), 'Competition for scenario of a film'.
65 G. R.Volkert, 'A cine travel society'.
66 S. Chalke, 'Animation explorations'.
67 R. Shand, 'Amateur film re-located'.
68 T. A. Bromley, 'Personalities – No. X'.
69 Productions by Stockport Amateur Cine Players' Club include: *1928/9: *The Emperor's Sapphire*, NWFA Film no. 6077 (b/w, silent, 36 min. 33 sec.); 1930: *The Last Gift*, NWFA Film no. 6076 (b/w, silent, 14 min. 36 sec.); *1930: *Billy of the Barge*, NWFA Film no. 6079 (b/w, silent, 14 min. 35 sec.); 1931: *The Secret Enemy*, NWFA Film no. 6078 (b/w, silent, 17 min. 44 sec.) (unfinished); c.1933: *The Night of June 17th*, NWFA Film no. 6075 (b/w, silent, 38 min. 20 sec.). Later fictional club output also survives on video.
70 Newcastle ACA Film and Video Makers (narrated by Michael Gough), ... *And Still We Meet on Tuesdays. Celebrating 75 Years of Amateur Filmmaking*' DVD (2002) kindly loaned by Doug Collender, June 2007.
71 Salford Cine Society, 1933: *Easy Come*, NWFA Film no. 182 (b/w, silent, 19 min. 54 sec.).
72 Richards, 'Cinema-going in Worktown', 151.
73 See, for instance, club productions by members of the Mid-Cheshire Amateur Cinematography Society [MCACS], including 1938: *Bank Holiday*, NWFA Film

no. 4320 (b/w, silent, 16 min. 47 sec.).
74 MCACS, *1939: [*Double Strength*], NWFA Film no. 4322 (b/w, silent, 9 min. 57 sec.).
75 MCACS, c. 1937: *Flag Day Fancy*, NWFA Film no. 4328 (b/w, silent, 15 min. 5 sec.).
76 (Anon.), 'Black and KKK'.
77 Rob Evans (Warrington Cine Society), Correspondence with author, June–July 2007.
78 V. Toulmin, S. Popple and P. Russell, *The Lost World of Mitchell and Kenyon*.
79 Bolton Local News, 1913: *The King in Bolton*, NWFA Film no. 964 (b/w, silent, 3 min. 22 sec.); Manchester Film Company, 1921 *H.R.H. The Prince of Wales Visit to Bury*, NWFA Film no. 241 (b/w, silent, 7 min. 50 sec.); Tatler News Theatre, 1937: *Merseyside Progress*, NWFA Film no. 435 (b/w, silent, 2 min. 30 sec.); see also L. McKernan, *Yesterday's News*.
80 See note 77.
81 *Ibid.*
82 *Ibid.*
83 Gerald Mee (Stoke Cine and Video Society), Correspondence with author, June–August 2007; conversations at *A Day to Remember. The 75th Anniversary IAC Film and Video Institute*, National Media Museum, Bradford, 30 June 2007.
84 Gerald Mee (Stoke Cine and Video Society), Correspondence with author, June–August 2007.
85 See also Chapter 3.
86 G. S. Malthouse, 'Editorial', *Amateur Cine World*, 6:7 (1939), 309.
87 G. S. Malthouse, 'Cinematography in wartime', p. 32.
88 Discussions with film archivists and also with amateur filmmakers whose memories extend to years covering the Second World War and National Service inform this interpretation.
89 See note 77.
90 Gerald Mee, *Amateur Film Memories – The First 30 Years!* Draft publication and email correspondence with author, June 2007.
91 (Anon.), 'Making films in the home'.
92 Arthur Smith interview, 21 June 2007.
93 See note 77.
94 See note 92.
95 *Ibid.*
96 I. Watson, 'Meet the winners'.
97 D. Rendell, *Photographers in the Altrincham Area*, pp. 130–1.
98 Alan Coulter. Conversation with author, 8 June 2007. See also notes 92 and 96.
99 J. Cook, 'This is not Hollywood'.
100 Charles Chislett correspondence files, Yorkshire Film Archives.
101 P. M. Williams and D. L. Williams, *Hooray for Jollywood*.
102 B. Hornsey, *Ninety Years of Cinema in Manchester*; see also Richards, 'Cinema-going in Worktown'.
103 F. Dyson, "Sightings of a "Lost Continent"'?

104 (Anon.), 'Better demand for camera'.
105 See note 77.
106 Ashby Ball (Southport Movie Makers), Correspondence with author, July–August 2007, and conversations at *A Day to Remember*, 30 June 2007; see also A. Ball, *Britain's Amateur Filmmaking during the Twentieth Century*.
107 A. Ball, 'Problems of the propaganda film'.
108 A. Ball, *Southport Movie Makers. A Brief History, 1949–2007* (club publication).
109 Keith Maxwell (Hoylake Cine and Video Club), Conversation with author, 14 June 2007.
110 Terry Ashworth (Bury Cine Society), Correspondence with author, June 2007; see also T. Ashworth, *Forty Years On. A History of Bury Cine Society 1959–1999*.
111 Ashworth, *Forty Years On*, p. 1.
112 *Ibid.*, pp. 3–6.
113 *Ibid.*, pp. 7–10.
114 *Ibid.*, pp. 12–13.
115 *Ibid.*, p. 12.
116 Angus Tilson (Swan Movie Makers), Correspondence with the author, 12 June 2007.
117 Peter Copestake (Pendle Movie Makers), Conversations with the author, June and July 2007.
118 Pauline Harrison (Preston Movie Makers), Correspondence with author, June 2007 and conversations at *A Day to Remember*, 30 June 2007.
119 (Anon.), 'Movies for the home'; see also S. Black 'Shopping guide. Fool-proof home movies'.
120 Arthur Bickerstaffe (Pendle Movie Makers), Conversations with the author, June – July 2007.
121 Tom Sparks (Pendle Movie Makers), Conversations with the author, June 2007.
122 Peter Copestake (Pendle Movie Makers), Conversations with the author, June–July 2007.
123 G. S. Malthouse, 'Introducing *ACW* Weekly'.
124 Alan Coulter (Altrincham Video Society), Conversation with the author, 8 June 2007.
125 See note 92.
126 See note 77.
127 J. Wright, 'Club commentary', *Movie Maker*, 7:11 (1973), 780.
128 J. Wright, 'Club commentary', *Movie Maker*, 4:6 (1970), 368.
129 J. Wright, 'Club commentary', *Movie Maker*, 5:2 (1971), 111–112.
130 J. Wright, 'Memberships melting'.
131 R. Miller, 'Letter', p.782; see also note 120.
132 (Anon.), 'Screen communication'; M. Wilkinson and L. Mchain, 'When oriental clichés hide western ways'; see also Arthur Sandles, '100 years of recorded sound'.
133 I. Watson, 'Super 8! Never heard of it!'; see also the anticipation of miniaturisation and of how 'our treasured collections of records, tapes, video-discs and movie movies will soon give way to a simpler but less romanticised ['1984–ish'] world centrally stored in a … ['audio-visual bank'] to be recalled at the press of a button

and the flash of a credit card', in Sandles, '100 years of recorded sound'.
134 G. H. Sewell, 'London Film Festival'.
135 (Anon.), 'Amateur sound for the 1970s'; see also 'Press release use of copyright music by amateur filmmakers', in Coad, *The IAC*, p. 99, and 'A new category of IAC membership, in Coad, *The IAC*, p. 105.
136 L. Rodgers, 'Editorial – Is it my imagination or are members of cine clubs getting older and older?' Cited in Coad, *The IAC*, p. 90–1.
137 (Anon.), 'Cinema prosperity ahead'.
138 S. Chalke, 'Animated explorations: the Grasshopper Group, 1953–83'.
139 A. Cleave, Untitled note, 615.
140 J. Harvey, 'Letters'.
141 T. Rose, 'Editorial', *Movie Maker*, 9:1 (1975), 11.
142 J. Wright, 'Club Commentary', *Movie Maker*, 4:6 (1970), 368; Coad, *The IAC*, p. 106.
143 I. Watson, 'Comment'; see also Bunting, 'Holiday with a camera'.
144 D. Sandbrook, *White Heat*, p. 792. See also Richards, *Film and British National Identity*.
145 Sandbrook, *White Heat*, p. 792.
146 *Ibid.*, p. 792.
147 Staff Reporter, 'Home movies will help BBC to recreate 1930s', 16.
148 'History from below' and 'hidden from history' were terms used to describe the challenge to academic historical study that gathered momentum during the 1970s. Interests in the democratisation of history, and exploration of broadening historical experience and perspectives, brought new visibility to the study of women, the working classes and other hitherto excluded and unrepresented, underrepresented or misrepresented social groups that had been marginalised in traditional forms of historical enquiry from local to international level. See the writings of Raphael Samuel, Edward P. Thompson, Gareth Steadman Jones, Alun Howkins, Sally Alexander, Susan Bullock and Anne Summers and others associated with the *History Workshop Journal*.

3

The rise of a hobby press

'This paper is an entirely amateur one, published by amateurs to serve amateurs and we trust you will help us to make it a success ... Its future is very largely in your hands and we hope, with your assistance, to develop ... a periodical that will ... help to put the English amateur cinematographer in the position he truly deserves.'[1] In August 1928, the ACA (the precursor to the still-surviving IAC) issued the first British serial publication aimed at amateur filmmakers. George H. Sewell, founding editor of *Amateur Films* (*AF*), sought readers and contributors for a specialist magazine on technical and topical aspects of taking, making and showing motion pictures. *AF* grew from a twelve-page newsletter into a well-illustrated thirty-six-page monthly by 1934 when it was replaced by *Amateur Cine World* (*ACW*). Written in an accessible style that was neither patronising nor overly 'highbrow', *AF* appealed to an intended readership of men and women. Early content was partly single-authored but *noms de plume* provided scope for variety, as did the mix of instruction, humour and critical response. *AF*'s combination of comment, features, film reviews, club news and advertisements provided a model that persisted for the next fifty years.

This chapter examines the role and character of amateur cinema's hobby press between the later 1920s and 1977. Attention focuses on two key British publications: *ACW* (1934–67), and the first ten years' publication of its successor, *Movie Maker* (*MM*) (1967–85).[2] Because of limitations of space, short-lived specialist offshoots including *Amateur Movie Maker* (1957–64), *Cine-camera* (1960–64) and *8mm Movie Maker* (1962–67) are not considered, as they were absorbed into the two main publications already mentioned. From 1927, a cine section within an expanded weekly and retitled newspaper *Amateur Photographer and Cinematographer* (*APC*) provided a sceptical voice within a broader photographic press.[3] The monthly *Home Movies and Home Talkies* (*HMHT*) also offered perspectives that helped to counter the more evangelical views elsewhere within the early advisory literature.[4] Other early short-lived publications are mentioned as their tone, format and existence highlight the sense of novelty that accompanied the technical developments which brought cameras and projectors into people's homes. Their brief flowering, in contrast to the longer-lived publications, epitomises the fickleness of attracting readers and heady optimism for amateur cinematography. The vicissitudes of this hobby press highlight patterns of cultural consumption and leisure practice as well as the risks of market saturation, especially against a backdrop of interwar recession and political instability. Cheaply reproduced wartime newsletters issued to IAC members strike a feisty note of resilience that evokes oft-cited national determination and public spiritedness.[5]

A review of published books would further understanding of nascent discursive practice on amateur activity. For brevity, all but the earliest are excluded here other than where writers contributed in both magazine and book form. Some critical distance occurred in newspaper and magazine coverage although references to amateur practice, found in early correspondence or comment, may also derive from people eager to promote amateur interests. The *Manchester Guardian*'s film reports hint at the social and intellectual networking that shaped local news-gathering in the paper's home city where the Cambridge graduate Peter Le Neve Foster, the founder of Manchester Film Society, gave prominence to local amateur activities by his regular press contributions.[6]

Communities of readers

A thriving specialist literature accompanied the emergence of early amateur cinematography in many countries. Overseas publications, particularly from the United States, and also those published abroad in English became available to early cine enthusiasts in Britain.[7] Unlike the American press that, according to Zimmermann,[8] was heavily influenced by rival companies' commercial interests, much of Britain's specialist literature thrived more independently and offered idiosyncratic but commercially more impartial advice on amateur practice. This home-grown cine press rapidly matured into a well-regarded, focused and distinctive genre of hobby literature.[9] Its existence provides a literary context for amateur activities and places non-professional filmmaking within a broader understanding of visual practice, leisure and national cinematic history.

The hobby literature hints at a specific reading public and complements film productions. It offers routes towards understanding the 'making' of amateur cinematic knowledge as an evolving body of disseminating ideas, practices and responsibilities. Viewers' expectations and experiences are indicated too. Print runs, sales outlets and longevity disclose past publishing and retailing histories and geographies that inform our sense of amateur activity at regional and national level.[10] Text, advertising, layout and cover design hint at the buying public too. Clues about the social experience of watching films in public and private settings supplement other fragments of now distant personal memories or surviving written records. Texts reveal how publishers, editors and contributors collectively shaped and tested the credibility of amateur activity. Over time, evolving ideas, content and vocabularies – technical, non-technical and aesthetic – contributed self-awareness, shared identities and ranges of expression as well as experiential knowledge that shed light on how and why people became involved in amateur film and who they were.

Undoubtedly, many prewar and postwar enthusiasts used their cameras quite unaffected by the amount of print devoted to their hobby, particularly if they were not club members. Unless copies of cine magazines are handed in with other ephemera to film repositories, clues to past familiarity with the advisory press usually remain unknown, especially if filmmakers' names and productions never got into print. Notwithstanding such limitations, these writings highlight changing societal moods and contexts within which cine practice occurred during its first half-century. Contributors were varied, as were their specific areas of interest, and they espoused values, attitudes and assumptions that reflect a broadening of middle-class identities, lifestyles and aspirations.

Practical and technical guidance was matched by articles on film composition and aesthetics. Help for makers of the oft-derided 'baby on the lawn' home movies and poorly shot holiday films occurred alongside advice on different gauges and reviews of technically competent and award-winning films. Some themes and debates on suitable subject matter for filming recurred, but editorial comment, features, news and printed correspondence also reveal wider social and cultural changes. Wartime restrictions, changing colonial relations, postwar opportunities, freedoms and concomitant anxieties about concerns as diverse as conservation, Cold War politics, sex, psychosis, public safety, urban redevelopment and the effects of past or future conflict all occur in published discussions about amateur practice between 1940 and 1977. Production during wartime was equally responsive to prevailing conditions that affected the taking, making and showing of films.

Contemporary writings on amateur cinema disclose changing patterns of involvement as the hobby outgrew its early use predominantly among the well-to-do. Real and imaginary women contributors to the amateur press, including Iris Fayde, disappear almost entirely over the fifty years surveyed here other than as occasional correspondents to letters pages or sometimes as suppliers of news in their role as club secretaries.[11] The increasing technical preoccupation hints at a gradual shift towards a predominantly male readership, although the increased use, in advertising or on covers, of young women, with or without a camera, may reflect other shifts in attitudes towards consumerism and sexuality. The hobby's changing appeal, according to gender, background and age, may be traced through years of publication. Debate on issues of amateurism versus professionalism in film production persisted too, as did discussion of the hobby's affordability, and suitability to fiction, documentary or animation.

Features on innovation and obsolescence prompted analytical ripostes and challenges over safeguarding visual quality, using colour, sound, film gauge and replacing equipment. Terse editorial responses to manufacturers' pricing structures and retailing strategies point to commercial independence and advocacy on behalf of cine users. This press did not simply represent a cosy coterie of leisured enthusiasts escaping into a fantasy world of cinematic production. As with coverage of festivals and competitions, from local to international level, in which judges' decisions, short-lists and award-winning came under close scrutiny, hobby publications assumed significance as official mouthpieces for the movement's disparate practitioners.

Dissenting voices were important amidst the approbation and, at times, somewhat self-promoting rhetoric. Some early critics were scathing in their derision of 'screen aspirants' and other over-ambitious amateurs who tried to emulate professional work.[12] Later, in defiance of more consensual tones, the occasional cynical voice questioned whether amateur film shows could really boost morale and retain evacuees in rural areas. Through this writing by, and for, amateur practitioners, meanings were thus constructed, disputed and promoted. Its discursive processes recorded and represented rivalries, regional and local particularities, patterns of collaboration and the commitment of enthusiasts. Arguably, just as the visual legacies of amateur filmmaking articulate particular social relations and cultural practices, so too do these associated printed texts.

Balancing tone and content

Although serial publications aimed at the home enthusiast did not appear until the later 1920s, they had antecedents. In the early 1900s, there was such rapid innovation and rivalry between manufacturers of early motion-picture equipment that amateur and professional interests in cinematography were very blurred. Everyone was a novice in the new craze for motion pictures, even commercial exhibitors. Successive improvements to home projection prompted advertising that supported an early trade press, and manuals on amateur cinematography began to appear before the First World War. *Cinematography for Amateurs* was aimed at the 'cultured craftsman' interested in the 'fascinating art-science' then attracting the 'increasing number of amateur photographers … making their first experiments in motion photography'.[13] Its author offered ideas for film plots and picture plays drawn from everyday actions and daily newspapers. He advised that 'topical cinematography is both fascinating and lucrative and should readily commend itself to the amateur' as images had 'immense journalistic value' and 'gay and pathetic incidents in connection with the war abound everywhere'.[14] 'Producers should insist on pretty actresses', offered one tipster, while, for users of nitrate film, home projectors should be 'as isolated as possible, away from draperies and curtains, and fenced round with chairs if children are about'. It made sense to 'Keep a bucket of sand handy'.[15] Ten years on, *Popular Cinematography* addressed 'those realising that this is "the hobby" and interested in "the fun of the thing" and 'possibly eager to make money by an occasional topical'.[16] Amateur film generated its own genre of practical self-help publications that combined wit, opinion and instruction.

The historiography of amateur cinema started early too. Marjorie Burgess first championed amateur film while writing for *The Era*, an arts magazine, in the late 1920s.[17] For her, the rapid growth of clubs (she cites over twenty in the London area and a further seventy in the provinces by 1932 although this figure is inconsistent with other evidence) meant that 'the films become a sort of league of nations in themselves'.[18] Amateur interests were, for Burgess, 'a cry for individualism at a time when machinery appears to be having everything its own way'.[19] She warned against imitation and urged her readers 'to build boldly a technique of our own, to maintain and make vital traditions, to learn all we can from the professional cinema and then if necessary to forget and quite happily to experiment on our own lines'.[20] Burgess recorded that, during *The Era* Challenge Cup presentation in 1932, one of the earliest press-sponsored competitions, the cine movement was praised as a 'vigorous adolescent'. She noted that 'the amateur might yet light the way of the intelligent cinema'.[21]

This rhetoric exudes a self-reinforcing optimism strengthened from different directions, converging circumstances and agendas. The Russian director

Pudovkin provided an inspirational 'Amateurs organise yourselves' for the first National Convention of Amateur Cinematograph Societies of Great Britain and Ireland (1929).[22] Echoing the idealism of other early Soviet thinking, his collectivised vision envisaged how amateur collaboration 'can produce work of quite exceptional quality', even though British cine users lacked Russia's state-sponsored studio system. Patronage, rather than politics, was probably more influential in how Britain's amateurs organised themselves (see Chapter 2). Meanwhile, Kenneth Mees, in his preface to Norris Gleason's *Scenario Writing and Producing for the Amateur*, claimed that 'inevitably, the work of the amateur, must have an influence, perhaps a very great influence, upon the future development of motion picture art'.[23] Matching the imported eloquence with a home-grown equivalent sustainable and acceptable to British readers was one of the many challenges facing those developing serial publications for the amateur market.

From the outset, Britain's hobby press combined practical guidance with topical considerations. Amateur cinema featured alongside discussion of new films coming from Europe, comment on imported films available for exhibition and home rental, and reports on local watch committees.[24] A three-part 'glossary of cinematic terms' was reassuring about 'this thing called montage' and stressed that 'one need not be "high brow" to understand and employ Russian film technique'.[25] Cine enthusiasts were urged to emulate European directors' use of composition, aesthetics and editing, and were offered unpretentious tips for self-improvement. Writers declared that critical viewing would benefit amateur practice which, in turn, would revitalise British cinema. Le Neve Foster cited Chaplin's *A Woman of Paris* when discussing realism and shadow effects.[26] 'Amateurs don't need to make big sets', he argued in praise of aesthetic gains compelled by budgetary restraint. 'One of these days, some amateur will make a film whose art will stagger the world.'[27] The hope that amateur activity might produce future professional talent threaded through the advisory press for decades. Moving from unpaid to paid filmmaker status perhaps remained a private aspiration for many hobbyists. It found later expression in an occasional series on talented amateurs entering professional and television work, including Kevin Brownlow, Bob Godfrey, Nat Crosby and, of course, Peter Watkins. Perhaps such hopes underpinned the success of periodic television appeals for personal films to broadcast?[28]

Within Britain's long-established photographic press, the shift from occasional to regular comment on amateur cinematography occurred in the appropriately retitled and expanded *APC* in mid-1927. The decision signalled acceptance that motion pictures could no longer be dismissed as a passing photographic novelty. Available from news-stands, the weekly paper offered an illustrated mix of practical information and opinion. Short features covered all aspects of cine use, and there were tips on buying equipment and other accessories. Readers received advice on writing 'amateur cine plays',[29] 'profitable everyday cine subjects',[30] showmanship and the home exhibitor,[31] setting up clubs,[32] and music for films.[33] 'The Walrus' poked fun too: 'I am beginning to think of instituting a search for discarded hurdy-gurdies, coffee mills and other articles with a handle to be turned so as to find something as a basis for constructing a home made movie camera. The addition of odd parts from grandfather clocks, and a metal drum or two ought to put me well on the road to assembling a complete instrument.'[34] Humour was a vital part of the advisory press. It occurred in letters, occasional satirical poems, the droll tones of regular columnists and the long-running Jeeves cartoon series in *ACW*. Self-deprecation helped to offset more trenchant criticism about 'aping professionals', being 'innocuous fans', 'thorough nuisances' and cine clubs being little more than 'a glorified casting agency'.[35] Nearly a decade later, Sewell was still reassuring amateur filmmakers that they were not merely 'over-ambitious church mice' who lacked the skills and resources to 'embark on a crusade for the betterment of the world'.[36]

Testing the market

Although short-lived, *AF* encouraged and enhanced the hobby's reputation. According to its founders Sewell and Sonin, *AF* was 'Independent – Interesting – Indispensable' and aimed at professionals and newcomers to the hobby. Citing material in *The Cinema*, Sewell reported that the British film industry was 'definitely interested' in amateur activity and 'watching its growth and development very keenly'.[37] Launching *AF* during a difficult year for commercial cinema was another indication that amateurs expected to be taken seriously. 'A country's industry cannot be in too bad a state when the general public band themselves together into experimental producers' quoted Sewell from *British Studio Gossip*.[38] *AF* had a clear mission: 'the cinema is now such an integral part of modern existence [that] members of the outside public desire to explore its mysteries'.[39] Self-justification brimmed with optimism: 'Amateur filmmakers, in their own way are developing the art of cinema. They have the time and inclination to experiment; they can produce a film with other considerations in view than its box office appeal.'[40] Amateur cinema would create a more demanding market: 'any movement that educates the public and makes it require only the best and most worthy films is eminently worthwhile'. Class interests in raising standards of popular taste and cinema entertainment seem embedded in such worthy desires that echo the social, educational and charitable mission of Sewell's earlier publishing with the RSPCA.[41]

Notwithstanding widespread unemployment and economic depression, the amateur film press was in ebullient mood during the early 1930s. Friction within the ACA prompted a break away group that became the founding members of the IAC in 1932, and *AF* ceased production. The new group included Percy Harris, who edited *HMHT* (published by George Newnes) briefly as the organisation's official magazine until the IAC launched a member-only publication, known first as the *IAC Bulletin* and still surviving as *Film and Video Maker*. As Vice President of the IAC, Sewell's contribution to the first issue of *ACW* in April 1934 was a welcome endorsement to the latest addition to a fast-growing hobby press scene.

Becoming a cornerstone

Costing 6d, with a cut-out back-page coupon for ordering the next issue, and forty-eight pages long, *ACW* strove to broaden cine activity's appeal: 'we seek to … popularise and widen its field. We want to see the projector as much a feature of the home as a wireless set or a gramophone. We want to see the cine-camera as popular as the snapshot camera.'[42] Sewell urged readers that 'Home movie-making is NOT expensive. Tell this to your doubting friends.' He cited his own modest beginnings using a 9.5mm on an income of £4 a week, and mentioned a recent meeting with a keen cinematographer, a (woman) florist earning 35s a week (i.e. £1.75 and less than half his own princely wage). Sewell enthused that 'amateur cinematography can be a hobby even for people with small incomes'. Careful practice, he reasoned, would bring 'more value for money than any other hobby'.[43] Claims and counterclaims about affordability recurred for decades. The availability of second-hand equipment and a growing range of equipment across a broad price range gradually reduced costs and widened social access particularly after the Second World War.

During the 1930s, *ACW* established itself as a cornerstone of amateur cine journalism. The editorial team promised wide subject coverage, independence from advertising and product promotion, and that contributors would be specialists in the emerging field of amateur cinematography – 'a who's who of the amateur cine world'.[44] *ACW* also offered technical advice and a free film review service to readers in the form of published critical response to films, including amateur film plays, submitted for comment. *ACW's* initial promise to 'give the same serious attention to the review of amateur film as the daily press gives to professional films'[45] proved unsustainable as the demand rose but it indicates the level of commitment and relationship between publisher and reader. The service was not for the faint-hearted: 'there are some really wild panoramas ... He should try using a pair of scissors', opined one reviewer after watching *A Fortnight in Wales*. If anonymity protected aspiring producers, it gave scope to be critical too, as shown by one damning response: 'There is a certain want of variety and repetition ... which betrays the haphazard shot and insufficient editing while the waving of the camera in front of the cage bars ... is quite distressing to the eyes.'[46] Club productions were reviewed too: Bolton Amateur Cine Association's *At Face Value* apparently showed 'the usual blood and thunder beloved of the amateur carried out rather better than usual'.[47] Public exposure was double-edged and prompted no doubt by a wish for approval conferred by *ACW's* growing reputation. 'A little gem of simplicity' was rare praise indeed.[48]

Readers were advised to learn from other film directors and keep up to date with cinematic developments. Professional works drew criticism too. One writer observed that Robert Flaherty's 'pictorially beautiful film' on the Aran Islands apparently 'missed' something while graciously conceding that 'this film can teach more to the amateur cine maker than any other that will be seen for a long while'.[49] Another contributor urged watching Paul Rotha's *Rising Tide* (1934) for ideas on editing: '[the film] repays study for not only does it contain much that can be pointed to as a shining example'. Thus 'the titles are used very intelligently' but, the writer continued, the 'hectic cutting is too quick'. As a result, 'shots are pictorially strikingly beautiful but rarely are they held'.[50] Fourteen years on, Donald Alexander exhorted readers to 'go miles' to see *The World Is Rich*, produced by Rotha as part of a Central Office of Information film trilogy. 'You will be more moved by it and get more technical lessons than you would from any other film I might have covered this month.'[51]

Amateur exponents believed that their critical responses to current cinematic work would strengthen their own reputation as serious filmmakers. It reveals their own sincerity and self-belief. Strategic positioning brought strength too. Just as the IAC's founding members helped to secure the organisation's place within cinematic and photographic circles through patronage, banquets, competitions, awards and participation in debates on topical film-related issues, *ACW* recognised the value of nurturing allies within the film industry.

Members of Britain's documentary film movement championed amateur activity repeatedly during the interwar years and beyond, as shown by their regular role as judges and adjudicators at events and their readiness for their comments to appear in print. Grierson, Wright and Rotha were of particular importance for their encouragement and, in turn, the amateur movement paid tribute to the quality of their own work. In 'It began like this' Basil Wright described his amateur activity and early work with Grierson.[52] He appealed directly to amateurs: for 'most of us in the documentary movement, they represent a potential force of social and civic value. They have in their power … the possibilities of technique (unbound) by bulky apparatus [and thus] denied the intimacies which go with a light and easily worked hand camera'.

A sense of purpose

In reality many hobbyists were less ambitious. From the outset, debates occurred over the purpose and identity of amateur filmmakers, reaching unprecedented forcefulness during the 1940s. Restraints were imposed on filming in sensitive locations, as were bans on imported equipment. Supplies of filmstock, paper and developing materials were limited. Blackout conditions and restricted movement after dark, petrol rationing and fewer public meetings all produced uncertainty over the possibility and even the propriety of pursuing the hobby during wartime. Debate focused on amateur cinema's potential contribution to boost public morale and as a means of escapism.

Editors adopted broadly similar positions, as they defined and defended their magazines' interests, and those of their readers. *APC* gradually reduced its wartime cover of cine-related topics. *ACW* was more typical, in identifying the 'substantial contribution that amateur film can make to the national cause'.[53] Amateurs might 'contribute instruction and propaganda films' and their activity could 'offer solace and relief' too. The editorial appeal was forthright: 'You will be performing a real national service by arranging short film shows and talks.'[54] Similarly, *HMHT*'s editor urged filmmakers to 'make a record of the 1939 Christmas' and to share 'equipment and skills where necessary', as part of the amateur movement's contribution 'to relieve the handicaps and mental stress of wartime'.[55] Manchester Film Society apparently tripled its film screenings by enabling members to cycle out with shared projector equipment to different venues.[56] 'Never since amateur filmmaking and showing began has there been a time when we more urgently needed home entertainment' one writer declared.[57] Enthusiasts should use their hobby to stop evacuees returning into urban areas, and to entertain Civil Defence groups and local military personnel.[58] This was their 'chance' to benefit the 'community at large' and 'stop the raiders achieving their purpose of breaking our nerve'.[59]

Such topical suggestions outnumbered those who, like 'Anti-organiser of Kew' begged 'do for goodness' sake, let us keep our hobby from interference'.[60] A 'cine war diary' format was ideal to film 'Digging for victory' schemes as land was converted into allotments, 'the busy sandbag activity around a vulnerable spot', ration books, emergency timetables and air-raid instructions on a railway carriage window.[61] 'Have you recorded', the same writer asked, 'the desolate appearance of the cinemas and theatres ... when they were closed' and 'the disintegration of those sandbags, the painting and boxing which has since taken place?' Readers were reminded that 'these pictorial opportunities only belong to wartime'. 'Sprocket's New Gate', a columnist who sustained writing through evacuation, encouraged close observation especially when filming new (or changed) surroundings, recognising the power of visual memory: 'Don't miss your chances – these are the things you will wish to remember when peace comes.'[62]

Such attitudes echo *ACW*'s editorial advice. 'You cannot cover the war with your cine-camera' even at a local level, readers were cautioned.[63] 'You cannot adequately show how war affects the other person. You can only show its effects on your own immediate circle of friends and relatives.' Given that 'most people bought cine-cameras to film the family', that task is more necessary than ever, *ACW*'s editor wrote, now that 'the war has so permeated our lives, brought abut the breakup of the family, restricted our movement, dampened our pleasures'.[64] 'Making a record of the war as it affects our home life', he reasoned 'will bring distraction and pleasure', create 'a valuable record' and is practical with limited filmstock.

Such comments encapsulate much of what is now valued about amateur film: its capacity to provide incidental testimony. Visual details reveal how people get on with their daily lives even when circumstances become extraordinary. This focus on documenting wartime reality removed personal filmmaking from any suggestion of being escapist and, in its emphasis upon purpose, tended to reinforce amateur use of realism as a dominant aesthetic mode.

War impinged directly upon production of the hobby press too. Publications reduced their size and number of issues, use of photographs and overall quality. Others, including *HMHT*, ceased production in c.1940. Advertisements became wittily topical in text and image. Film reviews and critical comments reflected prevailing conditions and new commercial releases. Published litanies of permissible amateur film topics at times seem to enjoy probing at the boundaries imposed by authority. Did gentle irony underlie encouraging IAC members to remain active when reporting the ban on filming 'fortifications, battery, searchlight … or other work of defence, aerodrome or seaplane … aircraft or the wreckage of any aircraft, building, structure, vessel or other object damaged by enemy action or as a result of steps taken to repel enemy action, hospital, treatment centre, ambulance or convoy on injured persons, reservoir, gasometer, [and] transport vehicles for evacuation'?[65] Different editors offered their own recommendations too: 'close-ups of headlines … shots of lamps being hooded, curtains measured for blackout material … close ups of your book of petrol coupons, your ID card, respirator, food ration coupons, headlamp mask'.[66]

Amateur wartime fiction thrived too. One series on 'Wartime plots for filming' outlined short shooting scripts for comedies variously involving a blackout, rationing, evacuation or air-raid shelters.[67] Political comment was guarded and expressed predominantly through correspondence pages. *ACW* advised its readers that, although the magazine was 'not a platform for the dissemination of political view', the 'filleted' letters selected for publication would 'retain some of their pungency and forthrightness'.[68] The vibrancy of the letters pages and the evolving polemics of regular columnists persisted well into the postwar years. Arguably, such characteristics helped key players to retain loyal readers within a fast-changing publishing landscape.

Postwar resurgence

The specialist press reinforced the movement's sense of postwar reinvigoration. Celebratory tones claimed the hobby's survival as testimony to its innate value. It symbolised wider national resilience and triumph over adversity. Older readers relished reconnecting with familiar names and welcomed the boost that newcomers brought to circulation and amateur practice. The regular output of news and comment, like the new readers' badges,[69] conferred a sense of belonging and also carried associative value. Continuity with prewar activity ensured that pioneers' expertise and enthusiasm would not be lost. Editors also realised that their publications had to be innovative and responsive to a new, changing and more varied readership with different experiences, expectations and interests. Satisfying both constituencies proved increasingly difficult and led to highly individual and provocative editorial styles as well as lively correspondence. Through the pages of *ACW* and its successor *MM*, as the now dominant voices shaping amateur cinema within a more consolidated hobby press market, Britain's postwar personal filmmaking movement emerged.

Amateur activity thus presented itself as a vibrant, self-reflexive and adaptive set of diffuse interests within which occasional hobby filmmakers, committed club members and independent enthusiasts could co-exist. The targeted appeal of contemporary leisure publications now makes the breadth of content within postwar cine publications seem anachronistic, as does their continuing combination of practical self-help and informed discussion of topical cinematic matters. Yet correspondence, news items and features indicate that *ACW* addressed a wider readership. Its influence in shaping lifelong interests has recurred in conversations with filmmakers who still treasure magazines purchased with pocket money or first earnings in the early postwar years.[70]

'Let it be the "year of the renaissance of the amateur film"', urged Gordon Malthouse, still *ACW* 's editor in early 1948.[71] The BFI's co-operation with the British Amateur Cinematographers' Central Council (founded in 1937 to represent British interests in UNICA) boded well (see Chapter 2). So did the BFI's encouragement of amateur activity as 'a social and cultural force ... a stimulus and aid to intelligent film appreciation and as a nursery of recruits to the professional film industry'.[72] The BFI's application to the Treasury for £6,500 to stimulate amateur productions was viewed positively despite some doubts: 'Is an amateur still an amateur if an amateur film receives money for its making? Is it still an amateur film? What if it only covers expenses?' Malthouse also saw how the use of amateurs might take away much-needed work from small professional film units. Monetary gain from amateur activity was nothing new as cash prizes for filmmaking competitions dated to the early 1930s but amateurs needed to differentiate and remember the UNICA ruling and definition of non-professional film activity 'remaining free from financial or commercial objective'. Malthouse's discussion has a contemporary note but also captured the new complexity of amateur activity in a climate already attuned to the potential of visual media and fast adjusting to the new challenges of television and advertising.

In practical terms, amateur film's postwar rebirth may have started earlier. *ACW*'s war time quarterly output resumed its monthly production cycle in 1947 as a 'heartening augur of a return to normality when filmstock and apparatus become readily available'.[73] Film competitions provided fresh impetus too. ROSPA ran its first postwar competition on road safety, and national contests attracted entries from established filmmakers and newcomers. Entries to a script-writing competition apparently gave 'an astonishing picture of the amateur film movement'.[74] Dilys Powell spoke of 'A Considerable Advance' in the quality of entries to the *ACW*'s Ten Best competition and praised the movement's creativity: 'Amateurs are important in the cinema: important because they are not merely passive and receptive. They are the adventurous critics; and it is encouraging to see how far and in what various directions their adventures are leading them.'[75]

Successive technological innovations prompted much advice, evaluation and opinion to appear in print. Filmmakers responded to the widening availability of equipment as imports returned, new products emerged at more affordable prices and a swelling second-hand market brought down the relative costs of capital outlay. Topics covered experiments with different gauges, stereoscopic cinematography,[76] sound,[77] the relevance of innovations in electricity, optics and chemistry for amateur film,[78] transferable techniques from television,[79] children's newsreel[80] and comparisons with commercial cinema. 'There's too much talk of technique', and 'whether to press, push or jab camera buttons' complained one writer who rejected the 'stranglehold of technique [that] generally seems to have amateur cinema well and truly in a death grip'.[81] Instead, 'craftsmanship, freshness and [a] vital sense of adventure' should replace the prevailing 'over-absorption in the physical mechanics of filmmaking'. It was a plea for amateurs 'to sense the magical possibilities of [their] medium'.[82]

For many amateurs, a cine-camera offered undreamed-of opportunities to capture family, friends and the details of every day life and special occasions in moving image. It was an effective means to retain links while working overseas and offered new educational potential at home[83] and abroad (see Chapter 1).[84] In an attempt to reach filmmakers who were not part of existing club networks, *ACW* set up cine circles in 1951. This 'invitation to lone workers' using different film gauges also sought to offer support and strengthen individual practice where clubs did not exist or meet particular needs.[85] Cine circles involved an identified group of correspondents who were willing regularly to share ideas, comment and questions about any aspects of shooting, editing and showing their films. They were invited to circulate a 'Cine circle notebook', to share films for critical response and to build up closer contact. By mid-1955 there were over thirty such notebooks circulating and some were 'treasure troves of information'.[86] One notebook evolved into an eighteen-page monthly newsletter, *The Link*.[87] Reference to cine circles seems to have disappeared from the hobby press by the early 1960s; they were possibly superseded by the IAC's own developing regional support networks and newsletters (including

Wide Angle in the North West), the continuing expansion of cine clubs and wider social changes including car ownership. Although documentary-style productions were more feasible than many fictional pieces to tackle alone, the need for an audience prompted many enthusiasts, beyond those content to screen to family, friends or local groups, to link up with other practitioners. The hobby press continued to include many articles on such initiatives, particularly as they gained acclaim or notoriety through annual competitions and public screenings.

Changing equipment, film length and prices widened the scope of amateur activity during the 1950s. While major national events, including the Festival of Britain (1951) and the Coronation (1953), provided impetus for new and established enthusiasts, others ventured into varied forms of documentary, fiction and animation at home and abroad. Examples of non-fiction documentary-style work are considered in other chapters. Here attention focuses more upon published attitudes towards shifting subject matter and other concerns within the hobby literature. Survival and future direction lay at the heart of comment, particularly when *ACW* celebrated its twenty-first anniversary in 1955.[88] As shown in Chapter 1, tributes flowed in from staunch supporters involved in film, theatre, television and the printed media. Generous praise for amateur cinema's contribution to national visual awareness and its nurturing of potential professional filmmakers, as well as its benefits to individuals, families and whole communities, brought encouragement and further momentum to the hobby's postwar recovery.

New influences

After the accolades came further self-reflection as key authors took stock of the changes that were affecting their readers and their film-related activities. Generational differences were widening as Sewell had pointed out as early as 1950: 'Undoubtedly our work was cruder … we pioneers enthusiastically took up a new and untried thing … [but] we were no less ambitious than those who follow us.'[89] Audience interests were changing too as people became more mobile but also less prepared to venture out to watch amateur holiday films.[90] Sponsorship was a recurring concern for some commentators who felt that amateurs would damage the overall reputation of the movement by producing substandard material.[91] 'The bedevilment of amateurism by commercial interests' would undermine the movement's ethos if individuals or clubs began to charge to hire out films.

Television's early interest in screening amateur material provoked mixed reactions. At its best, broadcast amateur material could reach out to new audiences and boost amateur activity, as shown by the endorsement of the BBC's plans for its *Vanishing Britain* competition.[92] Comparison of camerawork and shot length appropriate for different sized screens was an unwitting foretaste of later concerns about making and screening amateur footage on VHS.[93] Television advertisements were praised by some as example of how to 'make it snappy'.[94] Discussion occurred over whether amateurs should involve themselves in producing commercials, echoing not merely disquiet over sponsorship, but also perhaps broader anxieties about amateur activities and payment as found in sport. Concern about how inappropriate broadcasting without appropriate contextualisation might harm amateur filmmaking's reputation is not unlike recent worry over electronic access to archive footage stripped of metadata.[95]

Over the next decade, new concerns joined older debates. The so-called gauge war persisted.[96] The roles of UNICA and the IAC attracted critical attention.[97] So did the fundamental purpose and direction of amateur activity,[98] as well as its relationship with professional productions.[99] As early advocates of amateur cinema, including Grierson and others from Britain's documentary film movement, gradually retired from their much-valued role as competition adjudicators, questions arose over appropriate forms of evaluation and calls for 'the disinterested voice' of peer-reviewed judging gained widespread acceptance.[100] Editors found themselves refereeing discord over club activity, debates about affordability and elitism, the risks and rewards of amateur footage appearing on television,[101] and defending the increasing use of young women on magazine covers (on the basis of an increasingly male readership).[102] Concern mounted at the commercially driven pricing and availability of cine products that threatened the hobby's long-term health.

Despite the widespread belief that commercial rivalry was now jeopardising more filmmakers' opportunities to pursue their hobby, *ACW* greeted the 1960s optimistically. Describing 1960 as an 'annus mirabilis', one writer enthused about the 'new wave among the non-professionals ...made up of people who care rather a lot about the things they film ... love the cinema and want to make a contribution to it. These are not the "hobbyists", they're artists'.[103] New clubs continued to spring up and *ACW* relaunched as a weekly publication, after twenty-six years of monthly production.[104] Despite expanding sales figures and continuing popular interest, *ACW* survived only another six years and, after January 1967, *MM* took over as the new mouthpiece for Britain's amateur film movement.[105]

In retrospect, perhaps much of the agenda for the next decade had already been established. *MM* brought together a British postwar hobby press that had become overextended. During the years 1957–67, its predecessor's publisher, Fountain Press, had also launched *Amateur Movie Maker* (later to become *8mm Movie Maker*) aimed at the newcomer to Standard 8 (and later Super 8), and absorbed *Cine-camera* from a rival publisher.[106] This proliferation coincided with a trade recession that destroyed the existing amateur film press in the United States, and also with the demise of other serial publications in Britain where television had made continued production unsustainable. Closures included the distinctive photojournalist *Illustrated* (1958) and *Picture Post* (1957), the latter already terminally sick through internal strife.[107] Indeed, *ACW*'s six-year survival as a weekly cine magazine was a tribute to its tenacity, according to Ivan Watson, one of *MM*'s columnists who realised that the new publication's success rested, in part, on retaining a loyal readership.[108]

Under the editorship of Tony Rose, *MM* assumed a modern style although many familiar names and issues continued. Different type face, greater use of colour, large format dealers' advertisements and more idiomatic, informal writing styles characterised the editorials and many articles in the upbeat seventy-page publication. Innovations within the first few issues included a series that profiled amateurs who turned professional including Kevin Brownlow, Jonathan Ingrams, Peter Watkins and Christopher Miles. Peter Watkins's *The Forgotten Faces*, a reconstruction of the abortive 1956 Hungarian uprising filmed in the backstreets of Canterbury involving local people, was hailed as 'not just a mountainous physical achievement … [that was] one of the 'most memorable amateur films of all time'. It also made 'the majority of professional features' look 'puny, inconsequential and old hat'.[109] Miles's detailed locations in *The Virgin and the Gypsy* likewise gained approval, as in the village shop interior that was 'almost painfully nostalgic in this age of the supermarket'.[110] Such success stories, drawn from film and television, doubtless offered encouragement to readers aspiring to turn professional, although in reality relatively few amateurs crossed over into professional work, or benefited from emerging regional and independent production networks.[111]

Magazine writers continued to offer advice drawn from old and new material. The release of *Who's Afraid of Virginia Woolf?* (Nichols, 1966) offered readers a reminder that black and white was not just a poor man's substitute for colour [but a medium] 'with its own particular aesthetic'.[112] *Kes* (Loach, 1969), on nationwide release after many months' delay, was a 'film to see and savour and see again'.[113] Such comments maintained amateurs' critical awareness even if some fellow columnists regularly chided those 'many amateur movie makers ([who] ... live in a kind of artistic vacuum' and did not go to the cinema but merely 'played a 'jolly grown up game where [they] play at being a film director, collect equipment, join a club ...'.[114] Over time, columnists contradicted themselves and cautioned their readers. Even the staunchest advocate Watson could praise cine film as personal expression yet warn of the 'un-crossable chasm' and 'yawning gap' between hobby and professional filmmakers. Readers were ticked off periodically by a press still shaped by authoritative experts: 'Start imitating the professionals ... and you're the worst kind of amateur because you will have been doing a clog-dance where angels fear to tread.'[115]

Accommodating change

MM offers insights upon amateur preoccupations during the 1970s. Despite its cover of festivals, competitions and international activities and its reviews of individual and club productions, anxieties steadily grew. Falling club membership drew concern as early as mid-1970.[116] Intergenerational differences unsettled club relations, as shown by a seven-month acrimonious rankle started by one reader accusing Wakefield's cine society of being allegedly 'run on the lines of an Old Ladies Social Club'.[117] Content could be very provocative too: one book review about an American cine club told readers, 'No one wants to be associated with a bunch of stuffed shirts nor do they want to be among a group of deadheads'.[118]

Ongoing discord within and sometimes between clubs alluded to the 'battle of the formats' and highlighted continuing tensions between users of different film gauges. Rising film, equipment and developing costs, as well as purchase tax, provoked much heated comment.[119] The declining availability of older film gauges and technologies as manufacturers promoted Super 8 caused much worry.[120] So did the loss of specialist retailers and the wide range of cine merchandise as photography shops diversified into audio, colour television and other goods.[121] Uncertainties over the effects upon clubs and individuals of price rises,[122] decimalisation and postal charges swelled into broader concerns about the impact of worsening unemployment along with inflation, devaluation and other fiscal policies during the 1970s.[123] 'How many more people will have to join the dole queue before manufacturers like Kodak Ltd and the Price Commission come to their sense and allow people ... like me to pursue creative hobbies after we have earned our mortgages, rates payment, food for our families and other essential outgoings?' berated one correspondent.[124] Wider societal changes resonate through an increasingly outspoken press.

While a new generation of writers advised on how to film at home and on holiday, the changing nature of some amateur activity prompted comment too. Criticism over what some saw as regrettable digressions from amateur interests in the mid-1960s seems mild when compared with later outrage over sex and nudity. The *ACW*'s Ten Best winning entries for 1965–66 focused unduly 'on the gloomy and sordid aspects of life', one correspondent complained. Amateur films should not deal with 'children dying in a sunlit wood, husbands either brutally treating their wives or planning to kill them, perverted social misfits and so on'.[125] *MM*'s warnings about nudity in *Because that Road is Trodden*, one of the Ten Best films for 1969, sparked concern that amateurs now made films unsuitable for general entertainment. Although 'this autobiographical film essay' about 'adolescence, growing up and transmogrification' was unlikely to prompt a 'spate of amateur sex films', readers' unease remained.[126] The Ten Best's first prize-winning entry in Super 8 format, *I'm Furious – Red* by Cecil Satariano, an amateur filmmaker from Malta, unleashed further controversy. For one reviewer, it was simply 'eroticism through a red filter'. Presented supposedly via 'the eyes of a voyeur', the 'brilliant' award-winning photography could not mask that this was 'just gimmicks galore with nothing underneath'.[127] Phillips, writing on behalf of protesting club members, saw visual technique as no excuse for the 'distasteful and objectionable content' in the Ten Best's 1969 selection; 'with the continual display of sex and nudity and the permissive society on television and in newspapers, one was hoping that the films would provide some clean, fresh and pleasant viewing'.[128]

Allowing himself a jibe at the prominent and self-righteous guardian of contemporary British morality, Watson advised that interests in broader cinematic trends were part of a healthy amateur movement: 'Mary Whitehouse can always take comfort from a showing of amateur films in the Village Hall'. He was not always so conciliatory.[129] *Once upon a Sunday*, a film by Bill Davison, prompted one judge to speak of its 'post-coital tristesse'. While others noted that the film was 'an expressionistic study of a young man disappointed in love who after administering a dose of drugs in a derelict house slashes his wrists with a piece of broken glass',[130] Watson made his criticism obliquely: 'Militant Mary would not regard this as a subject suitable for home movies.'[131]

Editorial direction on *MM*'s stance had to balance sustaining a loyal readership with the unpalatable reality (for some) that amateur activity urgently needed to broaden and attract 'new blood' for its own survival. Davison's decision to film in the alleyways of Leeds,[132] and Altrincham Cine Club's film *And on the Eighth Day*,[133] about a survivor of a nerve gas attack who leaves his hospital oxygen tent to discover that he is the last person on earth, were simply indicative of younger filmmakers' use of the medium. The columnist, John Wright sensed that complacency was ill-judged. His rallying call for new members ended with 'So wake up man. Get the proverbial digit out now!'[134] reflecting how the language of Britain's amateur film movement, along with its content, were clearly adapting to changing times, even if some trends were short-lived.

MM's brief brush with 'the skin trade' was one such case. After reviewing *Helga from Copenhagen*, *Monique* and *Skin Show*, in response to readers' requests, Gifford wrote, 'now perhaps we can get back to the real stuff of home-movies for another decade'.[135] In its early issues, *MM* accepted advertisements from Studio Film Clubs 'for your own private library of glamour movies' and illustrated publication lists from *Sun and Health* to promote nudity and naturism lists, but use of cine-cameras for pornography gained relatively little attention in the hobby press. *MM*'s liberal direction in the late 1960s and early 1970s fuelled the letters pages: one reader reported his need to 'put the magazine out of the way of the children in case they get the impression that making films consists of something not very nice'.[136] When *MM* devoted a whole issue to filming the body, Rose applauded a film called *The Body* for 'not degenerating into a sticky mix of pseudo science and pop mysticism' and warned against productions that tried to promote 'sex under the guise of education'.[137]

Rose later used his editorial role to defend the right of individual creativity and reiterated that films merited critical review, regardless of subject matter: 'we simply aim to provide a shop window for the best films that are made anywhere in the world whatever their tastes and interests may be'.[138] Should judges act as unofficial censors and select films on their basis as suitable family entertainment, Rose queried in response to members at Truro Cine Club who 'even manage to detect pornographic undertones in the quietly charming *Summer with Monika*'? Do 'they want the title of Ten Best for ten year olds?'[139] Mrs Bagnall of Blackburn (calling herself 'not a prudish old lady but a young member of today's so-called permissive society') was unconvinced. She felt that the filmmaker responsible for *Eurynome* – selected as one of 1972's Ten Best – 'could have put his skill to better use than plasticine pornography'.[140] Watson also took to task, the ever prolific Davison for the subject of *Zenith*, another selected for the Ten Best – 'in which we have a sick creature with a penchant for little girls – a kinky misfit who needs treatment' and who, viewers later learn, 'needed a headshrinker rather than prison bars'. Watson argued that 'there are bigger injustices, broader themes and less cliché ridden moral issues for anyone with Bill's talent to deal with … [than a paedophile's psychiatric needs]'.[141] Such opinions are indicative of a mature specialist hobby press that both tackled and at times seemed to enjoy controversy. This breadth of discursive engagement also distinguishes the amateur cinema press from many other publications devoted to leisure and hobby activities.

Social changes and other topical concerns thread through *MM* in less sensational forms too and reveal that a sizeable number of amateur filmmakers had interests in subject matter that went beyond family and travel. Ideological concerns prompted occasional comment: why such censorship of sex when 'capitalism's face was scarcely a subject suitable for the kiddies' queried one writer who also pointed to the absence of films on war.[142] Although valid as a criticism of films about contemporary conflicts, *Baskeyfield VC* (1967–69), Bill Townley's epic feature-length film shot on 8mm about a forgotten Second World War hero, a young soldier from Staffordshire who was awarded the Victoria Cross posthumously, attracted much attention for the scale and ingenuity of its filming. It was hailed as a 'highly emotive portrayal of a terrifying and bloody battle and [of] one young man's courage', 'pain, weariness and frustration'.[143] Like the fictional film about a stranger returning home to a world no longer recognisable,[144] the detailed reconstructions of actual military manoeuvres using models,[145] and other films of the early postwar years, later productions on aspects of war had contemporary resonance for their makers and audiences in the 1970s when clashes between soldiers and civilians on the streets gained daily cover in national and international news.

Occasionally, published cine-related news items linked amateur activities directly to contemporary politics. When Grigori Rochal, a professional film director and president of the amateur section of the Union of Soviet Cinematographers, came to meet the Grasshopper group, *MM* reported that his companion, the director Igor Ivanovitch Elsov, 'walked out of hotel and demanded political asylum'.[146] Tourists venturing eastwards, meanwhile, were often unsure about what the Soviet authorities would permit them to film but echo other instances of internationalism found within the amateur film movement.[147] One contributor regretted 'the many deep conversations we had with ordinary Russians [that] just could not be caught on film.'[148] *MM*'s report on UNICA's 1967 congress advocated resuming membership on behalf of a 'younger amateur generation [of filmmakers] and those sharing the current desire for European and international unity'.[149] Rose argued that the amateur film movement could transcend language barriers and strengthen worldwide links. He advocated better financial support to promote British participation in international amateur festivals.[150] Closer to home, articles on documentary approaches to mental health, social disadvantage, steam railways, countryside change, forestry and wildlife likewise tied in with contemporary national concerns, as discussed in other chapters.

Cine footage occasionally became the actual visual source of news and a direct forerunner to contemporary forms of eye-witness reporting on new media technologies. Abraham Zapruder's 26-second recording on 8mm of 'the instant of death' had gained prominence in the Warren Commission's subsequent investigations into the assassination of President John F. Kennedy.[151] Fifteen years later, harassment of Czech dissidents shot secretly in Prague on Super 8 was central to a BBC *Panorama* programme.[152] Hailing it in the press as being 'well-suited to this sort of secret mission because of its compactness and convenience', the tone of *MM*'s report also instanced how the magazine endorsed the new film gauge, much to the annoyance of some readers still working with earlier technologies. Staff writers treated television's interest in amateur cinema more positively than their predecessors[153] although there was a growing sense of missed opportunities over how amateurs might contribute footage on topical concerns. Amateur wildlife films, based on local knowledge, might supplement the *Private Life* natural history series on BBC1 and boost popular interest.[154] Rose enthused about the impact of the BBC television series *Making Home Movies* in the summer of 1967: he reported that approximately 1.25 million viewers watched the first programme. This was, he wrote, the 'biggest break that amateur movies have had so far on television'. He suggested that 'the last programme offered a tantalising glimpse of subjects that might be covered in future series, pitched at a higher level'.[155]

Television production units began to realise the potential of amateur film for cheap programming and audience appeal. The BBC's *Holiday '70* competition attracted two thousand cine entries, including a winning entry that featured a family of four on a Mediterranean holiday plus underwater filming and sequences of volcanic activity on the Aeolian island of Stromboli.[156] By 1973, Rose sounded more cautious: 'the BBC has flirted intermittently with the world of amateur filmmaking'.[157] He praised *Film Club*, *Making Home Movies* and an even earlier 'instructive' BBC series called *Personal Cinema*, which had been commended for its decision to screen two short films at a time when it was 'indeed rare for amateur films to be televised in their entirety'.[158] Rose was critical, however, of more recent attention shown by television producers that had become a 'rather hit or miss affair with a good amateur film cropping up occasionally in a magazine programme like *Review* or *Late Night Line Up*' (no longer running by late 1973). He praised the BBC's *Search* competition for young makers of short films and the excellent work 'unearthed' through Scotland's *Scope* competition.[159] His editorship had ended by the time that *MM*'s Ten Best (1977) featured in a special bank holiday broadcast of Granada's *Clapperboard* but his alertness to links between amateur activity and television contributed importantly to the magazine during its first decade of publication.[160]

More recognition of amateur activity came from regional television: as older cine clubs approached significant fiftieth and sixtieth anniversaries, news items reported on their origins, illustrated by brief clips of early members' films. A one-minute montage of 16mm film clips and scenes of Mercury Movie Makers (Leeds) featured in a BBC *Community Night* programme.[161] Members from Warrington Cine Club were interviewed on camera.[162] BBC *TV North East* made a thirty-minute report on Newcastle ACA's golden anniversary which featured both a reconstruction of the club and much regional footage.[163] Articles about such programmes highlighted the significance of amateur cine material as visual local history, even prior to the setting up of the first regional film archives. In September 1977, the new BBC *North West TV* series, *Showing Tonight*, ran an early evening prime-time four-part series that featured 'a representative selection of films made by amateurs, individuals and clubs living in the BBC NW region'.[164] Its producer, Bob Mozley, selected the material from 150 films. The series, and also *MM*'s report on its transmission, drew attention to the amount and visual quality of non-professionally produced cine footage that was still largely unknown outside amateur circles.[165] 'The producers and their work were intelligently presented and without any of that awful "well-after-all-they're-only-amateurs" condescension', noted an editorial after the series ended. Recognition, however, was not uniform, as shown by the heartfelt 'Oh that the Beeb down south would give the amateur down south a similar break'.[166] Also in September, advance details of *Caught in Time*, a thirteen-part series on BBC1 and introduced by James Cameron, were released.[167] Home movies, gathered by national appeal, would 'provide a glimpse of fashion, family and political life as seen by the ordinary men and women of the time'. *MM*'s first decade of publication thus ended with clear evidence that amateur activity had achieved a new level of national awareness, ironically perhaps through the very same medium that gradually also affected people's leisure patterns and lifestyles and which helped to redefine amateur activity in the last quarter of the twentieth century.

Reading between the lines

Over fifty years of writing on amateur film have been traced through this chapter. As with any specialist press, it was essentially for its own devotees, yet its pages disclose that regularly it challenged and goaded its readership with jibes over complacency and visual quality. Reports on club and individual activities ensured coverage at grassroots level so that printed material portrays amateur activity accurately and not simply in promotional tones. Importantly, the hobby press records how some people expressed their own evolving interests in cine photography. Style and tone help to convey and locate significance. Amateur writings thus inform the reading of visual texts. They encode and transmit meanings, memories and values that might otherwise remain silent. Co-existing visual and written records sensitise interpretation to other social, cultural and circumstantial conditions and open up ways of thinking that reach into other realms of animating and exploring past actions and intentions. Many of the writers were not from literary backgrounds, nor were their readers. Indeed, as the opening quotation implies, overlap occurred between readers and writers. Experience gave writers the voice of authority and, over the years, successive newcomers arrived and established themselves as part of the writing landscape. There was much dissemination from expert to novice too as amateurs were differently situated in relation to their hobby and their respective abilities to become involved in the structured forms of communication and organisation required by publication. These publications, however, reveal that there was as much difference within amateur filmmaking as between the professional and their non-professional counterparts.

Some practitioners accumulated intellectual capital and became more professionally competent amateurs than others, depending on their interests and commitment. Their education and background, occupational status, geographical location and contact with like-minded enthusiasts were influential too. Hierarchies and patterns of influence occurred: some voices sounded louder and for longer than others as individuals gained and retained regular columns or feature slots. Some carved an earnest reputation for championing specific aspects of advice, gadget-making, film format or subjects. Others more cynically, sometimes under the protective mantle of anonymity and perhaps as part of editorial policy, raised controversy, and sustained readers' interests as they challenged what they saw as complacency and uncritical practice. Yet the hobby press also reveals that information flows were two-way, as some readers, in time, became contributors beyond the letters pages. Their films or clubs formed the focus for other people's comments. Together with the editors and regular columnists, these contributors provided the opinions, knowledge systems and film-related activities that constitute an interconnected amateur movement based upon active participation and a shared wish to develop non-professional visual practice. The hobby press, albeit modelled in part on professional organisations from which the early authors came, thus took shape through both top-down and bottom-up exchanges between filmmakers, audiences, writers and readers.

Arguably, the specialist cine magazines constituted a space where readers and writers could connect as a community regardless of other opportunities to meet. Within this space, beginners encountered others with varying levels of experience, learned new techniques and found opportunities to take part in screenings, club activities and competitions. For some readers, such encounters with people whose names were already familiar through print conferred status and reinforced a sense of involvement. As with fanzines, shared enthusiasms underpinned the success of sustained publication and, for the pioneer producers of serial amateur publications, the tone, mood and vision of amateur cinematography's future seemed limitless.

As memories of the First World War receded, probably many of the earliest subscribers came from a generation eager for innovation. Amateur cinematography connoted novelty, excitement and creative potential for those with time and money to indulge the craze for cine photography and its associated weekly, fortnightly or monthly publications. Names recur as people in their 1920s and 1930s wrote for an audience of a similar age. Twenty years later, members of another generation joined in and bought, read and, in turn, contributed to the postwar specialist literature that occupied both symbolic and real influence at the heart of Britain's amateur cinema. In evolutionary terms, *ACW*'s replacement by *MM* in 1967 represented a third generation moving into prominence on, behind and beyond the pages of the amateur press. The reality was not so neat. Demography, higher education, changing leisure trends, changes in work practice and healthier people entering retirement meant that both producers and consumers of the hobby press were growing older with fewer younger enthusiasts coming forward. Yet some still did and by 1977, despite real concerns about the survival of the hobby as well its specialist press, there was sufficient momentum in the writing and within the ranks of its readers for a hobby literature not simply to withstand the profound technological, societal and economic changes of the 1980s and 1990s but to enter the twenty-first century as a distinctive and still poly-vocal platform.

In short, the specialist press both chronicles and testifies to the evolutionary strength of non-professional filmmaking during the last century. It discloses prevailing thoughts about the breadth of amateur activities and offers its own terminologies and taxonomies. It points to amateur cinema's evolving relationship with film and television, as well as the enduring legacies of photography, which in turn offer pointers as to how this feisty record of amateur practice could be further interrogated.

Notes

1. G. H. Sewell, Letter to introduce *Amateur Films* (seven shillings annually [35 pence], Amateur Cinematographers' Association, August 1928 [British Library PP1912]).
2. *Amateur Cine World* (1934–67) incorporated *Miniature Camera World* and merged with *Amateur Movie Maker* (renamed as *8mm Movie Maker and Cine-camera* in 1967) to form the monthly issued *Movie Maker* (1967–85), thereafter renamed *Making Better Movies* (1985–89). Apart from reduced production during the Second World War, *Amateur Cine World* was published monthly from 1934 to 1961 (Vol. 1 to Vol. 24) and weekly from 1961 to 1967. *Amateur Cine World* and *Movie Maker* are available at the British Library.
3. *Amateur Photographer and Cinematographer* (1927–1945) is available at the British Library.
4. *Home Movie and Home Talkies* (1932–1940) is available at the British Film Institute (BFI).
5. *IAC Newsletters* are available at the British Library.
6. (Anon.), 'Personalities – No. II. "Foster of Manchester".
7. Most of the European contributors to *Close Up* (1927–33) wrote in English.
8. P. Zimmermann, *Reel Families*.
9. G. Malthouse, '21 years of amateur movies'.
10. See for example, recent scholarship and comparative discussions about the role of print and book-making in the shaping of social, political and intellectual histories including D. Finkelstein and A. McCleery (eds), *The Book History Reader*, and A. Grafton, *Worlds Made by Words*.
11. See for example 'A women's viewpoint', a series of cine-related articles by Iris Fayde that ran during the early 1950s, including 'A home of your own'.
12. Sewell, 'On the set'.
13. L. Donaldson, *Cinematography for Amateurs*, p. 11.
14. *Ibid.*, p. 82.
15. *Ibid.*, p. 73.
16. T. Langlands, *Poplar Cinematography*, Foreword, p. v.

17 M. A. Lovell Burgess, *A Popular Account of the Amateur Cine Movement in Great Britain*.
18 *Ibid.*, p. 4.
19 *Ibid.*, p. 4.
20 *Ibid.*, p. 28.
21 *Ibid.*, p. 6.
22 V. R. Pudovkin, *National Convention of Amateur Cinematograph Societies of Great Britain and Ireland*, 22–26 October 1929.
23 M. Norris Gleason, *Scenario Writing and Producing for the Amateur*.
24 See, for example, *Close Up*, Vols. 1–10 (1927–33).
25 (Anon.), 'Glossary of cinematic terms, Part 1'.
26 P. Le Neve Foster, 'Money or brains'.
27 *Ibid.*, 33.
28 See for instance T. Rose, 'Editorial', *Movie Maker*, 1:1 (1967), 8; A. Cleave, 'Editorial', *Movie Maker*, (October 1977), 783. See also Staff Reporter, 'Home movies will help BBC to recreate 1930s', 16.
29 G. H. Sewell, 'Amateur cine-plays'.
30 T. Langlands, 'Profitable everyday cine subjects'.
31 L. Cousselt, 'On giving that special show'.
32 F. J. Mortimer, 'Spirit of the times'.
33 P. Le Neve Foster, 'Music for films'.
34 'The Walrus', 'Piffle – a satirical column'.
35 Sewell, 'On the set'.
36 G. H. Sewell, 'The editor to his readers', 226.
37 See note 35.
38 *Ibid.*
39 G. H. Sewell, 'Talks to the tyro – I What is it all about?', 253.
40 *Ibid.*, 253.
41 (Anon.), 'Obituary: George H. Sewell (1899–1971)'.
42 (Anon.), 'Editorial', *Amateur Cine World*, 1:1 (1934), 5–6.
43 G. H. Sewell, 'Home movie-making is NOT expensive'.
44 See note 42.
45 (Anon.), 'Free services offered to readers'.
46 (Anon.), 'Critics' review ', *Amateur Cine World*, 1:1 (1934), 30.
47 (Anon.), 'Critics' review', *Amateur Cine World*, 1:5 (1934), 221.
48 (Anon.), 'Critics' review', *Amateur Cine World*, 1:7 (1934), 350.
49 J. Straker, '*Man of Aran*: a lesson for amateurs'.
50 (Anon.), 'Editing ideas for amateurs in new documentary film'.
51 D. Alexander, 'Experiment in an unusual film style'.
52 B. Wright, 'It began like this'.
53 G. Malthouse, 'Editorial', *Amateur Cine World*, 6:7 (1939), 309.
54 *Ibid.*
55 P. Harris, 'The editor's newsreel', *Home Movies and Home Talkies*, 8:7 (1939).
56 (Anon.) 'News of cine societies'.
57 P. Harris, 'What about Christmas?', 231.

58 P. Harris, 'The editor's newsreel', *Home Movies and Home Talkies*, 8:10 (1940).
59 '1914–18 of Gidea, Essex', 'Letters'.
60 'Anti-organiser of Kew', 'Letters'.
61 M. C. Grimshaw, 'Digging for victory'.
62 'Sprocket's New Gate', 'Short ends'.
63 G. Malthouse, 'What shall I film in wartime?'.
64 *Ibid*.
65 The *IAC Newsletter* editor also cites the June 1940 issue of the Australian Amateur Cine Society's official paper, *Movie News*, when discussing the need to maintain amateur film practice despite the lengthy official wartime restrictions: *IAC Newsletter* (August 1940).
66 See note 63.
67 A. Strasser, 'Wartime plots for filming'; 'Auntie and the blackout' ('a little comedy to show how our own life is affected by war'); 'A war, a dog and a bone – a script for food rationing and a dog'.
68 G. Malthouse, 'Letters' page – Editor's note'.
69 Aimed at readers who wished to meet 'fellow enthusiasts', the two styles of badge available were to link 'amateurs all over the world. Be sure you wear yours when you go on holiday' [Advertisement], *Amateur Cine World*, 19:1 (1955), 35.
70 Arthur Smith (see Chapter 2).
71 G. Malthouse, 'Editorial', *Amateur Cine World*, 11:10 [New Series 4:1] (1948).
72 *Ibid*.
73 G. Malthouse, 'Editorial', *Amateur Cine World* (Double quarterly issue), December 1946, 23.
74 G. Malthouse, 'Editorial', *Amateur Cine World*, 12:1 (1948), 137.
75 D. Powell, 'A considerable advance'.
76 A. L. M. Sowerby, 'Stereo cinematography'.
77 B. Carleton, 'There's too much talk of technique'.
78 J. Caunter, 'Inventor's delight'.
79 G. Malthouse, 'Editorial', *Amateur Cine World*, 11:12 [New Series 4:3] (1948), 93–4.
80 (Anon.), 'TV lessons for amateur filmmakers'.
81 Carleton, 'There's too much talk of technique'.
82 *Ibid*.
83 H. Maynard Hackett, 'A successful amateur movie maker asks "Coming my way?"'.
84 G. H. Sewell, 'Tracing projector troubles under an African sun'. See also G. Malthouse, 'Markets for your films'.
85 (Anon.), 'Cine circles get under way. An invitation to lone workers'.
86 (Anon.), 'Cine circles continue work keeping movie makers in touch'.
87 *Ibid*.
88 *Ibid*. The anniversary issue marking twenty-one years of publication was 102 pages long and advertisements filled almost half the magazine.
89 G. H. Sewell, 'Odd shots', *Amateur Cine World*, 14:1 (1950), 1.
90 (Anon.), 'The TV threat'; G. B. Tait, 'Audiences are so contrary'.
91 (Anon.), 'The lure of sponsorship'.

92 (Anon.), 'BBC-TV competition'.
93 G. Malthouse, 'TV beckons the amateur'. See also 'Flying Spot', 'Telescan. News and views'.
94 K. A. S. Pople, 'TV commericals: a model for the amateur'.
95 'Lynx', 'But why not try to be better than professionals?'; C. Draper, 'Filthy lucre'.
96 I. Watson, 'Audiences and 8mm'.
97 UNICA was hailed anonymously as the 'focal point within the international movement for amateur cinematographers', see (Anon.), 'British films for UNICA'.
98 G. Malthouse, 'Amateur status'.
99 G. Malthouse, 'Why does the amateur filmmaker copy the prof?'.
100 G. Malthouse, 'The widening pattern of amateur filmmaking'.
101 G. Malthouse, 'TV beckons the amateur'; D. Days, 'A movie maker's diary'.
102 J. Wright, 'Club commentary' (launching the 'Pin-Up of the Month' competition), *Movie Maker*, 1:2 (1967), 117; J. Franklin, 'Keeping it from the kids'.
103 J. Smith, 'A new wave of non-professionals'.
104 The ambitious launch with a larger format as a weekly on 26 Jan. 1961, after twenty-six years of monthly production (reduced to quarterly issues during the Second World War) was hailed as 'forward looking' by G. Malthouse, 'Introducing *Amateur Cine World Weekly*', 784.
105 *Movie Maker* was launched as a quarto size, seventy-page colour magazine, under the editorship of Tony Rose in March 1967.
106 T. Rose, 'Why we are launching *Movie Maker* and what's in it for you?'.
107 S. McDonald, *History of Picture Post Hulton Archive – History in Pictures*, 15 October 2004, at http://corporate.gettyimages.com/masters2/conservation/articles/HAHistory.pdf, accessed on 14 January 2010.
108 I. Watson, 'No need to say goodbye'.
109 T. Rose, 'Running, jumping and never standing still', 262.
110 T. Rose, 'Other peoples pictures', *Movie Maker*, 4:9 (1970), 548.
111 A. Cleave, 'The Ten Best – and what's in it for you'.
112 A. B.-G., 'The varying moods of black and white'.
113 T. Rose, 'Other peoples pictures', *Movie Maker*, 4:9 (1970), 546–8.
114 I. Watson, 'Throw away the guidebooks!'.
115 I. Watson, 'Too big for our bootlaces'.
116 J. Wright, 'Memberships melting'.
117 P. Rodgers, 'So much for the clubs'.
118 J. Wright, Review of P. H. Cappello, *Life in a Movie Club*, *Movie Maker*, 4:8 (1970), 405.
119 I. Watson, 'Throw away the guidebooks!'.
120 I. Watson, 'Super 8. Never heard of it!'; P. Marsh, 'Predictions'.
121 G. Whitfield, 'Nine five in Super 8 cameras'.
122 J. Breeds, 'What price pleasure?'.
123 J. Harvey, 'Your comments', 351.
124 A. Lotts, 'Price rises'.
125 A. P. Hickie, 'A plea for purity'.
126 B. Clarke, 'Your comments'.

127 T. Rose and A. Cleave, 'Super 8 wins Ten Best trophy for first time', 345.
128 C. Phillips, 'Your comments', 390.
129 I. Watson, 'Comment', 40.
130 T. Rose and A. Cleave, 'Super 8 wins Ten Best trophy for first time'.
131 *Ibid.*
132 B. Davison, 'Movie making, my way'.
133 *And on the Eighth Day* was selected as one of the Ten Best of 1971. See Altrincham Cine Club, '*And on the Eighth Day*'.
134 J. Wright, 'Club Commentary. The year of the new member', *Movie Maker*, 1:2 (1967), 117.
135 D. Gifford, 'Report on the skin trade'.
136 Franklin, 'Keeping it from the kids'.
137 T. Rose, 'Comment', *Movie Maker*, 4:11 (1970), 685–7.
138 T. Rose, 'Comment', *Movie Maker*, 7:8 (1973), 362.
139 T. Rose, 'Comment', *Movie Maker*, 7:8 (1973), 363.
140 D. A. Bagnall, 'Plasticine pornography'.
141 I. Watson, 'The Ten Best'.
142 J. Higgins, 'What should we censor?'.
143 T. Rose, 'Other peoples pictures', *Movie Maker*, 4:4 (1970), 208–9.
144 Leigh and District Cine Society, 'Our Town', 676.
145 Blackpool ACC, 'Notes and news'.
146 T. Rose, 'Russian visits Grasshoppers'.
147 McKinley's suggestion for an international film showing a typical day all over the world two issues earlier prompted a pragmatic response by 'Double Run', 'The World at work and play'.
148 A. Reid, 'Exploring the magic of places'. See also Chapter 7.
149 T. Rose, 'Surprises galore at San Feliu'.
150 T. Rose, 'Making the whole world kin'.
151 D. Culbert, 'Public diplomacy and the international history of mass media', 427.
152 (Anon.), 'Behind the Iron Curtain with Super 8'.
153 (Anon.), 'BBC amateur movie series'.
154 J. Boswell, 'Wildlife filming for the BBC'.
155 T. Rose, 'The night home movies were seen by more than a million', 423–33.
156 T. Rose, 'A family for adventure'.
157 T. Rose, 'Memo to the BBC'.
158 G. Malthouse, 'Introducing *Amateur Cine World* weekly'.
159 T. Rose, 'Other peoples films', *Movie Maker*, 7: 9 (1973), 594–6.
160 (Anon.), 'BBC amateur movie series'.
161 (Anon.), 'Club news', *Movie Maker*, 7:5 (1973), 342.
162 Rob Evans (see Chapter 2).
163 J. Wright, 'Club commentary', *Movie Maker*, 11:7 (1977), 585.
164 (Anon.), 'BBC amateur movie series'.
165 *Ibid.*
166 A. Cleave, 'Editorial', *Movie Maker*, 11:12 (1977), 1005.
167 (Staff reporter), 'Home movies will help BBC to recreate 1930s'.

4

Family life as fact and fiction

'Rachel is no film star. She doesn't know a camera when she sees one but to her the world is new. ...With her you journey ... watch her discover her shadow ... Nothing which hundreds of children have not done before – but reviving happy memories for many.'[1] One proud father's words capture the nostalgic adult enjoyment that prompted so much amateur recording of young children at play. Yet, despite its affection, *Rachel (Aged 2 and a Bit) Discovers England* (1937) was no ordinary home movie, and Rachel's father was no ordinary amateur filmmaker. For over fifteen years, Charles Chislett (1904–90) from Rotherham, South Yorkshire, re-edited and screened this early colour film that, according to his own publicity leaflet, he recommended for 'only people who love children'. Chislett became manager at William Deacon's Bank in Rotherham, but he was a professional filmmaker in all but how he earned his living.[2] Over four decades, he made more than a hundred silent films on different subjects and gave hundreds of film shows each accompanied by a carefully scripted written commentary drafted for a particular audience. His publicity details hint at his sense of audience and purpose. Years later, his daughter recalled in interview how she and her younger brother rehearsed many of the apparently carefree scenes of playing at home or in streams, woods and flower-filled meadows during outings and holidays.[3] Chislett's family focus typifies other enthusiasts' initial forays into moving image but his approaches and audiences distinguish him from many other cine users.

The birth of children or grandchildren often provided the impetus to purchase or borrow amateur equipment. Occasionally, a family friend documented the new arrival and, during early visits to hospital or nursing home, captured on camera the emerging roles of both parents.[4] A filmmaker's emotional distance or visual interests affected such filming as seen, for instance, in shots to outside views, staff or details of bedside flowers, clock or babywear.

Others simply focused upon wife, mother and newborn child as if camera use was redefining fatherhood, even as motherhood was being altered by changing medical practice, delivery and science.[5] Coinciding with the interwar shift to giving birth in hospital, cine film seems to reclaim a family event to share subsequently with others. Scenes taken at the Tower Hill Nursing Home in 1945 by Betty and Cyril Ramsden, two amateur enthusiasts from Leeds, West Yorkshire, start what became a detailed visual history of close friends and their new family. Short films, shot initially in black and white and, by 1946, also including brief sections in colour, documented outings with prams, a christening service that included a humorous section on 'rules for godfathers', bath time, a succession of birthdays and the second child's arrival. Other significant filmic moments were captured too; independent walking, riding tricycles and later bicycles, outings, holidays and family gatherings.[6]

Camerawork and treatment point to the Ramsdens' competence as semi-professionals and their films made regularly over a nine-year period offer an intimate record of mid-century middle-class domesticity. Unusually, the Ramsdens focused mainly on the parents; scenes of the father pushing a pram, changing nappies and other aspects of childcare that at this period were more usually associated with the mother highlight how the filming of subject matter may affect its subsequent interpretation. Without knowing more about the particular family, it is not clear if some role reversal was taking place deliberately for the camera to challenge prevailing stereotypes. Certainly, the Ramsdems, who never had children of their own, enjoyed making amusing films about themselves and their adult friends, as discussed later.

Framing the family

Many amateur filmmakers started with family scenes even if their interests changed over time. Alan Coulter, one of the founding members of Altrincham Cine Society, used a newly bought Standard 8 cine-camera in 1958 so that he could send pictures of his baby daughter to his sister who had just emigrated to Canada.[7] Only later did he turn to making fiction or story films, which he continued to collaborate on as a sound recordist for the next fifty years. Family gatherings, unless individuals disliked being filmed, provided accessible subject matter and ready audiences too. For many filmmakers, the family was simply too important to ignore.

Screening family films extends earlier photograph album traditions although both the materiality and the essential capturing of stillness or action differ.[8]

While both shared the commitment to preserving memorable moments, cine users extolled the merits of moving imagery. Apart from Pudovkin, for whom *collaboration* between different filmmakers might move the family film beyond 'the fate of the family photo album found on drawing room tables', family films more usually prompted practical rather than ideological discussion. 'To state that the family projection machine will replace the family photograph album so dear to the hearts of the past generation is no exaggeration if the progress of amateur cinematography is maintained', urged one enthusiast.[9] 'Who of us would not like to be the proud possessor of a film of one or more members of the family taken fifteen or even twenty years ago?' this author mused. Sewell also advocated cine equipment's affordability in recording the 'old people who are passing, the phases of growth of the youngsters [and] events that pass fairy-footed through our work and play'.[10] These scenes, he urged, would be 'not merely as lifeless images on a piece of paste board but as living, moving, inspiring pictures glowing from the screen'. Sentiments disregarded any value attached to the materiality of albums and photographs, and, for the converted, film's superior strength in documenting the past was unquestionable.[11] When the President of the IAC addressed the Royal Photographic Society in 1933, he foresaw that 'the diaries of the future would not be leather-bound books but shelves of sub-standard film ... [as] an inspiring prospect'.[12]

Family footage was shown often on Sunday evenings, or at special occasions including birthdays and Christmas. Watching did not endorse passively lives pictured predominantly through male eyes. Viewers supplied alternative commentaries to the titled or uncaptioned sequences on screen and recalled aloud or privately other moments left out of the cinematic record. Nor did the making and watching of amateur material in its intended family setting occur in a visual vacuum, as sometimes inferred from its distinctive way of linking spectators and participants on screen.[13] Viewers subverted, laughed at or cringed at the novelty of, as one filmmaker's elderly daughter recalled, 'being able to see oneself up with the stars'.[14] From the early 1920s to the later 1950s, family film shows often included material available from rental libraries in formats compatible with home projection. Depictions of family, and children in particular, had soon become standard ingredients in motion pictures[15] and, as public debate about parenting, childcare, education and health grew, it is not surprising that amateurs focused on such accessible subject matter.[16] Carefree play and idealised family life offered reassurance and affirmed a family's sense of identity, at least to the filmmaker. Films also expressed family experiences that were beginning to be qualitatively different in many homes from either wartime years or the 1930s, once rationing ended and material comforts entered more people's lives from the mid-1950s.[17]

Advice on filming the family flourished in the specialist press. The 'reel' family had to feel comfortable about being shown in public and that meant satisfying audience expectations too. 'The family should be allowed to see itself properly on the screen' urged one contributor.[18] Writers cautioned against subjects that were 'undecided and embarrassed',[19] discouraged 'gaping and waving in the direction of the camera'[20] or 'the silly ass who "does things"'.[21] Lighting a pipe or knitting were ideal 'natural movements'. The 'distant view of flying figures at the tennis court' or a 'maid coming in with tea' were keys to the 'secret of success in cine portraiture', as well as indicators of where one commentator placed the hobby socially.[22] Portraits in action hint at an emerging awareness of movement bringing a distinctive visual aesthetic. They differed from static views of people facing or sideways to the camera that seem to link back to the long exposures and poses of studio still photography.

Advocates of using colour film warned about upsetting relatives too: 'Colour wins hands down in family films … If I take a family film in monochrome, at the subsequent showing, the family feels vaguely cheated and will tell you so.'[23] Yet, pleasing others might compromise a filmmaker's own preferences: 'So far as I would like to make the past live in the future, to look back on my family when they have outgrown their family days, I would turn to black and white every time.'[24] Cost and availability influenced amateur use of colour filmstock in the early postwar years, aside from individual aesthetic preferences. What nuances might underlie these guarded responses to the suitability of family scenes in colour? Were they prompted by technical knowledge about the long-term instability of colour or, simply, a reluctance to accept change? Alternatively, might familiarity with still images of earlier generations induce an aesthetic response to picturing the past that made monochrome seem a more appropriate medium for the shaping of visual memories?

Almost thirty years earlier, there was no such debate. Being able to record and project home-produced family scenes in large black and white moving pictures was still a novelty even though domestic ways to approximate family scenes in flickering movement trace to the late nineteenth century.[25] Amateur family footage is rare in Britain until the early 1920s. Gerald Mee, an award-winning amateur filmmaker with Stoke Cine and Video Club, recalled, when in his eighties, his own family's earliest use of cine-cameras: 'I have 9.5mm footage of me – as a baby – going back … to the year 1926. My father's friend, the late John Martin, was a pioneer in "home movies" and purchased a Baby

Pathé 9.5mm outfit when it was introduced into the UK from France in 1923. My father bought this ... in 1925 when John moved on to 16mm. It was with this hand-cranked cine-camera that Dad recorded some of my very early childhood. The films were projected on a basic Baby Pathé projector.'[26]

Early family films show how people told visual stories about themselves and others. At their simplest, they chronicled moments of personal and domestic significance for subsequent shared recollection. Moving images became the collective family memory, selectively shaping processes of remembering and forgetting. The resultant visual archive of festive occasions, parties, outings, holidays, playing in the garden and elsewhere disclose, recognisable aspects of family life (Figure 3). Given the predominantly middle-class nature of early amateur cinematography, these activities are reminders of the similarities and differences found within such backgrounds during the pre- and early postwar years. Cameras, cars, holidays, family pets that sometimes included ponies, and the size of homes and gardens where children played and adults sat construct specific domestic contexts within which amateur cinema occurred. Importantly, this book shows that early cine interests and ownership were not confined to the upper and middle classes. Until the early 1950s, the amateur

3   [*Sykes Family Holiday in The Lakes*] (Dir. Peter Sykes, 1949) Still supplied by courtesy of North West Film Archive at Manchester Metropolitan University, Film no. 4380 (b/w, silent, 5 min. 57 sec.).

record seems to foreground families associated with professional occupations, for instance in dentistry, medicine, pharmacy and the civil service. Yet family footage also discloses hobby enthusiasts drawn from the new emerging middle classes linked to retailing, industry and other forms of family-owned enterprise. Further evidence points to a regional scatter of cine users, including Sam Hanna (see Chapter 6) who left school to become apprentices or clerks in local firms.[27] Collectively these practitioners widen the cultural practice beyond the realm of the well-to-do where the hobby's own nascent discursive practice tended to locate it.[28]

Whose view?

Men filmed much of the family footage that survives from before 1939, reflecting wider gender divisions within British society, although exceptions exist and women's varied contributions to amateur activity are gaining visibility as films become better known, as seen in the privately archived 16mm films of Marjorie Alexander (1894–1983), from the Wirral near Liverpool that span four decades.[29] In material more usually shot by fathers, uncles or close friends, the dominant filmmaker often appeared only briefly in a family picnic, cricket match or behind the driving wheel.[30] After the war, spending time within the domestic sphere, after coming home from work, or at the weekend (often just Saturday afternoon and Sunday until the later 1960s), was part of modern progressive thinking about fatherhood.[31] Being in charge of the camera still shaped men's family involvement in particular ways, and, even when male family members handed over cine equipment, their brief on-screen presence often still linked to sport and driving.[32] Sometimes, when another filmmaker was present, sequences filmed using separate cameras, during the same occasion, may capture different individuals in charge of the filming. The Preston brothers from Stockport thus occasionally filmed each other, and sometimes seem to play with the visual effects and the responses of passers-by to their identical appearance. One particularly haunting instance of cameras being used together is represented by found 'orphan' footage of a large, unknown and well-dressed family group of laughing, dark-haired adults and children filmed in northern France during 1931–32.[33] The small case of 43 reels of 9.5mm film was purchased privately from Germany in 2003 via an internet auction and this anonymous disposal of personal material raises questions about the survival and interpretation of family footage.

Occasionally, wives or mothers filmed family members in a fictional piece.

Sometimes their sequences brought the main filmmaker more visibly into the family picture. During the Hindley family's outing to Blackpool in c.1936, the father appears at close quarters splashing in the sea with his two young daughters.[34] Subsequent shots record donkey rides, crowded beach scenes, distorting mirrors and the little girls' encounter with a puppet of Charlie Chaplin. The use of colour, experimental shots of reflections and the mother's lengthy shots of water play denote affluence and her own familiarity with the camera. Although only the bathing scene can be attributed to her with certainty, the couple had recorded holidays abroad together before their first child's arrival. Another mother, some thirty years later, seems to have been largely responsible for filming her family, perhaps owing to her own restricted mobility. Despite changing attitudes and gender roles, her record of family life is striking in showing the father being so actively involved with children's games and other aspects of childcare. These scenes from the early 1960s offer a record of everyday ordinariness that predates the provision of preschool care being widely available. Small groups of women, possibly from neighbouring families on a housing estate sit and talk together, while toddlers play in the small back garden and among the freshly planted borders of the new open-plan frontages.[35]

Mothers in caring roles featured frequently in early family footage, occasionally with a nanny present too. They were easy to film when seated with babies or toddlers, but, as children became more active, interest in the mother's visual presence tended to lessen, shots often capturing her focus on a child nearby rather than looking directly at the camera. Shots of women interacting with children abound during picnics, parties or playing together. Much early family footage features holidays, outings and being at home together in the garden as easier lighting conditions outside favoured outdoor shots. Yet, despite successive camera improvements, these prewar childhoods remained highly selective in what the filmmaker would show as well as where filming might take place. Children seem essentially happy as cameras capture moments of harmony. While Susan Aasman observes that 'home movies are about the happy life of happy people', probing further into the relationship between idealised family scenes and intentional family memory-making seems valid too, as seen in the reworking of amateur footage to uncover hidden histories by the Hungarian archivist and filmmaker Péter Forgács.[36] An upset child appears rarely in archive footage. Reel children on home movies seem mischievous, charming and imaginative. They tend not to cry, argue or have a tantrum on camera. The filming of fighting children, as shown by a British legal case in 2007, falls quite outside perceived standards of decency and acceptable behaviour.[37] More usually, past childhoods recorded through adult eyes tend to be visual representations of idyllic times that sustain notions of happy families and the myth of youthful innocence.[38] Like snapshots, family films become part of the collective glossing over that one or more parents collude in as part of maintaining family unity.[39] Family memories on film are about making good times last. Their actuality is stretched through time as a wish of how family, childhood, parenthood might be recorded permanently or, at least, for longer. Remembering is also about forgetting.

Life cycles in pictures

Successive phases of childhood and parental experience are traceable through amateur material. Home life, children's uses of domestic spaces and places, the changing nature of play and their increasing role as consumers of domestic goods and toys for indoor and outdoor use are captured in film. Scenes disclose how children move, interact, make eye contact, use their right or left hand, focus and relate to people. These micro-details usually go unnoticed except where circumstances or routine childhood development changes, as shown by pioneering clinical studies that used home-shot footage of infants later diagnosed with developmental disorders.[40] As children grow, the minutiae of children's lives captured on cine-camera life, often tends to become fewer, perhaps reflecting changing parental roles – and time constraints of a growing family – as well as a child's increasing independence.

As children mature, some family footage recentres on school and organised activities. The resultant visual patchwork of children's widening circles of interests supplements the domestic imagery that features so much in early childhood sequences. Scenes denote the changing patterns of adult involvement in children's lives as well as the licence to film in situations where status and hobby may command respect. Ralph Brookes's detailed portrayal of postwar childhood experiences in the terraced streets around his newsagent shop in Ordsall, Salford, rarely extended inside the school gate.[41] His restraint contrasts with other prolific filmmakers, including the woodwork teacher Sam Hanna (see Chapters 5 and 6) (Figure 4) and George H. Higginson, who was an art teacher at Bolton School and an early member of Bolton Cine Society. Amongst many other subjects, Higginson filmed his young family extensively from c.1925 and through the 1930s, first on 9.5mm and later on 16mm monochrone. His films include his young son and daughter at home and also abroad with their nanny,

Street Games We Used to Play (Dir. Sam Hanna, *1957–59).
Still supplied by courtesy of Bob Hanna and North West Film Archive
at Manchester Metropolitan University, Film no. 5294

variously involved in playing with skittles, prams and trying on adult hats. Later, at Bolton School, Higginson recorded young children playing games, dancing, doing exercises and gardening as well as reading, writing and learning number skills through playing shop. While providing a fascinating glimpse of private nursery provision in the 1930s, Higginson's filmic gaze gradually shifts from a parental to professional perspective.

Amateurs often featured other family members and friends too although clues to identities may no longer exist. Sometimes one or more families joined together for excursions or holidays, sharing cars or travelling together by public transport. Combined family outings recur as seen in silent footage by Peter Sykes in c.1949 outside a hotel in the Lake District before younger group members set off walking.[42] People react to the camera differently: while some adults stand stiffly, sharing sideways glances, others talk, laugh and perhaps perform for future amusement. Their light-heartedness celebrates convivial excursions, notwithstanding rationing and broader political concerns.

The Ramsden couple, mentioned earlier, made a number of films that show only adults together.[43] Their films span successive Christmas and New Year gatherings and provide an intriguing window upon the homespun entertainment of the early postwar years. People talk, sing, laugh, drink, smoke and perform uninhibitedly in front of the camera surrounded by contemporary domestic details. Only one film records anyone watching the television, and the early close-down of transmission ensured that filming continued longer into the night. Two generations are shown although the younger couples actively involve themselves more in games of charades, cross-dressing, music hall acts and singing around the piano. Imaginative fades and trick sequences, including a rapid overlay of hands and dates disappearing from a plate, point to visual interests that extend beyond recording genteel merry-making for future enjoyment.[44]

Adolescents feature less frequently in many family films, although more buried aspects of youth culture hidden in amateur fiction, such as reportage of scooter rallies and other events attracting younger audiences and participants, provide alternative ways to reclaim underrepresented teenagers outside the family sphere. Cine photography attracted its own younger following too. The independent filmmaker Arthur Smith started his own career when he traded in an electric train set to buy his first cine-camera at the age of eleven.[45] Other amateur enthusiasts trace their fifty- or sixty-year long involvement with cine film back to opportunities to make and project films at secondary school. Filming their own family did not particularly interest them. Nor did being on other people's family films. Perhaps, owing to novelty, or simply familiarity with 'the man with the camera', as he was known locally, young people did occur occasionally in films made by Ralph Brookes when he began to use silent colour Standard 8mm, after decades of documenting neighbourhood life in Ordsall with a still camera. Although they were not family members, these are now valuable glimpses of adolescents as they stand at street corners or beside their Vespa scooters decorated with mirrors, or as they exchange comments with passing constables or snowballs with younger children. These informal and non-confrontational scenes show youngsters still connected with the social tissue and rhythms of a locality as it was being affected by slum clearance and redevelopment between 1954 and 1973.

Brookes's affectionate local portraits include elderly people as they look out from the windows of the new purpose-built low-rise blocks into which they moved. He recorded his own relocation too, after compulsory purchase of his home and shop, and filmed his wife walking around in their new upper-floor flat. Elderly relatives recur in Brookes' scenes of family gatherings. Social contrasts in family life, including the tendency to live nearby or move away, may help to account for who was and was not shown on camera but other contextual considerations may also inform visual meanings. Perhaps some filmmakers respected older people's wishes not to be filmed. Seeing oneself young, healthy and active emphasised the process of growing older. Although often present in scenes shot in domestic settings, particularly shared anniversary teas, elderly people are less evident in footage of family excursions. Going out with one or more grandparents features less on family footage too, although Brookes's excursions with grandchildren again provide an exception. Comparisons, particularly from localities now associated with retirement, might also identify regional variations in age-related mobility and participation in family activities recorded on cine film by the seaside or elsewhere. Family activities defined by cultural practice might also offer different perspectives on where, when and with whom filming occurred.

Being apart

Wartime profoundly influenced patterns of family presence and absence. Despite the restrictions on availability of filmstock, some cine-owning households continued to record family memories during the Second World War. The emotional significance of scenes of young soldiers with family members during periods of home leave or posing for a final shot before departure may only be guessed at for the families concerned.[46] The apparent detachment of recording such charged moments is belied by the intensity of a mother hugging her sailor son, watching a distant figure approach or a troop train pulling away from the platform.[47] In later years, what associations were evoked by shots of a pram with two young people, including one in uniform? Such scenes may have been watched and rewatched or proved too painful to ever project again, depending upon subsequent events. For the occupant of the pram, it may or may not be the sole image of a parent never known and killed in action. Uniformed personnel, young children's imitative play as marching soldiers and trying on gas masks in the garden, or even the occasional shot of ration books or someone reading a newspaper with the headlines 'Hitler invades Austria' all directly acknowledge a filmmaker's decision to capture the minutiae of war's impact on family life.[48]

Equally frequent, however, are the scenes that approximate to normality and offer brief records of weddings, holidays, birthdays and other special occasions. These visual markers testify to people's attempts to ensure that, despite profound disruptions, some rhythms of home life continued as usual. Such family-building moments seem intended for shared rewatching and recollection when peacetime returned. Viewed now, optimism and determination seem to permeate these scenes of merry-making at home and elsewhere despite absences implied by the age and gender of those present on camera. Even within quite prosperous homes, the wartime record often seems fragmentary. The short shots of a visual diary may span several years, making economic use of limited 16mm, 8mm or 9.5mm filmstock. Such wartime family compilations include birthdays and other anniversaries, newly weds posing at the church door, seasonal activities and other family get-togethers. Aesthetic experimentation occurs rarely but these scenes offer alternative private versions of wartime childhood and family experience shaped more by personal than public and official agenda. Perhaps these visual highlights of years spent apart also helped some families in the process of rebuilding lives together once peace returned?

Some family footage also survives from absences and relocations caused by more voluntary peacetime duties. Sometimes cine-cameras became important accessories when living overseas. Footage taken during twentieth-century missionary work and duties in former areas of colonial administration is often a powerful and distinctive expression of family life as experienced elsewhere. Expatriate non-working wives based at home might also have more time for filming while spouses were working. Domestic scenes of young children and family servants abound from some colonial postings overseas, shot by both parents, depending in part upon the colonial context, comfortable lifestyle and duration of living abroad. Scenes of formalities, captured on cine film, are plentiful too, sometimes disclosing incidental and telling details of local hierarchies, political expediency and gender relations. Unexpected gestures, eye contract and other interventions during a spouse's attendance at public engagements may hint at counter-narratives that particularise and challenge more official colonial histories.

Filming often depended upon supplies of filmstock being available and the reliable return of footage sent elsewhere for processing. In remote regions in Canada, for instance, months might elapse before films returned on one of the supply or hospital ships that linked scattered Inuit settlements in the High Arctic. Footage by the Arctic missionary John H. Turner combined scenes of domestic life with compelling scenes of pastoral care among 'these far-flung children of God'.[49] The promotional potential of such home movies was swiftly recognised and prompted the development of an influential 'Cinema for Christ' as it was called by its supporters that helped to raise money and promote Anglican missionary endeavour. Indeed, the Religious Film Society, founded in 1933, distributed material from home movies, shot in other remote mission fields, to spread its religious messages. Family, as the nurturing cradle of faith, becomes a potent symbol of spiritual outreach.

Amateur cinema also offered a valuable source of home entertainment and an eye-catching record of living abroad that could be shared with relatives back home. Scenes of children at play, or the family encountering local people and events, returning to Britain on leave, or even packing up during and at the end of a placement abroad all combined human interest with novelty. Whether depicting their servants or other workers, or being filmed by employees as invisible amateur cine-camera operators, such private films now seem eloquent expressions of privileged lives during late colonialism.[50] They were sometimes accompanied by scripted talks or captions that, just as parental pride and idealisation pervade Chislett's proud display of his daughter Rachel, disclose prevailing attitudes and perceptions. The family collection of one former district commissioner within the Indian Civil Service who then served in the administration of the Sudan Political Service before independence (1956) and returned to high-ranking positions within the ceremonial elite of the home counties includes scenes of family holidays, tea parties, weddings and hunting scenes as well as footage of local life.[51] Handwritten notes prepare viewers for 'these pictures of Northern Sudan … [and] some little background to the story of why the British were even in the Sudan and what we did while we were there for only fifty-six years'. Nomadic livestock herders are introduced as 'Kipling's 'Fuzzy wuzzy' wandering from well-hole to well-hole. You will see some of these later.' Further on, quotations from Macaulay, General Gordon and 'Ramsay Macdonald, the first socialist prime minister' construct a self-assured overview of British imperial endeavour. The historically sensitive nature of colonial film material – for both the colonised and the colonisers – has led to its relative neglect until recent years within the study of amateur films.[52] Yet these private records shot in and beyond the home constitute an integral part of the wider narratives about twentieth-century empire and authority. Issues of race, privilege and inequality permeate the home movies filmed in the final years of British rule in India and from other expatriate settings in areas of former imperial domination.[53] As de Klerk has found whilst working on archival footage from the former Dutch East Indies, such films provide another fascinating window upon the distinctive domestic experiences provided in the hybrid settings of upper-middle-class family lives relocated overseas.[54]

One absence from the visual family record is often that of death, but known exceptions expose how cine-cameras have, in different situations, chronicled moments of ritual associated with personal loss and mourning. Apparent rarity requires cautious interpretation. Despite film's ability to relive past times, most home movies tend to eschew direct personal references to death where visual memories seem gratuitous. Civic, state and military funerals all offer scope for spectacle, and even the development of a new civic crematorium provided interesting material for amateur filmmakers,[55] but personal grief remains private, and usually occurs away from the camera which may seem intrusive, or is that culturally constructed? In some faith communities, it may seem neither the time to film or to be on film, in contrast to the ghoulish fascination or aestheticism evident in various cinematic genres. Yet in others, or in specific contexts, scenes featuring the deceased among the living, either in the home or during the funeral, may have different significance. Such differences may link as much to the surviving family's sense of solidarity as to the dead person's age or circumstances of death. Ideologies may ascribe meanings, sometimes captured on film, that transform personal into community or political significance, as in footage from the North of Ireland. Within North West England, family bereavement only rarely features in the home movie record.[56] Brief panning shot across floral tributes laid out on a suburban front lawn reflect one filmmaker's wish to capture the ephemeral beauty of wreaths prior to the cortège's departure from a family home. Filmed during the 1960s, close-ups of personal messages have now faded and thus preserve anonymity.[57]

Filmed headstones and visits to family burial plots are often absent too as personal commemorations feature rarely in personal cine records.[58] Visual family histories of England's middle classes during the twentieth century seem to prefer the newly arrived to the departed. Attitudes no doubt affect where and when people feel moved to record times of family significance. They differ from those occasions when someone else's rituals were recorded for their aesthetic or ethnographic interest. It may be that cultural changes and new technologies more readily encompass grief and will bring about more inclusive future forms of personal memory-gathering. Might image-making practices found across the diversities of contemporary Britain provide future visual historians with images less troubled by taboos inherited from Victorian and Edwardian pasts? Even contemporary interpretation would be rather different in contexts where personal bereavement has been subject to more public gaze or normalised by its frequency.

Sifting facts from fictions

Let us now look beyond the visible record of framing family relationships. For many enthusiasts recording their family on film, motion brought an exciting and novel means of capturing significant moments. New converts to the hobby, including the Goughs from Newcastle, trace their interests to an occasion when friends showed their newborn on cine film.[59] The technical capacity to watch recorded movement confers even the most mundane imagery with value, be it a fly-on-the-wall presence to a moment of past intimacy and helplessness as in the image of the very young infant or more general scenes of domestic and familial experience. Supposed daily routines in the Sykes household, for instance, offer a gently amusing view of domestic interiors and family involvement in making the film. It shows Florence's parallel non-stop roles as wife, mother, child-minder, cleaner and cook running a well-managed professional and materially comfortable home.[60] No equivalent amateur footage about domesticity made by a woman filmmaker has surfaced during my research.

Wherein lies the appeal of making family films and who shared that appeal? Among some amateur club filmmakers, family footage is perceived, retrospectively, as a somewhat embarrassing first step in filmmaking, abandoned once other subject matter and different opportunities became available. Not all filmmakers, even at club level, are so disparaging and, while their public and collaborative film efforts later focused elsewhere, they still made home-movie footage of family and friends. Sometimes, footage spanned both public and private realms of life, as in the case of the award-winning filmmaker George Wain, who entered family material at the SAFF in 1950.[61] Outside the supportive network of organised amateur practice, family has remained a popular focus of attention, despite technological changes over the years. Its immediacy, human interest and the fascination for many of enjoying being able to look back at recognisable people, places and objects from times past ensures the frequent use of family material within television documentaries and other visual histories too.

Family footage has contradictory appeal too. The qualities that may cause derision in some quarters – its predictable, clichéd and domestic subject matter that may also combine with minimal skills in editing and camera handling – have also helped to marginalise amateur film within cinematic histories.[62] Most family footage, even at its best, tends to display visual competence and technical proficiency, rather than sustained creative, experimental or imaginative camera work, except perhaps in titling. Many of Chislett's family films were carefully scripted, shot-listed and staged, as mentioned at the start of this chapter, yet remained ostensibly naturalistic. His well-timed sequences of children and animals played on delighting their audiences as did the accompanying commentaries that he revised between screenings. Higginson's use of slow motion, animation and interesting camera angles replicates the inventiveness found elsewhere in his early film work, although his visual playfulness and cameo appearances doing somersaults, forward rolls and wild dancing is not typical of family material.[63] Such examples indicate how filmmakers used their cameras in different ways in and away from a cine club setting.

Other filmmakers considered in this book recorded their families in purely conventional ways, even if they made other films that now seem quite notable, as in the case of Sam Hanna (see Chapters 5 and 6). Family footage that lacks fancy camerawork, plotline or ethnographic appeal may have intrinsic value too, precisely through being less shaped by aesthetic or narrative concerns. The amateur filmmaker's picture-making impulse may often show little artistry but reflects the popular appeal of being able to capture brief moments of experience. Many amateur films are testimony to how thousands of families, within a very broadly based band of middle-class lifestyle, constructed cinematic versions of family life. Collectively, they comprise homespun visual narratives woven out of numerous, fairly unassuming stories that people have told about themselves and each other. This 'situational rootedness', in de Klerk's words, of most family footage provides an informal window upon past lives, places and activities that transcends individual memory-making and connects personal fragments into wider historical consciousness. These intimate family scenes reveal the textures of everyday living amidst inherited hierarchies of social order, cohesion and respectability even as new housing schemes, household gadgets and cars seem like visible harbingers of domestic, economic and ideological change. Collectively, they are part of society's cultural memory.

Family footage offers clues about former lifestyles and behaviour in and beyond the home. Incidentals of dress, decor, design, conduct, attitude and humour confer historical value simply because of what sequences may show about specific objects, places and peoples in the past. Such elements comprise, to borrow de Klerk's term, the 'upholstery' that has been often absent from mainstream history or sociology.[64] Amateur cinema's putative informality, disingenuous record of ordinariness and portrayal of daily minutiae in different settings makes it a window upon past social experience. Its visual associations trigger memories and ascribe meanings that extend far beyond those recorded on screen. Inevitably, there are similarities and differences as people, according to their backgrounds and beliefs, attach importance to festivals, rites of passages and other events. A Manchester wedding may be at a synagogue rather than a church. Ceremonies may differ but both represent specific moments of personal significance that connect family narratives told on amateur film to broader social and cultural processes.

What do these micro-histories disclose about families? One function was to unite across time and space. Setting up equipment in the living room for shared watching was a ritual that helped to consolidate the increasingly nuclear family unit. Imagery conferred individual and collective identities. The on-screen presence of family members no longer alive connected past to present, and the living to the dead. Home screenings accustomed children to loss and change over time too. Young children possibly grew to recognise relations whom they visited rarely via their screen identities. Watching films sent from relations living elsewhere maintained families spatially fragmented by war, migration or education and occupation. Annual compilations taken to show grandparents and friends elsewhere connected migrants, generations and lifestyles even if the screen and projector had to travel too. Older viewers could return to earlier phases of family-building and be reminded of times when they were younger. Likewise, children could see how others saw them before the start of their own conscious memory-making.

Family films occurred within specific socio-economic, political and cultural contexts. As filmmakers chose particular places, moments and family members, their footage mapped out the spatial geometries and micro-politics of family life. This visual testimony to life cycles and transitions helped to locate, authenticate and construct shared memories. The transformative power of cinematic intervention means that even ordinary occasions gain significance when captured on film. Being in charge of the camera changed the social dynamics too as one person was out of the picture framing others. Thus camerawork, for all its selectivity, also discloses subtleties about family narratives, identities and memory-shaping. Looking at and beyond its apparent ordinariness, we find embedded issues of domesticity, gender relations and family roles and identities. Family footage does more than simply confirm existing understanding of twentieth-century domestic dynamics as disclosed through abundant other sources. The captured successive movements, gestures and expression reveal more intangible aspects of domesticity expressed in spatial and visual form too.

Power relations, shaped by age, gender and status, inflect these cine visions too. Scenes of childhood may disclose as much about the adults in charge of making and showing the film as the children framed by the camera. Even rare scenes of an outing through a child's eyes shows the adults and siblings in conventional ways that would change as more child-centred visual cultures emerged.[65] Childhoods pictured through the lens may disclose notions about social order, home and parenting that were rooted in specific geographies, cultures and histories. No amateur filmmaker functioned in visual or cultural isolation: individual decisions about how to shoot, edit, splice and screen footage inevitably link back to prevailing attitudes and current ways of behaving.

Cine film families, just like other visual records, may contain pasts that fit uncomfortably within family narratives. A parent's attentive filming may sometimes seem too intrusive by later standards or unwelcome to the object of its focus.[66] The childhood spent on camera, or the father forever masked by cine equipment may come to symbolise other aspects of disunity within family life. People join and leave the family record in moving pictures, like the absences and additions within a photograph album. Family dynamics leave their visual traces over time. So too with the adopted child whose visual presence sometimes only starts as a toddler or young child. Reel families show departures as well as additions – the holidays after older siblings move away or waving goodbye to visiting relations. A child's serious illness, accident or death may end filming and watching altogether. The visual record may cease abruptly rather than trace rupture, trauma, loss or estrangement. Some visual family narratives may be unsettling for subsequent generations, or pose too many unanswered questions. Such films are simply left unwatched and, in time, they are passed on for others with more detachment and less circumstantial knowledge to explore and value. These may be some of the films that move into the public realm, along with others that find a new home in an archive because there is no longer the technical means to watch them in a family setting.

Another generation's filmic memories change their meaning as images become forgotten or abandoned. The technical specificity of cine film means that, unless or until it is transferred into another viewing format, these visual memories gradually become harder to view within their home settings. Although the shift from cine through successive types of video to varied forms of digital camera has been so swift, some amateurs have kept pace in reformatting their own early cine film. Other enthusiasts have given up as successive camera innovations have occurred and lost access to their own films. While memories exist of a relative who once used a cine-camera, details of filmic content are forgotten. One grandson could only recall the time spent with his granddad mending old tapes rather than any images.[67] Stored memories trapped in technological obsolescence become a branch line of collective family narrative-making. Both the memories and the means of accessing them lessen over time. Their centrality to a family's sense of self passes.

If family footage reaches an archive via descendants, reformatted cine material reconnects with other family memories with younger generations. It gains new prominence in family narratives. The journey of any film, from domestic setting to archive, may also disclose attitudes and relationships. While some material is entrusted by relatives who recognise its broader potential appeal, other films survive only by chance. Such orphan films reach the archive with little metadata, which opens different routes for subsequent interpretation. Permission for others to use the film may pass to the archive as trustees or remain with the family.

Within the archive, family footage is recontextualised. Its personal value gives way to social, cultural, historical or aesthetic significance. These are the reasons that it is deemed worth acquiring. Its earlier private and personal messages to, by and for the family and friends originally intended as its viewers may become secondary to what it may now contribute to wider patterns of understanding about broadly similar social groupings. Particularities give ways to generalities. Meanings are remade, redefined and transformed as new eyes look at images, distanced by time, space and standpoint. The images tell different stories. Such alteration is inevitable. In the archive, footage gains a new identity despite the acquisition officer's best attempts to elicit background details and relevant associated materials and to make contact with surviving family members and friends. Footage acquires an accession number, catalogue description and key words that affect its new significance. Other designations, according to technical quality, subject coverage and rarity or otherwise, help to shape its subsequent value and reputation. Serendipity also plays its part in influencing the family film's prospects and potential for onward journeys into dust-gathering obscurity, marketability, resource value for television productions, exhibition and academic research.

Rehoming family films

Family footage comprises a significant amount of the amateur material now held in Britain's regional film archives. It seems appropriate to conclude this chapter by raising some of the issues that occur when private and personal imagery move beyond their natural, original and intended home and becomes publicly available. How might such material be understood without risking historical condescension and speculative abstraction? What claims can be legitimately made for images made by others, often many decades ago? Details need verification wherever possible. Caution accompanies processes of contextualisation. Individual visual historians have preferred ways of working but all, in individual ways, acknowledge the transformations that occur when intimate material often intended only for limited domestic viewing reaches different audiences in classrooms, museums and other settings. While critical comment abounds on the creative and aesthetic effects of screening reworked family footage, exhibiting raw family footage merits exploration too as it assumes new frames of reference whether as a prototype of reality television, unedited and unrehearsed, or the precursor to self-documenting via mobile phones. These personal stories enter new settings on new terms, understood through a mesh of past and contemporary reference points and experiences.

Scrutiny of these glimpses into other families starts with detachment but forensic visual detective work make these strangers more familiar. Their smiles, gestures and body language become recognisable as do their turns to the camera and how they spend their time and relate to each other. Responsibility for how they will appear in any edited snippets passes from the filmmaker to the user whose own professional interests converts them into source material for fresh enquiry. Academic or creative visual appropriation of past lives requires caution. Presentations or publications should reclaim rather than reduce these remembered lives. The on-screen identity and public integrity of reel families becomes reliant upon another's authority. A sense of obligation requires that these camera-ready people are fairly treated on screen in subsequent public viewings. Borrowed moments from their lives, to support an argument or creative effect, require sensitivity. Visual quotes require acknowledgement. Of course, there are also contractual obligations and permissions sought from descendants or family friends who may hold the copyright. Use, in any form, involves undertaking to play fair with these filmic identities and their living representatives.

Other ethical and intellectual issues also arise as family film moves into and beyond the archive. Someone else's memories may trigger more subjective patterns of association. Events, occasions and localities may elicit personal responses that also shape interpretation. Stepping into other people's lives captured on cine film invites us as viewers, however briefly, to engage with the lives and lifestyles shown on the screen. Is this not why family films are so appealing to programme makers? They invite audiences to join them on nostalgic journeys. As Garfield writes of Kynaston's *Family Britain 1951–57*, we can see ourselves in every frame and make comparisons.[68] Or can we?

Family films show scenes that are partial, incomplete and unrepresentative of actuality. Childhood, families, holidays, weddings and so on are not all like those depicted on camera. Imagery reinforces differences, absences, gaps and contrasts. Not everyone has families that look, behave, move or sound like those on screen. Within the North West, people of all ages with visual, mobility or other disabilities, for instance, feature more in institutional settings than amateur home movies, disclosing social and family attitudes in the hiding of disability (see Chapter 9).[69] Footage of disability in home settings is invaluable because of its overall rarity.[70] While researchers may pursue unique or representative aspects of specific footage, exhibitors may have different concerns about appropriateness and messages conveyed. Elevating one set of experience captured on film should not eclipse or negate the value of other underrepresented or absent experiences. Visual memories have become important aspects of family histories but should not exclude those who may have no little or no past visible presence but still important stories to tell. Many families never featured in amateur cine film, apart from as anonymous walk-on parts in other people's home movies as servants, employees, passers-by or faces in a crowd. Other families' visual histories still await the links and trust building necessary to bring them forward into the public domain.[71] Picture-making featured less within some sections of mid-century Britain than others, for economic reasons, but film archives have yet to achieve a fuller pattern of national and regional diversity.[72] Underrepresentation of non-white or mixed-heritage families in postwar Britain is one such gap, and amateur family footage by Dr Hira Kapur of family life in Lancashire[73] and Raj Malhotra in Coventry is an important exception.[74] Archived footage of middle-class Jewish family life, even in Manchester, one of England's oldest and largest Jewish communities, similarly seems underrepresented, apart from a scatter of filmed gatherings for weddings, Rosh Hashana, Passover and other family occasions.[75]

Taking once private material into public settings poses risks and obligations. The risks involve misrepresentation and misunderstanding. There is scope for getting so many things wrong about who, where, when, what and why particular people, places and events were shown on camera. Family memories that are no longer uppermost in people's minds or passed on via a member of another generation or a family friend may be fragmentary. Interpretation combines past and present perceptions as the researcher and the researched – or their representatives – engage with each other.[76]

Venues and footage vary in their levels of intimacy, and audience responses to material differ according to setting. Amateurs were exempt from censorship laws but contemporary sensibilities may affect what is screened today. While the naked intimacies of young children filmed in the home, on the beach or at nursery may now prompt a sense of voyeurism, the politics of representation may be central to why other footage seems significant for its now problematic depiction of gender, sexuality, ethnicity, occupation and so on.

Separating fact from fiction within family footage is complex. Any attempt to frame lives on camera is incomplete unless the camera remains permanently switched on. Disentangling fictive and factual elements may be particularly hard when trying to retrace an amateur's ethnographic foray into other people's home or personal life. Yet those resultant family scenes, sometimes taken by an outsider with very different notions of domestic life, may now hold profound meaning if reconnected to their provenance through direct or online virtual repatriation. Such products of unequal visual exchanges may now provide unique ways to see relations, places and events known only through oral tradition.[77] Such imagery abounds from many former colonial contexts.[78] Despite the fictive distortions, sometimes unwittingly imposed during filming, visual reconnections with its 'home', even via YouTube, offer scope for repatriation within cultural memory elsewhere.[79] Such online links and intergenerational work may nurture important family and community links and involve ethical decisions and sensitivity.[80] Visual memories, like other ways of sharing family narratives, convey meanings across time. Making sense of these diverse private stories seems well worth the effort of judicious probing among the facts and fictions found in amateur footage of family life.

Notes

1. Charles Chislett (undated), *Light Hearted Lectures* (publicity leaflet), YFA.
2. H. Norris Nicholson, 'Seeing it how it was?'.
3. H. Norris Nicholson, 'Framing the view'.
4. Betty and Cyril Ramsden, 1944: *Fear Family Year One*, YFA Cat. no. 3121 (b/w, silent, 18 min. 0 sec.).
5. For a wider discussion see J. R. Gillis, *A World of Their Own Making*, pp. 172–3.
6. Betty and Cyril Ramsden, 1950s: *New Years Eve Parties*, YFA Cat. no. 3101 (b/w, separate magnetic, 60 min. 0 sec.).
7. Alan Coulter (Altrinham Video Club), Conversation with author, 8 June 2007.
8. E. Edwards, and J. Hart (eds), *Photographs Objects Histories*; A. Kuhn, *Family Secrets*.
9. (Anon.), 'The cinema family album', 30.
10. G. Sewell, 'Home movie-making is NOT expensive'.
11. G. Willumson, 'Making meaning. Displaced materiality'; see also E. Edwards, *Raw Histories. Photographs, Anthropology and Museums*, p. 16.
12. Duke of Sunderland, cited in G. Sewell, 'Here is advice on filming baby'.

13 See, for instance E. de Kuyper, 'Aux origins du cinéma: le film de famille, and R. Odin, 'Le film de famille dans l'institution familiale'.
14 Sheelagh Simpson (daughter) and Peter Simpson (grandson), Correspondence with author, August 2002.
15 See for instance, A. Katelle, *Home Movies*, p. 58 (Fig. 83), although it might also be suggested that this was commercially motivated and thus, fundamentally, not intended for personal use.
16 M. Abbott, *Family Affairs*, pp. 22–42; H. Hendrick, 'Constructions and reconstructions of British childhood'; J. Lewis, *Women in England 1870–1950*; S. Todd, *Young Women, Work and Family 1918–50*.
17 D. Kynaston, *Family Britain, 1951–1957*.
18 (Anon.), 'Appeal to the filmmaker'.
19 H. Dolphin, 'Home portraits'.
20 G. Collyer, 'Composing a cine picture'.
21 H. Lomax, 'Plan a scenario for filming the family'.
22 *Ibid*.
23 L. Barry, 'Comments on colour'.
24 *Ibid*.
25 In the 1890s, the Filoscope, Kinora and Mutoscope were domestic versions of the 'what the butler saw' type machines used in amusement arcades. As table-top, hand-cranked models with easily changeable picture reels, their suitability for home entertainment had novelty appeal.
26 G. Mee (Stoke Cine & Video Society), 'Amateur film in the twentieth century', Correspondence with author, 13 June 2007.
27 See for instance Sam Hanna, 1930s: [*Larkholme Farm, Bob's First Steps, at the Beach*], NWFA Film no. 5200 (b/w, silent, 8 min. 24 sec.); *1937/56/59: [*Family Christmas, Holidays, Golf and Swimming*], NWFA Film no. 5192 (b/w and colour, silent, 14 min. 58 sec.); 1938: *Holidays of the Hanna Family 1938*, NWFA Film no. 5196 (b/w, silent, 10 min. 13 sec.); see also films by Ralph Brookes, discussed in various chapters.
28 See for instance work by Sam Hanna cited in note 27.
29 One example at the North West Film Archive includes Constance and Edith Butterworth, both former members of Preston Cine Club, who filmed on Standard 8 and Super 8 in and around the local area during the 1960s–80s, according to their nephew who recently made contact and expressed a wish to donate 58 films (not yet catalogued at time of going to print). Films by the late Mary Corner, formerly a member of Burnley Cine Club, have also been donated to the North West Film Archive. See also Marjorie Alexander, www.valleystream.co.uk/alex%20youtube.htm, accessed on 24 March 2011.
30 See, for instance, Charles Chislett, 1942: *Dale Days*, YFA Cat no. 328 (colour, silent, 64 min.).
31 John R. Gillis, 'Your family in history: anthropology at home'.
32 H. Norris Nicholson, '"At Ilkley they sell lovely"'.
33 S. Tenkanen, 'Searching for a 9.5mm family'.
34 John Hindley, *1936–44: [*Hindley Family Scenes and Blackpool*], NWFA Film no.

3636 (b/w and colour, silent, 13 min. 30 sec.).
35 Anonymously reviewed amateur footage and interview for uncommissioned independent television production, August 2006.
36 S. I. Aasman, *Ritueel van huiselijk geluk*. See also J. Kedward, 'On Péter Forgács', www.forgacspeter.hu/prev_version/eng/main/press/articles/jessica_kedward.html, accessed on 24 March 2011.
37 L. Salkeld, 'Named and shamed'.
38 M. Citron, *Home Movies and Other Necessary Fictions*.
39 Abbott, *Family Affairs*, pp. 2–3; see also J. Spence and P. Holland (eds), *Family Snaps*; Kuhn, *Family Secrets*, pp. 157–8.
40 J. Osterling and G. Dawson, 'Early recognition of children with autism'.
41 H. Norris Nicholson, 'Two tales of a city: Salford in regional filmmaking. See also Chapter 5.
42 Peter Sykes, 1949: [*Sykes Family Holiday in the Lakes*], NWFA Film no 4380 (b/w, silent, 5 min. 57 sec.).
43 See note 6.
44 *Ibid*.
45 Interview with Arthur Smith (see Chapter 2).
46 See for instance Alfred Siddall, 1943: [*Holiday Scenes and Army Officer*], NWFA Film no. 4336 (b/w, silent, 1 min. 48 sec.); Ernest W Hart, *1940–42: [*Norma's Birthday Party and Family Get-together*], NWFA Film no. 4426 (b/w & colour, silent, 9 min. 35 sec.)
47 J. E. Hallam, c. 1940s: *All Pals Together*, NWFA Film no. 875 (b/w, silent, 11 min. 0 sec.).
48 George Wain, 1944–47: *Now We Are Five*, NWFA Film no. 4399 (colour, silent, 12 min. 24 sec.); Harold Wild, c. 1940: [*Oldham – Outside*], NWFA Film no. 4044 (b/w, silent, 6 min. 23 sec.); Unknown, c. 1940s: [*Royal Visit to Warrington / Family Scenes*], NWFA Film no. 2223 (b/w, silent, 6 min. 40 sec.).
49 H. Norris Nicholson, *Screening Culture*, pp. 93–9.
50 N. de Klerk, 'Home away from home', pp. 154–5; see also D. Hertogs and N. de Klerk. *Uncharted Territory*.
51 (Undated), *Eygpt and Suez*, Finlay Personal Film Collection, British Film Institute.
52 See, for example, N. de Klerk, 'Home away from home'.
53 See, for example A. Motrescu, 'British colonial identity in amateur films from India and Australia, 1920–1940s'.
54 De Klerk, 'Home away from home'.
55 See for instance *Halifax Crematorium Progress* (1954–56) and *Halifax Cine Club Newsreel* (1961–62), YFA Cat. no. 3474 (b&w and colour, silent, 10 min.).
56 Note that unusual private funerary practice, like public commemorations, might attract attention, as evidenced by R. Rudd, 1969: [*Gypsy Funeral at Portwood, Stockport*], NWFA Film no. 3257 (colour, silent, 9 min. 0 sec.).
57 See note 35.
58 See also Lt Col. James Fitzwilliam O'Grady, 1934: *Gallipoli Revisited A Pilgrimage Cruise 1934*, NWFA Film no. 1795 (b/w, silent, 9 min. 51 sec.); 1934: *Gallipoli Revisited A Pilgrimage Cruise 1934 Part 2* (b/w, silent, 12 min. 40 sec.).

59 M. Gough, 'The movie making career of Linda and Michael Gough', Correspondence with author, 14 August 2007.
60 Peter Sykes, 1949: [*Domestic Scenes at 30 Devonshire Road*], NWFA Film no. 4371 (colour, silent, 6 min. 11 sec.).
61 George Wain, *1949: *Devon Holiday*, NWFA Film no. 4401 (colour, silent, 9 min. 43 sec.).
62 See note 54.
63 G. H. Higginson, *1927/33/34/37: [*Higginson Family Holiday*], NWFA Film no. 2769 (b/w and colour, silent, 19 min. 57 sec.); 1930–35: [*Sylvia and Derek Playing*], NWFA Film no. 2768 (b/w, silent, 10 min. 45 sec.); *1949–57: [*Titles and Miscellaneous*], NWFA Film no. 2778 (colour, silent, 9 min. 49 sec.).
64 See note 54.
65 Mr Kaye, 1931: *A Picnic in Whitby*, YFA Cat. no. 2714 (b/w, silent, 2 min.); 1933: *A Sunday Morning*, YFA Cat. no. 2730 (b/w, silent, 2 min.).
66 See, for instance, discussions by Kuhn, *Family Secrets*, pp. 161–8.
67 Peter Simpson, Correspondence with author, August 2002.
68 Kynaston, *Family Britain 1951–57*. Review by Simon Garfield, *Observer*, 1 November 2009.
69 See also the discussion of living with disability and family representation through home videos by P. Tarrant, 'Planet usher: an interactive home movie'.
70 Dwight L. Core, *Think of Me First as a Person* (restored and edited with sound narrative by the filmmaker's grandson, the 16mm film portrays an American father's response to raising a son with Down's Syndrome in the 1960s and 1970s), www.homemovieday.com/news/2006/12/27/, accessed on 23 November 2010.
71 See, for example, J. Stewart, 'South Side history in locals' home movies'.
72 *Moving Memories* and *Reel Revolutions*, undertaken North West Film Archives with partners during 2009, linked with communities in central Manchester and Burnley. See also S. Gulzar and S. Manthrop, *Black and White in Colour*.
73 Dr Hira Kapur's films of family, friends and overseas holidays span the years 1971–85 and document birthdays and other anniversaries, seasonal activities including Halloween, Christmas and winter snow scenes, outings and longer visits within Britain as well as Spanish package holidays and extended visits to see relations and sightsee in India. See NWFA Film nos 6651–6658 and 6743–6759.
74 R. Malhotra and N. Puwar, 'Selections from Raj Malhotra's (Indian Workers Association) cine collection'.
75 Sefton Samuels, c. 1966: *Autumn in Delamere*, NWFA Film no. 1511(colour, sound, 27 min. 48 sec.); for Hubert Wiener's films of Passover and Rosh Hashana, visits by overseas relations and domestic scenes, shot between 1963 and 1975, see NWFA Film nos 4159–4184.
76 H. Norris Nicholson (2009), 'Moving pictures'.
77 Norris Nicholson, *Screening Culture*, pp. 96–7; see also T. D. Schneider, 'The role of archived photographs'.
78 See note 54.
79 See note 76.

80 Pam Wintle (Human Studies Film Archives, Smithsonian Institution), Conversation with the author about posting footage of the Bamiyan sculptures online, September 2010; see also *Alaska Natives on Film* (2003) undertaken by the Alaska Film Archive and University of Alaska, http://library.uaf.edu/alaska-natives-film-project, on accessed 27 March 2011.

5

Local lives and communities

'The English have gone out to look at England, and the English in the resources of amateur cinematography are learning to bring England home ... Every yard of this fair land is being shot by the amateur cine movement.'[1] Thus wrote Atkinson in 1932 as he introduced one of the earliest books to trace the rise of Britain's amateur cinema. Its author, Marjorie Lovell Burgess, an established commentator on amateur film in the London-based arts magazine *The Era*, linked cine activity with nationhood: 'I believe the amateur cine movement is helping English people to love England; or perhaps it would be more accurate to say that the movement is becoming a medium through which English men and women can express their love of England.'[2] Prevailing hopes that amateurs might help to revitalise Britain's film industry are apparent. Like others, she believed that, through creating more critical audiences and nurturing home-grown talent, amateur interest in *making* film would help to rekindle popular interest and markets for films produced outside the USA.[3]

Against a backdrop of political, social and economic instability at home and abroad, many British intellectuals were attracted by the avant-garde ideas and aesthetic practices in mainland Europe. Yet here Lovell Burgess's words affirm the national cultural symbolism of Britain's (and specifically, *England*'s) historic rural and urban landscapes.[4] As an early cinema historian, she doubtless knew that films showing local people and places were early staple ingredients in many cinema programmes.[5] Factory gate productions, topicals, roll of honour films and other early forms of actuality had attracted audiences eager to see familiar faces and places projected on screens that showed exotic other real and fictive worlds too.[6] Turning their cameras to the world around them seemed an obvious next step for many amateurs after recording family and friends.[7]

Out and about

Filming local life was recommended in early manuals. In 1916, Donaldson recommended the 'endless ideas for film plots' that might be found in daily newspapers, 'one's immediate surroundings' and 'our everyday actions'.[8] He observed that 'interesting events are occurring hourly in every town and village, and gay and pathetic incidents in connection with the war abound everywhere'. These images have 'immense journalistic value' and are 'in many instances secured by amateurs'. This prototype 'citizen journalism' made practical sense too: the local amateur might arrive early enough 'for obtaining a scoop'.[9] Access was cheap and easy, particularly if fickle weather required a return visit to finish filming. Outside light, when bright enough, avoided elaborate and expensive additional equipment. As shown by the flourishing regional culture of small professional outfits, locally produced material readily attracted audiences, public attention and press coverage. Not surprisingly, the first generation of postwar amateurs looked around them for their subject matter.

Much of the contemporary interest in such local footage ostensibly concerns its evocation of past routines and once familiar daily occurrences.[10] Amateurs also soon realised the visual potential of specific incidents – fires, floods, overturned trams, derailments or other dramatic and unusual event. Eye-catching subjects stretched their own skills, reinforced their local role as visual news providers and made material more appealing to others. Early films were often very short and their producers had to offset careful editing and adding captions against the time taken to shoot and bring processed eye-witness material to an audience while it was still newsworthy. Some amateurs edited together local news-stories, as evidenced by Harold and Sidney Preston, two brothers who made topicals for friends and employees of the family-owned tailoring business at their home near Stockport in Greater Manchester.[11]

One typical example of the Preston brothers' *Glengarry News*, produced for their own cinema in the family home, is fourteen minutes long and spans four months in 1929.[12] It includes scenes of destruction at the site of Southport's Palladium cinema (26 March), a fire at a large cotton mill at Shaw (17 April) and another fire (1 July), the White Star cruise ship, *SS Albertic* leaving Liverpool docks for New York and the arrival of an electric train at Liverpool railway station. These sequences combine with family excursions to Southport and footage of their father, Joshua Preston, greeting football players in his role as Mayor of Stockport. Enjoying such material probably involved identifying different locations and occasions. The Prestons' newsreels routinely covered a geographical range of over twenty miles, and sometimes more distant events. These films thus capture how wider transport, commercial and other links thread through local lives and experiences.

The Preston brothers made over twenty other newsreels and compilations outside their 'Glengarry Topicals' series over the next eight years. They featured ceremonies for laying foundation stones and opening buildings, regional shows, royal visits and ship launches at Liverpool and commemorative mercantile reviews. They documented an air crash, the collapse of a six-storey building, fires and floods as well as various regional modernisation projects.[13] This blend of disaster, novelty and the more mundane in what might be termed 'a cinema of local catastrophe' is characteristic of other amateur newsreels.[14] Tending towards spectacle, civic occasions (covering their father's and sister's duties) and transport (an interest shared by both brothers and other early cine enthusiasts), this footage discloses how unusual occurrences punctuated more predictable routines of daily life. Nearly eighty years later, the chance to glean any audience insights directly from past employees has probably passed,[15] but such newsreels possibly enhanced status and authority. They provided amateur alternatives to more metropolitan-based news and were forerunners of regional television. Reworking the aesthetic possibilities of this early amateur genre prompted postwar attention too among a new generation of emerging independent and experimental filmmakers, as shown by Lindsay Anderson's *Wakefield Express*.[16]

The Prestons' privileged role in the family business offered them flexibility and freedom.[17] Their own mobility enabled them to film visiting dignitaries[18] including Sir Robert Baden-Powell at a major scouting jamboree in Birkenhead,[19] presentations of sporting trophies[20] and many events further away.[21] Formal occasions suited some amateurs well. Planned events had pre-set routes, timetables and procedures that were invaluable and local connections often enabled access to ideal filming positions. Unlike the Prestons with their naturalistic style, another early enthusiast combined civic reportage with playful visual experimentation too, as in the quirkily finished film *Miss Middleton Visits Radcliffe*.[22] Civic procedures, horse-drawn dignitaries and a shop-window dressing competition chart the town's Charter Week celebrations, and the eponymous Miss Middleton officiates while the local Cotton Queen was 'indisposed'. The filmmaker then films himself briefly in front of a mirror before lowering the camera to reveal his face just as 'The End' comes on to the screen. The gothic ending is an instance of how early amateurs might break documentary conventions and also find ways of stepping into view.

Local lives and communities

More generally, local events enabled amateurs to produce actuality-style footage. Slow-moving motorcades or cavalcades between people-lined thoroughfares and the procedural etiquette of prolonged arrivals and departures were straightforward in visual and practical terms. These filmed civic traditions and grandiose welcomes on northern town hall steps are redolent with inherited pride. They appear unthreatened by processes of industrial and commercial change that were already transforming the economic and social fabric at local and regional level, and they recur throughout early amateur footage. Arguably, making and sharing such sequences were acts of affirmation even as traditional structures of public life and regional economic systems were coming under increasing strain during the later 1930s.

Notions of nationhood

Capturing royalty on tour appealed to some amateurs too and their footage of local pageantry and choreographed ritual might now be studied for its coded private, public and regional expressions of patriotism. These clichéd images may be seen as parts of the national imaginary and hint at how more personal acts of remembering interweave with public histories and consciousness.[23] Watching such scenes perhaps reinforced familiar symbols and protocol and helped to bind members of provincial Britain's middle classes into broader narratives of shared meanings and values. Grand ceremonies may be understood as tokens of unity and commitment to a larger identity. They recalled important non-work time, even if for others they were a distraction from unemployment. Viewing filmed events as a family or with a wider audience perhaps also conferred a social and participatory sense of belonging. Public memory-making of collective experience thus fitted in with mid-century middle-class notions of active citizenship.[24] Although an estimated twenty to twenty-seven million people watched the coronation of Elizabeth II in June 1953 live from Westminster Abbey on television sets hired or bought for the occasion[25], cine-camera sales and the rise of interest in amateur filmmaking indicate that many enthusiasts went out filming.[26] The local presence of visiting royalty continued to attract filmmakers' attention well into the later twentieth century, and may point to a lingering conservatism within some amateur circles.[27]

National events prompted some early cine users who could afford to visit London to make their own records on film.[28] By the 1950s, many more amateurs documented events closer to home. Their films provide a visual patchwork of how people in villages, towns and cities across Britain were swept along by populist enthusiasm.[29] Unlike the London-focused Festival of Britain in 1951, amateur coverage of the 1953 Coronation suggests that localised participation had both real and symbolic significance.[30] Many people equated the accession of the young queen with the start of a new Elizabethan era that would mark the end of postwar rationing and austerity and the dawn of new opportunities beyond the capital.[31] Across the North West, festivities were filmed in colour, in black and white, and on all film gauges. Scenes of crowds in Manchester's decorated central streets, squares and Piccadilly Gardens[32] contrast with the smaller fancy-dress parades, historical pageants and tableaux, marching brass-bands, acrobatic displays, fetes and floats that occurred.[33] Filmmakers recorded different aspects of this late flurry of nostalgic patriotism that, unlike the exhausted elation in 1945, seemed to herald – and even symbolise – the idea that Britain's wartime strength could at last bring a brighter future and fresh opportunities for all. People lit fireworks and held torchlight processions.[34] Souvenir medals and mugs were handed out to children.[35] Elderly residents at a nursing home enjoyed a garden fete.[36] Traditional rose queen corona-tions became alternative centre pieces for village green dancing and other celebrations,[37] while one Coronation film committee oversaw the recording of an 'Old Folks Tea', Coronation Ball, motorcycle race and 'Cowboys and Indians' show.[38] The details disclose how national occasions provided legitimate breaks in daily routine when people might film and be filmed in distinctive community settings.[39]

Such gatherings provided scope for filming unexpected incidents. Trying to capture defining moments on camera enabled amateurs to imitate or compete visually with professional newsreel reporters. Imagery illustrates how local subjectivities intertwined with national narratives. In one film, as different age groups take part in a tug-of-war, balloon race and fancy-dress parade of costumes, floats and decorated prams and tricycles, one banner with the words 'Long May She Reign' points to the reason for the underlying holiday mood.[40] This good-humoured vignette contrasts with more distant pageantry. It typifies how local cine memories inform wider debates on the dynamic relationship between memory and history.[41] Raphael Samuel's notion of memory as an image bank of the past readily applies to amateur cinema's role in determining what is remembered and forgotten.[42]

Personal and public memory-making connect in footage of veterans' anniversaries and ceremonies of remembrance. High levels of fatality from the Lancashire and Yorkshire regiments during the First World War left few families and localities untouched, so public commemorations attracted younger filmmakers as well as friends and relatives of those who had seen action.[43] While local production companies and cinema owners eagerly recorded the public presence of veterans at the unveiling of war memorials in the immediate aftermath of the war,[44] amateurs were more likely to film such commemorations ten years on. Detailed footage of successive Armistice Days shot by the Preston brothers coincided with their father's role as mayor.[45] Scout troops, brass-bands, veterans, police, women collecting money and placards urging 'wear your poppy' as well as numerous well-dressed wreath-bearers form processions.[46] No longer so newsworthy for professional and commercial interests, amateurs continued to chronicle these community acts of collective remembrance, unwittingly charting how participants aged and lessened over time even as film sequences lengthened. Some towns commemorated specific campaigns too, as at Bury, where cine club members filmed the Gallipoli veterans' parade on the fiftieth anniversary of the 'Lancashire landing', as part of their *Bury Pictorial 1965*.[47] Over time, public and personal rites converged and key dates change their symbolic significance, as instanced by one proud father who recorded his son's first seaside steps on Armistice Day in 1930.[48]

The solemnity of much amateur commemorative footage contrasts with scenes of sporting events. Improved focal quality prompted more filming at matches, even if most close-ups occurred as players entered or left the field or posed with trophies. Early exhibitors soon recognised that sport on film was a lucrative crowd-puller and some amateur filmmakers eagerly imitated the commercial pioneers with their own attempts to document local teams and major matches.[49] Amateur sports footage, while not developed here, links with histories of popular culture and, as shown by Dave Russell's work on northern identities, represents another enduring expression of belonging and affiliation.[50] Amateur interest in recording children's involvement in junior competitions and sports leagues also testifies to how family ties shape local connections and inform its filmic framing. Study of school-related sports footage could further understanding of young people's health and evolving physical educational practice within the state and independent sector.

Festive occasions

May Day celebrations and other local festivities attracted amateur interest during wartime, particularly where such activities involved children or charities. Carnival footage captures some of the exuberance that briefly inverted the normal social order and daily routines of northern industrial peacetime and wartime life. Long reabsorbed into the dominant structures of civic power and cultural life, carnivals had once been more subversive temporary invasions of public space and working time. They remained important public holidays for those in and out of employment during the Depression and beyond, and united people in lengthy preparations. Elaborate fancy-dress parades and large imaginatively designed floats contrast with the simplicity of other participants' costumes and accompanying prams, bicycles, carts, buses and horse-drawn vehicles.[51] Local brass-bands, dance troupes, majorettes and different uniformed groups participated too. The mayoral party riding in an open-roofed car or carriage and the police presence, on horseback, or dispersed amidst onlookers point to how controlled modern carnivals had become. Yet the possibility of unexpected incidents for bystanders, filmmakers and later audiences – a high-wheeled delivery van breaking an axle, horses agitated by balloons, ribbons or bunting – or impromptu moments of staged transgression heightened atmosphere, tension and excitement.

Carnival spectacle appealed to filmmakers of different abilities. Filming required steady shots and controlled camera movement, and worked well without intertitles although edited captions added to audience enjoyment. The huge heads of masked dancers, exotic costumes hinting at distant places, exposed bare skin smeared with body and face paint, banter with bystanders and children playing amidst strewn flower heads, burst balloons and tattered ribbons were ideal to film.[52] Many onlookers and participants were familiar with each other, even if assuming an unfamiliar role that allowed them to behave differently. The unpredictable performances of jesters or strong men maintained the brief possibility of misrule, while the presence of jazz musicians within larger carnivals hinted at strands of visual and musical complexity that were entering northern popular culture even while various folk traditions persisted.[53]

Some amateurs filmed carnivals repeatedly, recording the mix of old and new and changing annual themes. Local entrepreneurs advertised their services through participating or offering rides in liveried vans, carts and wagons. Named organisations sponsored or benefited from carnivals although other events involved more general fund-raising.[54] Processions included suburbs, town centres and country lanes although Morecambe's deckchair-lined route and Blackpool's tiered seating were uniquely seaside characteristics.[55] Footage captures the bustling atmosphere of waiting crowds and the bodily proximity of people enjoying themselves. In Urry's words, these spectators' 'co-presence' or 'collective tourist gaze' transformed familiar streets – and open spaces if linked with funfairs – briefly into somewhere (and something) else.[56] Unlike still camera imagery, filming from ground level offered viewers a mobilised gaze upon passing fairground rides, carnival floats and other people. Cine use thus extended visual perception beyond 'phantom ride' effects or seeing from the windows of a moving train or tram since it enabled filmakers to record motion without being in motion themselves.[57]

Amateur carnival footage evidences popular imperialism found in attitudes and entertainment in interwar Britain (Figure 5).[58] Body paint and parodies of borrowed cultural dances recur as do costumes, flags and floats representing different countries.[59] Just as such unproblematic depictions of imperial rule and economy were central to national self-image, tableaux of happy natives and produce affirmed regional status within patterns of colonial finance and trade. Older fairground and music-hall traditions persist too, as shown by acrobatic troupes, or 'Rainbow Fairies'.[60] The carnival 'drag queen' at Hebden Bridge evokes a pantomime dame tradition that continued into early silent comedies.[61] Themed pageants and civic anniversaries provided welcome distractions from the continuing austerity, fears at home and wider geo-political concerns that

[*Trains, Carnival and Dog Show*] (Dir. Harold and Sidney Preston, 1934). Still supplied by courtesy of North West Film Archive at Manchester Metropolitan University, Film no. 1186 (b/w, silent, 11 min. 8 sec.).

5

characterized the early postwar years.[62] Street decorations, torchlight procession and firework display all featured in Leigh's jubilee celebrations for fifty years of borough incorporation.[63]

Carnivals within North West England occurred within a relatively short and unreliable summer season but this did not lessen their frequency, popularity or filmmakers' enthusiasm for visual novelty.[64] Carnivals, like Whit Walks and other regional festivities, expressed civic identity and local pride, and united local people despite differences in race, religion and ethnicity. Distinctive Catholic and Anglican occasions attracted some filmmakers too.[65] Secular events ran competitions for the best float or costume, and being crowned Cotton, Rose or May Queen (and occasionally King) brought pride, local celebrity status and occasionally naming in amateur footage.[66] Inevitably, background details of buildings, vehicles, advertising, fashion or other aspects of material culture may now hold as much interest as foregrounded spectacle. How people behave together and respond to the camera, or with symbols of authority and legitimised burlesque (however sanitised) provides other routes into exploring these cine-scapes of local leisure consumption.

More routine rhythms and textures of local life attracted filmmakers too. Domestic scenes relied on good lighting and were most easily captured within their own homes, although professional standing or contacts sometimes allowed entry into other people's houses as seen in Charles Chislett's filming poorly housed families in Leeds and Mike Goodger's later scenes of slum clearance in Salford.[67] More frequently, amateurs documented other people's everyday worlds in exterior shots. Although visually limited in their disclosure of people's lived experiences, such scenes reveal how localities have changed. For over five decades, amateurs recorded what has been described as 'the murmuring of the everyday'.[68] Often they crossed social and physical space to film in the lived worlds of others, but occasionally they were insiders. They sought to document how days passed, as people greeted their neighbours, did routine chores or made local journeys. This imagery captures some of those processes and patterns of recognition, co-existence and familiarity that structure the micro-realities of human experience. Ideally, such filming involved being on foot, knowing the locality, being accepted and being able to record in uninhibited ways. Miss Lucy Fairbank was one such amateur.

Local worlds

For over thirty years, Lucy Fairbank (1890–1983), the daughter of a West Yorkshire business man, maintained her interest in amateur film. She filmed at home and abroad, with her 16mm camera, and showed her cine material to audiences in the Pennine textile settlements of the Colne Valley where she had been born and later taught at a primary school.[69] Her local films exemplify the fine-grained intimacy possible to find in amateur material. *Views and Personalities* (c.1935) recorded a series of encounters with people of different ages as she walked around her own straggling valley-side mill village, Wellhouse, during the early summer.[70] We see the hesitant awkwardness of a young workman standing in a cottage doorway and the polite dignity and operatic gesture of an elderly man who raises his hat and stiffly stands upright for a camera technology that was faster than he seemed to realise. The only adults shown on camera who ignore her presence are the driver of a small lumbering bus and a team of road workers in the village centre. A similar indifference to being on film is shown by children who spill out from school as they shrug themselves into coats, run off and skip away sometimes holding hands. They disappear from view watched only by the filmmaker, whose familiarity makes stopping and staring unnecessary for all but a few.

Generally, women appear relaxed as they laugh, smile, wave and turn from or towards Fairbank's camera. Her filming seems candid and prompts amusement and comment as women sit or stand on cottage steps darning, watering flowers, knitting and holding or caring for young children. These silent cameos record the social mix, networks and interactions of village life. People were her focus, even though the materiality of living conditions and physical landscape is ever-present. Shots reveal the varied age and structures of dwellings with and without front gardens; the attention to fashion and personal appearance; and the importance of apron and tabard for both indoor and outdoor work. No one seems idle or posed; even the young woman whose expressions register embarrassed pleasure and playful coyness in a series of shots from different angles was apparently interrupted while reading a book in her garden. Women with prams and toddlers pause and pass by, talking, smiling and interacting with their infants and each other as much as with the filmmaker. Fairbank's gaze was inclusive and respectful: elderly male residents – perhaps her father's contemporaries – turn towards her with apparent good humour as she films in close-up, their mouthed comments passing unrecorded. A quizzical expression flickers across the lined face of a frail but carefully dressed elderly woman with wispy hair scrapped back into a bun. Apart from her fingers tatting, she sits almost motionless, on a raised balcony, her angular features profiled against the blurred industrial landscape below, uninterrupted in her task by the younger woman's close presence and camera equipment.

Purposeful self-assurance pervades these scenes of women whose daily responsibilities and repetitive tasks confer knowledge and ownership of the village lanes. Shared steps, doorways, alleys and yards privatise the edges of public space. Boundaries seem even less clear where physical topography creates impromptu meeting places on roadside flagstones, or by water troughs and low walls. Scenes that seem to exemplify 'the wordless histories of walking, dress, housing, cooking [that] shape neighbourhoods' recur through many of Lucy Fairbank's films.[71] *Wellhouse, Hub of the Universe* (1935), a film about 'walking out on May Day', suggests local people's acceptance of the camera's presence and their familiarity with being filmed.[72] The valley floor brims with semi-rural and industrial messiness as terraces, mills, weaving sheds and chimneys vye for space with the river, canal and railway. Higher up, the footage shows that bank holiday pleasures still require much effort. Brass-band members puff their way along the steep village sides, as do men and women behind the prams and trolleys that bear younger family members. There are no bystanders for this community event. Youngsters take short cuts down flights of steps to avoid some of the road bends. When walkers pause for breath or to accompany the musicians as they play at a stopping point along the route, filming is possible too, sometimes from above or below so that expressions are clearly seen under brimmed hats and bonnets. Winter coats worn over summery printed dresses, suits and jackets as well as swaying trees and tightly held song sheets are visual clues to the chilly conditions even if many purchase ice-creams during the event. These scenes of walking, talking and laughing people and unsupervised children who weave through the small procession as it makes its halting journey exude a sense of pleasurable ordinariness. It typifies an occasion experienced by people who share the proximity of living and working together, just as countless generations had before them.

Fairbank's gaze penetrates into more enclosed space in another short film, *Fun and Frolic at a Garden Party Given by Miss Gledhill*.[73] Although probably shown for fund-raising like her other films, this footage presents local women of different ages unrestrainedly enjoying themselves playing games within the intimacy of a medium-sized back garden. Its character derives from her relationship and physical proximity to her subjects. Much of the garden party was shot in close-up and captures the sense of merriment as well-dressed women sit, eat and play different games that include throwing quoits, inflating balloons, and trying to attach pegs single-handedly to a violently flapping washing line. Lucy Fairbank is shown briefly with a cine-camera, plus lighting meter around her neck. Filming at close quarters occurs as women dance, smoke, eat or drink, specifically turning and performing or talking to the camera. Identities are constructed playfully for the filmmaker, as in the sequence of a young woman eating indulgently with a teaspoon.

Quick cutting captures the women's self-confidence and the concurrent nature of activities as they sit absorbed in conversation, or watching each other's antics. Fairbank focused repeatedly on hand movements, facial expressions, the occasional adjustment of hair or clothes, shared glances and at times the concentration of private conversations as women, unrestrained by family responsibilities, enjoy time to talk, regardless of the laughter, noise and jollity around them. Intimacy and informality characterise this private paper-streamer-filled back garden world of women into which one elderly man just briefly steps. Improvised entertainment using gendered tropes of daily life differently – pegs, washing line, indoor tableware and household furnishings set outside – enables these women to redefine an unprepossessing domestic space for relaxation, quite independently of the structures and timetables required to support more organised leisure time. Fairbank's footage salvages the ephemeral memories of past social practice and reinstates the emotional traces of remembered and forgotten places that link smaller stories of gender, class and locality into larger narratives of change.

Another filmmaker whose 'insider' relationship confers an immediacy upon his footage is Ralph Brookes (1900–97) who began to film people in and around Ordsall, Salford, during the later 1950s.[74] Brookes was born in Smith Street, Ordsall, into a family of six. After naval service during the First World War, Brookes worked at Salford Docks but joined the family-run newsagency during the 1930s. For decades he documented life in the terraced streets around the newspaper shop in New Park Street using a still camera. His work and hobby made him a well-liked and familiar figure, and he became known as the 'Man with the camera'.[75] Exemplifying the widening social access to amateur filmmaking, he bought his first cine-camera in the later 1950s, possibly prompted by the desire to record his young grandchildren during family gatherings and outings. Between 1957 and 1974, he made over ninety home movies using silent, colour Standard 8mm gauge cine film.[76]

Brookes never intended his films for more than home viewing. Yet his gaze upon family life extends beyond the domestic and is a reminder of how images are saturated with culturally and historically embedded meanings. John Berger's notion that a 'radial system' of 'personal, political, economic, dramatic, everyday and historic' processes co-exist around any image readily applies.[77] His footage offers an intimate portrayal of a working-class locality that has now disappeared. Although middle-class film enthusiasts across the Greater Manchester area had been telling stories on film about themselves at home and abroad for decades, Brookes's films offer a unique portrayal of Ordsall's terraced neighbourhoods through local eyes.

Brookes's vignettes of local life coincided with socio-economic and physical transformation. Scenes occur against a backdrop of economic decline and worsening unemployment among Salford's dock-workers and deserted quaysides. Adults go about their daily routines while children live and play surrounded by the effects of environmental decay, neglect and council-led rehousing schemes. Brookes's imagery has a sense of place rooted in local knowledge and a trusting relationship with people he also knew as customers and neighbours. Youngsters sometimes perform for the camera but mostly the footage represents his unobtrusive and unassuming gathering of informal impressions filmed at street level, indoors or from upper-storey windows. The resultant visual patchwork reflects personal inclinations and his opportunities to roam. Gender, age, interests and experience shape where, what and how he films rather than any predetermined message, plan or imposed storyline. His unedited footage offers a discontinuous narrative of community events and encounters. This montage of Ordsall's rhythms and micro-geographies contrasts with how other contemporary middle-class amateur and professional filmmakers constructed Ordsall – and equivalent localities – as a slum.[78]

Brookes recorded what made his life and locality distinctive. He filmed meals, arrivals and the exchange of gifts during family gatherings and weddings or christenings, picnics, playgrounds, open-air concerts in the local park or walking by the deserted docks during a strike. Carnivals and funfairs, brass-band competitions and Whit Walks point to locally focused lives punctuated by outings to Belle Vue Zoo or the centre of Salford and Manchester. Longer journeys, by car and public transport, maintained contact with family and friends living within the region. Their focus on people, particularly his grandchildren, contrast with the tourist attractions filmed during successive family holidays at favourite destinations in Dorset, Cornwall and the Lake District. His spatial networks, like his ways of seeing, denote the particularities of time, place and circumstances.

Brookes's version of life in Ordsall's old streets was less impoverished and more fun than is sometimes suggested.[79] Children play inventively outside amidst clearance debris or building materials. A hand-made go-kart confers status on its young driver and brings speed and greater freedom. A miniature ironing board briefly converts paving stones by the front door into an outdoor playhouse.[80] Activities are shaped by age and gender. As children grow, their improvised play shifts to street corners, alleys and open areas where games and fantasy develop away from adult supervision. Panning shots over household bric-à-brac, cleared land and harmless trespass on to building sites under the apparently casual gaze of two policemen suggest an affectionate older person's appreciation of youthful independence rather than concern about urban squalor.[81] Repeatedly we sense Brookes's pleasure of filming as seen in scenes of bonfire-building for Guy Fawkes' Night on land newly cleared of housing. Despite the dull autumnal light and drab colours, the mood is lively as one mischievous masked grandchild peeps around a corner before joining different-aged youngsters and excited dogs as they scramble precariously over a heap of house timbers and abandoned furniture.[82]

Whit Walk processions and other church festivals feature in Brookes's films too. These shared outdoor events punctuate the community's calendar and involve young and old as costumed musicians, dancers, marchers and standard bearers. By the late 1960s, his Whit Walk scenes included children of Caribbean and Asian background. Young Sikhs and Muslims stand among other smartly dressed pavement onlookers, as children parade past holding banners and streamers. These brightly costumed figures, like the funfair crowds found in other Salford footage, attest to the neighbourhood's residential diversity. As in similar dock areas, demography reflected patterns of contact and settlement that reflected the changing linkages of empire, dominions and commonwealth. Such glimpses are significant in reclaiming the visual histories of Black and Asian neighbourhoods in the city.[83]

Street processions illustrate the role played by inner-city churches during years associated with spreading secularisation. Religious festivals supplied many locally supported organised activities until urban churches were closed, demolished or severed from their earlier congregations by redevelopment schemes. As Ralph Brookes filmed the closure of St Cyprian's Church and its demolition, he unwittingly captured the evolution of faith communities.[84] The presence of Black and Asian children and families denotes an inclusivity and tolerance during locally celebrated festival days not readily found within more official records of 1960s Britain. These cinematic streetscapes denote changing local identities in which culture, ethnicity, race and class would become increasingly significant. Other religious events also chart regional demographic change. Surviving footage of Corpus Christi, Trinity Sunday and other Catholic festivals within areas of Bolton, for example, is a reminder too that Lancashire's Irish communities were rapidly being assimilated during the postwar decades.[85]

The amateur eye for local detail meant that attention often focused on scenes that have now disappeared. Displayed pigs' trotters, hams and sausages in a butcher's shop perhaps allude to another local business, also lost through redevelopment. Did shots of horse-drawn ice cream carts serving children in the middle of the street prompt personal memories of childhood and less traffic?[86] As girls dress in adults' clothes to dance around an improvised maypole in a deserted terraced street they link with traditions that, by the 1970s, were more usually associated only with rural areas.[87] Such insider perspectives reveal the omissions in official narratives that labelled such localities as problematic within planning and welfare circles.

Novelties prompted camera use too, whether it was seeing a motorised Mr Whippy ice cream van, displays in department stores or at outdoor markets, or Mrs Brookes visiting a shiny new self-service cafeteria. As rehousing and relocation gradually reshaped Ordsall's physical and social fabric, Brookes filmed closer to his home. Perhaps the pace of neighbourhood change coincided with his grandchildren's growing reluctance to feature in their grandfather's home movies. As Brookes never edited intertitles, his shots of named streets and building memorialise specific moments and places of transformation. One sequence shows cleared streets, then the compulsory purchase order served by Salford City Council on his own property, followed by footage of the site where the newsagent's once stood.[88]

The demolition of churches, pubs and, ultimately, the newspaper shop removed familiar landmarks and changed patterns of activity. On new housing estates, entrances to flats and maisonettes meant fewer doorsteps where adults might stand and toddlers play, perhaps signalling a retreat indoors. Brookes documents his wife in their own new flat and shows older people's faces at windows. Tracking shots follow younger residents as they create informal paths, passing places and meeting places. His gaze encompasses evolving identities against a background of emerging youth culture and fashion, changes in leisure, mobility and car ownership, social mores and demographic change. These biographical snippets capture the vitality within the ordinariness of their world. Notwithstanding the socio-economic hardships and prolonged uncertainties of multi-phased urban redevelopment, Brookes's films highlight the idea that, for those that lived, worked and played there, these old neighbourhoods were much more than the mean streets perceived by contemporary professionals. Loss and regret underlie scenes that chart how local character, meaning and identity radically alter. Footage of his wife and oldest grandchild as they walk through deserted dock areas has poignancy too. Such subjectivities enrich the historical imagination and trace how ideologies impact upon individual lives. Amateur film's fragmented visions of local and regional life, as seen here, reclaim the emotional geographies of memories and experiences that endow places with significance.[89]

Local histories on amateur footage highlight the serendipitous quality of visual memories. Some hobbyists, despite the warnings that occurred in the specialist press, joined material into a single reel. John Turner's use of three- and four-minute-long spools of Standard 8mm silent colour film illustrates the idiosyncratic nature of such visual jottings and economical picture-gathering. Over almost fifteen years, Turner filmed extensively, documenting his family and business, Palatine Paints Limited, based in Leigh, Lancashire. Amidst scenes of local occasions, other imagery fits less readily into a father's visual family narrative. Who were the teenagers waiting on a Wigan street corner or the train-spotters at a station? Why did he film someone donkey-stoning her front doorstep, a blacksmith shoeing a horse or cooling towers? What prompted the shots of newspaper vans delivering the *Daily Worker* and the sign outside a Ministry of Labour and National Service? Did personal or business interests spur the numerous scenes of houses being demolished and new building during the later 1950s and 1960s?

Numerous cine users created similar visual montages creating personalised versions of local and regional identities.[90] Although reasons for particular shots are now lost, as are their meanings for any intended audience, such material uncovers relationship between gender, family life, locality, memory-making and visualisation. Cine-cameras extended the snapshot record of single-shot camera techniques to motion photography. Such visual eclecticism contains fascinating gems and hints overall at wider patterns of practice but these fragments have less coherence than planned productions that, by contrast, prioritised capturing local character over personal meanings.

Local club productions

Amateur cine clubs soon recognised the benefits of making and screening films shot locally too (see Chapter 2). Some clubs, founded during the 1950s, produced local-interest documentaries from the outset, possibly because television comedy began to undermine their own belief in producing fiction. Perhaps the arrival of televised regional news cover also shifted cine groups away from magazine-style news compilations. Recorded over twelve months, and edited from different filmmakers' material, such productions were popular with paying audiences. Bury Cine Society's *Portrait of Wednes*day offered 'a cross-section … [of local life] from the moment when the sun breaks over the skyline of gaunt buildings and mill chimneys to the hour approaching midnight when the last light goes out in a row of terraced houses'.[91] Filming sought to portray 'the town at leisure, making music, acting, painting, playing bingo and twisting' (the dance craze of the time).[92]

Pendle Movie Makers, founded in 1960, focused on local documentaries too. Its early members submitted a five-minute entry to the BBC's *Vanishing Britain* competition that was subsequently shown on *Panorama*.[93] A restrained and elegiac soundtrack highlights 'the mood of change [as] old customs and ways of life vanish [and] new ones take their place' within a Pennine mill town. Regional imagery recurs: vibrating wire filaments rattling on upper window panes as the knocker-up passes by; mill workers operating huge machines; a woman in clogs and shawl white-stoning her doorstep before visiting the corner shop and children delivering wide-necked milk bottles from a horse-drawn cart. Tilted shots or low angles heighten later scenes of dereliction and demolition: the cloth-capped labourers using mallet and pickaxe; twisted machine parts heaped for scrap collection in an overgrown mill yard; gaping interiors where broken glass and discarded lampshades and chairs occupy cavernous and silent iron-pillared weaving sheds. Scenes evoke wider changes too as in a cluttered dark interior with high tin-stacked shelves behind scales and meat slicers on the wooden counter. A shopkeeper finds it 'increasingly hard to compete with supermarkets' in spite of the 'varied stock and personal service'. An elderly couple play the piano and violin and then worn hands place a vinyl disc of classical music on the turntable of a small record player as a narrator says, 'electronics have come of age'. Succinct and well-composed, this vignette displays filmmaking skills that were to establish the club's reputation for tackling social issues.

The next production, entitled *Nelson 62*, comprised a fifty-five-minute record of local life and events, filmed in colour over twelve months. Members filmed the town council proceedings, agricultural show events and visiting celebrities including Miss World and Marty Wilde all in close-up. Station scenes of holidaymakers leaving for their annual two-week summer break and lengthy sequences about educational provision, policing and other services signalled gaining official permission too. Using tripods produced steady, well-shot images that were edited to run along the reel-to-reel taped commentary. Sequences of fairground rides and shop frontages at night and unexpected moments sustain interest; a judge's awkward embrace of winners in a baby competition; a celebrity shedding a warm wrap for a brief public appearance, and the sagging guy ropes and strewn litter after an event. Details evince amateur aesthetics and filmmakers' sense of audience too, whether the anonymous gentle shove assisting someone on to an excursion bus or wrestlers relaxing after a combative display of muscle power.

This ethnographic gaze is rooted in place and time. It ties locality and region into national and global processes. Immigration, for instance, had yet to make a visible presence. Non-white faces are absent from the crowds and annual walk to Pendle Hill, schools and summer camps although practical courses at the local technical college show greater diversity. Other changes are mentioned, including rising car ownership and continental holidays in the sun. Mills where 'work is going on but not an operative in sight' reveal how contraction and automation affect the town's staple cotton industry. Old local firms being taken over by southern businesses prompt comment. So does the emergence of a small plastics factory within the town's former fresh fish market. Self-service is transforming shop interiors, and changing frontages herald the early erosion of independent retailers. Such signs give temporal specificity.

Nelson 62 captures the particularities of everyday living. Images reveal smoking chimneys, coal deliveries and blackened buildings indicative of an era before legislation on clean air. The market's predominance of British over imported fresh produce predates distribution patterns brought in by refrigeration and containerisation. Pupils are channelled by the eleven-plus into secondary schools that shape careers according to academic and practical ability. Scooters are ridden without protective helmets. Apart from an occasional nylon headscarf, innovative synthetic fibres have yet to affect everyday clothes. Even the children's chapped cheeks and legs suggest homes without central heating and lives reliant on walking and waiting at exposed bus stops.

This foregrounding of the everyday situates amateur film within the realm of social and local history, and also visual history. Just as pioneering cine-camera users imitated newsreels and locally produced topicals, the advent of independent and regional television opened later possibilities for imitation and occasional participation. Amateur cinema's close association with actuality reporting gained endorsement by key figures within Britain's prewar and postwar documentary film traditions. Despite vibrant alternative approaches attracting amateur attention during the 1950s, realism remained influential upon two generations of cine users and sustained local interest in films as a dominant strand of non-fiction amateur cinema.

Looking beyond the mundane

As this chapter's start suggested, cinematography offered a means to affirm continuities with national traditions that persisted despite the material and more invisible psychic and demographic traumas of war. Just as the 1920s witnessed a spate of publications by H.V. Morton[94] and others aimed at newly mobile travellers eager to explore and rediscover aspects of Britain, the postwar years again saw much printed encouragement to film locally. 'Opportunities await in the sphere of civics, social relations, the life of towns and villages, industries of the past, education, the economic, cultural and pictorial pattern of the countryside' enthused Gordon Malthouse.[95] The impetus for recording aspects of vanishing national life grew and, increasingly, during the 1960s and 1970s, the hobby press encouraged filmmakers to record aspects of Britain's disappearing hedgerows, vernacular buildings, woodlands, market towns and fishing fleets.[96] While some individual filmmakers and cine groups perceived film as a means to offer counter-narratives about contemporary society, others specifically responded to these exhortations. Some amateurs simply used their equipment to record daily lives in less structured ways. What these diversities disclose, however, is the mix of survivals, revivals and innovations that characterise late modernity. Everyday life necessitates negotiating and, to some extent, accommodating the contradictions of continuity and change. The resultant patchiness is what brings local distinctiveness and situates the visual plethora of micro-realities within broader frames of reference.

In the work and practice of Georg Simmel, Walter Benjamin and other early cultural theorists who focused on the everyday, their focus was quintessentially urban.[97] For them, the impact of modernity was most apparent and most compelling in towns, cities and metropolitan life. Owing to their own intellectual and philosophical lenses, and perhaps because of lingering urban romanticism found within different strands of mainland European critical thought, their focus was on the daily practice of city dwellers. Other realms of lived experience were overlooked. It might seem from the preceding discussion that amateur filmmakers in Britain similarly focused primarily on local life within built up areas. This was far from being the case even within the heavily urbanised and industrialised North West, and much footage of rural scenes exists as seen in outsiders' visits to country areas (see Chapter 7) and discussion of working lives (Chapter 6) and social issues (Chapter 8).

This chapter has highlighted amateur interests in local material. Whether their principal audiences were family and friends or more organised groups of viewers, much amateur activity expresses the localism that still dominated many people's experiences. Local knowledge, interests and connections affected how, where, who and when some enthusiasts were able to film even if their own status distanced them from specific scenes. Their capacity to contribute to and shape shared visual texts of collective interest perhaps helped to strengthen notions of community and imagined togetherness even as unprecedented patterns of mobility were altering people's lives and experiences. Amateurs also functioned in spheres of daily practice that extended beyond the boundaries of the local. Many, as discussed in this book, travelled with their cameras beyond the local area and sent their films for processing elsewhere (unless they developed them at home), and some enthusiasts became members of larger associative networks through club membership, competitions and their involvement as readers and contributors to the specialist press. Their records of local life, as well as their own day-to-day living sensitises us to the pluralities of everyday experience embedded within amateur practice even within the socio-cultural specificities of regional and historical experience in North West England.

Amateur imagery of local life is more than an accumulation of disparate everyday phenomena. Rather, its tissue of similarities and differences, continuities and changes define the heterogeneity of social life. Local details intermesh with other regional, national and global structures and dynamics. It offers visual cues that can reconnect with contemporary audiences and open fresh ways of working. Exploring local imagery comparatively and cross-culturally reinvests the particularities of past times with meaning and theoretical rigour. Revisiting these inherited visible and material worlds can help in understanding the contested identities and experiences now often associated with (and constituted through) particular places, types of spaces and people's relationships with their surroundings.

Notes

1 G. A. Atkinson, 'Introduction', in M. A. Lovell Burgess, *A Popular Account of the Amateur Cine Movement*.
2 Lovell Burgess, *A Popular Account*, p. 65.
3 *Ibid.*, p. 6; see also P. Le Neve Foster, 'Money or brains'; see also L. Cooke, 'British cinema'.

4 Lovell Burgess, *A Popular Account*, pp. 62, 65–6.
5 See detailed discussions of early film producers, dealers and exhibitors in J. Barnes, *The Beginnings of the Cinema*, and also V. Toulmin, S. Popple and P. Russell, *The Lost World of Mitchell and Kenyon*.
6 See, for example, M. Gomes, 'Working people, topical films, and home movies'; M. Hammond, '"The Men Who Came Back"'.
7 T. F. Langlands, 'Profitable everyday cine subjects'.
8 L. Donaldson, *Cinematography for Amateurs*, p. 17.
9 *Ibid.*, pp. 80–1.
10 R. Shand, 'Theorising amateur cinema'.
11 H. Norris Nicholson, 'British holiday films of the Mediterranean'.
12 Preston Brothers, 1929: [*Glengarry Local Newsreel*], NWFA Film no. 1891 (b/w, silent, 14 min. 6 sec.).
13 133 separate entries are listed for the Preston Brothers, starting from 1926 so individual films mentioned only in passing are not detailed in full. See catalogue entries, www.nwfa.mmu.ac.uk:591/search/FMPro, accessed on 12 October 2009.
14 The earliest film established the characteristic format of these topicals, as seen in Preston Brothers, *1927/31/33–34: [*Glengarry News and Family Footage*], NWFA Film no. 1903 (b/w, silent, 10 min. 52 sec.).
15 H. Norris Nicholson, 'Handle with care!'
16 (Anon.), 'They call it free cinema'.
17 Preston Brothers, *1928/32–35: [*Around the Capital*], NWFA Film no. 1914 (b/w, silent, 16 min. 38 sec.); 1931: [*A Trip to London 1931*], NWFA Film no. 1889 (b/w, silent, 15 min. 8 sec.); 1931: *Paris International Colonial Exhibition 1931*, NWFA Film no. 1895 (b/w, silent, 10 min. 29 sec.); 1931: [*A Visit to the Paris International Colonial Exhibition, 1931*], NWFA Film no. 1939 (b/w, silent, 15 min. 8 sec.).
18 See, for instance, Preston Brothers, 1928: [*1928 Greater Brighton Celebrations Duke and Duchess of York at the Royal Pavilion and Carnival Procession of Decorated Vehicles*], NWFA Film no. 1890 (b/w, silent, 15 min. 0 sec.).
19 Preston Brothers, 1929: *April 21st 1929. The Mayor (Mr Joshua Preston JP) with the Scouts,* NWFA Film no. 1183 (b/w, silent, 9 min. 22 sec.).
20 Preston Brothers, *1928–29: *The Royal Show Harrogate*, NWFA Film no. 1915 (b/w, silent, 15 min. 35 sec.).
21 Preston Brothers, 1929: *May 1st 1929 May Day in Stockport*, NWFA Film no. 1174 (b/w, silent, 13 min. 0 sec.).
22 Graham West, 1935: [*Miss Middleton Visits Radcliffe*], NWFA Film no. 6661 (b/w, silent, 9 min. 43 sec.).
23 Kuhn, *Family Secrets,* pp. 168–9.
24 For fuller discussions see A. Kidd and D. Nicholls (eds), *The Making of the British Middle Classes?*
25 P. Hennesey, *Having It So Good,* pp. 242–3; D. Sandbrook, *Never Had It So Good*, p. 44.
26 (Anon.), 'Better demand for camera'.
27 See also Chapter 9.
28 Preston Brothers, 1935: *July 16th 1935. The Late King's Silver Jubilee Review of The*

Fleet at Spithead, NWFA Film no.1892 (b/w, silent, 14 min. 6 sec.).
29 Pimlott, cited in Sandbrook, *Never Had It So Good*, p. 44.
30 See for instance, *Coronation Day in Godalming* and *Horley Coronation Fete*, Screen Archive South East Accession nos S 000621 and WS 000928/1.
31 See Kuhn, *Family Secrets*, pp. 79–82; see also Sandbrook, *Never Had It So Good*, p. 44-5.
32 Sandy Ricketts, 1953: *Manchester Coronation Decorations 1953*, NWFA Film no. 800 (colour, sound (sep.), 5 min. 8 sec.); A. E. Taylor, 1953: *E II R 1953*, NWFA Film no. 3458 (colour, silent, 3 min. 37 sec.); Harry Hill, 1953: *Coronation Celebrations May and June 1953*, NWFA Film no. 1684 (b/w, silent, 11 min. 6 sec.).
33 Mr W. E. Lynn, 1953: *Widnes Coronation Celebrations*, NWFA Film no. 321 (b/w, silent, 8 min. 46 sec.); Unknown, 1953: *Coronation Celebrations. Widnes Schools Pageant at the Wade Deacon Grammar School May 1953*, NWFA Film no. 722 (b/w, silent, 11 min. 18 sec.); see note 32, Harry Hill, 1953.
34 Sandy Ricketts, 1953: *Todmorden Coronation Day Celebrations*, NWFA Film no. 657 (b/w, silent, 4 min. 45 sec.).
35 W. L. Hall, 1953: *Ashton-U-Lyne Celebrates June 1953*, NWFA Film no. 4030 (colour, silent, 26 min. 1 sec.).
36 George Wain, 1953: *Pole Bank Hall – Coronation Garden Fete 20th June 1953*, NWFA Film no. 4479 (colour, silent, 6 min. 55 sec.).
37 Frank Finch, 1953: [*Parbold Rose Queen Parade 1953*], NWFA Film no. 4676 (colour, silent, 12 min. 7 sec.).
38 Great Harwood Coronation Film Committee, 1953: *Great Harwood Celebrates*, NWFA Film no. 4108 (colour, silent, 41 min. 28 sec.).
39 Sam Hanna, 1951: *Colne Parish Church. Historical Pageant of the Church of Colne by Members of Colne Parish Church. Narrative by the Rector: The Rev J. Ross Macvicar M.A.*, NWFA Film no. 5152 (b/w, silent, 8 min. 10 sec.); 1951: *Borough of Colne Festival of Britain Celebrations 1st July – 16th August 1951*, NWFA Film no. 5154 (b/w, silent, 25 min. 2 sec).
40 Unknown, 1953: *Coronation Celebrations Halewood*, NWFA Film no. 1542 (b/w, silent, 6 min. 40 sec.).
41 See G. Cubitt, *History and Memory*, pp. 26ff.; P. Ricoeur, *Memory, History and Forgetting*, pp. 385–93; P. H. Hutton, *History as an Art of Memory*, pp. 1–8.
42 R. Samuel, *Theatres of Memory*.
43 Major-General L. Nicholson and Major H. T. McMullen, *History of the East Lancashire Regiment in the Great War*; H. C. Wylly, The *Loyal North Lancashire Regiment 1914–1919*.
44 See, for instance, Manchester Film Co. Altrincham Picture Theatre, 1919: *The Earl of Stamford Unveils the Chapel Street Roll of Honour, Altrincham April 5 1919*, NWFA Film no. 44 (b/w, silent, 5 min. 15 sec.); Feature Films, Blackburn, 1919: *Whalley Peace Pageant*, NWFA Film no. 50 (b/w, silent, 5 min. 17 sec.); Palace Cinema, Uppermill, 1919: [*Saddleworth Returning Heroes*], NWFA Film no. 387 (b/w, silent, 3 min. 25 sec.); Manchester Film Company, 1920: *Altrincham and Dunham Massey War Memorial Unveiling Ceremony*, NWFA Film no. 46 (b/w, silent, 3 min. 10 sec.).

45 Preston Brothers, 1929: [*Remembrance Day 1929*], NWFA Film no. 3558 (b/w, silent, 4 min. 7 sec.); *1930/32: *St Julien Anniversary in Stockport 1930*, NWFA Film no. 1185 (b/w, silent, 7 min. 48 sec.).
46 See note 45 (Preston Brothers, 1929).
47 T. Ashworth, *Forty Years On*, p. 12.
48 G. Warburton, 1929/30: *Tom's First Appearance on the Movies*, NWFA, Film no. 1024 (b/w, silent, 9 min. 52 sec.).
49 D. Russell, 'The football films'.
50 D. Russell, *Looking North. Northern England and the National Imagination*; see also D. Russell, 'Sporting Manchester: from 1800 to the present'.
51 Preston Brothers, *1927–28: *Stockport Carnival Queen Crowned*, NWFA Film no. 1920 (b/w, silent, 10 min. 40 sec.); 1928: [*1928 Greater Brighton Celebrations Duke and Duchess of York at the Royal Pavilion and Carnival Procession of Decorated Vehicles.*], NWFA Film no. 1890 (b/w, silent, 15 min. 0 sec.); 1931: *May 9th 1931 Reddish May Queen Festival*, NWFA Film no. 1167 (b/w, silent, 11 min. 32 sec.); Mid-Cheshire Amateur Cinematography Society, 1937: [*Middlewich Coronation Celebrations 1937*], NWFA Film no. 4321 (b/w and colour, silent, 28 min. 29 sec.).
52 Unknown, 1919: *Peace Celebrations at Haslingden July 19th 1919*, NWFA Film no. 577 (b/w, silent, 8 min. 26 sec.); Unknown, 1923: *Haslingden's First Carnival*, NWFA Film no. 579 (b/w, silent, 9 min. 55 sec.).
53 See note 51.
54 Unknown, c1930: *The Infirmary Carnival*, NWFA Film no. 210 (b/w, silent, 1 min. 52 sec.); Preston Brothers, 1933: *Reddish Crippled Children's May Queen Festival May 13th 1933*, NWFA Film no. 1156 (b/w, silent, 17 min. 52 sec.).
55 Parkstone of Lytham St Annes, 1924: [*Blackpool Pageant*] / *Easter Fun*, NWFA Film no. 166 (b/w, silent, 9 min. 40 sec.); Preston Brothers, 1933–34: *Glengarry Topical Film No. 20*, NWFA Film no. 1922 (b/w, silent, 16 min. 34 sec.).
56 J. Urry, 'Globalising the tourist gaze. On tourist and tourism'; 'The place of emotions within place', p. 78; P. Stallybrass and A. White, 'Bourgeois hysteria and the carnivalesque'.
57 W. Schivelbusch, *The Railway Journey*; J. Taylor, *A Dream of England*, pp. 142–5.
58 J. M. Mackenzie, *Propaganda and Empire*, pp. 9–11.
59 Parkstone of Lytham St Annes, 1924: [*Blackpool Pageant*] / *Easter Fun*, NWFA Film no. 166 (b/w, silent, 9 min. 40 sec.); Arthur Waller, 1930–93: [*Stretford Pageants; Manchester Docks; School Sports; Rag Parade*], NWFA Film no. 4330 (b/w, silent, 12 min. 41 sec.).
60 Preston Brothers, 1932: *Wilmslow Carnival 1932*, NWFA Film no. 1154 (b/w, silent, 14 min. 5 sec.).
61 The Picture House, Hebden Bridge, 1925; *Hebden Bridge Carnival and Gala*, NWFA Film no. 529 (b/w, silent, 12 min. 51 sec.).
62 Unknown, 1929: *Wigan Carnival*, NWFA Film no. 1982 (b/w, silent, 9 min. 25 sec.); National Film Agency, Manchester, 1930: *Salford Historical Pageant and Charter Celebrations*, NWFA Film no. 27 (b/w, silent, 31 min. 13 sec.); South Manchester Amateur Cine Society, 1935: *Sale and the Charter Celebrations 1935*, NWFA Film no. 1336 (b/w, silent, 16 min. 29 sec.); see also A. Marr, *A History of*

Modern Britain, pp. 105–8.
63 Leigh and District Cine Society, 1949: *The Jubilee Celebrations*, NWFA Film no. 903 (b/w and colour, silent, 28 min. 12 sec.).
64 See, for example, the Preston brothers, who included carnival scenes from Winsford, Reddish, Altrincham, Alderley Edge, Wilmslow, New Brighton, Colchester and Douglas (Isle of Man) in their Glengarry topicals as well as footage of Stockport Carnival shot in successive years.
65 Thomas Magee, *1932: [*Catholic Procession, Bolton*], NWFA Film no. 582 (b/w, silent, 8 min. 5 sec.); *1932/33: [*Trinity Sunday Procession, Bolton*], NWFA Film no. 585 (b/w, silent, 13 min. 14 sec.); Sam Hanna, 1946–49: [*Whit Walk to Holy Trinity Church, Burnley*], NWFA Film no. 5290 (b/w, silent, 3 min. 54 sec.); 1949:[*Church Service, Military Parade, Procession of Witness*], NWFA Film no. 5343 (b/w, silent, 3 min. 55 sec.); Ralph Brookes, *1959/65–66/68: [*Manchester and Ordsall Scenes*], NWFA Film no. 2310 (colour, silent, 21 min. 52 sec); c. 1960s: [*Ordsall Scenes; St Clements Walk and Docks*], Film no. 2316 (colour, silent, 27 min. 33 sec.); c. 1960s: [*Mount Carmel Walk and Ordsall Park*], Film no. 2334 (colour, silent, 4 min. 26 sec.); 1969/72–73 [*St Marks Whit Walks and Cheetham Hill Scenes*], NWFA Film no. 1782 (colour, silent, 23 min. 13 sec.).
66 Named Rose Queens appear in some films, including: Preston Brothers, 1929: *May 1st 1929 May Day in Stockport*, NWFA Film no. 1174 (b/w, silent, 13 min. 0 sec.); *1934–35: [*Greek Street Baptist Rose Queen Celebrations*], NWFA Film no. 1935 (b/w, silent, 2 min. 58 sec.); J. E. Hallam, 1938: [*Gala Day / Armistice Day Commemoration Service 1938*], NWFA Film no. 861 (b/w, silent, 14 min. 0 sec.); Arthur Laycock, 1964/65: [*Wesley Church Rose Queen 1964*], NWFA Film no. 6166 (colour, silent, 27 min. 14 sec.); 1971: [*Wesley Church Rose Queen 1971*], NWFA Film no. 6167 (colour, silent, 10 min. 34 sec.).
67 Charles Chislett, 1951: *New Lives for Old – St George's Crypt*, YFA Cat. no. 822 (b/w, colour, 40 mins); Mike Goodger, 1968/69: *The Changing Face of Salford. Part 1, Life in the Slums*, NWFA Film no. 430 (colour, sound, 32 min. 0 sec).
68 L. Giard, M. de Certeau and P. Mayol, *The Practice of Everyday Life*, p. 7.
69 Information supplied by Yorkshire Film Archive.
70 Lucy Fairbank, 1935: *Views and Personalities*, YFA (uncatalogued).
71 Giard, de Certeau and Mayol, *The Practice of Everyday Life*, p. 7.
72 Lucy Fairbank, 1935: *Wellhouse, Hub of the Universe*, YFA (uncatalogued).
73 Lucy Fairbank, 1935: *Fun and Frolic at a Garden Party Given by Miss Gledhill*, YFA (uncatalogued).
74 Transcript of interview with Ralph Brookes, 6 December 1990, Salford Quays Heritage Project, Salford. Tape Nos 091–093; see also H. Norris Nicholson, 'Two tales of a city'.
75 *Ibid.*
76 The Ralph Brookes collection contains 93 films made c. 1957–74, of which 64 films were made during the 1960s, a time of significant redevelopment in Ordsall. See NWFA Film nos 1782–1793; 2308–2386; 2342.
77 J. Berger, 'Uses of photography'.
78 Norris Nicholson, 'Two tales of a city'; see also Chapter 8.

79 R. Hoggart, *A Local Habitation. Life and Times, 1918–1940*; see also note 67 (Mike Goodger, 1968/69) and note 78.
80 Ralph Brookes, c. 1960s: [*Salford Scenes; Morecambe; Alton Towers*], NWFA Film no. 2321 (colour, silent, 16 min. 4 sec.).
81 Ralph Brookes, *1968: [*Ordsall in Winter*], NWFA Film no. 1788 (colour, silent, 3 min. 49 sec.).
82 Ralph Brookes, *1968–69: [*Croal at Christmas, Santa's Grotto and Bonfire at Ordsall*], NWFA Film no. 1783 (colour, silent, 15 min. 29 sec.).
83 See note 78.
84 *Ibid.*
85 See for instance, May Castle, c. 1962: [*Catholic Whit Walks in Bolton*], NWFA Film no. 3479 (colour, silent, 29 min. 6 sec.); 1964: [*Catholic Whit Walks in Bolton 2*], NWFA Film no. 3480 (colour, silent, 14 min. 48 sec.); 1967: [*Catholic Whit Walks in Bolton 3*], NWFA Film no. 3487 (colour, silent, 25 min. 13 sec.); 1972: [*Catholic Ordination Service*], NWFA Film no. 3481 (colour, silent, 12 min. 28 sec.).
86 Ralph Brookes, *1968: [*Ordsall Scenes; Weddings and Belle Vue Zoo*], NWFA Film no. 2309 (colour, silent, 20 min. 43 sec.).
87 Ralph Brookes, 1963: [*Ordsall Scenes: Children and Docks*], NWFA Film no. 1792 (colour, silent, 4 min. 21 sec.).
88 Ralph Brookes, c. 1960: [*People and Places around Ordsall*], NWFA Film no. 2319 (colour, silent, 24 min. 56 sec.).
89 J.Urry, 'The place of emotions within place', p. 78.
90 See, for example, films by Graham West, a 16mm cine user from Radcliffe, Lancashire, made over four decades: NWFA Film nos 6558–6559 and 6660–6664; films shot on 9.5mm by Harry Hill from Waterfoot near Rawtenstall, Lancashire spanning almost two decades: NWFA Film nos 1681–1698; films shot on 9.5mm by Alf Frankland including ten years of scenes at home in Salford and on holiday at Blackpool and in North Wales: NWFA Film nos 3438–3442; and films shot on Standard 8 between 1960 and 1972 by Arthur Townsend a filmmaker from Ashton under Lyne, NWFA Film nos 3511–3527.
91 T. Ashworth *Forty Years On*, p. 5–10.
92 *Ibid.*, p. 8.
93 Pendle Movie Makers, *Vanishing Britain* (by courtesy of Pendle Movie Makers, 2008).
94 See, for instance, H. V. Morton *In Search of England*.
95 In 1948, according to Malthouse, the British Film Instutute requested a treasury grant of £6,500 to encourage amateur film production. It saw closer links with the newly set up British Amateur Cinematographers' Central Council as a means to 'encourage amateur film as "a social and cultural force, as a stimulus and aid to intelligent film appreciation, and as a nursery of recruits to the professional film industry"'. Cited by G. Malthouse, 'Amateur status'.
96 G. Haines, 'How about a movie with a message?'; 'Down in the forest'; 'To market, to market'; 'Filming along a lane'.
97 B. Highmore, *Everyday Life and Cultural Theory*, p. 74.

6

Gazing at other people working

Amateur cinema established itself within middle-class circles during the 1930s, when Britain's unemployment reached almost three million.[1] What prompted the making and showing of numerous films about working people during years of mass unemployment, particularly in the industrial regions of the North West? Government initiatives, public debate, media reports and the observable reality of people – specifically the young – losing jobs, claiming benefits and seeking work were all around, even if they gained little direct attention from most amateur enthusiasts. Newsreel makers, or cine users and photographers on the political Left, were more likely to document such experiences or of those joining marches and going to remote locations for controversial retraining programmes.[2] Yet the impact of economic recession upon ordinary people's lives meant that work-related issues were immediate and topical for amateur filmmakers and their audiences. As local entrepreneurs, or mill and factory owners, some families with interests in amateur cinematography were directly affected too. The vicissitudes of global and regional economic downturns reduced orders, deterred customers, broke supply lines and meant downsizing operations and greater all-round caution in business management. No income group was immune from changing economic realities even if more affluent social groups had greater protection from feeling hardship.

The prewar filmic gaze on working lives was more than voyeuristic curiosity upon daily routines of other people. Undoubtedly much was filmed with respect and sometimes considerable knowledge of the working processes involved. Some filmmakers recorded skills and methods already threatened with obsolescence. For others, making, showing and watching films about working situations connoted self-assurance and business acumen. Alongside the celebratory, perhaps there may also have been those films that were acts of faith and optimistic visions of conditions that could be returned to. Hindsight, however, may be misleading. Much filming was probably not prompted by a sense of looming change. Many amateurs simply turned the camera on aspects of the world around them, stepping into the material conditions of specific working contexts as opportunities and contacts arose. With varying levels of competence in camerawork, spelling, visual judgement and skill in portraying people, their footage now yields a rich if, at times, problematic gaze upon work routines.

Looking beyond humour

J. E. Hallam's *Following Horses. Our System* offers insights into Bolton's once thriving local urban brewery industry.[3] Filmed during the early 1940s at Magee, Marshall and Co. Ltd, then owned by another amateur enthusiast, it exudes humour from the opening image of a grinning road sweeper collecting horse manure in a cobbled street. Successive shots show employees as they enter and leave the unnamed premises during the course of a day. Captions indicate time passing; movements quicken and expressions brighten until at 5.00 pm, smiling workers briskly head for home. Time and motion, as tropes of modernity, provide the simplest of devices for framing working people. Instantly recognisable to local viewers too, the urban scenes also seem evocative of more generic northernness.[4]

Playful reversed sequences of casks back up the loading ramp and bowl fast across the brewery yard. Laughing workers watch a ritual barrel rolling and dunking meted out to an apprentice cooper, while stony-faced older employees interrupt their work to pose with tools for the camera and senior management stand nearby. Punch-lines usually follow images, as when the words 'Air Raid Precaution' succeed shots of older uniformed men carrying beer barrels. The caption 'Whose Feet? No Prizes Given' introduces imagery of men working underneath company delivery vehicles while 'May Day Parade 1940' displays finely harnessed drays and gleaming trucks with their proud drivers, rosettes and certificates. Elsewhere staff apparently struggle with fastenings while trying to hold on to gasmask boxes, evoking good-humoured wartime resilience. Such imagery cuts across occupational, gender and social delineations found in more formal portrayals of workplace relations.

Following Horses … is neither sophisticated nor exceptional. It typifies how enthusiasts tried out new visual techniques and tricks as they filmed to entertain friends and local people. It highlights how the presence of a cine-camera influenced people's behaviour in workplace settings, and cautions us about using visual sources uncritically as proof of past reality. Despite its artifice, ill-lit indoor sections and other technical shortcomings, Hallam's footage shows occupational practices within a once widespread urban industry that has virtually disappeared. It also indicates that amateur material was not isolated from the emerging visual conventions found within documentary, promotional and government information films. Verbal puns, which would not have been then permitted on stage,[5] visual ambiguities of physical propinquity ('Gas masks sometimes cover a multitude of sins') and staff relations are reminders that cinematography was, for many of its early affluent adherents, novel and mildly transgressive.[6] Indeed, filming others at work, especially during times of economic hardship, epitomises amateur practice as leisure consumption.

From the very start of amateur cinema, filming and watching scenes of work, along with family, holidays and animals, were promoted as legitimate and popular subject matter.[7] Physical exertion as seen in laborious routines and also in school-related films (see Norris Nicholson 2012) had an appealing exoticism too, perhaps resembling the appetite for scenic and cultural otherness that made travelogues and ethnographic films attractive. Films offered a peep inside premises known only from the outside, while the chance to see themselves or their workmates on screen brought pride and pleasure to some viewers. Filmmakers found that cinematic forays across social rather than geographical distance into workplace settings were feasible amateur alternatives during the economic austerity of the interwar and early postwar years. Leisurely opportunities for filming others engaged in distinctive occupations occurred too, especially when family holidays often coincided with highly intensive phases of seasonal outdoor rural activity.

Regional distinctiveness

This discussion concentrates on working people in the North and North West, although some occupation-related material, including health, features in other chapters. Amateur footage spans the region's maritime, rural and industrial economies and reveals the unevenness of modernising processes within and between different occupations. Changing social access to cine-camera usage and ownership altered the perspectives from which filmmakers recorded in the workplace. Informal 1960s scenes of employees eating, playing football and tug-of-war or being caught off-guard differ from the previously mentioned *Following Horses* ... or the informative documentaries made earlier by Hanna, Chislett and other amateurs.[8] Making and showing such material depended upon skill and a filmmaker's relationship to the subject matter, the owner or employees, and his (or her) sense of purpose and audience enjoyment.

Early workplace footage coincided with wider interwar interests in recording societal change, as seen in the documentary film movement, with which, the emerging hobby literature shows, there was some commonality and shared sense of purpose. While overlap between some amateur and early professional practice is well-evidenced in the specialist press, Mass Observation (MO)'s ambitious plans, in late 1936, to assemble an archive of everyday life, seem relevant in understanding contemporary amateur interest in filming the everyday world.[9] Certain similarities are apparent too. Among pioneering cine users, as changing interwar economic and occupational circumstances expanded the social complexity of regional middle-class identities, local relationships and connections permitted them to record informally in urban and rural work settings.

For some amateur filmmakers, like MO's survey-makers, accessible aspects of popular culture and daily occurrences widened interests in ethnography and anthropology beyond academic circles. Just as MO planned to use socially diverse respondents and observers, amateur footage mediated different perspectives and, specifically within the North West, recorded local livelihoods (including at Bolton and Blackpool, two key study areas for MO) through northern rather than southern eyes.[10] This is not the place to claim amateur cinematography as an autonomous visual offshoot to MO's data-gathering imperative. But it seems quite likely that the emergence of both movements was in response to specific cultural and material conditions: in particular, broadcast media's emerging role in articulating and circulating social meanings left many people's experiences off the screen. Evolving cine-camera technologies, even by the late 1920s, enabled cine users to make their own visions of daily life by venturing into different occupational worlds near where they lived. Such imagery complemented how life was fantasised in commercial cinema films or portrayed in news footage narrated by southern middle-class voices.

The early hobby press encouraged filming work-related subjects and acknowledged how Eisenstein's visual experiments in factories and elsewhere were transforming the face and reputation of Soviet cinema. Closer to home, successive technical innovations introduced different lenses and focal ranges that improved contrasts and lighting, and raised the quality of indoor filming. George Sewell was an influential early advocate of films on aspects of work,[11] and encouraged promotional filmmaking 'as a powerful aid to business'.[12] His preference for amateur-produced material was unequivocal. The amateur insider's perspective offered more to an organisation than any professional outsider; he urged, 'You live with it and all its ramifications, methods and processes' and can give 'your own angle on your personal affairs'.[13] Reprinting a *Daily Express* article in *Amateur Films* enabled Sewell to stress how screening promotional films could 'hit straight between the eyes' during a business visit.[14] If casting 16mm film gauge as 'the most useful assistant (the salesman) has ever had'[15] seemed unduly utilitarian, creative use could also record 'those old relics of a past age and its associations, the vanishing trades, the local celebrities'.[16] Such sentiments reinforced realism within early amateur practice.

While the British Council, Empire Marketing Board and industrial sponsors including the GPO, Shell and Gas boosted Britain's nascent documentary film,[17] regional promotions flourished too. Prewar cine pioneers thus grew up within a context of exhibited trade and industrial films produced by London and North West Railways, the North of England Film Bureau, Oldham Master Cotton Spinners Association Ltd and Manchester Ship Canal Company. Progressive businesses adopted film for marketing during the 1920s and early 1930s and, as in the case of Unilever and or Pilkington, amateur films preceded commercially produced promotional material.[18] Names, gauge, quality, style or even contextual details do not reliably distinguish between amateur and professionally produced early workplace film and highlight the problematic divisions found in early writing on differentiating between professional and sub-standard film.

Alongside amateur promotional films, some interwar workplace footage replicated early 'factory gate' sequences outside mills, factories, mines and other businesses. Outdoor physical work on roads, railways, docks or building sites suited early technical limits on focal length and lighting and expressed modernity directly albeit without, in the hands of most hobby enthusiasts, the celebratory visual aesthetic of social realism. Chance encounters reveal past employment or recruitment practice too, as in scenes of Lascars crewing 1930s holiday cruise ships. Imagery evinces patterns of rural electrification, pit closure or the extension of domestic telephone networks. Working people featured in footage of disasters and visiting dignitaries too although scenes recorded exceptional rather than everyday occurrences.

Footage of overseas visitors touring cotton mills offers reminders of Lancashire's globalised cotton production. If as, Todd convincingly argues, the world of work was central to people's lives, then those occasions that interrupted the routines of production in mill and factory were also memorable for employees.[19] Lengthy and courteous exchanges at managerial level contrast with the excited exuberance of young women mill workers who jostle and laugh alongside smiling overseas visitors. A filmed mill visit by a Nigerian delegation in 1950 captures an informal doorway pause for smoking and brief exchange with curious young onlookers. During jovial poses in the mill's nursery, infants seem overawed by the unfamiliarity of non-European formal dress and smiling black faces.[20] The apparent absence of contemporary prejudices is somewhat undermined by subsequent footage of blacked faces and people dressed in national costumes but it is not clear if the mill's fancy-dress competition was filmed during the same trade visit. Such scenes may be compared with contemporary amateur colonial footage of visits to plantations or missions in Nigeria and the Belgian Congo (now Democratic Republic of Congo) made to highlight Unilever's philanthropy and enlightened 'native–worker relations' and scenes taken while visiting plantations in Southern Rhodesia (Zimbabwe) that supplied cotton for mills in Rossendale.[21]

Much amateur footage of cotton mills survives from the 1920s onwards although dim interiors sometimes mar overall quality. Filmmakers detailed processes from unpacking canvas-wrapped bales of compressed cotton bolls through to carding, spinning, weaving and finishing. Differences reflect modernisation trends, patterns of inward investment and the persistence of older technologies, as well as individual filmmakers' interests. Higginson's mill scenes in Bury used angles, viewpoints (including an aerial shot) and focal range creatively, as well as simple graphics and elaborate calligraphy.[22] Abstract shots of cotton wisps, disembodied deft hands threading and knotting, or design punch-cards unfolding as they determine how shuttles criss-cross over a Jacquard loom, offer a visual richness that contrasts with the vagueness of 'another method of spinning and twisting' and other technically imprecise captions. Close-ups of rhythmically moving pistons, pulleys, levers, rollers, belts, bobbins, cones and cheeses transform raw material into finished products for different national and international destinations. Despite occasional cautions against showing machinery on screen, as offered by Major Notcutt (perhaps under pseudonym), as 'it so quickly bores the audience',[23] such sequences recur in non-professionally produced material over many decades and hint at an amateur aesthetic informed by wider contemporary cinematic developments.

Visual conventions emerged in the amateur portrayal of employees too but the focus is on the individual, or at most the workplace community, rather than the soulless autonomy of a large organisation. The camera's proximity may sometimes suggest that the cinematic gaze was sanctioned more by differences in status than by a shared enjoyment of informal relations. Such imagery, often filmed over the shoulder of an employee, also discloses a filmmaker's character, manner and relationship with senior management. Coy half-smiles, exchanged expression with others on the workbench, embarrassed demonstrations or self-contained indifference to the camera's presence occur too. Such clues to past interpersonal dynamics and workplace relations may now be the sole visual testimony to how age, gender and status influenced specific occupational settings and practices.

Thomas Magee, co-owner of the brewery discussed earlier, documented life in Bolton during the early 1930s.[24] In his films about local shoe and boot making, he shows a specialised work force engaged in processes that ranged from leather selection to displays of finished footwear.[25] His footage lacks intertitles and avoids step-by-step workplace processes yet he captures the employees' intricate skills and intense concentration. He filmed as an outsider invited into another local work situation. Many of the staff remain anonymous, occasionally smiling to the camera or holding an example – hand-stitched eyeholes for brogues – closer to the lens. As elsewhere, close-ups of male and female hands focus attention on the nimble dexterity of fingers as they stitch, heel, polish and pack finished articles. At times the lens is so close that chin hairs or a blurred sleeve are shown and only in the well-lit sewing workshop do women look up smiling from their Singer sewing machines. Yet even when shot and edited to make people laugh or smile, these films seem respectful of employees and their work.

Outings and visits

Works outings were accessible opportunities for filming that usually guaranteed an audience. Like other amateurs from the region's managerial circles, Magee recorded employees' families and management members posing informally or relaxing during annual excursions.[26] Visits to a wellington boot factory and sole leather tannery included playing bowls and leisurely strolls in nearby public gardens with convivial drinks and a raffle with the host firm. As high noise levels and potentially hazardous equipment often limited social contact at work, such scenes extend our visual understanding of workplace hierarchies beyond clues to dress code, task, work space and behaviour. The Preston brothers of Stockport made and showed films of excursions for staff and their families at Glengarry, their family home in Bramhall where they hosted visits for other occupational groups. One film records non-uniformed nurses taking part in races, dancing on the lawn to a wind-up gramophone and enjoying an elaborate buffet.[27] Like the occasions themselves, such filmed events evince company paternalism. They enhanced an employer's reputation and reinforced workers' sense of obligation and business loyalty.

Pilkington's Colliery Boys Go on Holiday epitomises how personal filmmaking might support a family business.[28] It details a private colliery's attempt to demonstrate social responsibility or even boost recruitment. The film's production coincides with a period of tense industrial relations between miners, private owners, trade unions and the government. Certainly, labour unrest and anger accompanied rising unemployment in Lancashire's mining districts as production fell.[29] Ameliorative government schemes had done little to generate alternative sources of sustainable work and new training opportunities. Contemporary pressing concerns about health, training and youth employment thus combine as both subject and context.[30] Lengthy captions explain why and how young colliery employees attend a scout-run camp during the mine's annual holiday week. The film's stated message is to demonstrate the colliery's social obligation 'as part of the welfare activity at St Helen's [sic] Colliery'. Intertitles stress how subsidised rest and healthy recreation by the sea for all employees under the age of eighteen accords with recent agreements between management and trade unions following the 'Holidays with Pay' legislation (1938).[31]

Captions detail union negotiation, and dramatised scenes show the colliery's general manager submitting a letter for consideration at a directors' board meeting where the proposal meets approval with a requirement that 'the boys will be asked to pay £1.00 towards the cost of the camp' and an undertaking that the company will meet all other costs. Stiffly re-enacted deliberations between seated well-dressed men where the only movements on camera are typing, leafing through ledger books and a smiling secretary (the only woman in the film) distributing paperwork contrast with surface shots of mine and miners and the subsequent intense regime of camp life. Text establishes location, main features of the pit-head workings (the 'Power House', 'Winding House') and key surface operatives, including 'the Winder', in charge of the metal cage that moved miners between the surface and underground galleries. Phrases introduce sequences of plant procedures and surface equipment but seem irrelevant for any local audience already familiar with these scarred and messy mining landscapes. Apart from the possiblility of miners seeing themselves on screen during a social evening film show, this material seems to have been intended less for the company's own colliery workers than as instructive or promotional material for other audiences and company shareholders.

The film thus offers an owners' perspective on company provision for young colliery workers at a time when mining was dirty, dangerous, poorly paid and desperately in need of modernisation. As part of 'the general desire to improve the lot of juvenile labour', which obliged private colliery owners to respond to wider union demands, viewers learn that 'all boys have to work for three months at the pit bottom. Doing their job.' Scenes of men with lamps stooping to enter and leave the cage at the start and finish of each shift lead on to sequences in which booted and clog-wearing teenagers (undersized through generations of poor diet and general health but no younger than the minimum working age of fourteen) drag coal tubs to the surface entrance. After stopping the heavy tubs from rolling back and crushing boys behind, they take out their 'snap boxes'. White bread, teeth and eyes show bright against coal-dust-smeared hands and grinning faces. 'The last shift before camp' shows youths leaving the cage, twelve at a time, waving or tilting hard hats towards the filmmakers. They visit the shower house where several towel-wrapped figures shyly find themselves caught on camera amidst silent laughter before heading home.

After filming the young miners departing excitedly by train, the filmmakers motored to the camp site in North Wales. Camp life scenes include 'Potato Peeling', meal queues, washing up, drumming on pans, basins and jugs for the morning wake-up call, tent inspections and eventually packing up for the return home. Beach scenes reveal an intense physical schedule of rigorous races, tugs-of-war and games of rugby league while their leaders chivvy, instruct, referee and participate in roughly equal amounts. Camera shots emphasise camaraderie, teamwork and the leaders' good humoured buffoonery during 'off-duty' moments. More reflective moments include close-ups as young campers relish brief opportunities to sunbathe between tents, fly kites or listen to one of their group playing the accordion.

Self-discipline, exertion and athleticism in healthy, natural outdoor settings were part of established reformist responses to the perceived excesses of working-class urban male culture.[32] Their absorption into aspects of interwar welfare provision as part of 'improving juvenile labour' was attractive to owners and directors who could enhance a company's reputation and workplace relations whilst improving productivity through better health and workers' well-being. This particular experience was a far cry from the controversial reconditioning camps in operation elsewhere but part of prevailing social pathologies about health, labour and youth.[33] While relocating young miners between two contrasting exclusively single-sex settings may have done little to challenge more entrenched notions of northern 'manly identities', the Pilkington Colliery film's window upon young miners in their knitted jersey swimwear at Borth in the months before war is another reminder of how regional industrial histories and working lives intersect with national concerns. Across Britain's coalfields, thousands saw military service as an opportunity to escape an industry desperately in need of restructuring and modernisation, but many from mining districts soon became trapped by Bevin slapping an Essential Work Order on the coal industry. As with so much amateur footage, one is left wondering what happened to the people on camera.

Changing employment patterns

Amateurs filmed working people well into the 1970s. Sometimes clues to impending historical changes are discernible only through hindsight, but explicit references occur too. *Nelson 62*, for instance, highlights the cotton industry's postwar contraction and automation in East Lancashire.[34] Viewers are informed that 'work is going on but not an operative in sight'. Chislett re-edited his footage of steel production during the industry's early postwar restructuring, although his interest lies more in the religious symbolism and awesome aesthetics of foundry work than the politics of short-lived nationalisation.[35] Views of life aboard the steam-powered North Atlantic fishing trawlers that operated out of Fleetwood conveyed nothing about the impending collapse of a regional economy.[36] Rather, the footage testifies to the disposable income available to Lancashire's trawler-men ironically just as their industry was about to end decades of local dependency on fishing and associated shore-based industries. Whether through the gaze of an insider or onlooker, these informal perspectives inform how working lives have been understood and mediated independently of newsreel and television.

Amateur actuality reportage was not without its critics, who lamented the missed opportunities for more creativity and experimentation. Some advised that amateur equipment and resources were simply unable to match professional production methods. While cine film's mimetic potential prompted many amateurs to shoot and share, the social documentary imperative remained influential. Public screenings of public information films had increased in number rapidly during the Second World War.[37] Free film shows offered reassuring messages about national productivity, self-sufficiency and the population's indomitable determination and resourcefulness. One week alone in March 1942, according to Ministry of Information figures, saw almost thirteen hundred film shows, mainly in rural areas, reaching out to 243,000 people.[38] Such activity influenced amateur activity after the war, and, where enthusiasts sustained filmmaking through the 1940s, people at work featured within officially permitted subjects available for filming.

Prewar initiatives and shifts in Soviet filmmaking, as already mentioned, provide other plausible contexts for the sustained amateur interest in documenting working people. Although some early Left-wing amateur filmmakers adopted film as a tool in wider class struggles as it was unfettered by laws of censorship, many featured strikes and union-led rallies more than routine work patterns during the interwar years.[39] Less polemical self-depictions of working-class life remained rare until social access to cine equipment widened after 1945. In contrast, prewar depictions of working people through middle-class eyes coincided with wider debate on the instructive benefit of film.[40] Discussion of film's use in scientific, medical and technological advancement as well as in colonial and educational settings strengthened middle class interests too.[41] Encouragement to make films on social and public topics came from the specialist press and from champions of amateur activity including Raul Rotha and others (see Chapter 8). Initiatives led by the British Film Institute (BFI) also boosted amateur documentaries, although later wartime loss of institutional records prevents tracing how some projects evolved. One such example concerned recording Britain's 'dying craft industries' on film.[42]

Disappearing worlds

An appeal by the BFI's History and Arts Committee to film national crafts and trades that were 'in danger of extinction but which are still being carried on' was published in *ACW* in early 1939.[43] *ACW* reprinted the BFI's list of threatened traditions that included over forty crafts and trades, mainly from rural localities in southern England. Northern entries included stone-walling in Derbyshire, Westmorland and Cumberland (now Cumbria), snuff-making in Kendal, clay-pipe and clog-making in north Staffordshire, Lancashire clog-making and handloom-produced fire-hoses in Salford. Although twenty trades and crafts under threat had no specified locality, some individual practitioners were identified with details of age, reputation as master craftsmen and uniqueness as (supposedly) 'one of the last'. Entries highlighted those who might be filmed using distinctive 'primitive tools' or 'primitive apparatus'. Accompanying notes covered particular processes, raw materials and the purpose of specific finished products. They suggest that specialist terms associated with such activities were also becoming unfamiliar, at least to staff at the BFI. *ACW* stressed how amateurs would bring 'more care and patience' than commercial filmmakers and stressed the BFI's preference for sound as 'in practically every case a commentary in local dialect would be extremely valuable'. Recognising that this might deter the majority of cine enthusiasts, the magazine suggested that interested filmmakers might 'draft a kind of commentary which should accompany the film should it ever be possible to put sound to it'. In this way the films 'may serve as records of our present-day civilisation'.

Wartime concerns eclipsed the BFI initiative, although it may be likened to Sir Kenneth Clark's *Recording Britain* project, launched later the same year.[44] As morale booster and a celebration of the nation's natural beauty, architectural heritage and cultural character, the later scheme's directive to commission painted scenes was prompted by threat of invasion but widened to documenting against broader vulnerability and loss caused by 'progress' and included many rural industries in decline. No evidence of relevant new films subsequently appears within the BFI's annual catalogues, although the next seven years saw more films on rural industries and agriculture, perhaps in part also prompted by the wartime relocation of the Film Council and Ministry of Information's film collection to Devon.[45]

Clogs in Lancashire (1943) exemplifies amateur skill in tackling such subject matters. It offers a portrait of an elderly clog-maker making clogs using alder bases from wood felled, dried and roughly shaped in an unidentified hilly woodland setting.[46] Scenes of children wearing clogs at school (where their teacher runs a clog fund for children from poor families) and mill scenes (which contrast with other mid-century films where spinners are still barefoot) are intercut with close-ups of the clog-maker. We watch as he hollows the wooden sole, shapes heel and edging grooves, nails on factory-supplied iron caulkers and then cuts, stitches and adds a button fastener before lasting the clog into shape for its final polish. Intertitles identify tools, terminology and processes involved at each stage of production. Camerawork combines information with aesthetic interest, strong contrasts of light and shade, and carefully composed frames.

The documentary films of Sam Hanna (1903–96) on rural industries and crafts possibly occurred independently of the BFI and *Recording Britain* initiatives but also began in the late 1930s.[47] Rural occupations form a significant part of his prodigious output of 9.5mm and 16mm footage produced over sixty years of filmmaking. Hanna was a qualified furniture designer and cabinet-maker before becoming a woodwork teacher in his home town of Burnley, where his innovatory classroom approaches and his early recognition of film's potential as a learning tool brought both respect and controversy. County educational officials viewed his film work as a distraction from teaching but Hanna's wartime training material for the Home Guard strengthened his personal convictions about film's peace time pedagogical role. Later contact with the National Committee for Visual Aids in Education reinforced Hanna's commitment. He believed that 'craftsmanship was an essential part of our tradition and heritage'. All pupils 'should be given the opportunity to use tools and materials both wood and metal', he urged so that they would gain a practical understanding of historical and social change.[48] Despite their inconsistent quality, Hanna's vignettes of individual craft workers are tributes to work practices that have now disappeared.[49]

If the wartime 'revival of rural crafts' inspired Hanna to film traditions 'in danger of dying out',[50] his films fitted in with subsequent attempts to sustain interest in regional traditions and practice.[51] Sam Smalley and his daughter Emily shaping wood for clog soles, chanced upon when driving through Grindleton near Clitheroe, feature in one of his earliest rural films, *The Clog Block Maker*.[52] Hanna later wrote that showing the film locally required waiting until electricity reached the village. Its projection on the kitchen wall to the family and a group of local children was how Sam Smalley first encountered cinema and discovered that the image would not disappear after its first screening. Back at school, Smalley exemplified 'the craft skills and the life style of a Master craftsman'.[53] Subjects of Hanna's films include a clogger and cooper in Burnley, pirn-winding (bobbin-winding) at Nelson, a blacksmith tyring a wheel, and slate quarry workers near Skipton. His notes record how he also chanced upon one of Yorkshire's last working tanneries.[54] 'Before filming any of the craftsmen I visited, I would watch them at their work and in my mind's eye I would visualise the whole of the film which I wanted to produce.'[55] He recalled that 'with the appropriate lens – wide angle, telephoto or normal – I would switch from one lens to another so that the one and only "take" required the minimum of editing'. Although pioneering, his methods were both idiosyncratic and at times visually unsuccessful as a result of technical mistakes that occurred either during the shooting or the processing of the film.

Hanna wrote notes to accompany his 'Old English Crafts' series. Some films were subtitled 'recorded for posterity' and claimed as 'invaluable in their research in conjunction with the static exhibits of our museums ... for historical accuracy'.[56] Comments about a barrel-maker reveal Hanna's sense of visual history: 'If I did not record him on film he would be forgotten ... He was using tools that most people had only seen in museums.'[57] Hanna believed that film could bring such 'curious objects to life'. Rapid postwar changes meant that this filmic record of northern occupations under threat soon more than doubled the BFI's own initial list of occupations at risk nationwide. Longer films were pared down to comparative compilations that captured diverse and distinctive practices, particularly in Lancashire, Yorkshire and the Lake District, but also further afield. One film reconstructs charcoal-burning processes in Grizedale Forest but the other films all recorded activities that were still extant. Hanna's imagery and commentary emphasise the effects of automation, mechanisation, loss of resource materials and an ageing workforce. Fewer apprentices meant dwindling specialist workers in the regional production of oat cakes, besoms and bespoke brushes, hay-creels, rush-seats, snuff, spelt baskets and stained glass.

Hanna believed that crafting practices produced exceptional artefacts and derived from experience. Innovation was unnecessary where continuity in design, production methods and tools had proved successful over generations. Crafting traditions involved dignity and integrity. 'Just let us watch the apparent simplicity of this form of weaving' urges one commentator.[58] Conversational digressions and idiomatic asides, as in sound footage of the Kendal Snuff Factory, typify voice-overs: 'That's another shot of the shaft', 'to put it bluntly' and 'as I said before'.[59] It is not clear whether the commentary was recorded separately as Hanna filmed during or more probably when later watching the footage. These commentaries also capture the subtleties of regional cadences and speech patterns that, like the activities under scrutiny, may have lessened or disappeared in the past fifty years.

Hanna contrasted regional practices too. One film included a small redundant upland Lancashire bobbin mill that offered space and convertible equipment suitable for automated rake making. 'Mechanisation has killed a handicraft yet it is mechanisation that has revived a dead one.'[60] Agricultural automation, however, and growing reliance upon silage for winter feeding, eventually ended hay-rake making altogether as mechanised harvesting and rough grazing spread over western Pennine pastures. Other disappearing local occupations recorded by Hanna include the hay-creel makers who supplied farmers in the Yorkshire Dales and Pendle district with frames for carrying loads of freshly cut hay to barns at lower level.[61]

Hanna records rural practices within a region whose predominant twentieth-century identities are associated with urbanisation and industrialisation. Imagery reveals the co-existence of rural and urban worlds, lifestyles and traditions that are now often hidden within less nuanced constructions of place meanings and identities. Hanna's preference to seek out rural cultural continuities may link to strands of prevailing postwar nostalgic romanticism for earlier times. His concern about the loss of intergenerational crafting expertise also connects to broader laments on disappearing ways of rural life by Hawkes, Hoskins, Priestley and others in and away from intellectual circles in the early postwar years.[62]

The amateur press gave encouragement too: 'Old country crafts are always a good subject particularly if they are one of the many now nearing extinction.'[63] Filmmakers should seek 'not to produce a lyrical study of the countryside or the seasons but a helpful practical record of agricultural activity'. 'Local knowledge' and 'availability of time' could give amateurs an advantage over professional filmmakers in recording marginal rural land ('now so much discussed' as part of wider debates upon postwar agricultural reform) that 'might start action to bring it into use'. Shifting concerns about the future of countryside, as well as broader concerns about conservation gradually, entered the hobby literature, as shown in a series by Haines, one of *MM*'s regular columnists, during the early 1970s. Rural occupations became visual routes into 'how you could show what is (and isn't) being done to preserve the beauties of Britain's green and pleasant land' and expose 'man-spoilt' scenes.[64] Country 'folk' engaged in 'ancient craft[s]' could be 'effective character studies' along with 'buyers in their hats', farmers, ringside dealers and 'the flat capped men watching, waiting, [and] leaning on walls' at a country auction or market. Rural workers were 'symbol[s] of permanence' and, like the recommended dramatic shots of prehistoric monuments in which light shafts fan from rain clouds 'as natural spotlights', high and low levels could even make a forestry worker seem like 'Gulliver inspecting young trees in his Lilliputian forest'.[65]

Amateur film had 'the power of showing what is actually happening' as urban growth, motorways, reservoirs and quarries and other consequences of modernity impacted upon rural lives and landscapes.[66] Haines's rhetoric was less polemical than Hoskins's impassioned outburst against the 'uglified' landscapes of 'England of the arterial by-pass, treeless and stinking of diesel oil' but it echoed interwar regrets for lost livelihoods and scenes.[67] He suggested collecting '"before" and "after" shots' that highlighted good practice, scanning local papers for topical issues, and referred to the weak powers of countryside protection. His authoritative tones suggest a readership that was still largely middle-class, educated and broadly in tune with the contemporary goals of amenity groups and liberal conservatism.

Filming family businesses

More informal views of work occurred too, reflecting widening cine use and the availability of 8mm colour film during the 1950s. Scenes feature alongside family outings and domestic or local material with minimal editing or titles. Intended like many postwar family films primarily as home viewing, such material was watched by people who had an interest in what was being shown or felt obliged to sit through a friend's or relative's screening of home movies. Less polished technically and often less visually creative than much prewar material, the immediacy of these films indicates a change in usage. As cine-cameras were simplified, their attractiveness for informal self-documentation grew. While costs and film length constrained use in comparison to contemporary visual trends in life-logging, more affordable equipment widened the amateur's propensity to record everyday incidentals in varied locations. Filming was particularly straightforward when home and work coincided, or where no one else's permission was needed.

Footage taken on and around the Walkers' family farm, at Audenshaw, now in Greater Manchester's eastern urban fringe, was one such instance.[68] Filming reveals the effects of modernisation and reform. A brightly painted horse-drawn float delivers milk around suburban roads of brick semi-detached houses built out into grazing land.[69] Slow-paced deliveries involve (possibly staged) neighbourly exchanges as housewives wait for milk and eggs. Heaving feed-sacks from a local merchant's small open truck contrasts too with later scenes of grain delivery by hydraulic truck.[70] The suction-pipe-filled feed hoppers and long poultry sheds reflect intensifying processes of national food production and consumption.[71] Family members deftly stack and wheel cardboard egg trays to dispatch areas and free-range hens give way to large-scale poultry production. Battery cages and high protein feeding regimes reliant on subsidised grain are filmed with care. Size and equipment denote modernity too as seen in skilful tractor work compressing grass for silage and huge sheds for machinery, milking facilities and indoor overwintering of cattle. Cutaways show children playing in a yard overshadowed by new structures and relatives relaxing outside the farmhouse, emblematic of a family-owned farm's absorption into an industrialised food system.[72]

John Turner portrayed changes within another Lancashire family business, Palatine Paints Limited, on the fringes of Leigh and Wigan. He recorded office practices, laboratory analysis and deliveries at his small manufacturing company during a period of expansion between c.1957 and 1965.[73]

Fluids churn and swirl through vats, tubs and pipes within the firm's mechanised paint production. Steady camerawork and adequate lighting illustrate production routines, spiced up by the occasional appearance of the factory cat. Dress code and fashion, office furnishings and interactions, manually operated machinery and laborious barrel movement disclose work practices and attitudes unaffected by concerns about health, safety or gender equality.[74] Building work reveals an absence of protective clothing, minimal scaffolding and the use of non-powered tools by elderly workmen. Turner's informal gaze thus has evidential value that extends beyond an owner preserving moments of personal importance.[75]

Other working lives and landscapes attracted Turner's attention too. His 'factory gate' scenes of employees leaving Leyland Motors echo earlier conventions, but his record of local collieries testifies to disappearing landscapes and working-class experiences.[76] Footage of miners wearing caps or hard hats as they return from underground shifts, move between buildings, visit the colliery nurse, sop up soup at long tables or queue for tea in the canteen memorialise a phase in the dismantling of the nation's coal industry. Careful camerawork captures aspects of surface activity. Winding gear is shown silhouetted against the sky. Pit wheels spin in opposite directions. Steam and smoke rise from chimneys and plumes drift above surface deposits. Warning signs, including the words 'Smoking strictly prohibited', together with shots of different working buildings, build a simple montage. These working scenes contrast with low-angle shots across wheel spokes discarded in deep grass, purple foxgloves foregrounded against boarded-up buildings and close-ups of glistening coal tips. The impending closures of Victoria Pit and others within the Atherton colliery complex and the associated redundancy of several thousand underground and surface workers confer significance upon these visual acts of bearing witness.[77]

Familiarity underpins Turner's footage of the Victoria Pit and Standish Social Club. Scenes include children dancing and people concentrating on dominoes and bingo. Elderly men with waist coats and fob watches smoke pipes as they play darts, drink or sit watching other people. Lancashire youth culture in the later 1950s is also briefly seen.[78] Although a smile is sometimes caught on camera, most young people seem oblivious to Turner's presence and absorbed within their own activities of playing cards and table tennis, or jostling for sweets at a tiny tuck-shop window. The self-conscious proximity and discreet hand-holding of different seated young couples contrasts with the exuberance of more frenetic dance sequences elsewhere in the club hall. This 'Variety

Night' brought together a brass-band, singer and various musicians on guitar, accordion, double bass and piano with band conductor and clergyman. Spotty youths, including a few with quiffs, drainpipe trousers and crepe shoes try to outdo each other as they rock'n'roll jive in limited floor space. Adolescent girls in wide-skirted dresses and cardigans dance together. The mix of teacups, Cola, Corona and beer glasses, fashions and activities suggests congeniality among employees and different age groups. Turner reminds us of the former vibrancy and versatility found in northern social clubs. Before teenagers acquired the mobility and financial means to seek out more independent niches away from family and adults, it was more usual to share social time and space. As the region's traditional occupations declined so did their associated networks that combined savings clubs and other forms of practical and family support with affordable, accessible and readily available ways, as seen at Standish, of having an evening out at 1s 6d (7.5p).

Working away from home

People's filmic memories sometimes informed other family members about their work elsewhere. Such camera users included the trawler men of Fleetwood who were well paid for their dangerous, contract-based two-week-long voyages into the then rich fishing grounds of the North Atlantic. Recording a fishing trip on cine film to show at home briefly became popular among trawler boat captains in the later 1950s and 1960s.[79] A thriving independent local camera shop supplied affordable photographic equipment for filming and projecting Standard and Super 8 films. Personal encouragement by its owners, Eleanor and Bill Curtis, made purchasing and developing films convenient and accessible during the two or three days onshore before trawlers returned to northern fishing grounds. With compact, lightweight and increasingly easy to use equipment, cinematography's novelty extended longer established interests in photography at sea and seemed well suited to the long hours of enforced inactivity during periods between fishing. No known links exist with the long-closed Fleetwood Cine Society, and the brief times ashore make active club involvement unlikely, so footage was primarily for family and friends.

Surviving amateur footage of Fleetwood's fishing industry was a consequence of circumstances. Briefly, amateur cine technologies coincided with disposable income among trawler owners whose working career spanned years when government grants and loans had supported the fleet's conversion to diesel and other forms of modernisation.[80] The resultant imagery combines the filmic gaze of insiders upon familiar tasks with the respected authority and licence to film that derived from having risen through the ranks. One such skipper and filmmaker was Jim Betty, who would open the wheelhouse window and record deck scenes from the bridge of his steam-powered trawler.[81] His footage, and that filmed by the ship's radio officer using the same camera, Eric Isaacs, never ventured to the crew's quarters below decks, perhaps because of a combination of easier daylight filming audiences being expected to have more interest in work rather than off-duty moments, and protecting what little privacy there was in cramped cabin conditions. As fish processing still took place on deck aboard a 'side-winder', sequences document how the fish catch was brought aboard over the boat's sides and its subsequent release from the nets for sorting, gutting and stowage on ice below decks for the return voyage.

Both cameramen's familiarity with their subject matter and the crew produced many well-timed sequences, filmed from above and behind. The final minutes of deckhands tugging and heaving nets aboard – sometimes during rough seas that splashed the lens – or the spectacular silver cascade of fish dropping on to the deck as the cod end of the trawl net opened, for instance, illustrate knowledge and economic use of filmstock without editing to capture key moments, as well as their on-board authority. Some scenes seem less frenetic, as when during calm weather men repair damaged nets stretched over the decks and jovially alert each other to the filmmakers' presence as they film from the bridge. Over-the-shoulder views also document aspects of routine ship maintenance as equipment is oiled, cleared, checked and stowed. Longer sequences show huge numbers of herring gulls and gannets dive-bombing and plummeting as the trawler nets were brought to the surface, or long views across broken pack ice when fishing off Iceland. Unwitting testimony to environmental change, such scenes in footage by Betty, Isaacs and other trawlermen also afford occasional glimpses of Icelandic gunboats and are reminders that the controversial succession of fishing limits introduced unilaterally around Iceland's waters further weakened the fishing fleets' commercial ability and hastened their decline at Fleetwood and the larger east-coast ports of Hull and Grimsby.

Amateur footage frequently combines self-conscious and more accidental recording of details that later acquire significance of impending change. Betty's and Isaacs' films span only nine years, yet their scenes of trawlers during construction and conversion from coal to diesel in Fleetwood's boatyards marked the final years of the town's postwar fishing boom. The lively quayside scenes of 'lumpers' unloading fish catches from the trawlers' holds ready for early morning auctions attest to the strong local economy too. Within a decade, most of the trawlers had been decommissioned, some younger trawlermen were seeking alternative offshore work further afield within the expanding North Sea oil industry and Fleetwood's associated fishing trades had virtually disappeared. Trawlermen's home movies became neglected visual evidence of past working lives. On-shore shots document making ice used to keep fish fresh on board the trawlers, scenes in the fish market and during deliveries elsewhere. They also include women as they sit or stand in the braiding rooms making nets. This footage thus offers a distinctive visual legacy of linked occupations that ceased as fishing virtually ended. These cine memories resurfaced only as part of an initiative to recover and commemorate lives associated with Fleetwood's former trawling industry. Direct knowledge of people's hard work and resilience, and their role in revitalising the town after wartime loss and hardship, were slipping from public memory. Technically competent although without the crafted aesthetic finesse or elegiac poignancy of earlier documentaries and radio ballads concerned with the fishing industry, trawlermen's amateur footage is a forthright tribute to the lives associated with the coast.[82]

Working out meanings

Framing other people working recurs through the history of amateur cinematography into the present and has varied over time. The simplest imagery comprises unplanned and informal impromptu glimpses of outdoor work chanced upon during a holiday or day's outing or sometimes filmed during a work break. Such scenes contrast with the details founds in scripted and edited films about particular work practices or settings that were made for documentary, instructive or promotional reasons.

Collectively, this unofficial visual record evidences economic activities that have been transformed or lost from many rural and urban localities. Some practices are now sustained or revived only as visitor attractions and photo-opportunities at heritage sites where role-play cannot quite capture the focus and dexterity of those whose skills derived from decades of experience. Even more rarely, the unwitting ethnographic gaze of early amateurs may have documented specialist processes that still persist.

Amateur visual eclecticism leaves more than simply a record of past activity. This footage recovers past experiences and marginalised memories that may be underrepresented historically. Such scenes may not feature extensively within commercial or feature films of the time. No obvious counter-narratives may be ascribed to the impassive faces or the silenced moving lips that recur in amateur material. Indeed, many of these glimpses into Britain's working past reveal mid-century establishment attitudes towards social and labour relations and notions of authority.[83] Early amateur visions of people at work were often framed by individuals who had economic, ideological and social dominance. The over-the-shoulder views in small and medium-sized businesses often offer workplace impressions more akin to a managerial inspection tour and convey little or nothing from an employee's perspective. Unlike the owner who *faces* the camera, most of the workers are shown from behind or sideways and often from above. Shots of smiling, friendly staff may suggest harmonious workplace relations as in a promotional or publicity film but as viewers we see nothing through the eyes of workers engaged in tasks at their own physical level. Shots of tired, unsmiling or expressionless faces found in some colliery and foundry sequences hint at prevailing strained worker–management relations more openly than other more obliging faces that turn to face the camera.[84] Inevitably, ideological differences are reflected in how subject matter was treated. The representation of workers and their activities is filtered through the eyes of those with access to camera equipment. Their ways of seeing determine how they understand themselves and how particular social groups find themselves depicted on screen. Only gradually did more widely available cine equipment permit more democratic workplace views. Thus amateurs may evidence under-represented aspects of work experience but much of its earlier cinematic gaze can also be interpreted as an act of marginalisation of other people's social experience.

These films derive from years when past certainties about region, community and class were in flux and when transforming economies elsewhere meant competitive local restructuring of production, supplies and distribution. Just as mechanisation, automation and workplace reorganisation altered work processes, wider societal changes affected labour relations, employees' expectations and working processes. Women provided a new, cheap and flexible peacetime labour force for manufacturing, although, outside the more flexible recruitment drives of both world wars, attitudes and customary practice still confined them to particular kinds of work and levels of promotion right through the decades covered in this book.[85] For decades, Lancashire women of different ages brought speed, skill and precision to highly repetitive and low-paid tasks. For younger women, waged work brought greater financial independence, and for all age groups the workplace had a social function, even if noise levels restricted conversation. Many women's sense of pride in specialist work, evidenced by oral histories, is visible too as employees demonstrate tasks or pose for a visiting filmmaker. During the 1950s, more women entered employment although even here the visual record still evidences primarily working-class women engaged in manufacturing. Women's changing professional opportunities are less well represented in this chapter although their expanding involvement in education, health and welfare features later (see Chapter 8 and bibliography). More women did clerical work by the end of the 1930s, and the male typist, successor to Victorian and Edwardian clerks, was rare by the 1960s.[86] Women's service sector employment during the 1950s and 1960s features less readily too, perhaps because of lesser perceived filmic interest (by amateurs who were still predominantly male) although some amateurs filmed female staff in canteen and shop interiors.[87]

Other workplace changes are discernible too. Modernisation is apparent too, as in the roadside scenes in which farm workers and a horse engaged in harvesting or hay-rick building are caught on camera during a day excursion by car.[88] Such recurrent images reveal regional farm work still reliant on anachronistic practices even as the passing presence of motorised transport and cinematography symbolise changing lifestyles and patterns of consumption. Elsewhere, co-existent continuities and changes recur. For some filmmakers innovation holds greater visual interest than tradition. Change and novelty take diverse forms. Hazardous occupations gradually gain more protective clothing, although the latter remains absent from much construction work well into the 1970s. Broader shifts in furniture design, fashion, building materials and the influence of health and safety codes gain visibility in different workplace settings that are better lit or where the still widespread practice of smoking at work is occasionally prohibited. Success and expansion may be variously expressed: for the Walkers of Audenshaw, the shift from sacks to automated poultry grain feeders points to commerical expansion.[89] Efficiency underpins every detail in *A Modern Bakery* shot by the Warburtons in their Cheshire–based family business,[90] and also in comparable footage of *Prestwich Co-operative Dairy*.[91] An owner's business proudly films new building while Joshua Preston's textile successes intermesh with his civic status and role as local patron.[92] Skipper Jim Betty's commercial strength simply is the size of the catch and its value back in dock. Such shots are personal celebrations of thriving enterprise, innovation and economic stability, and contrast with more elegiac and self-reflexive scenes of disappearing traditions,[93] or pit closures associated with recession and redundancy.[94]

Dress codes embody workplace hierarchies and disclose the unevenness of modernity's impact. Scenes may highlight regional dimensions within national narratives of economic and industrial change. In the North West, male supervisors, laboratory analysts and engineers in ties and jackets or white laboratory coats contrast with female workers wearing aprons or cotton work-dresses and men in overalls. Women wearing laboratory coats are rare outside regional promotional films even in the 1950s.[95] Sam Hanna's commentary singles out a female chemist making Victory V confectionery, although other shots of women involved in sweet production and packaging pass without comment. Footwear changes too as shoes replace clogs and the barefoot mill operatives at spinning looms disappear. Similarly, the distinctive white cotton shirt and woollen waistcoat of traditional craftsmen filmed mid-century pass along with their expertise. Synthetic fabrics reach the workplace less rapidly than metropolitan-dominated fashion histories, clothing catalogues, leisure magazines, feature films and the postwar development of chain fashion stores might suggest.[96]

Secretaries rather than canteen staff might testify, via their fashion sense, to wider shifts in social and sexual emancipation, but were also more likely to know in advance if management expected camera-holding visitors, and thus dress for their appearance on camera. Their walk-on roles holding papers for a meeting of men, or a typist's smiling upward gaze from behind her desk embody long-entrenched inequalities in the office. Uniform and authority testify to hierarchies of power in and beyond administration, in films of hospitals and maternity homes where, from the early 1950s onwards, overseas recruitment and discrimination further influence employers' status. Affluence as well as the mobilities of education, training, recruitment, occupation and better public transport all inform how and what different people wore and did at work. Occasional cutaway shots to men in suits beside parked cars are reminders too of gender and class differential, and sequences shows that, for rural and urban workers going home, travel on foot, bicycle or public transport still remained the main mode of travel.[97]

Escaping the daily grind

Amateur footage reveals prevailing employment conditions. The gendered and socially defined spaces of work are microcosms of wider power relations and spatial delineations in society. They evince the micro-geographies of everyday life both in and beyond particular settings. Entire working lives spent on specialised tasks from apprentic-hood to retirement represent now unfamiliar patterns of employment. Automation has reduced many long working periods or repetitive shared or individual heavy manual tasks. Work scenes in deafening and hazardous conditions point to the arduous nature of employment experiences that were once common within particular localities and communities.

Employment shaped social opportunities too, and amateurs regularly filmed relaxing occasions at social clubs or during works outings too. Earlier traditions of benelovent paternalism combine with modernising expectations and obligations on working hours. Opportunities for meeting workers from different occupations in many industrial localities were often limited, but employer patronage sometimes allowed workmates time to relax together. Films of employees enjoying a good day out reveal that owners and their family members or friends often went too, even if they travelled separately. Excursions by train, open charabanc or hired motor coach highlight socially differentiated mobilities and sometimes contrast with an employer's own family or travel holiday footage further afield. These spatial and temporal freedoms are direct expressions of economic status. Equally, the cine user's freedom to film inevitably provides a highly selective record of employees having a day away from work.

An amateur workplace aesthetic features rhythm, tempo and repetition as seen in moving hands, pistons and other pieces of machinery or equipment. Such recurrent visual tropes epitomise specific labour practices and settings. Their inclusion within professional footage during the period under consideration may be due less to prevailing visual aesthetic or amateur emulation of professional techniques and may simply reflect availability and practical reasons. In contrast, images of canteens, washrooms, medical rooms and nurseries are rarer and offer important visual clues to the piecemeal introduction of improved employee facilities in prewar and postwar Britain.

The politics of gender, class, culture, race and locality recur through these amateur scenes of waged work (see also housework in Chapter 4), although workers profiled in professional films have been similarly determined. Arguably, the possibilities for reclaiming past aspects of under represented social groups now come as much from amateur as from professional media sources, although existing archive material often requires better knowledge. One area of under representation, perhaps better represented in some regions other than the North West, is that of Britain's travelling communities, whose regional presence might link with seasonal fairs and other opportunities for informal employment as well as specific commemorative gatherings.[98]

Workers from abroad

Labour histories of Black and visible ethnic minorities also benefit from an exploration of amateur footage. Just as cine enthusiasts documented the diversifying nature of regional populations in their shots of public places and occasions, workplace scenes reflect changing demographics and employment. Recruitment policies and the widening participation of workers from the Caribbean, Africa and South Asia in new public sectors and the postwar rebuilding of key industries impact slowly upon the amateur record. Although widening cine use coincided with the early years of immigration and Britain's 'Windrush generation', most of its imagery so far contributes little to larger established oral and photographic histories of early postwar ethnic settlement and neighbourhood formation. Early cataloguing often omitted any mention of ethnic diversity, so detailed new research on archival collections is important in raising awareness of imagery within specific films. Although the workplace remained a popular focus for the region's amateur filmmakers, there is little material that reflects directly how demographic change transformed manufacturing and manual work and in areas of former heavy industry. Perhaps the jobs that white workers no longer wanted to do became less easy or attractive

The Burnley School of Nursing (Dir. Sam Hanna, 1960–63). Still supplied by courtesy of Bob Hanna and North West Film Archive at Manchester Metropolitan University, Film no. 5208 (colour, sound, 39 min. 32 sec.).

for non-professional filmmakers to gain access to. If so, such qualms contrast with the continuing fascination in filming 'native workers' within late colonial settings overseas.[99] Does the apparent absence of such material from northern industries hint at a broader domestic industrial confidence ebbing in the face of economic restructuring and competition? Overseas recruitment for long, unsociable work shifts in the competitive market repositioning in postwar Britain ultimately did not sustain long-term production. Many closures occurred except where investment and automation remained viable and where, as stated in *Nelson 62*, there was 'not an operative in sight'.[100] For whatever reason, few non-white employees feature in workplace sequences shot on Standard and Super 8. An important regional exception is Sam Hanna's film on nurse recruitment and training in Burnley (Figure 6).[101]

If race relations in 1950s and 1960s Britain were not conducive to white camera-touting amateur filmmakers among non-white workers, beyond hospitals and other public sector settings, is it possible to look elsewhere? Certainly there was an indigenous well-educated and professional camera-using elite within some of the Caribbean islands by the later 1950s.[102] It seems not unlikely that, along with letters, recipes, seasonal gifts of food and photographs, for some highly trained migrants specifically recruited to work in Britain's new key public sectors, cine-film occasionally became another means of documenting lives elsewhere for sharing with relatives and communities overseas. Accessing electricity and projectors were, however, major problems and, for many families, studio-taken posed photographs remained the more significant ways of sending images 'back home'. Recovering any visual stories of people newly arrived in postwar Britain is urgent before it becomes too late for elderly cine users to be identified and interviewed.[103] For some committed union activists, cine footage shot during rallies and demonstrations has gained attention within attempts to build more inclusive visual histories of labour relations during the 1950s, 1960s and 1970s.[104]

Outside political contexts, attitudes towards the contemporary value of amateur footage may well remain more sceptical among the elders of Britain's Black population. Opening doors via occupational groups may help to build more inclusive national and regional moving-image histories of former public sector employment as in public health and transport.[105] Emerging networks for community archive repositories, and also better co-ordination of oral history initiatives with visual archives, may foster the necessary links. The task of developing ways to identify and make available such informal amateur visual histories of Black and ethnic minority experiences within postwar Britain has barely begun. Such initiatives rely upon trust, openness and reassurances about the integrity and future ownership of any materials that may be transferred from private settings into more public contexts. Through appropriate cultural and other associative networks, the potential of such footage for strengthening understanding across social, spatial, generational and experiential differences is considerable. Such content is unlikely to disclose solely about working experiences but its wider glimpses upon the lives of non-white workers in living memory would create more inclusive employment histories at regional and national level. Long neglected within other visual histories, the amateur gaze on past working lives still has many untold stories to share.

Notes

1 Unemployment reached nearly three million in 1932. On the basis of published data, the unemployment rate peaked at 22.1 per cent that year, according to S. Constantine, *Social Conditions in Britain, 1918–1939*, p. 7. However, this figure would certainly have been lower on current definitions, perhaps in the range of 10–16 per cent. See: House of Commons Library, *A Century of Change*, p. 24.
2 D. S. King, *In the Name of Liberalism*, pp. 155–79.
3 J. E. Hallam, 1940s: *Following Horses. Our System by Fred Dawson and Jimmy Bee*, NWFA Film no. 877 (b/w, silent, 24 min. 0 sec.).
4 D. Russell, *Looking North*.
5 S. Nicholson, in conversation with author, August 2010.
6 See also H. Norris Nicholson, 'Floating hotels'.
7 H. Norris Nicholson, 'Authority, aesthetics and visions of the workplace'.
8 Frank Thorley, 1960s: [*Wagon Works and Blackpool Outing*], NWFA Film no. 1328 (colour, silent, 16 min. 8 sec.); Charles Chislett, 1948: *Men of Steel*, YFA Cat. no. 99 (colour, silent, 16 min.); 1947: *Hands of the Potter*, YFA Cat. no. 502 (b/w, silent, 27 min.).
9 T. Harrisson and H. Spender, *Britain in the Thirties*; N. Hubble, *Mass Observation and Everyday Life*. See also B. Highmore, *Everyday Life and Cultural Theory*, pp. 75–112.
10 H. Spender, *Worktown People*.
11 Leslie Froude, writing a tribute to George Sewell. Cited in Coad, The *IAC*, pp. 93–4.
12 G. H. Sewell, *Commercial Cinematography*, p. 1.
13 *Ibid.*, p. 5.
14 (Anon.), 'A waiting room cinema'.
15 Sewell, *Commercial Cinematography*, p. 176.
16 G. Sewell, 'Putting England on the film map'.
17 J. Chittock, 'Films to borrow', *Movie Maker*, 1:1 (1967), 35, 70; J. Chittock, 'Films to borrow', *Movie Maker*, 1:5 (1967), 380.
18 Lever Brothers, *1931: [*Port Sunlight*], NWFA Film no. 323 (b/w, silent, 23 min. 25 sec.) may be compared with the later film by Editorial Film Productions Ltd in

collaboration with Lintas Ltd, 1950: *Unilever News 1950 in the British Isles*, NWFA Film no. 1866 (b/w, sound, 12 min. 10 sec.); Pilkington Bros. Ltd., 1939: [*Pilkington's Colliery Boys Go on Holiday*], NWFA Film no. 161 (b/w and colour, silent, 36 min. 30 sec.); Norris Nicholson, 'Authority, aesthetics and visions of the workplace'.
19 S. Todd, *Young Women, Work and Family in England, 1918–50*.
20 G. Whittaker, 1948–50: [*Visit to Glen Mills*], NWFA Film no. 3500 (b/w and colour, silent, 16 min. 50 sec.).
21 Lintas, c. 1950: *The Tree of Life*, NWFA Film no. 329 (b/w, sound, 46 min. 40 sec.); Unilever/Editorial Film Productions in association with Lintas Ltd, *1953: *Portrait of a Man*, NWFA Film no. 4146 (b/w, sound, 18 min. 10 sec.); Frank Green, *1951: [*A New Twist to an Old Yarn*], NWFA Film no. 704 (b/w, sound, 25 min. 39 sec.).
22 G. Higginson with Edward D Andrew Ltd / R. W. Proffitt Ltd, *1949/50: *From Bale to Finished Cloth*, NWFA Film no. 515 (b/w, silent, 22 min. 45 sec.).
23 L. A. Notcutt, 'Ideas for documentary films'.
24 Thomas Magee, *1932: [*Catholic Procession, Bolton*], NWFA Film no. 582 (b/w, silent, 8 min. 5 sec.); *1932/33: [*Trinity Sunday Procession, Bolton*], NWFA Film no. 585 (b/w, silent, 13 min. 14 sec.).
25 Thomas Magee, *1931/33: [*Bolton Boot Trades Association Outings*], NWFA Film no. 584 (b/w, silent, 12 min. 46 sec.); *1933/4: [*Shoe Making*], NWFA Film no. 583 (b/w, silent, 9 min. 41 sec.).
26 See note 25.
27 Preston Brothers, 1929: *A Nurses' Outing in 1929*, NWFA Film no. 1182 (b/w, silent, 9 min.58 sec.).
28 Pilkington Bros. Ltd., 1939: [*Pilkington's Colliery Boys Go on Holiday*], NWFA Film no. 161 (b/w and colour, silent, 36 min. 30 sec.).
29 G. Timmins, *Made in Lancashire*, pp. 278–9.
30 King, *In the Name of Liberalism*, pp. 155–79.
31 C. L. Mowat, *Britain between the Wars*, p. 501.
32 M. Tebbutt, 'Rambling and manly identity'; see also Tebbutt, *Working Class Masculinities in the Interwar Years*.
33 King, *In the Name of Liberalism*, pp. 155–79.
34 Pendle Movie Makers, 1962: *Nelson 62* (by courtesy of Pendle Movie Makers collection).
35 See note 8, Charles Chislett, 1948.
36 Jim Betty and Eric Isaacs, *1965/6/74: [*The Fishing Industry around Fleetwood*], NWFA Film no. 4441 (colour, silent, 15 min. 51 sec.); *1965/72/4: [*Fishing from Fleetwood*], NWFA Film no. 4448 (colour, silent, 31 min. 14 sec.).
37 British Film Institute (BFI), *The Film in National Life*, p. 6.
38 *Ibid.*, pp. 16–17.
39 B. Hogenkamp, *Deadly Parallels*.
40 See for example, Commission on Educational and Cultural films (CEC Films), *The Film in National Life*.
41 See for example, regular features from the mid-1930s, including a plea for non-professionals to make 'magazine-reels' or news newsreels: (Anon.), 'The news film. Attempt at intelligence needed'; and detailed reviews of screenings organised by

Manchester Film Society, including (Anon.), 'Novel exhibition'; (Anon.), 'Amateur films. A varied show in Manchester'; and (Anon.), 'Individuals' films'.
42 Using film to document disappearing traditions was suggested early in the amateur press. 'Before they go, get a record of those old relics of a past age and its associations, the vanishing trades' wrote (Anon.), 'Putting England on the film map'. Amateur scenes of rural change gained new resonance during wartime's focus on tradition and national identity. See for instance, (Anon.), 'J. and G. Wadley's Our Heritage ("Amateur Film Show")'.
43 (Anon.), 'Dying industries'.
44 Palmer, *Recording Britain*; see also Victoria and Albert Museum, *Recording Britain*.
45 Film Council of the South West, and Library, 1938–1942 DHTA, ref. nos. T/AF/1/A and T/AF/1/A/7, www.dartington.org/archive, accessed on 3 November 2010.
46 Dartington Hall Film Unit, 1943: *Clogs in Lancashire*, NWFA Film no. 610 (b/w, silent, 12 min. 2 sec.), attributed to the film unit's staff member Arthur Elton, DHTA, ref. nos. T/AF/1/E, accessed on 3 November 2010.
47 Sam Hanna Collection, NWFA, www.nwfa.mmu.ac.uk:591/samhanna/default.htm, accessed on 6 October 2009.
48 Unpublished notes and correspondence, Sam Hanna Collection, NWFA.
49 Special thanks are owed to archive staff during very early work on the Sam Hanna Collection.
50 Hanna, *The Lowry of Film-making*, ch. 19, p. 1.
51 See, for example, (Anon.), 'Rural crafts at the Royal Lancashire Show'; (Anon.), 'Rural Industries'; (Anon.), 'Films of northern crafts'.
52 Hanna, *The Lowry of Film-making*, ch. 19, p. 1; see also S. Hanna, *1942–43: Old English Crafts. The Clog Block Maker*, NWFA Film no. 5128 (b/w and colour, silent, 6 min. 57 sec.).
53 Hanna, *The Lowry of Film-making*, ch. 19, p. 3.
54 Hanna's films include *Clog Making*, NWFA Film no. 5243 (*1942–43, colour, silent, 11 min. 13 sec); *The Clogger*, NWFA Film no. 5287 (*1946–51, colour, silent, 15 min. 2 sec); [*Pern Winding at Nelson*], NWFA Film no. 5274 (*1944, b/w, silent, 7 min. 50 sec.); *The Village Blacksmith*, NWFA Film no. 5142 (*1946, colour, silent, 8 min. 55 sec.); *The Slate Quarry*, NWFA Film no. 5104 (1945–46, colour, silent, 11 min. 53 sec.); *Old English Crafts Village Tannery*, NWFA Film no. 5120 (*1945, colour, silent, 8 min. 34 sec.).
55 Hanna, *The Lowry of Film-making*, ch. 19, p. 6.
56 Leaflets for Sam Hanna products and films produced as Brum Educational Films of Burn; see also Sam Hanna, 1980: *Old English Crafts Captured for Posterity. The Art of the Clock Maker. Craftsman Bill Allonby*, NWFA Film no. 5103 (colour, sound (sep.), 20 min. 18 sec).
57 Hanna, *The Lowry of Film-making*, ch. 19, p. 7; Sam Hanna, 1942: *Old English Crafts. The Cooper*, NWFA Film no. 5304 (colour, sound, 10 min. 5 sec.).
58 Sam Hanna, *1968: *The Craft of Rush Seating by courtesy: H. J. Berry and Sons*, NWFA Film no. 5241 (colour, silent, 10 min. 40 sec.).
59 Sam Hanna, 1942/66/68/70–72: *Old English Crafts* [*Extracts: The Cooper, Oak Spelk Basket Maker, Snuff Making, A Welsh Spoon, Clog Making, Haffe Net Fishing*],

NWFA Film no. 5163 (colour, sound, 11 min. 38 sec.).

60 Sam Hanna, 1946–50: *Making Hay Rakes Lancashire Type*, NWFA Film no. 5250 (colour, silent, 10 min. 20 sec.).

61 Sam Hanna, c.1945: *Old English Crafts Village Rope Maker Making Hay Creels*, NWFA Film no. 5111 (colour, silent, 4 min. 0 sec.).

62 R. Muir, *Approaches to Landscape*, pp. 108–11; see also R. Muir, '"A Land" revisited'; J. Hawkes, *A Land*; W. G. Hoskins, *The Making of the English Landscape*.

63 N. Dyer, 'Filming on the farm'.

64 G. Haines, 'How about a movie with a message?'.

65 *Ibid.*, 516; G. Haines, 'Down in the forest'; 'To market, to market'; 'Filming along a lane'.

66 Haines, 'How about a movie', 514.

67 Hoskins, *The Making of the English Landscape*, pp. 298–9.

68 Films were shot on or around the Walker family's dairy farms, Kings Road, Audenshaw, and Mill Lane, Woodley, between 1952 and 1966. See NWFA Film nos 2565–2571.

69 Walker Family, 1952: [*Walker's Dairy Farm – Milk Round*], NWFA Film no. 2566 (colour, silent, 1 min. 4 sec.).

70 Mr Walker, *1965: [*Farm Dogs*], NWFA Film no. 2567 (colour, silent, 3 min. 42 sec.).

71 Mr Walker, *1965: [*Walker's Farm – Poultry*], NWFA Film no. 2569 (colour, silent, 2 min. 5 sec.).

72 See, for example, Mr Walker, *1966: [*Walker's Dairy Farm*], NWFA Film no. 2568 (colour, silent, 3 min. 27 sec.); *1966: [*Walker's Farm – Horses and Cows*], NWFA Film no. 2570 (colour, silent, 5 min. 51 sec.); *1966: [*The Jones Family at Walker's Farm*], NWFA Film no. 2571 (colour, silent, 1 min. 9 sec.).

73 Films were shot on or around the Turner family's business, Palatine Paints, between 1957 and 1965. See NWFA Film nos 4593–4601, 4613.

74 John Turner, 1959: [*Walking Day; Palatine Paint Factory*], NWFA Film no. 4593 (colour, silent, 4 min. 5 sec.); 1959: *[Palatine Paint Factory]*, NWFA Film no. 4594 (colour, silent, 4 min. 39 sec.); 1960: [*Inside Palatine Paints*], NWFA Film no. 4595 (colour, silent, 1 min. 24 sec.).

75 John Turner, c.1960: [*Terraced Streets; Chester Zoo*], NWFA Film no. 4613 (colour, silent, 3 min. 40 sec.).

76 See for example, John Turner, 1957/58: [*Victoria Pit and Standish Social Activities*], NWFA Film no. 4598 (b/w, silent, 19 min. 42 sec.).

77 John Turner, 1958: [*Around Wigan*], NWFA Film no. 4599 (colour, silent, 4 min. 32 sec.); 1958: [*Open Cast Mining; Card Game*], NWFA Film no. 4626(b/w, silent, 3 min. 40 sec.); c.1965: [*Chorley Whit Walk; Standish; Leyland Motors; School Scenes*], NWFA Film no. 4589 (colour, silent, 14 min. 55 sec.).

78 See note 76.

79 Special thanks to David Pearce, for sharing his enthusiasm and his knowledge about Fleetwood's trawler industry and local history, and also to Eric Isaacs for his insights.

80 P. Horsley and A. Hirst, *Fleetwood's Fishing Industry*; J. M. Porter, *The Fishing Industry at Fleetwood*.

81 See note 36.
82 In 1957 the producer Charles Parker involved Ewan MacColl and Peggy Seeger in a BBC radio documentary project that resulted in eight hour-long radio ballads, broadcast between 1958 and 1964. *Singing the Fishing*, a tapestry of speech, sound and song dealt with the herring fishing industry.
83 Norris Nicholson, 'Authority, aesthetics and visions of the workplace'.
84 See, for example, Pilkington Bros. Ltd, 1939: [*Pilkington's Colliery Boys Go on Holiday*], NWFA Film no. 161 (b/w and colour, silent, 36 min. 30 sec.).
85 Todd, *Young Women, Work and Family in England, 1918–50*.
86 Unknown filmmaker, 1931: *CEAG Film*, YFA Cat. no. 1179 (b/w, silent, 5 min.).
87 G. Whittaker, 1948–50: [*Visit to Glen Mills*], NWFA Film no. 3500 (b/w and colour, silent, 16 min. 50 sec.); 1950: *Lancashire Pride*, NWFA Film no. 525 (colour, sound, 57 min. 20 sec.); John Turner, 1958: [*Palatine Paints Ltd*], NWFA Film no. 4600 (b/w, silent, 4 min. 29 sec).
88 See, for example, uses of horse-drawn plough and hay wain captured during excursions and family outing by Leonard F. Behrens, 1926: [*Holiday in Broadway; April / May 1926*], NWFA Film no. 2086 (b/w, silent, 5 min. 35 sec.); Preston Brothers, *1931–33: *The Lake District Windermere*, NWFA Film no. 1899 (b/w, silent, 10 min. 46 sec.).
89 See note 71.
90 Warburtons, c.1931–32: *A Modern Bakery*, NWFA Film no. 707 (b/w, silent, 6 min. 6 sec.).
91 Albert Todkill, c.1936–8: *Prestwich Co-operative Dairy*, NWFA Film no. 2502 (b/w, silent, 10 min. 56 sec.).
92 See, for example, Preston Brothers, 1927: *December 19th 1927 Earl of Crawford Met by the Mayor of Stockport at Edgeley Station*, NWFA Film no. 1936 (b/w, silent, 2 min. 0 sec.); 1928: *September 1st 1928 Bramhall Flower Show*, NWFA Film no. 1919 (b/w, silent, 11 min. 39 sec).
93 See note 61.
94 See note 76.
95 Sam Hanna for Red Rose Films, c. 1959: *Red Rose Films Present the Story of Victory-V [Camera Original]*, NWFA Film no. 5238 (colour, silent, 34 min. 19 sec.).
96 C. Buckley and H. Fawcett, *Fashioning the Feminine*, pp. 83–121.
97 Unknown filmmaker, c 1958: [*Workers Leaving Metrovic's*], NWFA Film no. 331 (b/w, silent, 10 min. 37 sec.).
98 See, for example, the opening sequence in the previous film, NWFA Film no. 4371; John Hindley, *1931: [*Devon Scenes; Outdoor Event and Racetrack*], NWFA Film no. 3619 (b/w, silent, 3 min. 36 sec.); R. Rudd, 1969: [*Gypsy Funeral at Portwood, Stockport*], NWFA no. 3257 (colour, silent, 9 min. 0 sec.).
99 See note 24.
100 Pendle Movies Makers, 1962: *Nelson 62* (by courtesy of Pendle Movie Makers).
101 Sam Hanna, 1960–63: *The Burnley School of Nursing*, NWFA Film no. 5208 (colour, sound, 39 min. 32 sec.).
102 See, for instance, the discussion of reworking family footage shot in Trinidad in R. Fung, 'Remaking home movies'.

103 *Moving Memories* and *Reel Revolutions*, two multi-partnership initiatives with North West Film Archives, undertaken during 2009, developed links to broaden diversity within regional archival holdings; See also S. Gulzar and S. Manthrop, *Black and White in Colour*.
104 R. Malholtra and N. Puwar, 'Selections from Raj Malhotra's (Indian Workers Association) cine collection'.
105 H. Norris Nicholson, A visual history of health worker recruitment from Africa and the Caribbean to Britain's National Health Service, c. 1948–83 (in progress).

7

An indispensable travel accessory

'I believe the amateur cine movement is helping English people to love England; or perhaps it would be more accurate to say that the movement is becoming a medium through which English men and women can express their love of England.'[1] Whether or not the amateur love affair with cine photography in the interwar years heightened notions of Englishness and regard for visual signifiers of national and regional identity, it did coincide with changing sensibilities towards landscape character.[2] It linked with the very changing patterns of mobility that fuelled some of the concerns about protecting rural areas from roads, housing and other aspects of modernity.[3] In practical terms too, filming outdoors suited the early handheld cameras designed for amateur use. From the first pioneering attempts at outdoor motion-picture making, filming the spectacle of everyday actions in natural light prompted amateur imitation and in 1901 a member of the Royal Photographic Society demonstrated his own attempts at making a 'scenic'.[4] Commercial exhibitors soon saw that shot scenes of local people enjoying a day out or waiting for an excursion train would appeal to those eager to see themselves or their friends on screen. Early home-movie-making manuals encouraged filmmakers outdoors.[5] Burgess likened them to troubadours and wandering minstrels who, 'instead of a lute or a harp, … take with them a cine-camera and bring home with them from their adventuring the raw material of the poet.'[6] Travel-related filming went on to become one of the most persistent strands within amateur activity. Over a century later, it remains prominent among annual amateur screen awards and receives much critical attention in the hobby press.[7] Of course, thousands of poorly made films of holidays and days out survive too, and they have contributed to the amateur movement's long denigration.

Finding ways to navigate this vast cine archive of leisured moments is this chapter's focus. Considerable scope exists for different ways of engaging with the imagery and its content as well as the varied contexts within which it was shot, edited and shown. This discussion identifies aspects of amateur practice that seem germane to the regional lens broadly adopted in this book. The filmmaker's identity, relationship to subject matter and opportunities for screening material for family, friends and wider audiences dovetail with other local, regional and national considerations considered in adjacent chapters. The micro-geographies and temporal patterns of where, when and how people visited particular localities become clearer when considering family collections in their entirety, as do the evolving character and range of individual life cycles of pleasure consumption. Wider leisure trends and the impact of changing access to different modes of private and public transport and holiday entitlements, as well as broadening options in accommodation, visitor attraction and holiday destination thread through these personal narratives of individual and family time spent 'somewhere else'.

Framing the view

Undeniably a powerful visual tool in tourism and travel histories at varied levels, the popularity of recording days out and holidays on film connects to wider social, cultural, economic and geo-political change.[8] While many influences affected the choice of destinations, recreational and holiday opportunities and even the character of the group captured on camera, the visual politics of representation discloses the interplay of gender, age, physical well-being and ethnicity. Status, whether in familial terms or as a figure of authority within civic, occupational or associational setting, either at home or abroad, contributed to how, where and when filmmakers were able to frame and present themselves and others.[9] Privilege accompanied the impunity with which many early pioneers filmed other people, whether it was a 'quaint character', herding sheep in the Lake District[10] or an 'exotic' street performer encountered overseas.[11] The filmmaker's recreational licence to record others at work conferred significance as unfamiliar routines – both mundane and highly specialist – assumed extraordinary status trapped in time and space for future recollection.

Appropriating other people and places as visual backdrops for personal narratives, in posed or cutaway shots, aligns much travel-related footage with other twentieth-century patterns of consuming spectacle.[12] Such shots connect the picture-making impulse to issues of individual and collective identity formation and memory-shaping too. Some filmmaking during excursions and holidays reflects tendencies for early cine users to follow already established routes. In and beyond Britain, even the earliest cine users visited and filmed in localities where existing visual conventions informed visitor expectations and mediated responses.[13] Getting the 'right view' was, for some people, integral to the success of the holiday narrative, as well as its effectiveness in impressing subsequent audiences. Choosing specific views at particular destinations was influenced by formal viewpoints, guidebooks, photo stops during tours and tips offered in the hobby press.[14] Adding introductory montage or animated sequences using printed holiday brochures or souvenirs was a cine variant upon earlier scrap-booking conventions that added tickets, postcards and other travel memorabilia to family album-making. Both remained popular among hobby filmmakers well into the 1960s. Playful use of signage and existing visual motifs avoided adding captions too, as in a 1928 shot by the Preston brothers of their sister beside a poster for a bullfight used to introduce a Spanish section in a cruise-holiday film.[15] Notwithstanding such recurring clichés, using cine extended single snapshot responses into more encompassing sequences and offered individuals greater opportunity for creative camerawork. Examples of footage shot in unusual locations, as discussed later in this chapter, exist from the later 1920s and, despite the increasing availability of packaged tourism, persist as leisure horizons expanded during the twentieth century.

Varied personal and external influences affected each filmmaker's wishes and opportunities to shoot, keep and present a sequence recorded elsewhere. Archive collections, as Rose reminds us over still photographs, have only the films passed on to them that, in turn, are those that were not lost, damaged, discarded or even confiscated by authorities at some earlier stage.[16] As visual fragments of past leisures, they could never be comprehensive, even as more affordable filmstock encouraged making longer films. Filmmakers produced travel-related footage for different reasons and with different priorities in mind. Prospective competition entries, or films made during a business or work-related visit overseas to watch with family members afterwards, differed from those made for shared reliving of leisure time spent together. Some filmmakers prioritised humour, provided informative travelogues or crafted written and visual text, as in Higginson's linkage of poetry to Lakeland landscape imagery.[17] Carefully captioned and edited productions contrast with home movies that offer a spontaneous mix of family experiences perhaps punctuated by the unexpected visual encounter that became part of remembering a specific occasion. Where filming foregrounded a family picnic, paddling, cricket or beach games, location may be recognisable only by chance identification of a particular landmark. Other filmmakers highlighted a distinctive setting or combined a sense of place with sequences that celebrated family time together. Footage was sometimes a minimally edited miscellany that approximated to a family's visual diary perhaps representing cine use spread over many months. Alternatively, it could be a highly edited and focused piece that combined numerous reels with elaborate titling and credit sequences. Some journeys were undertaken, purely to document a particular event, as shown by Charles Chislett's film of the *Queen Mary*'s first transatlantic voyage in May 1936.[18] Such variety reminds us that cine-cameras were used differently, and amateur productions changed over time as people's interests in cine photography and travel opportunities changed.

Through until the 1960s, working on Saturday mornings in many occupations and church attendance still limited many people's opportunities for regular days out to statutory public holidays and annual weeks' leave.[19] Unlike MacMillan's observations about the family-filled cars making their way to the south coast on Saturday mornings,[20] for many in the North West, non-work was often spent at home or enjoying local occasions within walking distance. Across the region, Whit Walks, processions, parades, galas, fairs, carnivals, sporting fixtures and other public commemorative daytime or evening outdoor events thus feature in much early amateur footage. Slow-moving parades of floats, decorated delivery vans and horse-drawn vehicles were easy to film with or without a tripod from a kerb-side position. The accompanying mix of uniformed and elaborately costumed, masked or face-painted participants often combined civic, religious and military solemnity with burlesque and comedy and offered scope for different camera shots too. Pride, patriotism and pantomime briefly co-existed with broad social appeal while the occasional inclusion of jazz players added novelty and excitement to the more traditional sights and sounds of brass bands. The abundance of such material, produced by professional exhibitors, by local newsreel producers and then by amateurs, indicates its recognised attraction for subsequent audiences who enjoyed looking back at themselves or others they knew. Some enthusiasts, however, soon sought out other visual spectacles, particularly those with time and the newfound mobilities of private transport,[21] and, from the later 1920s, growing numbers of film enthusiasts in the North West motored to different coastal destinations.

Seaside excursions

Seaside footage complements other sources that testify to the importance of such pleasurable outings within popular culture.[22] Sequences sustain mood, character and emotional appeal for longer than the single image. Unedited, their linear connection evokes some of the visual complexity as the filmmaker's gaze surveyed the surrounding sights. In-camera editing conveys the heightened mood and dazzling variety that appealed to some amateur filmmakers. Prior to 1939, despite the limited availability of cine-camera use beyond the middle and upper classes, amateur footage reveals that enjoying the beach and rides at Blackpool and elsewhere had wide social appeal.[23] Many families with links to professional, industrial, commercial, managerial or finance-related occupations recorded taking their young children to the coast. From as early as 1927, they used black and white filmstock and sometimes colour from the mid-1930s to capture scenes of bathing, donkey-rides, eating ice-cream, Punch and Judy shows, contorting mirrors and enjoyment of numerous other seafront attractions. For the Grime family in the 1930s, Blackpool's bulky Noah's Ark and its encircling train of smiling nursery animals had an eye-catching simplicity, shape and bold paintwork that were worthy of filming in black and white even if their seated children were hidden from view.[24] It was notable too, to watch at home again, as its scale differed from the temporary rides available more locally by travelling funfairs, and its design owed more to current film animation than earlier showground traditions. Family footage of seaside visits, whether filmed in monotone on 35mm during the late 1920s or Standard 8mm in the mid-1950s in Kodachrome, shared many similarities, even if attractions became more sophisticated and built-up areas stretched further and deeper inland along the coast. Families with young children depicted themselves involved in varied activities within easy reach of railway, bus station and parking. Social differences occur in that wealthier families frequently combined seaside activities with a country cottage or hotel in a quieter setting.[25] Footage shows how children might spend more time exploring rock pools and being in or on the water, although day excursions by car to nearer resorts might also take place.

Footage of groups of adults and young people visiting Morecambe, Cleveleys, Blackpool, Southport, New Brighton and elsewhere tended to depict fewer beach scenes although playful sequences of face pulling, leapfrog, cricket and other ball games exist. The Preston brothers filmed themselves on Blackpool's Big Dipper, Water Chute, a merry-go-round and other rides, as well as walking on the promenade and the pier between 1926 and 1934. Images of the

Tower, Pleasure Beach and Stanley Park denote the resort's socially differentiated pleasure landscapes.[26] Posed shots beside gift shops and refreshment stalls recur, as visual tropes of holiday consumption in both prewar and postwar footage.[27] *Magnetic Blackpool*'s (1955) images range from advertisements for oyster and shrimp stalls, playing beach football, boat-trips, the casino and ornate night-time illuminations to the calm of playing bowls, and flowers in the municipal gardens and conservatories.[28] The montage seems to celebrate postwar abundance, variety and opportunities, even if the vibrancy is muted by being shown in monotone.

Floodlit fountains, illuminated trams, static displays and mobile floats of incandescent light were exciting subjects to film and screen. The structural details of roller coasters, the Reel, and other attractions had novelty appeal but were visually compelling too. The resort's carnivalesque character contrasted with the character, form and routines of urban and industrial centres across the region and symbolised non-work-time freedom.[29] Even when rides were filmed from solid ground rather than as a passenger, they still suggest these early amateur filmmakers' fascination with modernity's speed and electrification. Rhythmic mechanical movements and motion are recurring motifs, perhaps echoing the shots of looms and mill machinery recorded in textile settings (see Chapter 6). Rails, twisting cars and track-ways, towering stanchions, and the criss-crossing beams and overhead girders outlined against the sky worked well in monotone and permitted playful engagement with the technologies of funfair and pleasure grounds. So too did the views of and from the moving lifts on Blackpool Tower. Panoramic sequences filmed from the tops of moving trams and aerial vistas shot of or during flights from Squire's Gate airfield, echo other contemporary interests in 'airmindness' and imaginative ways of presenting England from above.[30] They disclose too how modernity's thrilling spectacle could be savoured in affordable ways by some of Lancashire's cine-touting day-trippers and their home audiences.

Some distinctive moments of recorded pleasure focused on entertainments that, although unrelated to the seaside itself, increasingly contributed to a resort's reputation. Unlike the quieter, socially discriminating and smaller settlement of Lytham St Annes further south, Blackpool's rapid evolution of large-scale permanent entertainment facilities fostered the co-existence of contrasting specialist activities. They attracted different interest groups and heightened filmic opportunities as seen by scenes of gun displays, air shows, boating at Stanley Park, show jumping and gymkhanas. Footage of stunt artists on interweaving motorcycles, for instance, evokes Hobbs's encouragement of catching 'the swift rush on the newest motor-cycle'[31] while filmed motor rallies are reminders that changing transport technologies held novelty value, and attracted a dedicated following, as well as being a more affordable means of freedom than the car.[32] These scenes of daytime and illuminated attractions point to Blackpool's visual appeal for cine hobbyists in search of spectacle. Dramatic tension was achieved too, as in the scenes of acrobats, lion taming and tiger displays recorded during performances by the resort's resident amateur filmmaker and internationally renowned circus ring master, George Lockhart.[33] His insider knowledge enabled him also to record processions, notable events and visitors. Memorable sequences include the popular singer and entertainer George Formby helping during a public charity parade and appeal, and keepers riding the Tower Circus elephants into the sea for bathing.

Day-trips galore

Exoticism and spectacle were also available at Belle Vue Zoological Gardens, Gorton, Manchester, as shown by Le Neve Foster's extraordinary fiction film with Manchester Cine Society in 1927.[34] More typically, amateur footage of its funfair rides and roller-coasters, speedway 'dirt track' circuit, circus, gardens and other attractions attest to the venue's enduring local and regional significance as a popular tourist attraction until its closure in 1977.[35] Visual extravaganza elsewhere attracted some filmmakers' attention too, ranging from flower festivals to naval regattas and reviews.[36] Air and agricultural shows, races and other equestrian events offered ideal trackside or ringside positions for setting up a camera tripod. Sports events feature within amateur footage and detail aspects of sporting history, as well as particular major national and international events. As lenses improved so did the capability to record players involved in the game, rather than merely entering and leaving the field or parading for spectators. An excursion was still enough of a novel occasion for cine users to take their camera, and some independent filmmakers arranged excursions primarily for filming. Early club histories also identify the importance of outings as social occasions that combined specific opportunities for filming with car-sharing and a picnic.[37]

Published advice was plentiful: explore England with a cine-camera. One tipster recommended the 'cine bike' as, by 'steering a zigzag course a wonderful panning effect is obtained' from the cine-camera 'fixed on the handlebars'.[38] The novelty of motorised travel prompted reminders to include 'views of rear seat passengers and shots through the front windscreen as the car moves'.[39] An early 1939 editorial assumed rising motor use among its readers: 'I carry my camera everywhere in my car …'[40] Proud owners filmed their cars being polished or parked ready for an outing, featured them in static and mobile shots on country roads and included them in picnic scenes. Embodying modernism and consumerism, driving brought status and unprecedented freedom to explore and experience the region. The distinctiveness of northern rurality could be discovered, celebrated and shared.[41] Even if its appearance did not fit with the softer aesthetics of southern domesticated and productive landscapes, for regional residents the act of framing the visual variety of Cheshire's pastoral scenery, or the contrasting coastlines and uplands further north through car windows for later armchair tours, celebrated each motor excursion. The cine-camera was included along with children, picnic hamper and the family dog during days out and as part of holidays within areas adjacent to the North West or further afield during the interwar years. Such outings continued under the impetus of wartime exhortations to have 'Holidays at Home', and a number of reputable amateurs produced high-quality footage, despite wartime restrictions on film and petrol.[42]

Country air

Widening access to the countryside promoted more active ways of filming. In 1930, Atkinson enthused that 'These are the days in which half the population goes forth on wheels and the other half, or a large section of it, goes forth on its own sturdy legs in "hiking" and camping parties'.[43] Burgess advocated the versatile appeal of cinematography among the 'earnest grim faced young men on hiking tours or just a party of gay young things who are realising they have never seen the stars before'.[44] The 'pleasure of the cinematic ramble' was stressed in the first issue of *ACW*.[45] Amateurs, with varying ability, recorded themselves on hilltops, posing beside water and rustic bridges, or clambering over stiles and ambling through woods and fields. Their attempts to capture light on water, frame vistas, or compose views focused on a distant landform recur. These images in colour and monotone hark back to the celebratory ruralism of preceding decades. Filmmakers recorded village scenes and local residents working with livestock or engaged in other countryside tasks, on their outings from industrial and urban centres. Crooked signposts, rickety footbridges or lakeside jetties, broken down vehicles or tumbledown walls and buildings represent the visual serendipity of chanced-upon tropes of picturesque neglect. An eye-catching local dweller who 'makes a few pennies opening gates for passing motorists', seems more of a chanced-upon embodiment of an older rural world than an object of sympathy or middle-class humour.[46]

Amateurs' filmic forays in search of nature, tradition and fresh air rarely challenged countryside encroachments of modernity. Excluding pylons or electrical generators from these pastoral and upland visions sustained earlier pictorial conventions.[47] While landscapes of electrified illumination opened new opportunities for seaside filming, amateurs captured older kinds of individuality, character and spontaneous enjoyment during country excursions. Men and women shared in this robust wholesome outdoor world that had lost some of its earlier pre-eminent association with masculinity.[48] Cheery interwar and even late 1940s scenes of impromptu paddling, resting against stone walls, pausing to retie bootlaces or for a photo-opportunity testify to an era of rambling and outdoor activity recorded also by Mass Observation (MO).[49] Windswept hair, smiling faces and muscular thighs and calves refute the bleakness of some contemporary written commentators too, and offer a conservative and untroubled gaze upon the identities of healthy individuals who seem materially untouched by the nation's domestic industrial and economic woes. After 1939, resilience to change readily transformed into defiance of external threat, and taking an outdoor break from the domestic reminders of wartime prompted friends, families, schools, clubs and other organisations into making varied forms of short excursion and overnight stay using tents, youth hostels, caravans and other accommodation. Examples include Ernest Hart's record of Manchester Amateur Photographic Society members hostelling in North Wales,[50] and the films *Rope* and *Torch on Helvellyn*.[51]

Footage in the late 1930s reveals rural areas seemingly untouched by impending concerns about national security, food self-sufficiency and agricultural efficiency. Filmed forest walks in young maturing plantations alone stand witness to the military and economic imperatives of albeit an earlier generation's emergency planning. A decade later, modernising forces still seem largely absent from the uplands of Snowdonia, the Lake District and Yorkshire as excursionists increasingly ventured out using public or, when petrol permitted, private transport. These idealised versions of rurality perhaps offered escapist reassurance and a sense of continuity with an older world order still unshaken by nuclear threats, independence movements and Cold War politics. Repeatedly, amateur film's often comfortable memory-shaping and portrayals of families at leisure intermesh recreational and lifestyle trends with the intricacies of unevenly paced regional change. Equally, cine footage reminds us that the imperatives of ordinariness become means to negotiate living as well as a lens through which, retrospectively, to understand larger historical narratives.

Changing circumstances

Postwar road building, rising car ownership and the end of petrol rationing allowed people to travel further afield after the mid-1950s. Distinctions between excursions and holidays blurred, as access to both car and cine-camera changed profoundly in the decades following 1945. Just over half of Britain's population took some kind of holiday in 1950 although the vast majority still involved travelling by train to the seaside.[52] One family's regional day-trip destination increasingly overlapped with another family's annual holiday location as pleasure peripheries and social mobilities began to widen. A filmmaker's composite footage might record different outings and holidays over one or more years, revisiting and changing destinations, and combine colour and monotone filmstock, according to availability. Cheaper cameras, the growing market in second-hand equipment and other indicators of changing patterns of leisure consumption and material wealth ensured more varied cine practice too. Holidays based with relatives elsewhere had long provided domestic footage in extended family settings as part of the annual vacation cycle for wealthier families. For first-time cine users, the cost-cutting option of staying with relations on holiday began to lose its appeal during the postwar years. As preferences for affordable independent accommodation grew, a new generation of amateurs using Standard 8 recorded stays at holiday camps and caravan parks as well as holiday flats and overnight serviced accommodation at seaside boarding houses, inns, farms or cottages. Films feature widespread use of train and coach travel but also growing use of the family car as numbers doubled from 2.3 million (including vans) during the 1950s and more than tripled by the early 1960s.[53]

Family footage recorded an increasing range of attractions, events and destinations as national campaigns to promote domestic tourism evolved to offset the emerging attraction of affordable holidays abroad. Traditional costumes, horse-drawn trams and canal barges, the maturing landscapes of Portmeirion, Clough Williams-Ellis's pastiche Italianate village in Wales, begun in 1925, and castles, abbeys, gardens and other historic sites increasingly feature among other visitor destinations captured on film. Footage suggests that avid consumption of tradition and national symbolism persisted alongside politicians' contested visions of modernisation. National park designation in 1951 did not unduly affect cine activity at regional level as both the Lake District and the Peak District were already well-established destinations, although more footage might appear in archive holiday footage from other regions. Motorway building, after its experimental eight-mile stretch around Preston, opened up the first long stretch in 1959, and sections of the M6 and M60 in 1960–63, thus launching twenty-five years of almost continuous road building and improvement that profoundly altered patterns of mobility including recreational travel. For some filmmakers, the democratic sleekness and plastic functionality encountered at motorway service stations became part of the holiday record in the 1960s.[54]

Holiday memories

Broadening cine ownership is reflected in postwar holiday footage. Away from his newsagency, Ralph Brookes recorded outings and family holidays that combined stays with relatives and sightseeing.[55] His films ranged from a single holiday reel to compilations spanning different aspects of family and local life over a number of years. This inconsistency perhaps reflects available time, interest and skill as blurred sequences suggest minimal editing. His material identifies shifts in domestic recreational travel.[56] Museums, high-street shopping and market stalls, wildlife, heritage attractions, archaeological excavations, local funfairs and parades intermix with visits to the Lancashire coast and holidays in different parts of Britain. His repeated use of travelling shots – sometimes speeded up – hints at his pleasure in recording landscapes en route to new destinations by coach and car. Mr Brookes's films of days out with his wife and grandchildren perhaps also point to a new pattern of intergenerational care that links with the postwar rise in mothers seeking paid part-time and full-time work. The couple's unprecedented mobility and ability to spend money on leisure activities with their children and grandchildren combine, for their generation, with public health care provision and the beginnings of more active and healthier retirements. While relatively cheaper filmstock and processing meant that amateurs could record more of their holiday memories on film, Mr Brookes's eclectic mix of leisure-time-related activities and interests also points to widening notions of pleasure and 'a good day out'.

Particularly memorable excursions occurred when relatives visited from abroad. The last century's demographic shifts meant that the first two postwar decades also saw a rise in cine use among families with international connections. Emigration to colonies and old dominions exceeded in-migration well into the 1960s.[57] Footage of a cousin visiting from South Africa and of North American relations features within Hubert Wiener's detailed thirteen-year visual record of family events at different synagogues, festivals and holidays.[58] Overseas visitors gave filmmakers an opportunity to share their home area. Familiarity with local sights and attractions implicitly conveyed a sense of rootedness and well-being that could be shared via the visitors to other members of an extended family. Screening films made during such outings and visits might also help to unify and maintain family bonds across distance. Dr Hira Kapur, a doctor trained in Jaipur, India, and who worked for over forty years in north-west Lancashire, similarly portrayed overseas visitors within his fifteen-year record of family life and travel.[59] Excursions up the Lune Valley, into the Lake District and locally around Heysham and Lancaster reveal the family's gradual exploration of different localities as the children grew older and they expanded their choice of places and picnic spots that suited the age, mobility and interests of visiting relations and friends. Although his films feature recurring visits to family and friends in West London and Kent, and major holidays that introduce his wife and children to relatives and sites of personal significance in India, much of Kapur's footage highlights his love of landscapes, architecture, gardens and visual delight in travelling to different places in Britain, the Mediterranean and elsewhere. Kapur's imagery also contributes importantly to a more inclusive picture of regional life in its portrait of domestic detail within an ethnically mixed professional home during the 1970s and early 1980s.

During the 1920s, after years of restricted mobility, widening opportunities for foreign travel coincided with the rise of amateur cinematography. Journeying by train, boat, car and even the occasional plane gave unprecedented opportunities to see and be seen elsewhere, albeit in changing geo-political and societal contexts. New patterns of recreational mobility and (in)activity, as well as changing ideas about the relationship between work, fatigue and the benefits of sunshine and being outdoors, offered camera-wielding enthusiasts fresh opportunities for taking and showing films.[60] Overseas footage, formerly shot during missionary, medical and governmental duties abroad, increasingly extended a touristic gaze over other localities, landscapes and lifestyles, as holiday cine films allowed those able to indulge the twin costly pursuits of travel and amateur film to shoot and share scenes of their vacations abroad with audiences back home.[61] While the novelty soon palled for more reluctant younger audience members who, particularly after the first screening, were more likely to enjoy any hired animations or other films included in the family film show, reliving and sharing holiday memories became an enduring part of amateur practice. Clearer lighting conditions in southern Europe allowed filmmakers considerable scope for camerawork. So did fresh subject matter and, when filmmakers strayed on to unfamiliar ground in the pursuit of visual difference, their handheld equipment could reassuringly distance them from those in front of the lens.

Within an eclectic range of travel footage made between c.1925 and 1939, hobbyists avidly recorded diverse aspects of overseas holiday experience ranging from pre-departure packing to the return journey and arrival at home. As peacetime international holidaying resumed after 1945, overseas travel and its associated opportunities for documenting self and surroundings in unfamiliar settings altered under the impact of package holidays.[62] Over the new two decades, changing holiday entitlements and improved material wealth combined to extend the tourist periphery still further.[63] More varied long-haul destinations became more accessible by air. Cine users ventured further afield both independently and as members of organised groups, collectively amassing a vast body of unofficial imagery about being somewhere else. Paradoxically, home audiences eager to consume other people's amateur travel footage projected on living room walls and screens diminished over the same period. Even as more people were able to enjoy overseas holidays themselves thanks to rising personal mobility and cine-ownership, watching television began to affect leisure time and patterns of hobby activity.[64] Nonetheless, holiday films remained an integral component of many cine club programmes and an important strand of the hobby press until 1977 and well beyond.

Picturing places

Comparing prewar and postwar overseas holiday footage discloses qualitative differences too, as much unedited and poor-quality material resulted from the rapid expansion of cine-camera use after 1950. More people, for whatever reason, contented themselves with projecting unedited footage without adding often the time-consuming captions and titling sequences found in the 1930s. Experimenting with gadgetry lessened too as ready-made products became available, but challenges remained, as shown by those filmmakers who combined animated maps, or explored ways of adding sound and improvised sequences to their travellers' tales. Colour foreign holiday footage appeared from the early 1930s, and was sometimes edited into black and white footage, to highlight a specific sequence, as for instance in Barker Scarr's on-board swimming pool scenes during a Mediterranean cruise.[65] Filming entirely in colour was expensive and difficult between late 1939 and 1949, owing to the limited availability of filmstock. Political circumstances placed travel restrictions upon taking camera equipment or new and used film across borders, as shown by advice in the hobby press, early campaigning by the IAC[66] and the documented experiences of filmmakers who travelled to Soviet Russia in the early 1930s[67] and to Spain during the Spanish Civil War.[68] In contrast, some enthusiasts took their cameras overseas during the Second World War, but practicalities frequently limited their use. Interestingly, few limitations appear to have been placed upon Geoffrey and Dorothy Haworth during their extensive visits to Soviet Russia at the height of the Cold War. Moreover, Haworth's footage of the 1959 May Day Parade suggests that he filmed from a prime position and his resultant colour footage of passing troops and interballistic missiles contrasts with official newsreel footage recorded for international audiences in black and white.[69]

Some overseas holiday footage was shown repeatedly to family, friends and wider audiences over a number of years but other footage was rarely seen after its first viewing, particularly if it involved borrowing a screen and projector. Opportunities to screen holiday films varied beyond the home, depending upon people's work-related or social networks, and other affiliations to political, religious or civic amenity groups at and beyond the local level. Cine clubs remained critical settings for screening material, and even the earliest amateur competitions encouraged travel-related entries (see Chapters 2 and 3). Both were bolstered by a hobby press that tried to balance its steady flow of practical tips on well-worked themes with more innovative and sophisticated ways of representing holiday experiences. Away from the club scene, some independent pioneers used their cine interests as an educative tool. The Manchester politician and businessman Sir Leonard Behrens showed his films within liberal, geographical and charitable circles,[70] while Dr Taylor from Bolton and his travel companions made various presentations across the North West combining travel notes and his 1932 cine footage of Soviet Russia.[71] Travelling extensively from Rotherham in South Yorkshire, Charles Chislett gave numerous lectures and accompanying re-edited versions of his travelogues to schools, church groups and other audiences within and beyond the region on behalf of the Church Pastoral Aid Society, for whom he also made training films.[72] Well into the 1970s, the Haworths gave film shows to Women's Institutes, Liberal Party and Rotary Club gatherings across the North West.[73] Generating this appetite for vicarious travel were gradually ageing audiences of active working people, retired people as well as dwindling numbers of younger individuals from a mix of occupations, self-improvement and formal education who maintained established habits of supporting organised events in their leisure time.[74]

Concern over touristic voyeurism and intrusion into other people's lives penetrated amateur cinematography no faster than other branches of photography. Cine users sought out spectacle and difference specifically as subject matter. Hobson, for instance, urged filmmakers to 'sandwich in a few picturesque natives or the snake charmer and his sinuous snakes; the one eyed beggar, be-trousered beauties of the harem and the donkeys [to] add zip that makes your movie attractive.'[75] Capturing on camera distinctive dress-codes, everyday routines and material culture conferred status upon filmmakers who ventured into alien places. Street scenes, animal-drawn transport, domestic tasks undertaken in communal space or public view, could satisfy an audience's desire for exoticism and enhance viewers' own sense of connectedness with the actions on screen through being in the filmmakers' presence.[76] Ethnographic fascination with visual distinctiveness recurred throughout the interwar years, giving a double-edged quality to some sequences in that such imagery undoubtedly now contributes to a film's historical significance as record of local life whilst also being problematic in terms of appropriation and objectification.[77] Cine-travellers' capacity to fix other people's time and space could also mislead in offering historicised and pictorialised views of material culture elsewhere. Tropes of tradition contrasted with the modernity of home life. Time travel accentuated the sense of physical distance travelled. Disadvantage, decrepitude and dilapidation also attracted the unquestioning gaze of filmmakers who might in other contexts be considered to be liberal and progressive. The camera's scopic vision could transform an unusual detail into being representative of being somewhere else, as outsiders alert to recording visual novelty included eye-catching moments within their holiday memories. Home audiences could indulge in armchair travel unperturbed by the cine-enthusiasts' essentialising gaze.

While for some early users a cine-camera was a fashionable travel accessory, for other enthusiasts the shift from still to motion-picture technologies heralded new possibilities for making aesthetic responses to their material surroundings.[78] Holiday films permitted alternative mimetic techniques. Admittedly, realist, rather than abstract techniques soon dominated emerging shooting approaches as enthusiasts often framed and held a snapshot image simply for longer than needed for a single exposure. Cine-camera poses at viewpoints, beside statues or bridges, on beaches or promenades or in gardens or pavement cafés often differed from their still predecessors only by being longer. Adjusting clothes, gestures, facial expressions and an individual's moving lips signal the shifting awareness to other possibilities of using film. Through trial and considerable error, early hobbyists identified their cine-camera's strengths and limitations on holiday. Strong lighting contrasts, perhaps unnoticed by the human eye, were ineffective when trying to shoot from darkened doorways, through arches or branches. Swinging shots across panoramic views failed as a result of speed and early camera limitations on depth of field and focus. Undifferentiated monotones reduced visual complexity to a blur, and resisting the logical wish to make pictures with plenty of movement required entirely new ways of handling and understanding the cine-camera's capabilities.

Successive holiday films reveal how some individual filmmakers technically improved over time. Experimentation with night-time illuminations, attempts at filming indoors or in low light, and the seemingly irresistible desire to film from a moving vehicle, recur through interwar footage as hobbyists found, after developing their films, what their visual efforts had successfully recorded. For the postwar generation of 9mm, Standard 8 and later Super 8 filmstock users, the growing body of expertise available in print and evolving camera design sometimes helped to avoid some of the earlier frustrations. Many more newcomers ultimately abandoned their hobby as their holiday efforts failed to match the increasing wealth of travel-related material offered in popular fiction, films and television during the 1960s.

Attention now focuses on more detailed examples of how filmic sightseeing evoked the pleasures of holidays abroad for subsequent recollection. Like all amateur cine activity, holiday footage did not occur in a visual vacuum and may be set against other visual meanings and representation circulating during the middle decades of the last century. Amateur overseas holiday imagery, no less than its professional counterparts, helped to valorise specific moments, feelings and situations. Less sophisticated than feature films undoubtedly, its content now offers often compelling visual historical evidence. Its very existence is a reminder too that newfound opportunities for travel, through the cine-camera's mimetic intervention, retained an umbilical cord with home. Modernity's contradictory promise of relocation required insulation from its overwhelming threat of dislocation. Framing difference overseas for later home consumption could simultaneously empower and console during years when mediated versions of national and international life brimmed with uncertainties.

Peacetime travel

The worrying contraction of Lancashire's textile export market, for example, and the need to understand changing customer demand and production methods abroad motivated John Hindley's nine-month return trip to East Asia in 1927.[79] With fares paid by elder brothers already established in the family's extensive textile operations around Nelson, east Lancashire, the twenty-one-year-old embarked on a journey by steamship and train to visit business agents and other contacts. From Hindley's detailed letters home and his diary entries, reporting back seems to have been a self-assumed dutiful response to his sponsors. His surviving cine-films reveal that his travels combined holiday with adventure. His camerawork, like his dairy entries, improved with practice, but from the outset the mix of palpable excitement and anticipation are apparent. Accompanying his letters, diary and film, there exist postcards, photographs and other items that trace Hindley's travels but here the focus is primarily on how his approximately sixty-six minutes of cine footage disclose a still unmodified map of Britain's empire and overseas dominions.[80]

Short intertitles punctuate the footage, perhaps reflecting the months of delay between filming and editing material and constraints upon Hindley's time after returning home. Their brevity contrasts with much of his filmmaking. His leisurely delight in documenting visual novelty points to the slowness of travelling by ship and train. His images evoke other ship-based imagery, found in promotional films from Cunard and other companies, as well as the emerging cinematic genres of mysteries, murders and melodrama located aboard cruise vessels.[81] Shipboard filming, whether on long sea crossings or coastal port-hopping during organised cruises in the Mediterranean or northern Europe, relied upon recurring motifs for decades.[82] The receding figures on the quayside and harbour frontages, views over the bows and stern of breaking waves, and the departing pilot boat and other vessels that often formed informal flotillas of farewell as liners headed out to sea, became stock ingredients of amateur filming afloat. So too were the cutaways to birds overhead and sightings of passing vessels, whales, dolphins and other fauna. Using medium to close-up shots of decks, superstructure, funnels and vents became ways of remembering the most distinctive feature of the cruise traveller's temporary home and floating hotel.

Hindley focused less on shipboard scenes than some of his immediate successors, for whom recreational sea travel soon became part of the holiday rather than simply a mode of transport. Perhaps, as a solitary traveller, Hindley felt awkward in recording fellow passengers, although they featured in his diary.[83] He left no filmic record of his visits to merchants, factories and commercial premises either. Instead, his footage reflects an outsider's opportunistic gathering of visual clues about being in different places, whether filmed over the ship's rail or during excursions and longer periods ashore. Lengthy sequences brim with contemporary detail about daily activities, livelihoods and physical well-being. A Maori mother and child feature in an organised excursion to a village where curious tourists stroll among carvers.[84] Medium-range shots record men working together on boats, wagon trains, plantations or construction camps. Roadside stalls and open-air urban markets co-exist within an eclectic mix of temples, mosques and Victorian warehouses and industrial buildings. Wandering livestock and drying clothes among unpaved alleyways and huddled roof-tops hint at the impoverished residential districts that underpinned life in the tree-lined roads and well-tended garden settings of comfortable suburban living across the British Empire.

Hindley's not untypical mix of traveller's sympathy and distaste for poverty, detailed in writing, was shaped by his own background, education, upbringing and attitudes.[85] He was already familiar with management issues and scenes of efficient labour and urban enterprise repeatedly drew his attention.[86] He filmed the frenzied bustle of street vendors, rickshaws and porters in Singapore, Manila, Hong Kong, Shanghai, Bombay (Mumbai), Colombo and elsewhere. The sight of workers heaving, hauling, balancing on scaffolding, moving freight by water, wheels, draught animals or their own effort, prompted extensive recording and note-making, although few intertitles. Although adults knowingly caught on camera exhibit indifference and restraint, teenagers, as in New Zealand, sometimes gather exuberantly in front of him, and posed groups of young children, filmed in South Africa and elsewhere, stare with as much wide-eyed curiosity as he observes them. Notwithstanding the unequal forms of looking, Hindley's ethnographic gaze discloses an outsider's fascination with the spectacle of late colonialism, even as his own overseas business encounters were revealing how changes were beginning to weaken imperial political and economic domination.

From the mid-1920s, cruise holidays offered affluent cine-enthusiasts alternative opportunities to encounter unfamiliar worlds too.[87] As shipping companies reconsolidated after wartime losses, newly commissioned and refitted vessels increasingly reflected a shift towards recreational travel at prices that the affluent middle classes were willing to pay.[88] One- to three-week-long cruises to the Mediterranean and northern Europe combined shore visits, on-board activities and entertainment with the recognisable rituals and comforts of hotel service.[89] As protective floating bubbles, cruise vessels combined the possibility of transporting passengers between well-known locations with minimal danger and controlled exposure to exoticism. During holidays afloat, cruise ships represented transport, accommodation and an integral part of the recorded holiday experience, as shown in a number of films made by passengers from Lancashire between 1928 and the mid-1930s.[90] Interwar cruise holidays were an innovative component of changing leisure patterns that transformed commercial peacetime maritime activity and opened a new chapter in tourism history. Advice on filming holidays afloat flowed from the hobby literature, and *MM* organised cruises for cine-enthusiasts during the late 1960s and 1970s.[91]

Scenes of leaving Liverpool, London or Southampton started many interwar cruise-films. Quayside loading and boarding plus views over deck-rails emphasised the size of these vessels as they towered over harbour facilities and waving onlookers. Early safety drills routinely introduced passengers in life jackets as well as the ship's officers and crew to home audiences as did a short cinematic tour of decks, and seating areas.[92] Subsequent on-board filming of deck games, promenading, reading or fraternising with other passengers and antics around the swimming pool disclose the effortless and repetitive nature of being afloat. Offsetting the ennui of much motionless ship-based travel – once safely across the Bay of Biscay and through the Straits of Gibraltar – south-bound cine-enthusiasts avidly recorded their travelling companions, passing ships, porpoises, seabirds and any prominent landforms. Approaching landfall prompted attempts to document shorelines and the skylines of ports and cities. Such material reflects the amateur's close observation of local practice and their impressionistic portraits of economies adjusting to tourism – young men and boys diving for coins, quayside performances by musicians, acrobats and fire-swallowers, postcard, lace and carpet sellers clustering around gang planks, the opportune drivers of cars, charabancs and horse-drawn carriages ready for trade and the waiters eager for custom.[93] Shots reveal an amateur's delight in the sudden deluge of visual stimuli after the restrictions of being afloat.

As a break to the frustrations of filming at sea, cine users revelled in the more stable conditions for recording quayside encounters from a moored vessel.[94] Upper decks offered clear overhead views, avoided the crowds attracted by the ship's arrival and were safely out of reach from the much-touted threat of local pickpockets. Deck-level filming orientated excursionists prior to going ashore and afterwards as notable street-level buildings could be identified as sites of personal exploration. Visits ashore ranged from independent wandering to organised excursions further inland. Flânerie broadened the holidaymaker's scopic vision as chance encounters with street traders, children, animals, and other local people provided collectible visual trophies that helped to differentiate between places.[95] Overseas holiday films, like their domestic counterparts, disclose the patchy, partial and incomplete nature of visual remembering. Personal records of being somewhere were accumulations of incidental sights and moments impulsively framed as asides from the standardised tourism agenda. Pigeons in St Mark's Square, decorated donkey harness in Ibiza or a flock of sheep in the shade attracted amateurs' interest as routinely as did Baedeker's recommended churches, bridges and other monuments.[96] Doubtless, an awareness of prospective audiences affected some filmmakers' propensity to make seemingly random recordings of animals and children plus other signs or amusing incongruities. Perhaps these visual tendencies also reveal more about emerging patterns of tourism consumption. In some family groups recorded on film, carried guidebooks clearly feature[97] but cine-cameras also enabled amateurs to construct alternative narratives about the places they visited and their own sensibilities while they were there. For some enthusiasts, showing was proof of having visited particular places, perhaps replacing the need to display knowledge too. For others, lengthy titling to convey information occurred, as in Barker Scarr's footage of Rome.[98] Much later, enthusiasts also attempted spoken commentaries during filming, as heard in Kapur's repeated invocations to 'look carefully' at Hindu carvings and temples.[99]

Travel politics

Interwar holidays afloat appealed less to families with younger children, so while some hobbyists satisfied their ethnographic impulse by documenting crew, travelling companions and local life ashore, other early filmmakers, including Higginson and Behrens, first recorded their own offspring during overseas holidays in the Swiss Alps, Italy and Ireland.[100] Over time, touring vacations gained popularity and European motoring holidays increased during the 1930s.[101] The inclusion of Nazi officers posed alongside a filmmaker's family and scenes of gliders, pleasure boats and timber-framed houses bearing swastikas as tail symbols, ensigns or on banners points to how the touristic gaze could neutralise political activity into photo-opportunities or omit it altogether. Glimpsing Hitler among crowds watching passion plays at Oberammergau, or titling a group of Jews in transit as 'excursionists' and filming younger family members as they parodied Nazi salutes and marches[102] are reminders too of how such holiday imagery and encounters perhaps helped to anaesthetise some audiences against fuller implications of political developments in Germany.

Political indifference depended on individual interests that may be no longer verifiable. For the Preston brothers, uniforms of colonial police and soldiers at crowded stations filmed during an inland excursion to Ceuta may simply have contrasted with the djellabas and other regional garments around them.[103] Yet, such footage unwittingly alludes to the European authorities' prevailing disquiet over mobilising nationalist factions. Was the banner-bedecked frontage of Mussolini's headquarters spotted during Barker Scarr's filmic tour of Rome's imperial monuments shot as a visual curiosity or an overt link to contemporary political ambition?[104] Some amateur filmmakers travelled more knowingly into contested space on holiday. Package tourism took increasing numbers to Franco's Spain during the 1950s but politics gained visibility and comment most obviously in shots of graffiti, control posts and gateways between Gibraltar and the mainland.[105] Perhaps the military presence, although never filmed, also sensitised British visitors to the Rock's colonial history. In contrast, those capturing the abundant folk-dancing displays provided for tourists were oblivious of how Franco manipulated such representations of national culture.[106]

Visitors' impressions of Soviet Russia were among the most overtly political, owing to the specific character of encouraging western tourists under Stalin and during the Cold War years (Figure 7).[107] Cine footage made between 1932 and the mid-1960s by filmmakers travelling from north-west England is a reminder of the complex attitudes towards Russia during these decades.[108] It offers a regional rather than metropolitan glimpse of international relationships and, although Left-wing filmmaking traditions and intellectual interests were active in the region, neither Horace Wilfred Taylor nor Geoffrey Haworth had communist sympathies. Importantly, their films, discussed in Chapter 8, acknowledge more liberal and less partisan interests in internationalism that found middle-class expression in travel and activities which were concerned with cultural and educational exchange, civic association and local societies.[109] Changing opportunities for air and overland coach travel broadened visitors' travel experiences, as shown by Walter Holden's *To Moscow by Motorcoach* (1958) in which he recorded impressions of Warsaw and Krakow as well as religious processions and scenes of Polish rural life and his return from Russia via Prague.[110] Collectively, such amateur holiday footage helps to reposition

Tour in the USSR, Part 2 (Dir. Horace Wilfred Taylor, 1932). Still supplied by courtesy of N. R. and Dr B. S. Taylor and North West Film Archive at Manchester Metropolitan University, Film no. RR852/35 (b/w. silent, 19 min. 38 sec.)

east–west travel relations within a wider understanding of cultural relations and twentieth-century tourism history.[111]

During the 1950s, greater freedom to travel was accompanied by a broadening range of holidays in ever more varied locations. By 1958, about two million Britons had foreign holidays, almost double the number in the late 1930s.[112] Three years later, 3.5 million Britons went abroad on holiday, almost double the figure for 1950.[113] As overseas family driving holidays gained popularity, imagery of cars being transferred by crane from quayside to ship's deck became widespread.[114] Coach travel catered for more cautious travellers.[115] Amateurs documented their train journeys, cruises, coach tours, package trips, Club Mediterranean holiday villages and organised tours too.[116] Young independent travellers and backpackers were largely absent from this swelling record of consumer affluence during the later 1960s although this might differ in regional patterns of surviving material. Perhaps, since becoming parents often triggered buying cine equipment, the holiday record was bound to be underrepresentative of recreational travel among younger adults. Nonetheless, alongside continuing interest in luxury cruises to the Caribbean, or bespoke travel to such long-haul destinations as Mongolia,[117] Ethiopia,[118] Australia,[119] and visits organised by the English Speaking Union,[120] newer holiday locations and experiences supplemented more conventional vacation patterns.

Filming in the sun

Sunbathing proliferated from the Caribbean to Tel Aviv and transformed southern Europe's pleasure periphery. At emerging Mediterranean resorts, local fishing fleets gave way to beach towels on the sand along coastlines where tourist hotels and apartments invaded more fields, orchards and olive groves each year. Lengthy coach transfers ceased as regional airports developed to accommodate new seasonal influxes brought by charter flights. Amateur sequences showing hotel façades and gardens or dining areas, individual balconies and en-suite facilities lessened as the novelty and pride in such visual tropes of holidaying abroad shifted to recording more organised excursions and beach time. Tourist facilities proliferated too, alongside the growing presence of holidaymakers in street scenes, at local markets and strolling among stretched-out nets or racks of drying spaghetti. Yugoslavia regained some of its prewar popularity among filmmakers too, as an affordable and distinctive holiday destination filled with historic towns, picturesque coastal and inland communities, regional costumes, markets and other photo-opportunities. Among cine users, Greece, Turkey and Israel all featured on cruise itineraries not yet affected by simmering regional geo-politics, while nascent airborne tourism rekindled interest in Egyptian antiquities and began to offer more than a brief stopover before or after journeying through the Suez Canal.

Unprecedented levels of overseas holiday filmmaking occurred from the mid-1950s onwards. Jack Wells and his wife, for instance, toured around western Europe, in an Austin J2 Camper van for over fifteen years and joined organised tours too. They combined their holiday footage with additional material and commentaries recorded at home with the help of friends using reel-to-reel tape decks. Improvised scenes, based upon receiving an invitation abroad, being inspired by a radio programme or planning a holiday route show contemporary domestic interiors, furnishing and design and tourist brochures but also brim with the delight of making films together. Their holiday camerawork discloses good-humoured self-awareness of themselves sitting alone surrounded by home comforts in different scenic overseas locations. *Sunny Morocco* (1954–58) reveals intriguing aspects of the early package holiday experience, including pre-boarding and in-seat filming of the propeller-driven plane and its flight from a former military airfield at Hurn near Bournemouth.[121] As forerunners of much later tourist enclave development, early coach and air tours used town centre hotels that were ideal for filming street scenes from balconies. Scenes of travelling as part of a group using cars rather than a coach offer other clues to the nascent package tourism infrastructure then available in Morocco, despite its up-market interwar appeal.

As the cost of foreign holidays to island, coastal, mountain and other locations became more affordable to families, for whom going overseas had only ever been associated with migration or war, the desire to share and relive 'once in a lifetime' experiences spurred new interests in using cine-cameras. While 'foreign travel off the peg' became part of unprecedented material affluence for some British families, recording a holiday away from home every year or every two years became an established part of more family experiences from the late 1950s onwards. This does not deny that holidays of any kind remained beyond the financial reach of many families far beyond the decades considered here, and that discrimination also prompted many non-white families not to venture beyond their neighbourhoods.[122] The Wells's material, as in footage shot by many of their white contemporaries, captured the printed frocks, headscarves and flannel trousers of Britons on holiday. In Morocco, the colourful designs and printed fabrics of holiday wear contrasted with many local women's garments, although numerous men and children are shown in western clothes. Holiday imagery routinely juxtaposed imported cars and motorbikes with animal-drawn carts and other images of modernity and tradition. Filmmakers varied in their focus upon secular and religious buildings, although Jack Wells seems to have been intrigued by the concrete modernity in Casablanca and elsewhere. His varied use of close-up and medium-range filming, slow pans and short sequences of brief shots of arches, window patterns, tiling and local signs in Arabic also hints at his sense of visual aesthetic even if overall quality varies. Footage of inserted maps, holiday brochure imagery and souvenir pennants that replicated sights captured on film also suggest that making such productions helped to 'extend the holiday into … cold winter evenings' even before screening the finished version.[123]

Some newcomers to amateur cinema during the 1960s showed their holiday footage within a cine club setting where tips on film technique, editing and splicing abounded. Taking their recent film of honeymooning in Tangiers, Gibraltar and Spain, to a local cine club launched Linda and Michael Gough in 1967 into a lifelong fascination with amateur film practice from local to national level.[124] They were teachers and their interests soon focused on editing footage into documentaries for general audiences rather than family and friends. Even where holiday memories and their children were obvious, Michael's observations of other people enjoying themselves and interest in places enriched his visual focus. A juxtaposed crucifix and brief passing political reference offer early clues to his sensitivity to cultural setting. Over time, travel destinations broadened and more opportunity to become familiar with guidebooks, novels and music associated with different holiday destinations informed how the Goughs experienced the places they visited and their subsequent film editing. Transferring from cine to video and later digital technologies enabled the Goughs to develop many award-winning travel documentaries on a variety of ecological, historical, musical and other cultural themes. Michael's accompanying self-reflexivity upon his own filmic practice and the enduring appeal of screening travel footage disclose a close understanding of changing amateur practice from the later years of cine use, although many of these reflections lie outside the present book's timescale.[125]

Narratives of family outings and holidays were not exclusively shaped by men. Opportunities to step aside from childcare and other gendered conventions of domesticity occurred more readily for women when they were away from home. Examples of travel-related films made by women are gradually surfacing in the North West as elsewhere. Lucy Fairbank (see Chapter 5) filmed extensively at home and abroad from the mid-1930s, while Leonora Bichard, an art student at the Harris Institute School of Art in Preston, also briefly experimented with film during the 1930s.[126] Her thirteen surviving films, each less than two minutes long, include striking details, whether recording family and fellow students during excursions, a honeymoon departure by plane and a parachutist's descent and parade by open-topped car also at Blackpool, or visits to York. Other cameos include school-age children on a swing, a mechanic checking a plane, people throwing confetti and adults informally standing alone and in groups. Her vignettes of a school playground in Ypres, people exploring overgrown trenches, military installations and shelled buildings and posing beside an abandoned tank testify to the informality of 1930s battlefield tourism on the western front.[127]

Closer to home, fathers occasionally stepped into view as wives and mothers recorded husbands driving the family car, on the beach, playing cricket or during a family picnic. Similarities persist well into the postwar years, even if fathers' on-screen family role varied over time. Parents sometimes exchanged roles within adjacent shots, so that they had a record of being present with the children at the same time. Beyond the immediacy of family groups, it often remains harder to identify who was in charge of the camera by imagery alone. Changing attitudes and technologies helped to broaden women's involvement in making holiday and other types of film once video and digital technologies became more widespread.

Recording relaxation – continuity and change

For over fifty years, the cinematic gaze of the amateur, no less than the professional, reinforced particular ways of seeing and being seen or shown to others. Image-making framed people behind and in front of the camera in sociopolitical space and, however seemingly innocuous, their images encoded specific values. Consequently, amateur travel-related footage, whether shot at home or abroad, sometimes discloses as much about the individuals in charge of the camera as about actual destinations. Whether made primarily for family consumption or wider general interests, screenings of amateur holiday-related material provided a significant source of contemporary place and cultural imagery in the decades before and immediately after the introduction of widespread television viewing. Along with advertising, commercial films, popular fiction and an upsurge in travel-related publications, amateur imagery helped to shape and define people's sense of themselves and the world around them.[128] It extended the picturing impulse of previous generations and the conventions of the nineteenth-century illustrated travel lecture. Epidiascopes, magic lanterns and early home projectors paved the way for domestic consumption of commercially available and personally produced imagery. Audiences adjusted to seeing familiar and unfamiliar people and places through the selective gaze of the camera. Many amateur filmmakers were voracious observers – image collectors who leisurely gathered on camera visual signifiers of difference, much as their predecessors had acquired other travel souvenirs. Collectively the detailed visual histories to be found in this material, whether filmed by the British seaside or in distant locations, complement our understanding of the diverse cultures of travel and travel narrative during the last century.

From the outset, the cine-camera's technological intervention in memory-gathering, sharing and preserving was also a product of modernity. It embodied the increasingly complex mesh of science and technology with aspects of popular culture and everyday life. It symbolised outlook as well as affluence. Its competitively evolving design, materials, weight and components paralleled broader changes in manufacturing, production and international distribution. The cine-camera conferred on early owners, undeterred by their critics, the status, power and authority to depict others or, at the very least, a changing sense of selfhood and personal confidence about being in the world. Yet its illusory power to defy, suspend and rewind time also suggests another lasting aspect of its appeal as a means to gaze backwards and relive the past.[129] Imagery of time spent together as a couple or as a family became part of how people told stories about themselves and each other. As visual anthologies of holiday moments, which were selected at the moment of taking and any subsequent editing stage, postwar footage offered nostalgic escapism from the tedium of some people's working lives. Its flickering scenes were a projected promise of equivalent future non-work time away from home. They helped to sustain everyday routines and the economic and social imperatives of paid and unpaid labour for the rest of the year. Despite all the unrecorded tensions and domestic disasters that might have occurred, imagery offered families a sense of visual cohesion and stability even as the experiences of growing up, home life and going to work were unfolding against the turbulence of wider societal change in later twentieth-century Britain. If early cine footage had helped the middle classes to reaffirm their affinity as a nation after the First World War, fifty years on amateur filmmaking was part of the increasingly nuclear family's attempt to hold on to a sense of itself within a country and a world that had become a very different place.

Notes

1. M. A. Lovell Burgess, *A Popular Account of the Amateur Cine Movement*, p. 65.
2. D. Matless, *Landscape and Englishness*; D. P. Corbett, Y. Holt, and F. Russell (eds) *The Geographies of Englishness*; W. J. Darby, *Landscape and Identity*.
3. M. Featherstone, 'Automobilities. An introduction'; T. Edensor, 'Automobility and national identity'.
4. Lovell Burgess, *A Popular Account*, p. 5.
5. S. Moir, 'New ideas in your holiday film'.
6. Lovell Burgess, *A Popular Account*, p. 62.
7. For instance, at *BIAFF 2009* (the IAC's annual British International Amateur Film Festival), six travel-related entries won 4–Star awards.
8. P. Brendon, *Thomas Cook. 150 Years of Popular Tourism*; J. Towner, *An Historical Geography of Recreation and Tourism*. See also Norris Nicholson, 'Moving pictures; moving memories'; 'Framing the view'; 'Floating hotels'.
9. D. Chambers, 'Family as place: family photograph albums and the domestication of public and private space'.
10. George Higginson, 1943–45: *The English Lakes*, NWFA Film no. 2753 (b/w and colour, silent, 38 mins. 5 sec.).

11 John Barker Scarr, 1931: [*Casablanca and Shipboard Scenes*], NWFA Film no. 3800 (b/w, silent, 14 min. 57 sec.).
12 C. Rojek and J. Urry (eds), *Touring Cultures*; K. Hetherington and A. Cronin (eds), *Consuming the Entrepreneurial City*; G. Crawford, *Consuming Sport*; J. de Groot, *Consuming History*.
13 J. M. Schwartz and J. R. Ryan, 'Photography and the geographical imagination'; J. R. Ryan, *Picturing Empire*.
14 A. Strasser, *Amateur Films. Planning, Directing, Cutting*.
15 Preston Brothers, *1928: [*Preston Family – Cruise Holiday*], NWFA Film no 1187 (b/w, silent, 10 min. 0 sec.).
16 G. Rose, 'Practising photography'.
17 George Higginson, 1946: *Autumn*, NWFA Film no. 465 (colour, silent, 12 mins. 35 sec.).
18 Norris Nicholson, 'Framing the view', 94–5.
19 A. Marr, *A History of Modern Britain*, pp. 85–6.
20 H. Fairlie, *The Life of Politics* (p. 250), cited in P. Hennessy, *Having It So Good*, p. 538.
21 J. Urry, *Sociology Beyond Societies*; T. Cresswell, *On the Move*.
22 J. K. Walton, *The British Seaside Holidays and Resorts in the Twentieth Century*; G. S. Cross and J. K. Walton, *The Playful Crowd*.
23 S. Braggs and D. Harris, *Sun, Fun and Crowds*.
24 Frederick Grime, c. 1930s: [*Motor Cycle, Horses and Military Displays*], NWFA Film no. 1858 (b/w, silent, 9 min. 19 sec.).
25 Leonard F. Behrens, 1925: [*Skerries, June/July 1925*], NWFA Film no. 2082b (b/w, silent, 8 min. 56 sec.).
26 M. Huggins, 'More sinful pleasures?'; D. Webb, 'Bahktin at the seaside'.
27 Thomas Eggles, c. 1930s: [*Boys and Girls Come out to Play*], NWFA Film no. 1822 (b/w, silent, 13 min. 9 sec.); Mr Morley, 1930–32: *Holidays – Morley Family*, NWFA Film no. 2547 (b/w, silent, 14 min. 7 sec.).
28 David Cayton, 1955: *Magnetic Blackpool*, NWFA Film no. 5969 (b/w, silent, 9 min. 20 sec.).
29 Webb, 'Bahktin at the seaside', 122–8.
30 C. Baldick, *The Modern Movement*, p. 308.
31 E. W. Hobbs, *Cinematography for Amateurs*, p. 14.
32 M. Featherstone, 'Automobilities. An introduction', p. 3.
33 George Lockhart, 1930–31: [*Tower Circus Elephants Bathing and Stanley Park*], NWFA Film no. 1772 (b/w, silent, 9 min. 38 sec.).
34 G. H. Sewell, 'Our cover picture'.
35 J. Cronin and F. Rhodes, *Belle Vue*; R. Nicholls, *The Belle Vue Story*.
36 See for instance: Preston Brothers, 16 July 1935: *The Pageant of British Sea Power. Submarines, Destroyers, Dreadnoughts ...*, NWFA Film no. 1892D (b/w, silent, 14 min. 6 sec.).
37 See Chapter 3.
38 'Professor Gumm Boyle', 'A new invention'.
39 Cine Smith, 'Putting the car on the screen',
40 (Anon.), 'Mr Never hits back'.

41 D. Russell, *Looking North*.
42 Norris Nicholson, 'Framing the view'.
43 G. A. Atkinson, 'Introduction', in Lovell Burgess, *A Popular Account*.
44 Lovell Burgess, *A Popular Account*, p. 66.
45 G. H. Sewell, 'Rambling with a cine-camera'.
46 George Higginson, 1931: *Derbyshire*, NWFA Film no. 2770 (b/w, silent, 2 min. 53 sec.).
47 William Wynne, 1953: *Wynne Scottish Holiday*, NWFA Film no. 3759 (b/w, silent, 11 min. 48 sec.).
48 Leonard F Behrens, 1925: [*Sandsend, 1st–6th June 1925*], NWFA Film no. 2081 (b/w, silent, 2 min. 45 sec.); See also M. Tebbutt, 'Rambling and manly identity'.
49 C. Langhamer, *Women's Leisure*, p. 77.
50 Ernest W. Hart, 194–43: [*Climbing and Photography in Wales*], NWFA Film no. 4416 (b/w, silent, 14 min. 40 sec.).
51 Gidlow School Cine Club, 1945: *The Torch on Helvellyn*, NWFA Film no. 909 (b/w, silent, 11 min. 36 sec.); *1945: *Rope*, NWFA Film no. 910 (b/w, silent, 17 min. 23 sec.).
52 A. Marr, *A History of Modern Britain*, p. 86.
53 *Ibid.*, p. 176.
54 Philip Taylor, 1963: [*School Holiday to Austria*], NWFA Film no. 3022 (colour, silent, c.18 min. 0 sec.); Mr R. G. Wilkinson, 1966: *Milnrow Community Centre Day Out, July 12th 1966*, NWFA Film no. 1529 (b/w, silent, 11 min. 8 sec.). See also P. Merriman, 'Driving places'.
55 Ralph Brookes made c. 95 films between the later 1950s and 1974.
56 Marr, *A History of Modern Britain*, pp. 85–9; D. Sandbrook, *Never Had It So Good*, p. 517.
57 P. Hennessy, *Having It So Good*, p. 225.; Sandbrook, *Never Had It So Good*, pp. 308–9.
58 See for example, Hubert Weiner, 1964: *Our Wedding*, NWFA Film no. 4163 (colour, silent, 35 min. 43 sec.); 1966: [*Rosh Hashana; David Weiner*], NWFA Film no. 4175 (colour , silent, 4 min. 13 sec.); 1972: *Judith and Bernard's Wedding*, NWFA Film no. 4169 (colour, silent, 3 min. 55 sec.) *1975: [*Farewell To Lois*], NWFA Film no. 4170 (colour, silent, 4 min. 26 sec.).
59 See, for example, Dr Hira L. Kapur, 1975 [*Bombay and Richmond Park*], NWFA Film no. 6746 (colour, silent, 3 min. 35 sec.); 1976 [*Christmas Morning*], NWFA Film no. 6655 (colour, silent, 3 min. 36 sec); *1975/8 [*India – Rajasthan*], NWFA Film no. 6652 (colour, sound, 19 min. 24 sec.); 1978 [*India – Punjab, Delhi and Rajasthan*], NWFA Film no. 6653 (colour, sound, 28 min. 20 sec.).
60 A. Rabinbach, *The Human Motor*, p. 274; see also Norris Nicholson, 'Framing the view', pp. 96–9.
61 H. Norris Nicholson, *Screening Culture*, pp. 93–9.
62 P. Brendon, *Thomas Cook*.
63 Sandbrook, *Never Had It So Good*, pp. 143–4, p. 441.
64 *Ibid.*, pp. 383–7; Hennessy, *Having It So Good*, pp. 534–5.
65 John Barker Scarr, 1935: *Mediterranean Cruise Arandora Star 1935 [2]*, NWFA Film

no. 3809 (b/w and colour, silent, 13 min. 36 sec.).
66 Institute of Amateur Cinematographers (IAC), *International Itinerary and Amateur Cinematographers' Year Book and Guide*, p. 35; See also *Amateur Cine World Diary*, 1941, compiled by Gordon S. Malthouse. 'Cinematography in Wartime' detailed reminders about where not to film and reported from the War Office that 'generally there is no ban upon the carriage of cameras in public places by persons other than enemy aliens who would need a permit for this purpose' (p. 32).
67 H. Norris Nicholson, 'Journeys into seeing'.
68 H. Norris Nicholson 'Shooting the Mediterranean'.
69 Sir Geoffrey Haworth, 1960: *USSR, May 1960*, NWFA Film no. 1575 (colour, silent, 27 min. 0 sec.); H. Norris Nicholson, 'Amateur filmmaking and Cold War tourism' (in progress).
70 Leonard F. Behrens, 1928: [*Société Nations I*], NWFA Film no. 2190 (b/w, silent, 0 min. 54 sec.). See also *Papers of Sir Leonard Frederick Behrens* (1890–1978), www.library.manchester.ac.uk/searchresources/guidetospecialcollections/atoz/behrensleonarpapers/, accessed on 8 February 2012.
71 See note 67.
72 See Norris Nicholson, 'Framing the view', pp. 109–11.
73 Alison Godlee, Correspondence with the author, 2 August 2002.
74 D. Wahrman, *Imagining the Middle Class*, p. xxvii; see also B. Harrison, *Peaceable Kingdom*, p. 241.
75 A. D. Hobson, 'How to make a travel film'.
76 H. Norris Nicholson, 'Telling travellers' tales'.
77 H. Norris Nicholson, 'Through the Balkan States'.
78 Norris Nicholson, 'Framing the view'.
79 John Hindley, 1927–28: *Go East Young Man, Parts I–VI*, NWFA. film nos 3638–3643.
80 Norris Nicholson, 'Framing the view', pp. 107–8.
81 Norris Nicholson,' Floating hotels', p. 49; 'Old world traditions … and modernity'.
82 Norris Nicholson,' Floating hotels', pp. 51–6.
83 V. Cutter, *Go East Young Man*.
84 John Hindley, 1927: [*Go East Young Man Pt. 3: New Zealand*], NWFA Film no. 3640 (b/w, silent, 10 min. 34 sec.).
85 See also 'Foreword' by Michael Grey, in Cutter, *Go East Young Man*, pp. 9–10.
86 Cutter, *Go East Young Man*, pp. 13–21.
87 Norris Nicholson, 'At home and abroad with cine enthusiasts'.
88 Norris Nicholson,'Old world traditions … and modernity'.
89 Norris Nicholson, 'Floating hotels', pp. 51–62.
90 Norris Nicholson, 'At home and abroad'; 'British holiday films of the Mediterranean'.
91 During *Movie Maker*'s second fifteen-day Mediterranean cruise, co-organised with Fountain Press and accompanied by key writers on amateur film, there were screenings of the '1969 Ten Best' and the editor's films as well as discussions on technical issues. The Maltese Amateur Cine Club met cruise members by cars and hosted a film screening during their time ashore. Source: T. Rose, 'A movie holiday to remember', p. 32.

92 Preston Brothers, 1928: *Royal Mail Line Cruise. M.V. Asturias (22500 tonnes) to Spain, Madeira and the Canaries*, NWFA film no. 1964D (b/w, silent, 15 min. 53 sec.).
93 See also notes 87 and 70.
94 R. Spillman, 'Holiday cruise'.
95 See for instance, footage of Casablanca that includes sequences of a young snake-charmer, local children and camels amidst more general views of mosques, markets and street scenes in Dr John Barker Scarr, 1931: [*Casablanca and Shipboard Scenes*], NWFA Film no.3800 (b/w, silent, 14 min. 57 sec.).
96 Norris Nicholson, 'Through the Balkan states'.
97 Preston Brothers, 1933: *Palma & Mallorca*, NWFA film no. 1985D (b/w, silent, 15 min. 39 sec.).
98 Dr John Barker Scarr, 1934: *Mediterranean Cruise SS Arandora Star May 1934 [1]*, NWFA Film no. 3805 (b/w, silent, 18 min. 5 sec.).
99 See note 59, Dr Hira L. Kapur, 1978.
100 George Higginson, 1925: [*Higginson Family – Holiday to Switzerland*], NWFA Film no. 2773 (b/w, silent, 7 min. 36 sec.); 1925: [*Sylvia Higginson*], NWFA Film no. 2775 (b/w, silent, 12 min. 34 sec.); Leonard F Behrens, 1926: [*Holiday in Italy; Sept./Oct. 1926*], NWFA Film no. 2091 (b/w, silent, 5 min. 45 sec.).
101 Arthur Riley 1934–5: [*On the Rhine*], NWFA Film no. 3272 (b/w and colour, silent, 11 min. 28 sec.); 1934–39: *Ideal Hotel Blankenberghe Our Host and His Daughter*, NWFA Film no. 3271 (b/w and colour, silent, 17 min. 48 sec); 1935: *July 1935 The Tour to Belgium and Holland leaving Dover*, NWFA Film no. 3265 (b/w and colour, silent, 15 min. 40 sec); George Higginson, 1937: *On Holiday in Germany and Switzerland*, NWFA Film no. 2784 (b/w, silent, 28 min. 57 sec.); Dr John Barker Scarr, 1937: *Touring Europe by Car June 1937 [1]*, NWFA Film no. 3810 (b/w and colour, silent, 15 min. 30 sec.).
102 See note 101 (George Higginson, 1937); see also Part Two of a 42-minute 16mm travelogue about western Europe, made by Lucy Fairbank, 1934: *Munich to Innsbruck*, YFA Cat. no. 3405 (b/w, silent, 16 min.).
103 Preston Brothers, 1932: *Peninsular and Orient Steam Navigation Co. Mediterranean Cruise 28 May 1932*, NWFA Film no. 1943D (b/w, silent, 13 min. 7 sec.).
104 See note 98.
105 Walter Holden, 1956: [*Spanish Holiday*], NWFA Film no. 6148 (colour, silent, 41 min. 11 sec.). Other Spanish-related material held at the NWFA features in 'Cine-cameras in and away from the classroom'. 1950s and 1960s footage shot in Spain was associated with the making of 'Packaged Holiday', *Nation on Screen* (2006). For earlier filming at the Spanish border with Gibraltar see Dr John Barker Scarr, 1933: *Mediterranean Cruise; SS Arandora Star May 1933 [1]*, NWFA Film no. 3802 (b/w, silent, 14 min. 13 sec.).
106 L. Dankworth, 'Performing paradise'.
107 Norris Nicholson, 'Journeys into seeing'. See also note 69.
108 For other amateur filmmakers' positive experiences of filming in Soviet Russia, see A. Reid, 'Exploring the magic of places', and J. Wright, 'Travellers' tale'.
109 Norris Nicholson, 'Framing the view', pp. 103–15; see also 'Cultural relations

and comfortable curiosity'.
110 Walter Holden, 1958: *Moscow by Motorcoach*, NWFA Film no. 6146 (colour, silent, 57 min. 25 sec.).
111 D. P. Koenker, 'Travel to work, travel to play'; A. E. Gorsuch and D. P. Koenker (eds), *TURIZM*.
112 H. Hopkins, *The New Look*, p. 461.
113 A. Sampson, *Who Runs This Place?*, p. 575.
114 J. H. Haffner *1948/50–52: *2400 Miles Continental Journey / The Car 'Mayflower'*, NWFA Film no. 670 (colour, silent, 28 min. 32 sec.); Doug Rendell, 1950: [*Paris 1950*], NWFA Film no. 4127 (b/w, silent, 12 min. 18 sec.); George Eastham, 1954: [*Eastham Touring Holiday in Belgium, Germany and Holland*], NWFA Film no. 4215 (colour, silent, 9 min. 0 sec.).
115 Dr John Barker Scarr, 1955: *A Continental Holiday July 1955*, NWFA Film no. 3796 (colour, silent, 18 min. 30 sec.) ; Walter Holden, 1955: [*European Road Tour*], NWFA Film no. 6144 (colour, silent, 10 min. 48 sec.).
116 Family Collection, 1963: [*In America with the English Speaking Union*], NWFA Film no. 4283 (colour, sound, 22 min.23 sec.).
117 Sir Geoffrey Haworth, 1965: [*Mongolia Aug. Sep. 1965 Part 2*], NWFA Film no. 1570 (colour, silent, 17 min. 18 sec.).
118 Sir Geoffrey Haworth, 1969: [*Ethiopia November 1969 Part 1*], NWFA Film no. 1556 (colour, silent, 17 min. 33 sec.).
119 The Hugh Hesson Collection including, c.1960s: [*Hesson Family Celebrations and Holidays Abroad*], NWFA Film no. 1436 (colour, silent, 35 min. 0 sec.); *1963–64/67–68: [*The Hesson Family on Holiday in Australia*], NWFA Film no. 1437 (colour, silent, 30 min. 0 sec.); *1966 [*The Hesson Family Holiday on Board a Cruise Ship*], NWFA Film no. 1438 (colour, silent, 35 min. 0 sec.).
120 See note 116.
121 Jack Wells, *1954/58: *Sunny Morocco*, NWFA Film no. 4472 (colour, sound, 18 min. 35 sec.).
122 Interview with Mavis Griffiths in *A Tale of Two Black Families* (1973), BBC Collection, NWFA Film B89/1.
123 M. Gough, 'The movie making career of Linda and Michael Gough', email communication with author, 14 August 2007.
124 M. Gough, 'A double take in Torremolinos', 18–19; Correspondence with the author, June–August 2007, including unpublished article, M. Gough, 'The movie-making career of Linda and Michael Gough', 4 pp.
125 M. Gough, *Michael Gough's Hawaiian Production Diary*, www.fvi.org.uk/training/gough/hawaii01.html, accessed 15 June 2009).
126 See Lucy Fairbank Collection, YFA Cat. nos 126, 3405, 3407–13, 3466 and above, note 102; See also Leonora Bichard Collection, NWFA film nos 4031– 4044.
127 Leonora Bichard, 1930s: [*War Memorials*], NWFA Film no. 4037 (b/w, silent, 1 min. 4 sec.); 1930s: [*War Relics*], NWFA Film no. 4041 (b/w, silent, 1 min. 5 sec.); 1930s: [*War Memorial And Trenches*], NWFA Film no. 4042 (b/w, silent, 1 min. 3 sec.); 1930s: [*Cathedral Ruins*], NWFA Film no. 4043 (b/w, silent, 1 min. 5 sec.); see also Lucy Fairbank Collection, YFA.

128 According to Sandbrook, Ian Fleming borrowed the enthusiastic prose of travelogues and tourism brochures in his evocations of settings and journeys, as part of locating his narratives and characters in postwar modernity and consumer society. Source: Sandbrook, *Never Had It So Good*, pp. 618–19.
129 See also consideration of filmmaking as a form of closure for First World War veterans in Norris Nicholson, 'Sites of meaning'.

8

Socially engaged filmmaking

'How strange so many Amateur movies still seem to reflect yesterday's world … [and] … thoroughly old-fashioned in a world bristling with social problems and fractured values where nobody is sure of anything and many people are desperately searching for some answers.'[1] Ivan Watson regularly linked Britain's amateur cinema movement to broader social issues. This outburst attacked readers 'who would prefer to live in a cosy little world where people don't get blown to bits, where no anthropoid disguised as a human ever maims a child, where married people are never clotted together in helpless misery, where doctors don't dispense 200,000,000 tranquillizers a year, where no sick and depraved people are roaming the streets at night'. Such criticisms spiced up the hobby press and prompted lively exchanges between readers willing and able to engage in such debates. Such polemics linked publications and possibly boosted sales too. Watson's remarks aptly described much amateur activity, but it would be unfair to overlook those films that did explore contemporary society.

Watson's wake-up call for more socially engaged filmmaking was not new.[2] Since the mid-1920s, some filmmakers had tackled topical concerns in factual and fictional forms. Social issues changed over time, as did how filmmakers approached particular topics. Perspectives differed too as cine use gained wider usage beyond its early adherents. Filming the observable world reflected available opportunities, so regional variations occurred. For all that it never made more than a modest contribution to overall output, sufficient evidence exists to justify an exploration of socially committed amateur activities as a vibrant minor strand of filmmaking that persisted far beyond the years of this survey.

Films about specific topics form only one kind of amateur societal comment. Visual comment occurred in footage that was ostensibly about something else. Family films thus disclose the micro-politics of power, status and authority.

Ideologies of race, gender and status abound even as cheaper cine-cameras were redefining who had the right to film. Social issues occurred in fiction too, particularly in cine club and productions. This chapter considers amateur material that exemplifies socially concerned reportage and how, as amateur practice occurred within specific cultural and social settings, even unintentional details might have visual significance. Such visual asides within family, holiday or local narratives, featuring election posters, demonstrators' banners, empty wharves during a strike or scenes of unemployed people, point to the sensibilities of time and place captured in personal footage.

Alongside films concerned with public rather than private concerns, this chapter links imagery to contemporary opinion and public mood evidenced by the hobby press. Listed amateur film shows to raise funds or entertain in prisons, hospitals, care homes and other needy settings broaden our sense of audiences beyond domestic, educational and cine club circles.[3] Printed comment also permits discussion of other forms of welfare, charity and social responsibility found elsewhere in the amateur repertoire. Collectively, the material emphasises the impulse to address social concerns in and away from cine club settings.

Picturing people

As the first amateur generation grew up, cinema exhibitors attracted audiences by showing films involving human interest, and actual or fictive acts of mercy. Two Mitchell & Kenyon films made and shown in the North West, for example, distilled military action, heroism and compassion into brief melodramas involving Red Cross nurses on the front line during the South African (so-called Boer) Wars.[4] Charity events featured in prewar topicals, and cinemas thrived on screening local footage that included unemployment marches and a civic health week amid the cycle of carnivals, parades, outings and other annual events.[5] Amateurs readily copied this eclecticism as they produced their own pioneering versions of local-interest films.

Writers in the embryonic hobby press promoted the social value of 'purposeful filming' as an alternative to making fictional film plays. George Sewell (see Chapter 3) promoted such interests too, having already made 35mm films for the RSPCA.[6] A decade later, Basil Wright (1907–87), whose career in documentary film began with Grierson spotting his amateur work, championed non-professional filmmakers: '[for] most of us in the documentary movement, they represent a potential source of social and civic value'.[7]

His opinion was not unique. 'The splendid pioneer work of Mr John Grierson is evidently influencing the amateur field and building up future documentary producers' declared a correspondent to *ACW*.[8] Acknowledgement of the blurred distinction between realism and fiction that often permeated many documentaries came only later.

As amateur activity organised during the 1930s and attracted the attention of Korda, Rotha, Grierson and others whose names became synonymous with Britian's documentary film movement, early enthusiasts were urged to record the world around them. They made films for varied religious, educational, civic, promotional, commemorative, humanitarian, work-related and other personal reasons. Much footage was tinged with the prevailing influence of a distinctively genteel and patronising English form of middle class liberalism and social consciousness, as found in writings by Christopher Isherwood, Stephen Spender and George Orwell. Such sentiments may be detected in advice offered to amateurs too. Buchanan's tips for 'creating human stories which really matter' included filming in hospitals and on themes of unemployment, housing and rearmament.[9] Brunel's appeal for 'fresh ground' likewise urged amateurs to tackle '*any* of the burning topics of the moment', including religious issues and war: 'Give us ordinary people, people we can be interested in and sympathise with ... something that will move us and leave a lasting impression.'[10] While it would be misleading to overstate the level of association between Britain's intellectuals, interwar documentary filmmakers and amateurs, the hobby press suggests that cine use should be viewed as an integral component of broader cinematic developments during these formative decades. Certainly, parallels existed between the widening amateur search for suitable non-fictional film topics and the breadth of films on documentary and educational themes as well as, in the words of Rachael Low, 'comment and persuasion'.[11]

Health and hospitals

Britain's prewar health system, based on a combination of voluntary-funded and newer municipal hospitals, many of the latter replacing earlier workhouses, offered accessible urban subject matter across the North West. While fundraising events attracted filmmakers' attentions, local authorities' growing involvement with hospitals meant the development of modern new facilities and public medicine. Even as the region's cotton and associated industries declined, investment in medical provision continued, not just in the specialisms of cancer and tuberculosis for which Manchester and adjacent areas were already known, but also in areas of mental health, orthopaedics and maternity care.[12] As discussions on health and welfare reform intensified, so did the use of film in medical research and training. Not surprisingly, amateur films date from these years. In 1933, for example, the twin brothers Harold and Sidney Preston made several films to promote their local hospital, Stockport Infirmary.[13] Interior and exterior shots detail wards, the operating theatre and close-up scenes of various patients receiving treatment. Their family status and father's former role as town mayor gave them freedom to film in the recently opened Sykes ward, as children wearing underwear and goggles, receive 'Sunlight Treatment' from portable X-ray equipment in the Violet Ray Department.[14] Other scenes include a nurse setting a girl's broken wrist, a young child having physiotherapy treatment and work in the laundry room and kitchens. Their shots of schoolchildren collecting and packing hens' eggs from around Stockport also record local fund-raising for interwar public health provision.[15]

Other amateurs, including doctors and dentists, filmed family members or friends during a hospital stay. Such scenes detail routine practices, nursing provision and medical arrangements for male and female patients, and other specialist groups as seen at a children's orthopaedic hospital.[16] A portrait of disability provision filmed at the Sir Robert Jones Memorial Workshop for Cripples in Liverpool probably served as promotional material as it ends with a plea to support 'this important and humane work'.[17] Its close-ups of medical care, therapy and rehabilitation, as well as different practical training opportunities for adults and adolescents, illustrate contemporary good practice, and contribute to the visual history of disability care.[18] Footage depicts people with varied physical needs taking part in gendered recreational and handicraft activities and at mealtimes in a highly structured charitable setting. Disabled young people with mobility and co-ordination needs are seen concentrating on bookbinding, leatherwork and needlework in contrast to camera-conscious shots of nurses and guests. Elsewhere, a dedication ceremony at Manchester's Duchess of York Hospital for Babies gently signals unexpected humour with its edited opening credit sequence.[19] Nurses stand stiffly for visitors before scattering back to their demanding charges in the rows of identical iron-framed cots arranged outside while photographers scramble to reposition tripods amidst mingling guests. The filmmaker's more continuous gaze captures 'behind the scenes' informality in between more official poses that brim with decorum and graciousness.

Amateur hospital films were made even as institutions began to make their own films for teaching and fund-raising purposes. Distinctions between interwar amateur and professionally produced material are not always obvious from either quality or credits, as a cine-using staff-member or trustee sometimes used an institution's name. Subject matter may offer clues, particularly where filming reveals specialist activities or alternatively where the level of informality and self-assurance between staff and patients suggests the presence of an insider rather than an outside professional. Footage that combined a royal visit and a Christmas party with more formal sequences recording an X-ray room, pathology laboratory, operating theatre and dispensary at the Royal Oldham Hospital has the hallmarks of an informed amateur 'insider', as does the film of patients taking part in different novelty races and competitions including a pillow fight whilst balancing on a greasy pole, shot at Deva Mental Hospital.[20]

Amateur club productions sometimes combined members' interest by using role-play within a naturalistic, issue-based setting.[21] One such collaboration, tackled by members of the Leigh Literary Society Cine Section, on behalf of the local Medical Health Officer, resulted in a technocratic portrayal of maternity care provision.[22] Successive indoor and exterior shots portray local services at The Firs, Leigh's central maternity unit, and local health team members outside their respective outpost clinics. Camerawork details the delivery room, premature infant and postnatal care facilities including breast-feeding and bottle-feeding, and a noisy nursery. Well-lit shots show nurses and the supervising matron in clinical and office settings and support staff in the laundry, kitchens and a sterilisation room. Even the midwife who cycles to a home delivery and returns smiling many hours later exemplifies dedication and efficiency. In contrast, a panic-stricken husband dashes from his house to a phone box to call for help. Other scenes show reunited parents with newborn infants proudly leaving the maternity home. Notwithstanding its dramatic shortcomings, the footage clearly illustrates prewar regional maternal and neo-natal infant care.

More sophisticated role-play within hospital settings occurred in the early postwar period, anticipating the popular appeal of hospital-based television dramas. By the early 1950s, recruitment films for nurses from both home and overseas emanated from both professional and amateur sources for British and colonial consumption.[23] One award-winning nursing story, featured in *ACW*'s Ten Best competition in 1949, was used subsequently by the Central Office for Information for national recruitment.[24] Huddersfield Cine Society soon produced its own amusing local version to illustrate staffing needs within the newly formed National Health Service.[25] *Service Partners* portrays hospital care and staff working in a locality where pending international migration had yet to make any visible impact. Indeed, racial concerns had no place in a filming location where, according to cine club historians, the presiding matron disapproved of the plot involving a romance developing between a young student nurse and the police constable who accompanied an accident victim into hospital. The overall support offered by the local ambulance service, police and medical staff demonstrates how amateur activity attracted respect and interest. Using actual locations now endows such club productions with historical significance even if their dramatic merit and social vision is slight. Sam Hanna's later recruitment film was similarly reliant upon local hospital co-operation. He combined role-play and documentary styles to trace a young woman's journey from spotting a local advertisement to qualifying as a nurse. Shot in colour and including local-interest footage as well as details of training, ward duties and medical practice, Hanna's material also gives visibility to the overseas recruitment of health workers that was so vital to the NHS's expansion.[26]

The national shortage of blood donors provided another early postwar opportunity for an amateur production that received support from local hospitals, the Red Cross and St John's Ambulance service. When George Monro, Liverpool's then regional organiser for the National Blood Transfusion Service (NBTS) approached Ashby Ball in 1951 to discuss making a sponsored 16mm film, Southport Movie Makers (then known as St James Film Unit) began a long commitment to producing documentaries.[27] Locally shot material, Monro believed, would have greater regional impact than a professional production, shot on 35mm and available from headquarters. Accordingly, Ball and a group of student friends, embarked upon a seven-month project. The message and plot of *Calling to You* were direct and developed in consultation with the NBTS. A young factory worker's indifference to an appeal for donors was overcome by meeting an older employee whose own life-saving blood transfusion, depicted via flashback, radically changed his attitudes.

Technically complex, the filming required high-quality indoor lighting suitable for convincing close-up shots. The blood transfusion sequence was shot on a well-lit set built in the local church hall but location shots in factories, streets and hospital settings used improvised lighting rigs. The local police stopped an interview with a long-service blood donor in a local park as filming for public use contravened a local bylaw. Inventiveness resolved other obstacles, so instrument and tea trolleys became dollies for interior-tracking shots, and a tripod on a van roof recorded outdoor scenes. Highlight exposure and filters offset the bright glare of white uniforms, gowns, overalls, bedcovers and towels and the cast included factory workers, medical staff and Red Cross volunteers. The production was well received by its sponsors and became one of *ACW*'s Ten Best in 1951.[28]

The film's success attracted extra further funding to add sound on optical tape, achieved with the help of the National Film Agency in Manchester, and soon afterwards, another commission from the NBTS's regional office. The resultant educational film on pioneering methods of post-natal transfusions was used in and beyond Britain. Medical interest returned with a film on pharmacy as a career in the late 1960s and the group's sustained reputation for high-quality productions prompted successive commissions. The local authority, Southport Corporation, requested publicity films that ranged from flower shows, mayoral inaugurations and royal visits to countryside protection.[29]

Aspects of medical provision, welfare and charity attracted amateur interest through the 1960s, although compelling details of contemporary practices, occurrences and attitudes sometimes simply crept into other scenes. Memorial services that combine personal and collective acts of remembrance feature the dismembered and injured veterans along with the absent re-membered. A uniformed woman unobtrusively fastens a good luck horseshoe on to a vehicle door amidst more formal proceedings as two new ambulances are donated to the Red Cross and St John's Ambulance Brigade.[30] Scenes of a grandchild with physical disabilities deriving from the thalidomide drug likewise mesh individual tragedy and wider societal experiences.[31] Colin Harding's *Where the Money Goes*, a student production detailing how Rag Week fund-raising supported a range of charities for needy people across the region, details post-natal clinics and residential children's homes. For decades, dispassionate recording of routine physical medical checks in nurseries, schools, hospitals, workplaces and relief centres captured compliant and almost stationary subject matter in the cine-camera's objectifying gaze as human interest for lay and specialist audiences. Although produced in mid-century Britain for charitable or educational purposes, these films often still normalised invasive acts of physical or behavioural scrutiny. They are reminders of how film extended earlier visual practices of building racial and ethnic taxonomies that still persisted in mainland Europe and colonial settings at the same period. Their unblinking gaze upon prevailing practice, nevertheless, offers invaluable insights to today's medical historian.

The medical interests of early cine users sometimes extended beyond Britain. For instance, Dr Horace Wilfred Taylor, from Bolton, filmed *Tour in the*

USSR while travelling with his grandfather in an organised group from the Manchester region to Soviet Russia in 1932.[32] His still photography and cine footage at clinics and hospitals reflect the official expectation that visitors should encounter 'creches, maternity homes and their Park[s] of Rest and Culture' along with other such sanctioned venues as state-run theatres, prisons, courts, construction sites and factories.[33] His subjects range from patients in landscaped sanatorium gardens overlooking the Black Sea to scenes of severe urban and rural material impoverishment and poor physical health. Taylor's imagery thus provides a striking visual record of conditions under Stalin. Three decades later, an informed outsider's objectivity again details health needs elsewhere when a young girl receives impromptu dental treatment during a filmed Himalayan expedition to mark the golden jubilee of the Manchester Rucksack Club.[34] Relief work in Catalonia was filmed by Cuthbert Wigham for fund-raising and educational purposes on behalf of the Society of Friends during the Spanish Civil War.[35] His informal gaze notes young medical volunteers relaxing off-duty amidst other scenes of displaced peoples, aid distribution and the transport convoys moving refugees from front-line hostilities. These images are stark reminders of how amateur films, as precursors to mobile phone technologies, communicated important visual information in many contrasting contexts.

Controversial content

The specialist press did not sanction every foray into needy or awareness-raising contexts. Alcoholism rarely provoked as much critical comment as in 1960 when *ACW* featured *A mouche que veux-tu* under the caption, 'Prize-winner but too horrific to be shown'.[36] This entry to an international film festival portrayed how an alcoholic waged war on flies, and sought to torture them before falling 'victim to the nightmares of his own deranged mind' with fatal consequences. Its description as 'revolting but enthralling' contrasted with *ACW*'s more customary caution although less severe critical judgement was not infrequent. One month earlier, two very different films about cerebral palsy had received severe rebukes for their portrayal of residential and community care for physically disabled young people and adults.[37] *A Helping Hand*, made in monochrome with sound by members of Carlisle and Border Cine Club, was considered clumsy in its sincerely meant but inappropriate references to 'poor little spastic hands' while praise for the 'much happier impression' offered in another colour film with subtitles was accompanied with a warning about over-sentimentality.[38]

Disability provision for older and younger people features in filmed excursions, social events and regular activities across the region during the 1950s and early 1960s.[39] Standard shots of out-patient care show swollen shuffling legs, passive expressions, lolling heads and unaccompanied parked wheelchair users waiting or watching entertainers.[40] A display of crafted soft toys with jolly faces, extrovert comic performers and the expectant expressions of pensioners as they receive civic Christmas hampers contrast with the passivity elsewhere. Apart from an occasional smile and affectionate greeting, these scenes lack the sense of autonomy that exudes from beaming faces filmed during a disabled people's excursion filmed a few years later.[41] The footage unwittingly denotes shifts in societal attitudes towards disability and geriatric care that, although important, often remain inadequate forty years on.

Amateur material points to changing sensibilities towards the vulnerable and disadvantaged. At the Glasgow Amateur Film Festival of 1939, *Man of the Road* provoked a controversial response, after its denunciation by one of the judges, the documentary filmmaker Alberto Cavalcanti.[42] Its producer, John Martin, an established filmmaker at Stoke and Leek Cine Clubs, cast another member as a tramp, after having 'toyed with the idea of a real one … [who] failed to show up [for filming]'. Cavalcanti maintained that the film was 'entirely thoughtless and irresponsible'. In his view it was an insult to 'human dignity' and treated vagrancy with insensitivity.[43] The decision to close workhouses, combined with unemployment and housing shortage, had become a pressing social issue by the late 1930s. 'The degraded classes' were not, in Cavalcanti's view, 'a fit subject for humour' but Martin defended the film's conception and production, stating that his research included talking with staff at the local workhouse and with homeless people.[44] Editorial comment fuelled the ensuing debate over how to assess a film's success and balance ethics about content over technical and creative quality. How to choose appropriate suitable subject matter and handle material in realistic and non-realistic forms were questioned too. Within months, issues of destitution and homelessness acquired a new national significance and the matter sank without a trace as filmmakers and their concerns adapted their interests to wartime conditions.

Ten years later, Charles Chislett produced *St George's Crypt*, a fund-raising piece to support a major Leeds church.[45] Its persuasive tale of spiritual and material renewal documented the church's provision for homeless people as part of its urban ministry and community outreach. Camerawork in black and white focused on one individual as he arrived, received practical assistance, prayed and left after dressing in a fresh set of clothes, metaphorically and visibly a new man. Chislett made numerous films that the Church Pastoral Aid Society used for years in training, fund-raising and educational contexts.[46] Christian beliefs informed how he filmed, titled, re-edited and devised spoken scripts for productions about early postwar social and urban experience. *St George's Crypt* has well-composed and often striking imagery shot within and outside the church, and is a fine example of an amateur passion for cinematography used to support personal convictions.

In contrast, *Cotton-eyed Joe*, an award-winning film in the 1973 Ten Best competition, reflected a younger generation's engagement with issues of inequality and lifestyle compounded with race.[47] Sensitively filming in and around Joe's improvised packing-case home in a tucked-away spot outside Los Angeles, John McDonald relied on developing mutual trust, understanding and insight over time. His glimpses into a day in Joe's life, plus the racially motivated attack that ultimately wrecked his hideaway, attracted as much social and political comment within cine circles as did the technical finesse that underlay the use of monochrome and colour in his camerawork, editing and soundtrack of recorded and original music mixed with downtown city sounds. At subsequent screenings, interpretations were varied but McDonald preferred a more open-ended response: 'I can never say what my exact intentions were in making the film because I honestly don't know.'[48]

Some of his contemporaries were more polemical, as shown by two prolific young enthusiasts, John Gresty and Mike Goodger, whose respective professional and amateur filmmaking interests inspired collaborative projects for over a decade.[49] Cine-photo, a production company set up by John Gresty's father in the mid-1940s, occupied premises close to the University of Salford by the later 1960s.[50] It was ideally placed for Goodger, then working as a lecturer, while completing his PhD. He established links that were to underpin his own ambitious films and later student projects on local social issues including elderly people's care and quality of life, traffic congestion and modernity, and in particular urban housing.[51]

For years, local authority responses to urban housing needs had prompted slum clearance programmes that periodically caught amateurs' attention across the North West. While numerous details exist within the annual compilations of domestic and holiday scenes made for family film shows, some filmmakers documented the process of demolition and rehousing more systematically for other audiences. Time has given such records of urban transformation and social relocation significance, especially where there have been further attempts at rehabilitation and renewal. Prewar footage from Preston records how residents vacate their home and load their possessions into a horse-drawn cart for fumigation and subsequent rehousing. This stark record then shows masked inspectors and workmen as they release poison gas through the condemned terraced dwelling.[52] Scenes from later urban clearances offer equally forthright records of relocation and prevailing attitudes towards social housing. Goodger and John Gresty junior, therefore, were working in a clearly defined realm of amateur social realism when they documented urban demolition in Manchester and Salford.

Goodger filmed the effects of local urban redevelopment, less than a year after *Cathy Come Home* was shown on BBC1.[53] Although that programme became part of broadening concern to expose the underbelly of social concerns that accompanied the so-called 'swinging sixties',[54] Goodger recalls that he was motivated more by a 'strong sense of disappearing history'.[55] He wished to record the fast 'changing face of Salford's housing'. He later wrote, 'Somewhat in a pioneering spirit, I took a simple 16mm camera into the slums of Salford with the original intention of supplementing the visual material I already used in my lectures on urban renewal. But I gradually became aware of the need to do a lot more than merely return with footage of slum houses.'[56] Goodger had made two short films previously, but over the next four years *The Changing Face of Salford* became an ambitious record of urban renewal and social change. *Part One: Life in the Slums* portrayed people just before and during demolition and as relocations took place. *Part Two: Bloody Slums* charted the area's growth and decline and local authority decisions to clear 'unfit dwellings' and depicted how individual homes were vacated and demolished to make way for redevelopment (Figure 8).

Making the films prompted considerable comment, and so did their screening. *The Changing Face of Salford* soon became more than subject matter for student seminars. Controversies generated local headlines and prompted a special screening for a House of Commons Select committee on housing.[57] Yet, retrospectively, the footage seems less didactic than how it was perceived at the time. Now its thoughtful engagement both with the locality and with current planning ideologies offers a visual conversation – a learning piece – in which Goodger explores ambiguities within planning decisions and establishment views on slum clearance and rehousing. Although he was an outsider, in terms of class, occupation and background, the footage remains sensitive to the complexities of belonging and sense of place. Despite his own later self-doubts about how he filmed covertly, Goodger's footage illustrate how having a home, friendship and valued familiar surroundings co-existed with material

The Changing Face of Salford. Part One, Life in the Slums (Dir. Michael Goodger, 1968–69). Still supplied by courtesy of Michael Goodger and North West Film Archive at Manchester Metropolitan University, Film no. 430 (colour, sound, 32 min. 0 sec.).

impoverishment and physical discomfort. His camera shots, use of voice-over, edited local opinion and a commissioned musical score situate his amateur material within recognisable film aesthetics and stylistic forms.

Goodger's collaboration with Gresty enabled students to make a series of short films on social concerns. Their visual playfulness in tackling issues of unemployment, traffic, river pollution, urban decay, friendship and other aspects of contemporary city living and making a statement in less than five minutes generated some well-shot vignettes of urban life in the 1970s. *Dirty Old Town*, for example, borrowed its title and soundtrack from the Salford-born folksinger, radical and poet Ewan MacColl in its focus upon a young couple among deserted docks, local canalscapes and the wastelands of partially demolished neighbourhoods.[58] Such social and visual motifs recurred in this period of working together before Gresty moved on to make promotional films for the new town of Skelmersdale and elsewhere.[59]

Risks and insecurities

Other young filmmakers across the North West turned their camera upon current concerns at different times. Like some of his contemporaries, Gresty senior made films about road and general safety for public information campaigns that responded to the rise in accidents during wartime blackout conditions.[60] Safety remained a priority as traffic levels and road-related accidents continued to soar. One forthright film opens with a funeral cortège and ends with a failed attempt at resuscitation on a canal towpath.[61] Made for Stretford's local safety committee, Gresty's semi-dramatised sequences, shots of billboards and intertitles pulled no punches: 'Dashing means danger'; 'Watch this silly boy turning right' and 'Here's a silly fellow that did not keep to the kerb'. Another film was shot at Avenham Park in Preston, where dramatic near-misses involved pushchairs, pedestrians and cyclists in collision with different motorised vehicles.[62] Lavishly staged stunt driving assumed summer spectacle status for the seated and standing onlookers, eager to find peacetime entertainment even amidst the cautionary placards and reminders of child mortality rates ('Five children die daily on the roads – warn yours') plastered along parked double-decker buses. 'Pause a second – save a life', 'Cut out that cutting in' and 'God made plenty of time. Why hurry to save it?' and other maxims are reminiscent of the painted slogans still found in more contemporary contexts of fast-rising motorised transport levels. Their instructive tones echo prevailing public campaigning and outreach using educational film at home and abroad.[63]

Amateur films on the risks of peacetime were not solely about transport or finding a stray unexploded bomb. The end of military hostilities lifted British wartime constraints on filming in sensitive locations. After the spate of amateur productions about air raid precautions, home guard training and other voluntary services, new opportunities were welcome.[64] Although National Service again required military personnel to serve overseas, including a generation that had been too young to see action during the Second World War, few enthusiasts took cine-cameras abroad and poor access to film limited their opportunities for photography.[65] In the late 1940s, amateurs avoided war-related topics and more typically concentrated on peacetime matters. So the decision to recreate a task force landing on a Pacific atoll using models and filming on Blackpool beach was unusual.[66] *Our Town* was a more introspective exploration of place and memory after someone's return from a long absence that readily connected with military service elsewhere.[67]

Emerging Cold War tensions unleashed fresh concerns about conflict and threats of annihilation that surfaced occasionally in amateur productions. Given the scale of anxiety at both domestic and international level over increasing capabilities for mass destruction by atomic, hydrogen and then nuclear means, the apparent absence of amateur attention to global insecurities might seem surprising, were it not for the preponderance of accessible and less serious domestic topics for consideration. The freedom to enjoy making films was of prime importance and, as with the box office hits of colourfully staged musicals and other forms of public entertainment, many amateurs willingly focused on more innocuous subjects. The unimaginable horrors and unprecedented scales of 'an enlarged arithmetic of death and destruction'[68] that Whitehall sought to calculate and plan for mainly in secret were real enough threats for Britain's anxious public in the early 1950s. Amateurs seemed to feel little need to venture into realms where *High Treason* (1951) and the hugely more successful *Seven Days to Noon* (1950) had already evoked, according to one reviewer for the *Daily Express*, 'all the nasty fears and terrors of the ordinary citizen'.[69] After the Second World War, recording the ordinariness of the familiar constituted a particularly satisfying and reassuring form of visual pleasure. As access to cine club archives collections widens, evidence of fictional approaches to such themes will become better known.

Nuclear proliferation

Nuclear concerns remained outside regional amateur interests until a film was produced in conjunction with Preston Borough Police as part of a civil defence exercise. It showed volunteers and emergency service co-operating in a smoothly co-ordinated rescue mission following the hypothetical explosion of a nuclear bomb in Euxton near Chorley.[70] This Lancashire example of preparedness for a nuclear catastrophe is interesting, in its echo of official civil defence perspectives.[71] Attlee had acknowledged the futility of civil defence back in 1946; atomic testing in the Pacific had prompted further Whitehall recalculations, and the publication of the Strath Report (1955) on the destructive impact of hydrogen bombs should have undermined any notions of replicating the emergency planning of the 1940s.[72] Perhaps the Euxton film illustrates how, despite the massive shift in official 'minds, measurements and imaginations',[73] there were still those who believed that nuclear warfare required only dealing with conventional bomb-induced disaster on a larger scale.

An important exception to this apparent complacency was Peter Watkins, who was no longer strictly an amateur by the time the BBC commissioned him to make *War Game*. Interestingly, *MM* ignored the ensuing controversy and broadcasting ban and emphasised Watkins's non-professional status when writing about another of his films three years later.[74] Indeed, Watkins's work reflects the fluidity between amateur and professional cinema and how, along with Ken Russell, Kevin Brownlow and others, emerging filmmakers took some of the characteristics of amateur cinema with them as they handled contentious topics and crossed into the professional sphere. More usually, amateurs seem to have avoided challenging the still widely accepted notions of civil defence based on 'protect and survive'. On the other hand, although national consciousness was yet to wake up to some of the implications of the arms race, arguably helped, according to Hennessy, by Ian Fleming's world of espionage reaching cinemagoers, Cold War politics had already confronted some regional amateur audiences.[75]

Visual opportunism within overseas travel in the Eastern Bloc, occasionally provided cine users with compelling first-hand observations. Resembling an apparently exotic detail within a foreign holiday setting, the significance

[*Ban the Bomb*] (Dir. Tony Iddon, 1964)
Still supplied by courtesy of Henry Iddon and North West Film Archive at Manchester Metropolitan University, Film no. 4396 (b/w, silent, 4 min. 11 sec.).

of such encounters for both filmmakers and their audiences is particularly hard to gauge retrospectively. Sir Geoffrey Haworth's views of Moscow's 1960 May Day parade, for example, documents state-sanctioned display of Soviet military hardware at the height of strained east–west relations.[76] He and his wife screened their startling eye-witness holiday encounter at Rotary Club meetings and other gatherings across the North West. Their colourful imagery contrasted with familiar black and white Pathé newsreel footage, preceded the BBC gaining permission to transmit live coverage of the event and illustrates how politics entered amateur film-sharing circles.[77]

Closer to home, amateurs also provided the occasional glimpse of public rallies and demonstrations that were more usually seen via newsreel and television. Tony Iddon's carefully shot record of a large well-organised anti-nuclear rally on Blackpool beach is one such example (Figure 9).[78] He was a member of Blackpool Cine Club, rather than a CND (Campaign for Nuclear Disarmament) activist.[79] His scenes of polite protest include women marshals briskly in charge of the final tidying up, and the police seem uninterested onlookers.[80] *Ban the Bomb* captures the social character of the anti-nuclear movement's appeal in the early to mid-1960s – ranks of tweed-jacketed, tie-wearing young men with pipes, middle-aged women in pleated skirts, and occasional toddlers in pushchairs waving tiny CND flags. Iddon's shots of banners and placards held aloft seem to be concerned more with their visual juxtaposition against the background frivolity of posters for seaside entertainment than with any thorough recording of platform speakers, protestors' affiliations or geographical identities. Even so, these long shots show slogans that denote a distinctive phase in both the membership and direction of the movement in the early 1960s when its avowedly single-issue focus was fracturing over concerns about class, socialism, unilateralism and notions of Britain as a still powerful world player. Despite the metaphorical significance of the 'Lost Children' sign, the cutaway shot to an entwined prostrate couple on the sand and a cloud that faintly resembles a mushroom, Iddon's interest seems to be the marchers' silhouettes shot against a hazy horizon and the hypnotic rhythms of their passing feet. Capturing a sea of billowing banners effectively against the horizon appears to be of greater interest than ensuring that their slogans – 'No Tests East or West' and 'Tomorrow may be too late' – are readable.

Two notable productions about war and catastrophe were made in the early 1970s. Arthur Smith, Alan Coulter and their friends at the Altrincham Cine Club created their own cinematic vision of an apocalyptic Britain with *And on the Eighth Day ...*, which went on to win in the Ten Best 1971 competition.[81]

Co-operation from the police, hospital authorities and general public, as well as after-hours opening at a local library and supermarket, enabled club members to make, in the words of one judge, Stanley Reed, 'a good variant on the now familiar theme of the last survivors of a holocaust'.[82] Watson, another adjudicator, felt that the plot's handling of a young man waking up in a hospital oxygen tent to find that he seems to be the only survivor of a devastating poison gas attack was 'a brave effort to put an epic into a half-pint pot' and considered the 'staging of corpse-littered streets … first class' even if he 'didn't believe a word of it'.[83] Protests, demonstrations and campaigns were becoming standard features of British public life and media news coverage as well as compelling strands within sections of popular music, theatre and commercial cinema. Yet the young scriptwriter and director Arthur Smith claimed in writing at the time that making the production was more about 'relaxing' without a hint that radicalism was part of the group's decision to make the film.[84]

Baskeyfield VC, Bill Townley's war epic, eschewed direct reference to current conflict although making and screening his film about a then unsung local hero of the Second World War took place against a background of ongoing bloody armed struggles on different continents.[85] Townley, a painter and decorator turned filmmaker, made a feature-length film on 8mm involving a young soldier from Burslem, in the Potteries, who was awarded the Victoria Cross posthumously after dying at Oosterbeeck during the Battle of Arnhem. The film was three years in the making, and Townley filmed in and around Stoke on Trent and in the rural borders between Staffordshire and Derbyshire. Like *The Forgotten Faces* (1961), Watkins's 16mm version of the Hungarian uprising, shot in Canterbury using local people, and his *Diary of an Unknown Soldier* (1959) – its significant predecessor in style, technique and career terms – Townley's film recruited soldiers from street corners and public houses.[86] Although far apart in almost every other way, both filmmakers empathised with the victims of war. Townley equipped his large cast with costumes, and military hardware, including guns and tanks, borrowed from the 16/15th Queens Royal Lancers. A local abattoir supplied blood. The production focused on the eponymous hero's pain, both physical and emotional and his death on the battlefield from a fatal injury. Tony Rose's review in *MM* acknowledged Townley's handling of human feeling as 'big and compelling'. The film's intensity derived, in Rose's view, from how he compellingly 'and without irony' portrayed the dying man's pain, weariness and frustration and, apparently, had an 'electrifying effect on the townspeople', prompting later commemoration.[87] Rose's percipient comment that 'few amateur films can have evoked such a response from their audience' was fulsome praise for a production that was also a technical achievement both in how it staged complex military manoeuvres and in its subsequent need for widescreen projection.

Screening social change

Between the later 1950s and early 1970s, amateur fictional films tackled social concerns other than disaster and war. As shown in Chapter 3, some amateurs, much to the dismay of more conventional cine-camera users, addressed issues of sexuality, violence and psychosis. They made documentaries as well as semi-dramatised and fictional films, according to their interests and abilities. Stylistic variations in handling particular issues may be set against broader shifts. In 1957, Robert Kennedy, writing in the *Daily Worker*, commented that the 'commercial industry shows little sign of encouraging' amateur filmmaking, and *Tribune* also lamented the industry's neglect of 'the wit, charm and individuality' evident in amateur productions. A decade later, Chittock wrote about older conventions of documentary filmmaking being 'toppled perhaps and making way for less of an exercise in realism'.[88] In contrast to the prewar pioneers who conceived many of their own projects within a context of sponsored documentary filmmaking, Chittock pondered whether amateurs better understood film's potential 'as a device for stimulating emotional responses'? Watkins's emerging use of handheld cameras and point of view shooting had an intensity and visual impact absent from the mainstream big screen that attracted praise also in amateur critical circles. Sydney Bernstein of Granada TV, allegedly commented that no one would believe newsreel again, in response to seeing Watkins's faked documentary style.[89] Taylor has suggested that changing postwar commercial priorities may have reduced the creative openings available to amateurs and professionals during interwar sponsored film production.[90] As seen here, it might be suggested that figures within Britain's amateur cinema movement contributed originality and perspectives into their later professional film work. Perhaps they occupy an underrecognised fringe of other experimental cinematic and cultural shifts in postwar regional Britain? After all, Free Cinema emerged from 16mm film production in semi-amateur conditions to challenge prevailing and previous screen practice. Chittock's words perhaps indeed point to how older conventions of emotional restraint still found within the ranks of middle England during the austerity and lingering interwar attitudes of early 1950s Britain were finally ebbing as part of bigger shifts in visual cultural practice.

Did television affect amateur approaches to social issues? Commentators identified that television was redefining the audience for amateur cinema, but was it influencing content and technique too?[91] Using monochrome 'as a medium in its own right with its own particular aesthetic' rather than colour to help 'mood and theme' may indicate a reawakened awareness of documentary realism due to television.[92] Chittock believed so when he wrote that 'Television is doing the telling nowadays, the reportage, the viewing of world events'. He also wondered if television's capacity to deliver reportage and actuality might reinvigorate amateur film as 'a real motivational instrument bypassing the intellectual senses altogether and leaving that job to the mass media'.[93]

In retrospect, socially engaged amateur film reflects more change than continuity, as younger cine users filmed differently and as more homes bought or rented television sets after the mid-1950s. Pendle Movie Makers staged door-to-door searches and filmed long lines of volunteers and police combing the bleak moorlands in their production *The Lonely One* (1968).[94] It seems likely that most of the filmmakers and their viewers had encountered at least some media coverage of the multiple disappearances of young people and their subsequent murders by Myra Hindley and Ian Brady in the so-called Moors Murders case, associated with uplands slightly further south. Temporal and spatial links are also reinforced by the use of textual understatement. The terse, understated dialogues and stark black and white camerawork evoke televised detective series of the time but also new cinematic interests in social realism and ordinary northern people.

Emotion and youthful confrontation with authority surfaced early in postwar amateur fiction. *A Letter to My Son*, the story of a condemned young murderer who refuses to see his mother but then calls for her when it is too late for her to visit, was one of the runners up in the 1952 Ten Best competition.[95] It is also hard not to see this film, not unconnected to re-emerging interest in social realism, outside the context of changing attitudes towards youth and capital punishment. Two teenage boys were arrested in November 1952 during a robbery in which a policeman was shot dead. Derek Bentley was hanged three months later. By the time *ACW* was offering comment on the film, the anti-hanging lobby was already taking shape even though abolition came a decade later.

Teenage years

Public disquiet about adolescents behaving badly recurs in mid-century amateur cinema. The experimental Scottish amateur filmmaker, Enrico Cocozza made *Chick's Day*, a fictional documentary film that dealt with the issue of 'juvenile delinquency'. Filmed in 1949 and 1950 in and around Glasgow, this award-winning film features teenage boys involved in a robbery. Cocozza explored some of the psychological complexity surrounding acts of crime as he incorporated background details of home and upbringing by an alcoholic mother. The film received further acclaim and Cocozza subsequently added a sound tape.[96] Some years later, *Flick Knife*, made by eighteen-year-old Hugh Raggett on 8mm and with added sound, was included as one of the Ten Best of 1957, again for its portrayal of rapidly changing realities for Britain's urban youth. From vibrant northern jazz club to country lane car crash on the way home, Bill Edgar's impressive *Short Stop* – a Ten Best winner in 1960 – portrays how an occasion when young people are having a good time goes fatally wrong.[97]

Even as freedom, independence and challenging conventions inevitably took young people beyond their own family's filmic gaze, less controversial youth experiences feature in mid-century amateur material too. Earlier reformist concerns about youth culture identified a postwar generation that had suffered absent fathers as a result of active service. Newly set-up youth committees used film to promote their aims and activities. They relied on local filmmakers and cine clubs to make recruitment material.[98] Alfred Siddall's *Birth of a Youth Club* (1949) exemplifies the redemptive potential of supervised activity.[99] His film starts with boys playing together on the edge of Cheshire woodland, then throwing stones and gambling until the gang's lookout spots a local police constable approaching. Parents and young people later meet to discuss the 'youth problem' and its apparent resolution by setting up cycling excursions, organised sport and a youth club.[100] Elsewhere, upbeat representations of youthful creativity, agility and prowess were recorded during Blackpool Youth Week (1948) and at regional festivals of youth.[101] Such footage extends earlier traditions of filming scouts and guides during excursions and organised camps or in local parades and processions. Some later youth-related footage may be traced to specific faith communities. Black teenagers' participation in sponsored country walks and other club activities feature in Sharon Full Gospel Church's visual record of evangelical ministry and outreach.[102]

The containment of regional youthful endeavour is paramount in scenes of organised craft workshops, quizzes, competitions, country dancing, plays, debates and simulated court trials.[103] This amateur footage of neatly dressed and often uniformed high achievers participating in organised public events discloses broader concerns about class, identity and education, as featured in the Albermarle Report (1960).[104] Its conservative gaze offered visual reassurance and conferred local and regional pride even as the music, manners and mores of British youth were contributing to the wider transformation of the establishment and society. Yet, collectively, these varied adolescents of amateur cinema perhaps offer a corrective visual note to the narratives of growing up in postwar Britain.

Amateur footage offers many clues about contemporary social worlds, concerns and experiences. It demonstrates the interplay of older traditions and new influences at local, regional and national level. Many of the preoccupations that prompted amateur productions have evolved rather than disappeared from contemporary life as seen in social and other visually based networking systems. More openness on subjects that were once taboo ensures greater public exposure to societal ills, but other concerns about personal safety and global (in)securities, health and welfare provision, housing and environmental sustainability, (anti-)social behaviour, equity of opportunities and equality within different sections of the population retain their contemporary prescience.

Other outlooks have altered. Amateur productions with a single narrative voice or all-seeing vision persisted into the 1970s as enthusiasts sought earnestly to inform and entertain their audiences. Intemperate utterances were not widespread within amateur productions. Amateur views on social issues tended to be liberal or conservative although some filmmakers experimented with content and camerawork. For others, however, the establishment only slowly lessened its influence upon style. As in television and newsreel, amateur material shows much continuity with earlier years until the late 1960s. Viewers of a Rag Week film produced by Manchester's students in 1962 were thus asked, by a narrator emulating conventional received English modulations and broadcasting style, to be tolerant of 'normally quite respectable students [as they] descend upon the Manchester populace'.[105] Student coverage of protests filmed on Oxford Road in central Manchester only eight years later discloses other societal shifts evidenced by its silent testimony of past policing tactics.[106]

Overseas endeavour

Britain's changing world role reshaped amateur practice too. As former colonial dependencies gained independence during the 1950s and 1960s, overseas postings ended for diverse groups of camera-using professionals, government administrators and others. Their return into a changing domestic scene meant that footage of comfortable family lifestyles maintained abroad with staff and accommodation more evocative of prewar times gradually lost relevance and appeal. Regrets over geo-political changes or affectionate nostalgia for aspects of expatriate privilege abroad tended to remain private yet survive in written or recorded oral testimony.[107] For descendants, now entrusting such material into archive care can be problematic as these filmic reminders of colonial condescension and racism expose family complicity with once unquestioned patterns of authority and superiority.

Footage shot by amateurs from North West England in former British colonial settings mainly focuses on trade and commercial visits, and home movies about living overseas whilst working for regionally based multinational companies, largely remains in private hands. Holiday films offer alternative visual routes into understanding colonial encounters abroad; travelogues form a distinctive strand for locating who watched imagery of foreign and unfamiliar lifestyles, and where. During the interwar years, representations of Empire and colonial subjects recurred in the region's carnival parades and amateurs filmed exotic sights at Empire exhibitions.[108] Elsewhere archive material points to the popularity of amateur cinematography among those who worked and lived abroad during the final decades of empire. Cine footage made by Britons abroad discloses much informally about relations under colonial rule as well as more personal experiences.[109] Its use for unofficial and personal interests gave cine users a freedom to record on camera that contrasts with other material from or for colonial contexts. While some hobbyists overseas confined filming to family or domestic subjects, others both at home and abroad perceived different opportunities and produced footage for wider consumption. Perceiving the value of film as 'an instrument of culture and education [that] merits the closest attention especially with primitive peoples' prompted the Secretary of State for the Colonies to set up a Colonial Film Committee as early as 1929.[110] The specialist hobby press also urged amateurs to aim specifically for an overseas market that was not considered lucrative enough to attract professional attention.

Notcutt, for instance, whilst acknowledging potential distribution problems, encouraged *serious* amateurs to make the affordable 'documentary style of film of English life that is so immensely popular overseas in the Dominions and colonies among older school children and native audiences'.[111] Malthouse opined that 'Africa offers a market for just those very films you thought could only be of interest to the family circle'. Such advice emanates racial assumptions and also late colonial self-confidence, as in the recommendation for 'simple films of English home life, manners, customs … pictures of the British Empire and occupations of its peoples, pageantry [and] royalty'. 'For the African market', we learn that 'films should be of slow tempo' and that producers should 'Err on the side of overstatement rather than understatement' with lots of close-ups and descriptive titles. '[R]emember that to the audiences, things that are familiar and commonplace to you, will be excitingly new and strange', Malthouse cautioned in launching *ACW*'s new service to review and distribute such material.[112]

Ten years later, Sewell's experiences in Gambia acknowledged greater audience understanding. '[O]ne might perhaps be excused for supposing that a high standard of projection is not so necessary out here as it is for better educated audiences at home but, in point of fact, African audiences vary greatly from the spruce Civil service clerk to the blue cloaked Mauretanian who walks many miles from the fringes of the Sahara Desert to pay his weekly visit to the white man's pictures.'[113] Seating arrangements are not disclosed but, from other colonial settings, segregation seems likely.[114] Humour does not mask more deep-rooted prejudices as shown in the self-deprecating sketch of himself and another European 'as two middle-aged gentlemen stripped to the waist and sweating like pigs trying to sort out problems before another show' as a result of 'some inquisitive African who had been playing with the controls during the afternoon'. Colonial rhetoric in amateur discourse, as mediated through the hobby press which had no avowed political agenda, remains an important corollary to the interpretation of visual records that survive from specific contexts both in and beyond mid-century Britain.

Missionaries were another group of overseas workers who travelled over many decades with their cameras into contexts that appealed visually because of being so different to the communities that they had left behind. Changing opportunities for evangelism abroad during the postwar years varied between different religious groups, and missionary activity lessened as secular models of delivering health, education and welfare services gradually evolved under independence. The importance of missionary film lies in its combination of ethnographic interest and its intended educational or fund-raising uses for home audiences. These portrayals of far-flung faith communities in settings that were often harsh, uncompromising and alien to their externally appointed spiritual guides often disclose much less about the people depicted on screen than about those in charge of the filming. They were shaped by prevailing attitudes about race, culture, ideology, gender and authority too.[115]

The footage created by these cine-enthusiasts, when film supplies, equipment and subjects permitted photography, now represent an important form of amateur activity, particularly as missionaries were often in situations where local people lacked the visual means to document their own lives. Such footage more usually reaches private or religious rather than public archives, and no regional connections have come to light during my research although a former Anglican Polar missionary and filmmaker, John Hudspith Turner, who worked for almost twenty years among the Inuit of northern Baffin Land has been traced to Leeds.[116] The Canadian film historian Peter Geller brings great sensitivity both to his interpretation of Turner's imagery and to the evolving colonial, ecumenical and spiritual circumstances in which local Inuit as Christians-in-waiting and missionary minister encountered each other on and off camera.[117]

Work by Geller and others, to find appropriate ways of engaging with material that derives from missionary contexts, as with films that derive from past colonial times, generates questions about working with amateur film.[118] Cine-enthusiasts repeatedly stepped unasked into other people's social and material worlds as they sought to tell stories on camera. Their perspectives are valuable even though they were often from beyond the situations and routines they sought to present or represent on screen. Their outsider status legitimised and helped to justify their camera use, and their authority undoubtedly affected how others behaved. Notwithstanding its eye-witness value, such amateur filmwork remains a selectively constituted gaze. Like those in the specialist press who sought to justify amateur activity as an instructive or fundraising tool, filmmakers who produced films with a message represent a social group that, in many cases, felt that their right to look was unquestionable. Concerns over authority and the politics of representation were not preoccupations for the bulk of these filmmakers.

Some amateurs believed they had sufficient camera skills and views worth sharing. As Bateman urged, amateur cinema allowed for individuality and freedom of expression: 'The guts of Meals on Wheels is not shots of the very noble women who tirelessly cart hot grub round in a van; it's the backgrounds of the lives of those who need the meals ... The problem of the unmarried mother is ... less the welfare worker handing over free gift nappies, than a terrified teenager in a shabby bedroom trying to pluck up courage to tell Mum.'[119] Other enthusiasts simply seized opportunities to use their cameras. In so doing, their erratic, spontaneous and at times experimental forays into different cinematic genres have also left a significant record of how people gave meaning to themselves and others in moving image.

Notes

1 I. Watson, 'Time for amateur movies to grow up'.
2 F. J. Mortimer, 'Amateur cinematography matters for social purposes'.
3 'Children from 'poorer parts of Manchester and Preston' watched home movies during their stay at summer camps, 'Club news', *Amateur Cine World*, 1951–54.
4 Mitchell and Kenyon, 1900: *Boer Attack on a Red Cross Outpost*, NWFA Film no. 250 (b/w, silent, 0 min. 45 sec.); 1900: *A Sneaky Boer [A Skirmish with Boers]*, NWFA Film no. 320 (b/w, silent, 2 mins. 0 sec.).
5 Unknown (possibly Palace Cinema, Leigh), 1920: *Leigh Pictorial News*, NWFA Film no. 572 (b/w, silent, 4 min. 11 sec.); St Helens Cinemas/St Helens Health Committee, 1923: [*St. Helens Health Week*], NWFA Film no. 91 (b/w, silent, 3 min. 4 sec.).
6 The Amateur Cinematograph Association (ACA) was founded in July 1927. George Sewell launched *Amateur Films* in August 1928, and made his own fund-raising films while working for the RSPCA. Source: L. Froude, 'Obituary note and tribute to George Sewell', in Coad, *The IAC*, pp. 93–4.
7 B. Wright, 'It began like this'.
8 N. J. Wadley, 'Letter to the editor'.
9 A. Buchanan, *Filmmaking. From Script to Screen*, p. 167.
10 A. Brunel, *Film Production*, pp. 4–7.
11 R. Low, *History of British Film: Films of Comment and Persuasion of the 1930s*.
12 S. Butler and J. Pickstone (eds), 'Medicine in Manchester', 30; see also E. L. Jones and J. V. Pickstone, *The Quest for Public Health in Manchester*, pp. 23–4.
13 Preston Brothers, *1933: *Stockport Infirmary Film*, NWFA Film no. 1178 (b/w, silent, 9 min. 25 sec.); *1933: *The New Sykes Ward opened in 1932 [Stockport Infirmary]*, NWFA Film no. 1161 (b/w, silent, 9 min. 15 sec.).
14 See previous note on film no. 1161.
15 *Ibid*.
16 Charles Taylor, *1933–45: [*Children's Orthopaedic Hospital; Boy Scouts*], NWFA Film no. 1231 (b/w & colour, silent, 14 min. 20 sec.).
17 Alex Briscoe, 1936/37: *Activities at the Sir Robert Jones Memorial Workshop for Cripples – Liverpool*, NWFA Film no. 477 (b/w and colour, silent, 18 min. 51 sec.).
18 A. Borsay, *Disability and Social Policy in Britain since 1750*.
19 Dr. F. Reynolds, 1935: [*Duchess of York Hospital – Dedication Ceremony*], NWFA Film no. 322 (b/w, silent, 3 min. 2 sec.).
20 The Royal Oldham Hospital [?], 1938: *Royal Visit: King George and Queen Elizabeth Visit Oldham, May 20th 1938*, NWFA Film no. 1452 (b/w, silent, 16 min. 9 sec.); 1938: [*Oldham Royal Infirmary 1938*], NWFA Film no. 1453 (b/w, silent, 18 min. 7 sec.); Deva Mental Hospital [?], 1937: [*Sports Day at Deva Mental Hospital*], NWFA Film no. 1292 (b/w, silent, 10 min. 13 secs.).
21 Outside amateur circles, Katy McGahan, Curator (Non-Fiction), BFI National Archive, also notes that 'The 1940s saw an increased integration of non-fiction and fictional approaches' that led on to actors, sets, and fictionalised dialogues contributing increasingly to the 'social problem films' of the 1950s *The People at*

No. 19 (Context) BFI (Inview), www.bfi.org.uk/inview/node/6343, accessed on 1 July 2009.
22 Leigh Literary Society Cine Section, 1937–38: [*Leigh Maternity Scenes Reel 1*], NWFA Film no. 3196 (b/w, silent, 13 min. 5 sec.); 1937–38: [*Leigh Maternity Services Reel 2*], NWFA Film no. 3194 (b/w, silent, 10 min. 19 sec.).
23 W. M. Essen, 'Planned from script to screen'.
24 *Ibid*. The Central Office of Information bought copies for the Ministry of Labour's nursing recruitment scheme.
25 Ernest Taylor (Huddersfield Cine Society), *Service Partners* (b/w, c. 30 min. undated). Re-edited by Trevor Spencer and screened at *Huddersfield Video and Cine Club Presents 75 years of The Way We Were, 1932–2007*, Huddersfield Town Hall, November 2007.
26 Sam Hanna for the Burnley and District Hospital Management Committee, 1960–63: *The Burnley School of Nursing*, NWFA Film no. 5208 (colour, sound, 39 min. 32 sec.); B. Jones and L. Snow, *Against the Odds*.
27 Correspondence between author and Ashby Ball, see Chapter 2.
28 A. Ball, 'Problems of the propaganda film'.
29 A. Ball, *Britain's amateur filmmaking*.
30 J. E. Hallam, 1940: *Home Movies*, NWFA Film no. 873 (b/w, silent, 15 min. 30 sec.).
31 Mrs. E A Richardson, *1959: [*Alder Hey Children's Hospital*], NWFA Film no. 816 (colour, silent, 4 min. 0 sec.).
32 H. Norris Nicholson, 'Journeys into seeing'; Horace Wilfred Taylor, 1932: *Tour in the USSR, Part 2*, NWFA Film no. RR852/35 (b/w., silent, 19 min. 38 sec.).
33 P. Le Neve Foster, 'A movie maker in Moscow'.
34 James Lovelock and Simon Clark, 1961: [*With Local People in the Himalayas*], NWFA Film no. 2786 (b/w, silent, 19 min. 50 sec.).
35 H. Norris Nicholson, 'Shooting the Mediterranean'.
36 D. M. Elliott, 'Prizewinner, but too horrific to be shown'.
37 *Scope* was founded in 1952 as The National Spastics Society and renamed in 1994.
38 'Double Run', 'Films about children'.
39 Rochdale and District Cine Society for the Inskip League, 1953: *Inskip Adventure*, NWFA Film no. 4587 (b/w, silent, 26 min. 51 sec.).
40 Crippled Help Society (?), 1964: [*Day Out and Fete*], NWFA Film no. 1043 (b/w, silent, 10 min. 40 sec.); 1964: [*Day Centre*], NWFA Film no. 1044 (b/w, silent, 10 min. 40 sec.); 1964: [*Christmas – Manchester Town Hall*], NWFA Film no. 1045 (b/w, silent, 14 min. 40 sec.); Announced in mid-1962, the 'full length feature film for the Crippled Help Society' aimed 'to show the disabled and their guardians and what can be done and what they can do for themselves', Letters page, *Wide Angle* (Journal of the North West region of the IAC) (Summer 1962), 13.
41 Alan Mannion with Sir John Deane's College Film Unit, 1968: *Isle of Man 1968*, NWFA Film no. 3867 (b/w, silent, 27 min. 14 sec.).
42 J. Martin, *Man of the Road*.
43 A. Cavalcanti, 'Mr Cavalcanti explains … why he banned *Man on the Road*'.
44 See note 42.

45 H. Norris Nicholson, 'In amateur hands'; '"At Ilkley they sell lovely"'.
46 H. Norris Nicholson, '"Seeing it how it was?"'; 'Telling travellers' tales', pp. 47–68.
47 J. McDonald, 'Filming a portrait from life'.
48 *Ibid.*, 460.
49 Collaborative projects by John Gresty and Mike Goodger included: 1973: [*Age*], NWFA Film no. 2283 (b/w, sound, 4 min. 29 sec.); 1973: [*Heaven and Hell*], NWFA Film no. 2284 (b/w, sound, 5 min. 20 sec.); 1974: *Dirty Old Town*, NWFA Film no. 2286 (colour, sound, 3 min. 13 sec); 1974: *From Old To New*, NWFA Film no. 2287 (colour, sound, 4 min. 40 sec.); 1974: *The Bell Tolls for Whom*, NWFA Film no. 2288 (colour, sound, 5 min. 7 sec.).
50 Background details provided by Geoff Senior, Archivist, NWFA, Sept. 2008.
51 Mike Goodger, 1968/69: *The Changing Face of Salford. Part 1, Life in the Slums*, NWFA Film no. 430 (colour, sound, 32 min. 0 sec.); 1967–70: *The Changing Face of Salford. Part 2, 1967–70 Bloody Slums*, NWFA Film no. 1366 (colour, sound, 33 min. 53 sec.); Goodger sought to overcome local criticism with; *1971: *Salford – The Other Side*, NWFA Film no. 1365 (colour, sound, 15 min. 21 sec.).
52 Preston Borough Council / Mr Green, 1938: [*Preston Slum Clearance*], NWFA Film no. 518 (b/w, silent, 5 min. 58 sec.).
53 Ken Loach, *Cathy Come Home* (1966), For the Wednesday Play, BBC1. Transmission 16 November 1966 (b/w, sound, 80 min.).
54 D. Sandbrook, *White Heat*, pp. 597–9.
55 H. Norris Nicholson,'Two tales of a city'.
56 John Michael Goodger, Personal correspondence file, North West Film Archive. See also note 52.
57 *Ibid.*
58 John Gresty and Mike Goodger, 1974: *Dirty Old Town*, see note 49.
59 Cinephoto Productions (John Gresty) for Skelmersdale Development Corporation, *1971: *Prospect of Skelmersdale*, NWFA Film no. 514 (colour, sound, 25 min. 1 sec.).
60 (Anon.), 'The national safety first competition'.
61 J. M. Gresty, 1950/54: *Camera on Safety*, NWFA Film no. 854 (b/w, silent, 10 min. 40 sec.).
62 Wallace and George Miller, Cyril Parkinson and Thomas Taylor, *1945: *National Road Safety Campaign: Accident Prevention Display Organised by Preston Accident Prevention Council*, NWFA Film no. 4668 (colour, sound, 17 min. 27 sec.).
63 See for example: G. H. Sewell, 'Tracing projector troubles under an African sun'. See proposal for schools and the colonies as two markets suited to distribution of amateur films in G. Malthouse, 'Markets for your films'.
64 See, for example, Stanley Hilton Snr, *1937–39/44: [*A.R.P. and A.F.S. Training*], NWFA Film no. 6117 (b/w and colour, silent, 12 min. 22 sec.); Alexander John Dodd, 1939–45: [*Gas Attack Drill*], NWFA Film no. 6133 (b/w, silent, 2 min. 3 sec.); Wallace Miller, c.1942: *County Borough Of Preston Invasion Exercises*, NWFA Film no. 6199 (b/w, silent, 13 min. 36 sec.). For examples of films made by an individual, a cine club and a local-authority-sponsored amateur production, see John Williams [?], 1942/46: [*Nelson Home Guard*, NWFA Film no. 1263 (b/w

and colour, silent, 14 min. 12 sec.); G. Dunkerley, J. Lancaster, J. H. Haffner, 1941 (for Burnley Borough Council), *Alert!*, NWFA Film no. 145 (b/w, silent, 21 min. 39 sec.); Warrington Cine and Video Society, *ARP 1938* (kindly loaned by Rob Evans, WCVS, Summer 2008); see also R. S. Kirkham, 'Filming for Victory'; M. C. Grimshaw, 'Digging for Victory', 350.
65 See Chapter 1.
66 Blackpool ACC, 'Notes and news'.
67 Leigh and District Cine Society, '*Our Town*'.
68 P. Hennessy, *Having It So Good*, p. 165.
69 *Ibid.*, p. 161.
70 Preston Borough Police, 1959: *County Borough of Preston Civil Defence Exercise 'Prestonian'*, NWFA Film no. 3160 (b/w, silent, 18 min. 7 sec.).
71 See, for example, D. Villiers, 1956: *H-Bomb* (1956), sponsored by Home Office for Civil Defence and Fire Services / R.H.R. Productions and Film Producers Guild, *BBC-Inview*, accessed on 30 June 2009 (see note 21).
72 Hennessy, *Having It So Good*, p. 165.
73 *Ibid.*
74 T. Rose, 'Running, jumping and never standing still' (see Chapter 3).
75 Hennessy, *Having It So Good*, p. 166.
76 Sir Geoffrey Haworth, 1960: *USSR, May 1960*, NWFA Film no. 1575 (colour, silent, 27 min. 0 sec.).
77 H. Norris Nicholson, 'Cultural relations and comfortable curiosity'.
78 Norris Nicholson, 'Journeys into seeing'.
79 Conversation with Geoff Senior, Senior Archivist, NWFA (April 2009).
80 Tony Iddon, c.1964: [*Ban the Bomb*], NWFA Film no. 4396 (b/w, silent, 4 min. 11 sec.).
81 (Anon.), 'Club commentary' (untitled note), *Movie Maker*, 5:3 (1971), 237. See also interview with Alan Smith (Chapter 2).
82 I. Watson, 'Meet the winners'.
83 *Ibid.*
84 Altrincham Cine Club, '*And on the Eighth Day*', 374.
85 T. Rose, 'Other peoples pictures', *Movie Maker*, 4:4 (1970), 208–9.
86 Rose, 'Running, jumping and never standing still.
87 (Anon.), 'John Baskeyfield, South Stafford's 1st Airborne', http://theairbornesoldier.com/johnbaskeyfield.html, accessed on 2 July 2009; BBC Stoke and Staffordshire, *Local Heroes: Jack Baskeyfield*, www.bbc.co.uk/stoke/content/articles/2009/08/24/john_baskeyfield_film_anniversary_feature.shtml, accessed on 9 February 2012. Ray Johnson, Staffordshire Film Archives, kindly supplied further details, September 2010.
88 J. Chittock, 'Films to borrow'.
89 J. Cook, '"This is not Hollywood": Peter Watkins and the challenge of amateurism'.
90 J. Taylor, 'Seeing and sustainability'.
91 T. Rose, 'The night home movies were seen by more than a million'.
92 'A. B.-G.', The varying moods of black and white'.
93 See note 88.

94 Pendle Movie Makers, *The Lonely One* (1968) (b/w, sound, 16 min. 0 sec.) received a Gold Star in the Ten Best award.
95 (Anon.), 'In the condemned cell'.
96 Enrico Cocozza (Connoisseur Productions), 1949–50: *Chick's Day*, Scottish Screen Archive Reference no. 1173 (b/w : 31 min. 55 sec.), http://ssa.nls.uk/film.cfm?fid=1173#header, accessed on 27 July 2009.
97 Bill Edgar, 1960: *Short Stop*, YFA Film no. 2341 (b/w, silent, 9 min. 16 sec.) www.yfaonline.com/, accessed on 1 May 2011.
98 Blackpool Youth Committee / R.Aird, 1948: *Blackpool Youth Week 3rd – 9th May 1948*, NWFA Film no. 512 (b/w, silent, 8 min. 0 sec.).
99 Alfred Siddall, *1949: *The Birth of a Youth Club*, NWFA Film no. 4355 (b/w, silent, 7 min. 20 sec.).
100 (Anon.), 'Amateur Teddy Boy drama pulls a punch'.
101 Blackpool Youth Committee / R. Aird, 1948: *Blackpool Youth Week 3rd – 9th May 1948*, NWFA Film no. 512 (b/w, silent, 8 min. 0 sec); Rochdale & District Cine Society, 1956: *Rochdale Centenary Newsreel*, NWFA Film no. 232 (colour, silent, 20 min. 16 sec.); Mr and Mrs Kenworthy, 1959/60/61: [*The Mayor's Procession 1959 and 1960 / Oldham Youth Festival 1961*], NWFA Film no. 698 (b/w and colour, silent, 10 min. 0 sec.).
102 Sharon Full Gospel Church Film Unit, 1969–71: [*Chorlton Road, Sponsored Walks And Youth Centre Construction*], NWFA Film no. 3074 (colour, silent, 10 min. 49 sec.).
103 J. Hill, *Sport, Leisure and Culture in Twentieth-century Britain*; J. Hargreaves, *Sport, Power and Culture*; J. A. Mangan (ed.), *Reformers, Sport, Modernizers*.
104 Ministry of Education, *The Youth Service in England and Wales*.
105 Tech Movie Group, 1962: *University of Manchester Shrove Rag Committee Presents 'Where The Money Goes'*, NWFA Film no. 771 (b/w, sound, 15 min. 56 sec.).
106 Umist TV Society, *1970: [*Work, Study and Leisure*], NWFA Film no. 783 (b/w, silent, 15 min. 48 sec.).
107 See, for example, the notes that accompanied the screening of films made during a period of duty as Deputy Governor of the Sudan Police Force prior to independence, Finlay Personal Collection (1928–67), British Film Institute, London.
108 Preston Brothers, 1934: [*Trains, Carnivals and Dog Show*], NWFA Film no. 1186 (b/w, silent, 11 min. 8 sec.); 1931: [*A Visit to the Paris International Colonial Exhibition, 1931*], NWFA Film no. 1939 (b/w, silent, 15 min. 8 sec.); Lucy Fairbank, 1938: *British Empire Exhibition in Glasgow*, YFA Cat. no. 126 (b/w, silent, 16 min.).
109 H. Norris Nicholson, *Screening Culture*, pp. 94–5 ; 'Telling travellers' tales'.
110 Commission on Educational and Cultural films (CEC films), 'The Cinema and Empire', *The Cinema in National Life*, paragraph 198.
111 L. A. Notcutt, 'Ideas for documentary films'.
112 G. Malthouse, 'Markets for your films'.
113 Sewell, 'Tracing projector troubles under an African sun', 56, 62.
114 Nico de Klerk (Nederlands Filmmuseum, Amsterdam). Mentioned in passing during discussion of links between colonial films, historical interpretation and

archive materials, with particular reference to former Dutch East Indies material (now part of Indonesia) at the conference, *Moving History: Film Archives and Academic Research*.
115 See note 109.
116 I am grateful to Faith Turner for the opportunity to watch and talk about *Arctic Pioneers in Baffinland* prior to and during *Screening Culture: Constructing Image and Identity*, held at University St John, York, October 1996.
117 P. Geller, 'Into the glorious dawn'.
118 H. Norris Nicholson, 'Moving pictures; moving memories: framing the interpretative gaze', pp. 71–80; 'Manchester's *Moving Memories: Tales from Moss Side and Hulme*: archive film and community history-making' (2012).
119 R. Bateman, 'Storylines'.

9

Moving pictures, moving on

'There is richness at every street corner, under every roof', enthused *ACW*'s reporter at 'Look at Britain!', the third Free Cinema programme, held at the National Film Theatre in mid-1957.[1] Readers were urged to see how the profiled filmmakers linked with amateur practice and to emulate their challenge to re-observe the familiar: 'to look at it with honesty and affection … relish its eccentricities, attack its abuses, love its people'. Encouraging amateur awareness of broader contemporary shifts in cinematic and visual practice recurred during the decades under review. Advocacy, in the hobby press, repeatedly positioned amateur activity in relation to professional cinema, as seen in published film criticism. Directors' profiles highlighted backgrounds in non-professional film production. Cinematic language, and the formalities of competitions, awards, festivals and other events that arose to shape the amateur calendar aligned some cine users with professional practice. Undoubtedly, amateur cinema became, for some of its exponents, visual practice unfettered by commercial considerations. Cine equipment and projection at home or in local club venues allowed freedom for personal expression and experimentation. Small-gauge film maximised scope for pursuing individual interests and available opportunities with limited resources. Undaunted by the pejorative tags and jibes aimed in their direction by doubters, some amateur enthusiasts pursued their activity with dedication. Sustained by shared interests and the companionship of fellow practitioners, their sometimes lifelong commitment gave rise both individually and collectively to considerable artistry, talent and endeavour as brought to new audiences by an emerging number of scholars in recent years.

At the other end of the amateur spectrum were numerous do-it-yourself cine-equipment users, whose commitment, skills, resources and motives varied. Understanding Britain's amateur filmmaking movement as a continuum stretching between casual usage and high-quality cinematography that reflects expertise and many years of experience helps to accommodate this vast range of output that exists within public archives and still in private hands. Finding ways to understand this disparate body of work that neither relegate footage as visually naive and banal nor bubble-wrap the aesthetically sophisticated production in narrow theoretical concepts lies at the heart of the present text. Writing has striven not to alienate the very constituency whose enthusiasms have sustained amateur activity against decades of rapid technological development and societal change. Some of those very practitioners, indeed, have contributed to the present project. Crafting a text informed by contemporary concerns and scholarship whilst ideally remaining faithful to the intentions and integrity of successive generations of amateur practitioners has been important.

Undeniably, amateurs and their audiences found something intensely compelling in the cine-camera's capacity to record moments of being there. Reliving particular events or the ability to join in as armchair travellers prompted part of the interest and delight. The shared experience of making and watching amateur films together, particularly beyond the family circle, but rather with friends, club members and local people, was not merely a 'social good', in sociological terms – a process of bringing people together. Its reassuring promise of belonging and shared involvement in affective pleasures created an intimate and empowering semi-public sphere that perhaps assuaged wider uncertainties of societal and political change, not unlike more contemporary interests in shared reading and choral singing.

For some people, the medium's visual pleasure existed precisely in recalling the transient enjoyments of the ordinary – the visual ephemeralities of the past, with the help of either known or unfamiliar filmmakers. Conversely, for others, the handheld camera and amateur's informal point of view, however compromised by poor quality, lighting or technical prowess, beckoned as invitations to step imaginatively into other worlds. Take, for example, the praise in *ACW* following the public screening in late 1952 of the explorer-anthropologist Thor Heyerdahl's epic Kon Tiki voyage across the Pacific on a papyrus raft.[2] There was jerky camerawork shot at sea level, scratched film emulsion, overly rapid panning, rusted film cans and water damage, and unmatched shots and sequences. Yet, the six crew members who used 16mm film for the first time – later blown up to 35mm for public screening – were commended for their 'triumph of teamwork', inspiration and capturing of 'remarkable thrills'. Amateur film, whether on the garden lawn, on the school playing field or in more exotic locations, invited its makers and audiences to sidestep time and, for the duration of the film, to inhabit alternative realities of various kinds. Produced alone or with others, amateur material stands as testimony to how people spent their time, sometimes engaged in 'serious leisure' and sometimes simply indulging a passing fancy for an activity that became available.[3]

Highlighting some of the scope and variety of amateur practice through offering a thematic lens and regional focus that, at times, has drawn up relevant material elsewhere, has been central to this project. No single area can encapsulate the variety of British or even English regional experience, but the diversities found within the main study location and periodic wandering across its boundaries to adjacent rural, industrial and urban localities offer a sufficiently coherent provincial focus suitable for future comparisons with other regions and metropolitan areas. The preceding discussion has drawn on virtually no material from Wales, Scotland or Northern Ireland, with the exception of the Scottish Amateur Film Festival. Claims that a regional focus offers a means for exploring a national movement seem valid, however, in that amateur practice has been related to aspects of national socio-historical, cultural and economic experience and has drawn upon the most continuously influential publications in Britain's advisory literature. A different regional setting, would inevitably skew the content differently but underlying the cited examples run themes, concerns and perspectives that merit a broader positioning of material, largely drawn from the nation's largest public regional film archive outside London, as a means to understand fifty years of twentieth-century British experience through amateur eyes.

Inevitably, the task has grown beyond its initial remit. Since its inception, developments in different areas of scholarship have been germane to the writing. Awareness and interest in amateur film has grown too, creating a shifting background for the present work. Educators, visual artists, filmmakers, broadcasters and other users have acknowledged the significance of amateur film footage in unprecedented ways. Archivists and collectors have become increasingly visible at the forefront of innovative partnerships that use amateur footage as part of broadening access to visual culture. Arts and heritage organisations have seen the potential popular appeal of flickering archive image on monitor screens even as the rise of multiple channels has precipitated a rash of independent producers searching for the unexpected, unmediated personal testimony and quirkiness believed to attract audiences.

Such activity is occurring against a background of shifting priorities in public sector spending and looming reductions to the funding of arts, culture, teaching and research. The explosion of digital technologies and their impact on personal image-making and the electronic implications for storing, accessing and distributing archive amateur materials pose challenges and opportunities that seem too important to ignore. Acknowledging the implications of such dynamic thrusts and turns within – and, as importantly, *beyond* academic enquiry, highlights the value underlying the interdisciplinarity and multiple standpoints that are now associated with understanding amateur film. Some thoughts on future directions in amateur film scholarship seem a fitting conclusion. If not an agenda, as scope for further study of different kinds has been identified in relevant sections already, the following comments may be seen as a positioning of this study in the emerging historiography and intellectual mapping out of amateur cinema studies.

Growing academic interest in amateur activity has broadened theoretical and methodological approaches. Exploration of surviving amateur footage now ranges across themes, formats, genres – including fiction, animation, historical, colonial, travelogue and documentary – and its textual and cultural practices. Yet, for some scholars, its relationships with other forms of moving image – and photography too – remain prime considerations. As the complex interplay of past links between amateur and professional practice is gaining recognition through emerging studies of individual filmmakers, or the role of support organisations, clubs, festivals, competitions and specialist literature, fresh attention is drawn to more theoretical concerns about how amateur films are talked and written about now and in the past.

For decades, Britain's specialist press reverberated with references to current films and terminologies used in film criticism in ways that were both eclectic and enthusiastic, as seen early on in Macpherson's idiosyncratic *Close Up*. While this short-lived magazine embodies how some writing about different cinematic forms was inflected with prevailing concerns about modernism, art, literature and society, much amateur activity occurred away from elite discursive practice, even if not totally isolated from wider trends in the viewing and screening of moving imagery. Other amateur publications had more middle-brow appeal in their mix of advice and criticism and yet, for some cine users, even these instructive tones were not part of how they practised their hobby. Indeed, commentators sometimes lamented the apparent gulf between critical awareness honed by actually going to the cinema and much amateur output. Issues of intentionality seem valid here, in remembering the breadth of amateur visual practice and the appropriateness of transferring critical perspectives between contexts. Even within later serial publications, contributions ensured different voices and a plurality of perspectives that would reach a wide readership.

As with any language, evolution occurs as expressions borrow, import, absorb and graft from different sources and give rise to new ways of communication. While some amateurs used art-house and mainstream film-related lexicons to strengthen the status of amateur cinematography – perhaps enhancing their own position too – it seems likely that language of film – and later television – also gained some popular acceptance too, as borne out by dipping into dictionaries and other verbal texts of the time. An aesthetic history of amateur practice could further develop the trajectories of these co-existent discursive forms within amateur settings. Contemporary approaches to amateur film may likewise gain from applying the critical vocabularies and constructs of film studies. Such steps might offer analytical lenses that assist with its repatriation within film studies, and have legitimacy among those wishing to further links with creative practitioners and scholars from film, media and visual backgrounds.

Adopting the language of contemporary film studies in the analysis of amateur practice may also help in repositioning the latter within more inclusive cinematic histories. Since the study of emerging national cinema remains an important element of twentieth-century film history, where amateur activity predates production at a national level, might amateur film be considered as an underacknowledged fledging step in the development of a country's cinema? Valuable contributions are being made by researchers who examine amateur film practice within specific national contexts, rather than conceiving it as an undifferentiated trans-national hobby contingent upon international marketing, publishing and organisational structures. Comparative studies on amateur activity will further our understanding of both content and context.

Connecting with other relevant areas of film-related study and, almost as importantly, regional television histories from the 1950s onwards need not eclipse the potential for other interpretative frameworks. Memory studies is one such burgeoning area of enquiry where concepts and approaches contribute to understanding processes underlying the making, sharing, and passing on of private and public visual memories. While digital technologies impact upon processes of remembering and forgetting, research into psychoanalytical, neuro-cognitive and biological systems broadens established socio-cultural, literary and artistic areas of interest in acts of recollection, forgetting, avoidance and erasure.[4] Long-established metaphors of memory as storehouse, archive and other forms of repository have undergone reappraisal as new vocabularies, springing from the previously hidden survivor narratives of conflict, disaster, trauma and genocide, have gained recognition.[5] This paradigm shift opens ways of understanding memory as being more fluid, dynamic and complex than hitherto implied by the fixity implicit in earlier cultural imagery.[6] For those working on questions of visual memory and identity, more transformative approaches to making sense of amateur material have become available.

Amateur film, and its video and digital successors, evolved against decades that witnessed total war, prospects of annihilation and the powerful role of human agency in creating landscapes of dereliction and ruin. As the capacity for obliterating traces of the past soared, mimetic means to record expanded from the early brief fragments of exposed film less than a minute long to the life-logging possibilities that digital media now permit. Exposing this mismatch between the recordable and the recording process highlights more philosophical concerns over the ultimately unknowable and incomprehensible nature of times past. Couching the significance of past amateur footage in terms of its evidential value as visual history continues to play an important role in establishing and furthering amateur film scholarship but more nuanced interpretations of memory-making offer exciting possibilities to the study of amateur materials at a point where the absences, gaps and discontinuities in recollection, and in time itself, seem to converge.

Dynamic notions of memory-making and shaping, like more multi-layered ideas about identity formation, selfhood and belonging, have greater relevance for some areas of amateur film than others. Both have seemed pertinent to the discussion of material broadly conceived within a realist tradition as considered in these pages. Such concepts seem least applicable to amateur animation, other than, perhaps, in oral histories of individual practitioners. While finding points of commonality may appear to undermine the breadth of amateur practice, it identifies scope for less obvious points of investigation, as in details of past social practice and gender roles that exist in the relatively small number of amateur fiction productions currently held in public archives and better represented within club collections. More generally, visual clues to past lives and landscapes offer amateur footage a focus on visibility and materiality that appears at odds with the elusive flickering nature of its projected image and beam of light. While the insubstantial nature of the image – as opposed to the mechanical presence, form and sound of cine equipment – distances it from the materiality of a photograph and the sensory encounter of holding an album, amateur film's frequent visual focus on people, places and objects creates an unlikely alliance with recent conceptual shifts in archaeology.[7]

Long seen as the poor relation to history, archaeology developed in part outside the frameworks and dialogues of its supposedly more intellectually significant and text-based superior. It offers an interesting parallel to the erstwhile marginalisation of amateur activity within broader cinematic study. Whilst being analogous to repositioning amateur film scholarship within discussions on film and cinema history, this comparison highlights the enriching insights available from elsewhere. Both subjects share an interest in fragments from the past and acknowledge the inherently selective process of making and leaving traces in time. If excavation has dealt with the discarded rubbish of the past, amateur activity, particularly in earlier dismissive notions about home movies, was viewed with similar contempt. Attempts to reinstate two once marginalised activities within more inclusive dialogues offer points of similarity.

Both fields of study share concerns with what survives and the problematic gaps in what is left unsaid, unseen and remains unrecoverable.[8] The omissions, absences, discontinuities and unseen presences are starting points for investigations that seek to step beyond the frame and widen the search for meaning. Issues of provenance, relocations, and agency and action, are of mutual importance, as shown by how archival discoveries, like those unearthed from the ground, gain fresh meanings when seen and shared in different settings. Ethical issues may arise as shifts occur from once private, or neglected and forgotten places to more public spheres. Intentionality, purpose, function, reception and value may be as elusive for the excavated artefact as for an amateur cine reel. Materiality, and chance survival, may confer on both a longevity that outlasts their original makers and users. They may even acquire their own narratives, memories and new significance.

Making sense of multiple stories and alternative perspectives has given rise to notions of multi-vocality within archaeology and cultural anthropology.[9] It offers a potential framework for accommodating the variety of past experiences found within amateur material too, particularly when dealing with the abundance of similar content within personal and family film recording. Multi-vocality offers a multi-stranded alternative to the constructing of historical memory-making. Different visual versions may be understood alongside each other as complementary traces of the past. Archived private footage is not simply the unofficial version of past experience made visible; it represents repeated instances of individual expression on a large scale. So, birthdays, beach scenes, picnics and tea parties, for instance, simply through their replication over time by different amateurs, gain value that extends beyond their individual worth.

Family stories, whether in words or pictures, communicate notions of self and situation and link past, present and future. Although an analogy with oral traditions can not be taken very far since footage lacks the malleability and longevity of being passed down by storytellers and their audiences, it does point to the importance of negotiated spaces in which presenter and audience may share in making disparate 'texts' meaningful. If excavated artefacts acquire significance through uncovering their wider setting, then the stories told on amateur film – just like oral traditions – gain from being related to their social, political and historical contexts. Both expose the subjective and sometimes provocative nature of interpretation, and are reminders of how the past is contested as it prompts fresh interests in contemporary social and political settings.

During decades when the acceleration of time generated new ways of experiencing, conceptualising, dominating and representing the world, amateur filmmakers explored their own ways to manipulate time, challenging and reworking logics of sequence and linearity. Archaeology likewise moved beyond narrow sequential framing of stratified layers to comparative approaches, entering into new dialogue with cultural anthropology, contemporary art, design and comparative indigenous studies, to bring new explanations and insights. Amateur footage similarly benefits as scholars, creative practitioners and varied audiences expose, juxtapose, locate and encounter its imagery differently. Meanings evolve and significances change as shown in the preceding chapters. Finding effective languages permits different kinds of conversation about past visual pursuits. Aesthetics, techniques, sounds, silences, intertitles and story boards may be understood afresh as amateur film scholarship engages with other areas of thought and practice.

The archaeological metaphor may be taken further by those who excavate media prehistory to recover the layers and genealogies of past practices and technologies of communication. Linking the record-making impulse between home movies and mobile phone technologies traces a desire to see and share technically from modernity to postmodernity and propels amateur film practice beyond a cinematic framework into narratives of communication history. Early cine practices legitimately nestle within more inclusive and unconventional histories of communication that embrace filmic histories as media archaeology.[10] Work on the role of home video technologies in the transition from cine film to digital image-making augments this evolutionary route still further. The 'hiddenscapes' of amateur visual activity – those patterns of meanings and details below the surface, invisible without careful investigation, await uncovering: imagery, like landscape, is inscribed with past ideas, assumptions and values that also inform contemporary sensibilities.

In the digital era, Witmore suggests, memory has become cheap.[11] Film length, development costs and album accumulation long constrained the taking of analogue photographs. Moving imagery was likewise limited by resources until video technologies arrived. New media's capacity for personal image-making moved from hesitancy to profligacy in under two decades, generating an explosion of visual mementoes, as well as an unprecedented facility to store, show and share picture memories. If digital technologies have impacted upon visual memory-making, they have also recast amateur film and video practice as direct visual antecedents to the mimetic processes of today. The British launch of Pathé and Kodak's camera and projector equipment for the home market in the early 1920s established precursors to contemporary media technologies. This fifty-year survey of amateur film may itself be seen as an archaeological intervention in mapping out Britain's personal image making practices and cultures over the past nine decades. While study of digital memories is evolving fast, the comparative perspectives offered by amateur activity help to position the digital turn within a wider understanding of visual memory studies. Grappling with the impact of digitisation upon memory at personal, public and collective levels may be new but the mental, emotional, social, cultural and practical consequences of technological shifts in mediating memories have happened before with the advent of printing and in relation to photographic and media developments. Arguably, different evolving communication technologies have each affected the human capacity to remember, so present-day technologies of the self, to borrow Foucault's phrase, are but the latest in a succession of ways to redefine the boundaries, conventions and constructions of autobiographical and collective remembering and forgetting.

This longer perspective informs comparison of past and present visual practices. Given current capabilities in digital capture of everyday visual flotsam, earlier dismissive treatment of amateur activity as parochial and limited in content now seems misleading. Far from simply recording the routines of daily life, the selective nature of past cine use appears striking when set alongside the infinite nature of today's digital self-recording pursuits. Using a cine-camera was a conscious but, for some amateurs, highly sporadic intervention, often prompted by an occasion being special for a particular reason. The resultant visual record may seem trivial in some of what it shows, but what promoted the moments of shooting had significance. Visual fragments of times past, precisely because of their capacity to show again, now acquire value simply for their distance from the present.

As instances of outreach to different communities in widely different contexts reveal, historical visual fragments are not merely animated versions of local history. Their gaze upon specific situations and experiences, which have been transformed or no longer survive, may help to offset patterns of myopia, erasure and severance that exist from domestic to global level. In different settings, working with amateur film and its successor video technologies, including those often problematic sequences shot by privileged outsiders, now offer the potential to help reconnect generations, overcome alienation and build bridges across physical, social, and psychic chasms. Virtual visual repatriation may involve no more than posting an archive clip and perhaps monitoring responses but its online presence may be a catalyst for gathering other evidence and renewed cultural visibility.[12] The challenges of such work are considerable while public funding for such schemes that seek to recover lost knowledge and rekindle hope tends to be limited.[13] From the Arctic to sub-Saharan Africa, there is scope for taking amateur visual imagery out of the archive, whether as part of widening access to collections or sensitive schemes of visual repatriation, knowledge-sharing or community empowerment. Far from being nostalgic indulgence, such ventures may enhance understanding within and between different peoples. Will family films in cine or video format once shot in and around the comfortable homes of Belfast, Bagdhad, Bulawayo or Bloomfontein – currently discarded, unloved or despised – one day have future roles and relevance in helping people come to understand their pasts and presents differently?[14] Can footage of communities and localities marginalised and divided by race, religion and reputation find alternative ways of understanding self, circumstance and sense of direction, though engaging with the visual snippets of earlier times?[15] Certainly, recent and ongoing initiatives offer some cautious encouragement as evolving technologies bring old formats to new audiences and venues.

While accessing digital and cine or video memories relies upon other equipment, digitisation has expanded image availability, far beyond the original personal sphere of domestic or semi-public club space. Scale poses its own challenges: individual storage of personal material was hard enough as cine reels and cassettes accumulated over time, with or without titles and re-editing. Digitisation throws open the once private archive of stored visual memories in new ways: imagery is shared, circulated and remixed even as some individual items are lost in the process. Beyond the challenges of organising data and its retrieval on a personal computer exist global possibilities of accessing data, as unknown amounts of material are streamed and made available online. The practical, ethical and conceptual consequences of such electronic abundance carry risks and rewards.

Opening archival access breathes fresh life and possibilities, and generates creativity, interest and new audiences for working with archive footage, in and beyond academic circles. Such strategies within archival practice highlight new emphasis upon visibility, outreach and self-justification, and overturn traditional roles as keepers and protectors of archive materials. Putting material online means it enters a global public domain. Inevitably, the online presence of archive amateur footage is skewed by resources, so that some repositories are more able to digitise than others. Changing patterns of availability emerge in new configurations of unevenness at regional, national and international levels. Whilst not forgetting the digital divide and those that lack access for different reasons at national and international level, digitisation enables wider access to moving imagery of all kinds from social networks too, as shown by the upsurge of archive footage on YouTube and equivalent sites since its inception. Arguably, archives have a greater longevity than YouTube and its equivalents, even in the present economic landscape.

How vulnerable could past amateur footage become through digital access? The extent of digitisation, availability and usage are as yet unknown. Amateur content and aesthetic is appealing to different users, but online availability should not make it any more exploitable than professionally made archive film. Often erroneously assumed to be freely available without seeking copyright permission from its owners or its archival home, streaming amateur material requires the same clearance by the archival host as needed by any user approaching via conventional routes. Although streaming offers greater visibility and easier access rather than making a quantitative change, in practical terms it seems to make more material available. The potential visual pick and mix available through electronic access seems to pose specific threats to amateur material but those risks relate in part to how data is digitised and appears on line, with or without contextual details. The integrity of imagery, and how it is found and reworked by users, forms part of an evolving agenda of online archival practice.

More and more collectors and archives, internationally, feel that open access ultimately raises awareness and contributes new significance as imagery gains fresh meaning in different contexts. Within what some might see as an emerging era of global visual commons, new notions of regularity practice have yet to gain consensus, let alone adoption and usage. Visual artists, archivists and scholars are still coming to terms with the sheer freedom of possibilities as hitherto unavailable materials become accessible. Issues of ethics, integrity and even the very basics of contextual research to establish provenance, intentionality and other details of origin rely upon the time, commitment and skills of individual image-searchers. Among those using, working with and responsible for archive footage, exemplary research and creative practice urgently deserves more publicity so that new interpretations and approaches do not take place in a critical or visual vacuum or sever amateur material from its wider narratives.

As digital scholarship offers alternative tools within the arts and humanities for collaborative ways to generate and interpret materials exchanged via digital means – with implications for teaching and learning, scholarship, knowledge creation and dissemination, and participation through virtual means – archive visual material acquires new potency. Archive amateur imagery is a means to question how people constructed ways of knowing about themselves, their families and friends, and others in the world. It is a means to reflect upon successive visual acts and interventions that constitute cultural memory and experience. Delving into the stories and meanings accompanying the amateur films considered in this book offers a reminder of the richness that those perspectives may also bring. As amateur film practice, historiography and scholarship approach their centenary, the delights and passions underlying its visual pursuits seem integral to understanding past amateur activity. Conversations about amateur film practices – in all senses – are entering a fascinating phase. This study seeks to be one step towards greater understanding.

Notes

1. (Anon.), 'They call it free cinema'.
2. T. Heyerdahl, 'How I filmed Kon Tiki', 780–1, 786; L. Wood, 'At your cinema – remarkable thrills'.
3. I. Craven, *Movies on Home Ground*.
4. A. Erll and A. Nunning, *Memory Studies*.
5. J. Brockmeier, 'After the archive: remapping memory'.
6. S. Nalbantian, *Memory in Literature: from Rousseau to Neuroscience*.
7. See for instance, I. Hodder (ed.), *Archaeological Theory Today*.
8. A. Gonzalez-Ruibal, '"The Dark Abyss of Time", accessed on 10 September 2010.
9. I. Hodder, *Symbols in Action*.
10. Elsaesser, T., 'The new film history as media archaeology'.
11. C. Witmore, 'Between media archaeology and memory practices: two recent excavations', accessed on 10 September 2010.
12. Conversation with Pam Wintle, senior archivist at Human Studies Film Archives, Smithsonian Institution, Washington DC. about streaming footage of Bamiyan Valley, 23 September 2010.

13 Caroline Forcier Holloway (Library and Archives Canada, Ottawa) kindly drew my attention to *Project Naming*, www.collectionscanada.gc.ca/inuit/index.html. Outreach to northern communities has used archive still imagery to foster intergenerational knowledge and memories-sharing and archive footage during the tenth anniversary of Nunavut (January 2009), Personal communication with author, 27 July 2010.
14 Passing reference to home movies during an interview by Gabriel Gatehouse, 'Iraq's growing disquiet at lack of infrastructure' in BBC Radio 4, 'From Our Own Correspondent', 3 July 2010.
15 H. Norris Nicholson, 'Moving pictures; moving memories: framing the interpretative gaze'; 'Manchester's *Moving Memories: Tales from Moss Side and Hulme*: archive film and community history-making' (2012).

Bibliography

(Anon.), 'A special plaque for cine clubs', *Amateur Cine World*, 5:5 (1938), 226.
(———.), 'A waiting room cinema' [reprinted from an undated issue of *The Daily Express*], *Amateur Films*, 1:4 (1928), 46.
(———.), 'Amateur films. A varied show in Manchester', *Manchester Guardian*, 6 December 1934, 18.
(———.), 'Amateur sound for the 1970s', *Movie Maker*, 4:3 (1970), 151–2.
(———.), 'Amateur Teddy Boy drama pulls a punch', *Amateur Cine World*, 21:7 (1957), 654.
(———.), 'Announcement for first ACW competition', *Amateur Cine World*, 1:5 (1934), 198.
(———.), 'Appeal to the filmmaker', *Amateur Cine World*, 15:9 (1952), 888.
(———.), 'BBC amateur movie series', *Movie Maker*, 11:9 (1977), 719.
(———.), 'BBC-TV competition', *Amateur Cine World*, 24:6 (1960), 549.
(———.), 'Behind the Iron Curtain with Super 8', *Movie Maker*, 11:9 (1977), 718.
(———.), 'Better demand for camera', *The Financial Times*, 9 June 1953, 7.
(———.), 'Black and KKK', *Literary Digest*, 16 September 1937, 6.
(———.), 'British films for UNICA', *Amateur Cine World*, 20:2 (1956), 269.
(———.), 'Cine circles continue work keeping movie makers in touch', *Amateur Cine World*, 19:1 (1955), 71.
(———.), 'Cine circles get under way. An invitation to lone workers', *Amateur Cine World*, 15:4 (1951), 379.
(———.), 'Cinema prosperity ahead', *Movie Maker* 7:1 (1973), 86.
(———.), 'Club news', *Amateur Cine World*, 1:3 (1934), 77.
(———.), 'Club news', *Amateur Cine World*, 6:4 (1939), 185.
(———.), 'Club news', *Movie Maker* 7:5 (1973), 342.
(———.), 'Competition for scenario for a film on the League of Nations', *Amateur Cine World*, 5:2 (1938), 85.
(———.), 'News of cine societies', *Home Movies and Home Talkies*, 8:9 (1940), 331.
(———.), 'Critics' review', *Amateur Cine World*, 1:1 (1934), 30.
(———.), 'Critics' review', *Amateur Cine World*, 1:5 (1934), 221.
(———.), 'Critics' review', *Amateur Cine World*, 1:7 (1934), 350.
(———.), 'Dying industries. Worthwhile subjects for documentary films – and where to find them', *Amateur Cine World*, 5:11 (1939), 566–7.

(——.), 'Editing ideas for amateurs in new documentary film', *Amateur Cine World*, 1:7 (1934), 324.
(——.), 'Editorial', *Amateur Cine World*, 1:1 (1934), 5–6.
(——.), 'Films of northern crafts. Schoolmaster's collection', *Manchester Guardian*, 10 March 1952, 8.
(——.), 'Free services offered to readers', *Amateur Cine World*, 1:1 (1934), 23.
(——.), 'George Newnes. Review of company's interests', *The Financial Times*, 8 July 1932, 4.
(——.), 'Glossary of cinematic terms, Part 1', *Amateur Films*, 2:4 (1929), 100.
(——.), 'In the condemned cell', *Amateur Cine World*, 18:11 (1954), 1145–6.
(——.), 'Individuals' films', *Manchester Guardian*, 4 December 1936, 13.
(——.), 'J. and G. Wadley's Our Heritage ("Amateur Film Show")', *Manchester Guardian*, 4 December 1939, 8.
(——.), 'John Baskeyfield, South Stafford's 1st Airborne', http://theairbornesoldier.com/johnbaskeyfield.html, accessed on 2 July 2009; BBC Stoke and Staffordshire, *Local Heroes: Jack Baskeyfield*, www.bbc.co.uk/stoke/content/articles/2009/08/24/john_baskeyfield_film_anniversary_feature.shtml, accessed on 9 February 2012.
(——.), 'Letters', *Amateur Cine World*, 6:12 (1940), 521.
(——.), 'Making films in the home', *The Financial Times*, 17 September 1957, 6.
(——.), 'Movies for the home', *The Financial Times*, 23 February 1955, 7.
(——.), 'Mr Never hits back', *Amateur Cine World*, 5:10 (1939), 505.
(——.), 'News from the societies', *Amateur Films*, 2:5 (1930), 121.
(——.), 'News of cine societies', *Home Movies and Home Talkies*, 8:9 (1940), 331.
(——.), 'Note on Federation of Cinematograph Societies', *Amateur Cine World*, 5:12 (1939), 615.
(——.), 'Novel exhibition', *Manchester Guardian*, 20 October 1932, 11.
(——.), 'Obituary: George H. Sewell (1899–1971)', *Movie Maker* 5:9 (1971), 565.
(——.), 'Our cover picture', *Amateur Films*, 1:12 [New Series, 1929], 294.
(——.), 'Personalities. – No. II. "Foster of Manchester"', *Amateur Films*, 1:3 (1928), 31.
(——.), 'Personalities. – No. V. "Frances Lascot"', *Amateur Films*, 1:6 (1929), 101.
(——.), 'Putting England on the film map', *Amateur Films*, 1:2 (1928), 21.
(——.),'Rural crafts at the Royal Lancashire Show', *Manchester Guardian*, 4 August 1950, 4.
(——.), 'Rural industries', *Manchester Guardian*, 20 December 1950, 4.
(——.), 'Screen communication. *The Financial Times* survey. The visual explosion', *The Financial Times*, 24 June 1969, 24.
(——.), 'The cinema family album', *Amateur Photographer and Cinematographer*, 64:2026 (27 September 1927), 30.
(——.), 'The lure of sponsorship', *Amateur Cine World*, 20:11 (1957), 1268.
(——.), 'The national safety first competition', *Amateur Cine World* 5:7 (1938), 368.
(——.), 'The news film. Attempt at intelligence needed', *Manchester Guardian*, 23 May 1934, 10.
(——.), 'The Ten Best of 1954', *Amateur Cine World*, 19:1 (1955), 55.
(——.), 'The TV threat', *Amateur Cine World*, 19:9 (1956), 970.
(——.), 'They call it free cinema', *Amateur Cine World*, 21:4 (1957), 356.
(——.), 'TV lessons for amateur filmmakers', *Amateur Cine World*, 14:11 (1951), 1070.
(——.), 'Weekend', *Amateur Cine World*, 1:5 (1934), 198.

(———.), 'What the societies are doing', *Amateur Cine World*, 1:7 (1934), 325.
(———.), 'What the societies are doing', *Amateur Cine World*, 6, 8 (1939), 371.
Aasman, S. I., 'Home movies, a new technology, a new duty, a new cultural practice', in S. Kmec and V. Thill (eds), *Private Eyes and the Public Gaze. The Manipulation and Valorisation of Amateur Images* (Trier, Kliomedia, 2009), pp. 45–51.
———., *Ritueel van huiselijk geluk. Een cultuur-historische verkenning van de familiefilm* [trans. *Rituals of Domestic Happiness: A Cultural History of the Home Movie*] (Groningen: University of Groningen Press, 2004).
Abbott, M., *Family Affairs: A History of the Family in 20th Century England* (London: Routledge, 2003).
'A. B.-G.', 'The varying moods of black and white', *Movie Maker*, 1:5 (1967), 366.
Abraham, A., 'Deteriorating memories: blurring fact and fiction in home movies in India', in K. L. Ishizuka and P. R. Zimmermann (eds), *Mining the Home Movie: Excavations in Histories and Memories* (Berkeley: University of California Press, 2008), pp. 168–84.
Aitkin, I., *Film and Reform. John Grierson and the Documentary Film Movement* (London: Routledge, 1990), pp. 182–3.
Aldgate, T., 'Loose ends, hidden gems and the moment of "melodramatic emotionality"', in J. Richards (ed.), *The Unknown Thirties. An Alternative History of the British Cinema, 1929–1939* (London: I. B. Tauris, 2000), pp. 219–36.
Alexander, D., 'Experiment in an unusual film style', *Amateur Cine World*, 11:10 [New Series, 4:1] (1948), 17–18.
Altrincham Cine Club, '*And on the Eighth Day*', *Movie Maker*, 5:6 (1971), 374.
'Anti-organiser of Kew, 'Letters', *Home Movies and Home Talkies*, 8: 8 (1940), 269.
Arnold, D., 'How television could yet bring a home movie boom', *The Financial Times*, 4 December 1974, 30.
Ashworth, T., *Forty Years On. A History of Bury Cine Society 1959–1999* (Bury: Bury Cine Society, 1999).
Atkinson, G. A., 'Introduction', in M. A. Lovell Burgess (ed.), *A Popular Account of the Amateur Cine Movement in Great Britain* (London: Sampson Low, Marston & Co., 1932), pp. xi–xii.
Bagnall, D. A., 'Plasticine pornography', *Movie Maker*, 7:6 (1973), 364.
Bailey, C., 'Cinema of duty', *Cine Action*, 28 (1990–91), 38–47.
Baldick, C., *The Modern Movement. The Oxford English Literary History, Vol. 10 1910–1940* (Oxford: Oxford University Press, 2004).
Ball, A., 'Problems of the propaganda film', *Amateur Cine World*, 16:7 (1952), 654–6, 662.
———., *Britain's Amateur Film Making during the Twentieth Century. Some Reminiscences by Ashby Ball* (Southport, A. Ball, July 2007).
———., *Southport Movie Makers. A Brief History, 1949–2007* (club publication).
Barnes, J., *The Beginnings of the Cinema in England 1894–1901* (5 volumes) (Exeter: University of Exeter Press, 1996–98).
Barry, L., 'Comments on colour', *Amateur Cine World*, 15:8 (1952), 807–8.
Bateman, R., 'Storylines', *Amateur Cine World*, 19 January 1967, 79.
Beavan, B., *Leisure, Citizenship and Working Class Men in Britain, 1850–1945* (Manchester: Manchester University Press, 2005).
Berger, J., 'Uses of photography', in J. Berger, *About Looking* (originally published by

Writers' and Readers' Publishing Co-op, 1980, then New York: Pantheon Books, 1980, and reissued London: Bloomsbury, 2009), 52–68.
Black, S., 'Shopping guide. Fool-proof home movies', *The Financial Times*, 16 October 1965, 7.
Blackpool ACC, 'Notes and news', *Amateur Cine World*, 19:1 (1955), 78.
Bolton Cine Society, 'Club news', *Amateur Cine World*, 1:3 (1934), 177.
Borsay, A., *Disability and Social Policy in Britain since 1750: A History of Exclusion* (Basingstoke: Palgrave, 2004).
Boswell, J., 'Wildlife filming for the BBC', *Movie Maker*, 7:9 (1973), 590–3, 632.
Bourdieu, P. (with L. Boltanski, R. Castel, D. Schnapper and J.-C. Chamboredon), *Photography: A Middle-brow Art* [trans. Shaun Whiteside] (Stanford, Stanford University Press, 1990).
Braggs, S. and Harris, D., *Sun, Fun and Crowds: Seaside Holidays between the Wars* (London: Tempus, 2000).
Breeds, J., 'What price pleasure?', *Movie Maker*, 11:9 (1977), 713.
Brendon, P., *Thomas Cook. 150 Years of Popular Tourism* (London: Secker and Warburg, 1991).
British Film Institute, *The Film in National Life* (London: BFI, 1943).
——, *Catalogue of the National Film Library* (London: BFI, 1936).
Brockmeier, J., 'After the archive: remapping memory', *Culture Psychology*, 16:1 (2010), 5–35.
Bromley, A. J., 'Sitting room cinema', *Amateur Cine World*, 5:10 (1939), 535.
Bromley, T. A., 'Personalities – No. X', *Amateur Films* 1:11 (1927), 252.
Brown, B., *Amateur Talking Pictures and Recording* (London: Sir Isaac Pitman & Sons, 1933).
Brunel, A., *Film Production* [Introduction by Alexander Korda] (London: Newnes, 1936).
Buchanan, A., *Filmmaking. From Script to Screen* (London: Faber and Faber, 1937).
Buckingham, D., *After the Death of Childhood* (Cambridge: Polity Press, 2000).
Buckley, C., and Fawcett, H., *Fashioning the Feminine. Representation and Women's Fashion from the Fin de Siecle to the Present* (London: I. B. Tauris, 2002).
Bunting, A., 'Holiday with a camera', *Movie Maker*, 4:8 (1970), 479.
Burleigh, J., 'BBC celebrates 50 years of television news reporting', *Independent*, 5 July 2004, 15.
Burton, A. (ed.), *The British Co-operative Movement Film Catalogue* (Trowbridge, Flick Books, 1997).
Butler, S., and Pickstone, J. (eds), 'Medicine in Manchester: Manchester in medicine, 1750–2000', *Bulletin of the John Rylands University Library of Manchester*, 87:1 (2007), 13–41.
Carleton, B., 'There's too much talk of technique', *Amateur Cine World*, 14:5 (1950), 421, 448.
Caunter, J., 'Inventor's delight', *Amateur Cine World*, 14:2 (1950), 131–3.
Cavalcanti, A., 'Mr Cavalcanti explains … why he banned *Man on the Road*', *Amateur Cine World*, 6:2 (1939), 60–1, 64, 104.
Chalfren, R., *Shapshot Versions of Life* (Bowling Green, OH: Bowling Green State University Popular Press, 1987).

Chalke, S., 'Animated explorations: the Grasshopper Group, 1953–83', in I. Craven (ed.), *Movies on Home Ground*, pp. 238–69.

Chambers, D., 'Family as place: family photograph albums and the domestication of public and private space', in J. M. Schwartz, and J. R. Ryan (eds), *Picturing Place. Photography and the Geographical Imagination* (London: I. B. Tauris, 2003), pp. 96–114.

Chittock, J., 'Films to borrow', *Movie Maker*, 1:1 (1967), 35, 70.

——., 'Films to borrow', *Movie Maker*, 1:5 (1967), 380.

Cine Smith, 'Putting the car on the screen', *Amateur Cine World*, 1.3 (1934), 163.

Citron, M. (ed.), *Home Movies and Other Necessary Fictions* (Minneapolis: University of Minnesota Press, 1998).

Clarke, B., 'Your comments', *Movie Maker*, 4:3 (1970), 128–9.

Cleave, A., 'Editorial', *Movie Maker* (October 1977), 783.

——., 'Editorial', *Movie Maker*, 11:12 (1977), 1005.

——., 'The Ten Best – and what's in it for you', *Movie Maker*, 11:10 (October, 1977), 783.

——., Untitled note, *Movie Maker*, 4:10 (1970), 615.

Coad, M. and J., *The IAC. The Film and Video Council. A History of the First Fifty Years* (Epsom: The Film and Video Council, 2007).

Collyer, G., 'Composing a cine picture. The rules of cine artistry', *Amateur Cine World*, 1:2 (1934), 25.

Commission on Educational and Cultural Films (CEC Films), *The Film in National Life* (London: George Allen and Unwin, 1932).

Constantine, S., *Social Conditions in Britain, 1918–1939* (London: Methuen, 1983).

Cook, J., '"This is not Hollywood": Peter Watkins and the challenge of amateurism', presented at *Small-gauge Storytelling: The Amateur Fiction Film*, University of Liverpool, 9 June 2010.

Cooke, L., 'British cinema', in J. Nelmes (ed.), *An Introduction to Film Studies* (London and New York: Routledge, 1996) [second edition, 1999], pp. 348–80.

Corbett, D. P., Holt, Y. and Russell F. (eds), *The Geographies of Englishness: Landscape and the National Past 1880–1940* (New Haven, CT: Yale University Press, 2002).

Cousselt, L., 'On giving that special show', *Amateur Photographer and Cinematographer*, 64:2032 (1927), 25–6.

Craig, B. L., 'Selected themes in the literature on memory and their pertinence to archives', *American Archivist*, 62.5 (2002), www.archivists.org/periodicals/aa_v65/v65_2/index.asp, accessed on 21 May 2010.

Craven, I., 'Introduction. A *Very Fishy Tale*: the curious case of amateur subjectivities', in I. Craven (ed.), *Movies on Home Ground*, pp. 1–33.

——., (ed.), *Movies on Home Ground. Explorations in Amateur Cinema* (Newcastle upon Tyne: Cambridge Scholars Publishing, 2009).

——., 'Neither fanatical nor lukewarm. Amateur cinema as middle brow culture', Paper presented at *Researching the Middle Brow: Resources and Archives*, Middlebrow Cultures Conference, Glasgow 14–15 July 2009.

Crawford, G., *Consuming Sport. Fans, Sport and Culture* (London and New York: Routledge, 2004).

Cresswell, T., *On the Move: Mobility in the Modern Western World* (London: CRC Press, 2006).

Cronin, J., and Rhodes, E., *Belle Vue* (Stroud: Tempus Publishing, 1999).

Cross, B., 'Mimeses and the spatial economy of children's play', in R. Willett, M. Robinson and J. Marsh (eds), *Play, Creativity and Digital Cultures* (New York and London, New York Press, 2009), pp. 125–44.

Cross, G. S., and Walton, J. K., *The Playful Crowd: Pleasure Places in the Twentieth Century* (New York: Columbia University Press, 2005).

Cubitt, G., *History and Memory. Historical Approaches* (Manchester: Manchester University Press, 2007).

Cuevas, E., (ed.), *La casa abieta: El cine domestico y sus reciclajes contemporaneous* [trans. *The Open House: Home Movies and Their Contemporary Recycling*] (Madrid: Colección Textos Documenta, Ocho y Medio, 2009).

Culbert, D., 'Public diplomacy and the international history of mass media: the USA, the Kennedy assassination and the world', *Historical Journal of Radio and Television*, 30:3 (2010), 421–32.

Cutter, V., *Go East Young Man* (London: Regency Press, 1985).

Dankworth, L., '"Performing paradise". Dance, identity and tourism in the Mediterranean island of Mallorca', presented at *Visualising Paradise: The Mediterranean*, Centre for Mediterranean Studies, University of Leeds, 13–15 September 2004.

Darby, W. J., *Landscape and Identity: Geographies of Nation and Class in England* (Oxford and New York: Berg, 2000).

Davison, B., 'Movie making my way', *Movie Maker*, 5:3 (1971), 235–7.

Days, D., 'A movie maker's diary', *Amateur Cine World*, 19:8 (1955), 796.

de Groot, J., *Consuming History. Historians and Heritage in Contemporary Popular Culture* (London: Routledge, 2008).

de Klerk, N., 'Home away from home. Private films from the Dutch East Indies', in K. L. Ishizuka and P. R. Zimmermann (eds), *Mining the Home Movie: Excavations in Histories and Memories* (Berkeley: University of California Press, 2008), pp. 148–62.

de Kuyper, E., 'Aux origins du cinéma: le film de famille', in R. Odin (ed.), *Le Film de famille: usage privé, usage public* (Paris: Meridiens-Klincksieck, 1995), p. 16.

Denzin, N. K., *The Cinematic Society: The Voyeur's Gaze* (London: Sage, 1995).

Dolphin, H., 'Home portraits', *Amateur Cine World*, 1:3 (1934), 171.

Donald, J., Friedberg, A. and Marcus, L. (eds), *Close Up, 1927–1933: Cinema and Modernism* (London: Cassell, 1998).

Donaldson, L., *Cinematography for Amateurs* (London: Iliffe and Sons, 1916).

Dorme, Y., *Images cachés – Hidden Images*. Exhibition catalogue (Dudelange: Centre national de l'audiovisuel, 2007).

'Double Run', 'Films about children', *Amateur Cine World*, 24:5 (1960), 475.

——, 'The world at work and play', *Amatur Cine World*, 24:1 (1960), 50.

Draper, C., 'Filthy lucre', *Amateur Cine World*, 19:6 (1955), 551.

Dyer, N., 'Filming on the farm', *Amateur Cine World*, 14:4 (1950), 318–19.

Dyson, F., '"Sightings of a Lost Continent"? A consideration of the activities of the amateur cine-club Ace Movies and amateur film genre', presented at *Small-gauge Storytelling: The Amateur Fiction Film*, University of Liverpool, 9 June 2010.

Edensor, T., 'Automobility and national identity. Representation, geography and driving practice', in M. Featherstone, N. Thrift and J. Urry (eds), *Automobilities* (London and New York: Sage) and *Theory, Culture & Society*, 21:4/5 (2004), 101–20.

Edmonds, G., '"Remember, remember ..." An amateur narrative film and its half-remembered context', presented at *Small-gauge Storytelling: The Amateur Fiction Film*, University of Liverpool, 9 June 2010.

Edwards, E. and Hart, J. (eds), *Photographs Objects Histories. On the Materiality of Images* (London: Routledge, 1999).

Edwards, E., *Raw Histories. Photographs, Anthropology and Museums* (Oxford and New York: Berg, 2001).

Elliott, D. M., 'Prizewinner, but too horrific to be shown', *Amateur Cine World*, 24:6 (1960), 544.

Elsaesser, T., 'The new film history as media archaeology', *Cinemas. Journal of Film Studies*, 14:2–3 (2004), 75–117.

Engelstad, E. and Gerrard, S., 'Introduction. Challenging situatedness', in E. Engelstad and S. Gerrard (eds), *Challenging Situatedness: Gender, Culture and the Production of Knowledge* (Delft: Eburon Academic Publishers, 2005), pp. 1–26.

Enticknap, L., *Moving Image Technology: From Zoetrope to Digital* (London: Wallflower Press, 2005).

Erll, A. and Nunning, A., *Memory Studies. An International and Inter-disciplinary Handbook* (Berlin: de Gruyter, 2008).

Essen, W. M., 'Planned from script to screen', *Amateur Cine World*, 14:5 (1950), 415.

Fayde, I., 'A home of your own', *Amateur Cine World*, 16:1 (1952), 63–4.

Featherstone, M., 'Automobilities. An introduction', in M. Featherstone, N. Thrift and J. Urry (eds), *Automobilities* (London and New Delhi: Sage) and *Theory, Culture & Society*, 21:4/5 (2004), 1–24.

Film and Video Maker – 75th Year Commemorative Issue, IAC 1932–2007 (May–June 2007).

Film Archive Forum, *The Moving Image Archive Framework: Policies, Standards and Guidelines* (Film Archive Forum 2005), www.bufvc.ac.uk/faf/MIAFv1.pdf, accessed on 13 May 2010.

Finkelstein, D., and McCleery, A. (eds), *The Book History Reader* (London: Routledge, 2002).

Fitton, J. S., 'Hyde Cine Society', *Amateur Cine World*, 1:8 (1934), 372.

'Flying Spot', 'Telescan. News and views on TV and film topics', *Amateur Cine World*, 24:7 (1960), 650.

Franklin, J., 'Keeping it from the kids', *Movie Maker*, 1:2 (1967), 159.

Froude, L., 'Obituary note and tribute to George Sewell (1899–1971)', in M. and J. Coad, *The IAC / The Film and Video Council*, pp. 93–4.

Fullerton, J., and Söderbergh Widding, A. (eds), *Moving Images: From Edison to the Webcam* (Sydney: John Libbey & Co., 2000).

Fung, R., 'Remaking home movies', in K. L. Ishizuka and P. R. Zimmermann (eds), *Mining the Home Movie: Excavations in Histories and Memories* (Berkeley: University of California Press, 2008), pp. 29–40.

Geller, P., 'Into the glorious dawn: from Arctic home movie to missionary cinema', in Norris Nicholson, *Screening Culture*, pp. 103–12.

Gergen, M., 'Life stories: pieces of a dream', in G. Rosenwald and R. Ochberg (eds), *Storied Lives* (New Haven: Yale University Press, 1992), pp. 127–44.

Giard, L., de Certeau, M. and Mayol, P., *The Practice of Everyday Life. Vol 2 Living and*

Cooking. [trans. T. J. Tomasik] (Minneapolis: University of Minnesota Press, 1998).
Gibson-Graham et. al., 'Introduction', in J. K. Gibson-Graham, S. T. Resnick, and R. D. Wolff (eds), *Class and Its Others* (Minneapolis: University of Minnesota Press, 2000).
Gifford, D., 'Report on the skin trade', *Movie Maker*, 5:7 (1971), 449.
Gillis, J. R., *A World of Their Own Making: Myth, Ritual, and the Quest for Family Values* (Cambridge, MA: Harvard University Press, 1997).
——., 'Your Family in history: anthropology at home', *Magazine of History* (Organisation of American Historians) *Family History*, 15:4 (2001), www.oah.org/pubs/magazine/family/gillis.html, accessed on 10 November 2009.
Gomes, M., 'Working people, topical films, and home movies' in K. L. Ishizuka and P. R. Zimmermann (eds), *Mining the Home Movie: Excavations in Histories and Memories* (Berkeley: University of California Press, 2008), pp. 235–48.
Gonzalez-Ruibal, A., '"The Dark Abyss of Time". A review of Laurent Olivier: Le sombre abîme du temps. Mémoire et archéologie. Seuil, Paris, 2008', *Archaeolog: Memory Archives*, posted 19 June 2008, http://traumwerk.stanford.edu/archaeolog/2007/12/between_media_archaeology_and.html, accessed on 10 September 2010.
Gorsuch, A. E. and Koenker, D. P. (eds), *TURIZM. The Russian and East European Tourist under Capitalism and Socialism* (Ithaca, NY and London: Cornell University Press, 2006).
Gough, M., 'A double take in Torremolinos', *Film and Video Maker*, March–April 2007, 18–19.
Grafton, A., *Worlds Made by Words: Scholarship and Community in the Modern West* (Cambridge, MA: Harvard University Press, 2009).
Grele, R. J., 'Oral history as evidence', in T. L. Charlton, L. E. Myers and R. Sharpless (eds), *History of Oral History: Foundations and Methodology* (Lanham, ML: AltaMira Press, 2007), pp. 33–91.
Grey, M., 'Foreword', in V. Cutter, *Go East Young Man*, pp. 9–10.
Grimshaw, M. C., 'Digging for victory', *Home Movies and Home Talkies*, 8:10 (1940), 350, 356.
Gullace, N. F., 'Memory, memorials, and the post-war literary experience: traditional values and the legacy of World War I', *Twentieth Century British History*, 10:2 (1999), 235–43.
Gulzar, S. and Manthrop, S., *Black and White in Colour. Films Made by or about Black and Minority Ethnic Communities* (York: Yorkshire Film Archive, 2009).
Haines, G., 'Down in the forest', *Movie Maker*, 4:11 (1970), 678–80.
——., 'Filming along a lane', *Movie Maker*, 7:6 (1973), 380–2.
——., 'How about a movie with a message?', *Movie Maker*, 5:7 (1971), 514–17.
——., 'To market, to market', *Movie Maker*, 4:12 (1970), 756–8.
Hammond, M., '"The Men Who Came Back": anonymity and recognition in local British Roll of Honour films (1914–1918)', *Scope*, 14 (June 1999), www.scope.nottingham.ac.uk/reader/chapter.php?id=7, accessed on 6 November 2009.
Hanna, S., *The Lowry of Filmmaking Better than Chalk and Talk*, www.sam-hanna.co.uk/chalk/Contents.ht, accessed on 11 November 2010.
Haraway, D., *Simians, Cyborgs, and Women: The Reinvention of Nature* (New York: Routledge, Chapman and Hall, 1991).

Hargreaves, J., *Sport, Power and Culture: A Social and Historical Analysis of Popular Sports in Britain* (Oxford: Polity Press, 1986).
Harris, P. 'The editor's newsreel', *Home Movies and Home Talkies*, 8:7 (1939), 229.
——., 'The editor's newsreel', *Home Movies and Home Talkies*, 8:10 (1940), 350.
——., 'What about Christmas?', *Home Movies and Home Talkies*, 8:7 (1939), 231.
Harrison, B., *Peaceable Kingdom: Stability and Change in Modern Britain* (Oxford: Clarendon Press, 1982).
Harrisson, T. and Spender, H., *Britain in the Thirties: Worktown by Camera* (London: Unicorn Press, Royal College of Art, 1975).
J. Harvey, 'Your comments', *Movie Maker*, 5:6 (1971), 351.
Hawkes, J., *A Land* (London: Cresset Press, 1951).
Hawley, S., 'The outsider: the films of George Higginson', in S. Hawley, *Art School! Manchester School of Art since 1838. Contemporary Reflections* (Manchester: Manchester Metropolitan University, 2009), pp. 3–6.
Hendrick H., 'Constructions and reconstructions of British childhood: an interpretative survey 1800 to the present', in A. James and A. Prout (eds), *Constructing and Reconstructing Childhood: Contemporary Issues in the Sociological Study of Childhood* (London: Routledge, 1990) pp. 34–62.
Hennessy, P., *Having It So Good. Britain in the 1950s* (London: Penguin, 2007).
Hertogs, D. and de Klerk. N., *Uncharted Territory: Essays on Early Non-fiction Film* (Amsterdam: Nederlands Filmmuseum, 1997).
Hetherington, K. and Cronin, A. (eds), *Consuming the Entrepreneurial City: Image, Memory, Spectacle* (New York: Routledge, 2008).
Heyerdahl, T., 'How I filmed Kon Tiki', *Amateur Cine World*, 16:8 (1952), 780–1.
Hickie, A. P., 'A plea for purity', *Amateur Cine World*, 13:3 [New Series] (1967), 71.
Higgins, J., 'What should we censor?', *Movie Maker*, 7:11 (1973), 734.
Highmore, B., *Everyday Life and Cultural Theory. An Introduction* (Routledge: London, 2002).
Hill, J., *Sport, Leisure and Culture in Twentieth-century Britain* (Basingstoke: Palgrave, 2002).
Hobbs, E. W., *Cinematography for Amateurs* (London: Cassell & Co., 1930).
Hobson, A. D., 'How to make a travel film', *Amateur Films*, 1:3 (1928), 29–30.
Hodder, I. (ed.), *Archaeological Theory Today* (Cambridge: Polity Press, 2001).
——., *Symbols in Action: Ethnoarchaeological Studies of Material Culture* (Cambridge: Cambridge University Press, 2009).
Hogenkamp, B., *Deadly Parallels: Film and the Left in Britain, 1929–1939* (London: Lawrence and Wishart, 1986).
Hoggart, R., *A Local Habitation. Life and Times, 1918–1940* (Oxford: Oxford University Press, 1988).
Hopkins, H., *The New Look: A Social History of the 1940s and 1950s in Britain* (London: Secker and Warburg, 1964).
Hornsey, B., *Ninety Years of Cinema in Manchester: A Chronological Essay in Celebration of the Cinemas* (Wakefield: Mercia Cinema Society and Fuchsiaprint, 1999).
Horsley, P. and Hirst, A., *Fleetwood's Fishing Industry: The Story of Deep-sea Fishing from Fleetwood, 1840–1990* (Beverley: Hutton Press, 1991).
Hoskins, W. G., *The Making of the English Landscape* (London: Hodder and Stoughton, 1970).

House of Commons Library, *A Century of Change: Trends in UK Statistics since 1900, Research Paper 99/111*, 21 December 1999, p. 24, www.parliament.uk/documents/commons/lib/research/rp99/rp99-111.pdf, accessed on 25 June 2010.

Houston, P., *Keepers of the Frame: The Film Archives* (London: British Film Institute, 1994).

Howe, M., '"The photographic hangover": reconsidering the aesthetics of the 8mm home movie', presented at *Saving Private Reels. On the Presentation, Appropriation and Rec-contextualisation of the Amateur Moving Image*, University College Cork, Ireland, 16–19 September 2010.

Hubble, N., *Mass Observation and Everyday Life: Culture, History, Theory* (London: Palgrave Macmillan, 2005).

Huggins, M., 'More sinful pleasures? Leisure, respectability and the male middle classes in Victorian England', *Journal of Social History*, 33:3 (2000), 585–600.

Hutton, P. H., *History as an Art of Memory* (Hanover, NH: University Press of New England, 1993).

Hyde Cine Society, 'Club news', *Amateur Cine World*, 6:8 (1939), 371.

Institute of Amateur Cinematography (IAC), *International Itinerary and Amateur Cinematographers' Year Book and Guide 1934* (London: Institute of Amateur Cinematography, 1935).

Jackson, A., *The Middle Classes, 1900–1950* (Nairn: David St John Thomas Publisher, 1991).

James, D. E. (ed.), *To Free the Cinema: Jonas Mekas and the New York Underground* (Princeton, NJ: Princeton University Press, 1992).

James, L., *The Middle Class. A History* (London: Little Brown, 2006).

Jimerson, R. C., 'Embracing the power of archives', *The American Archivist*, 69 (2006), 19–32.

Jones, E. L. and Pickstone, J. V., *The Quest for Public Health in Manchester. The Industrial City, the NHS and Recent History* (Manchester: Manchester NHS Primary Care Trust, 2008).

Jones, E. L. and Snow, S., *Against the Odds: Black and Minority Ethnic Clinicians and Manchester 1948–2009* (Manchester: Manchester NHS Primary Care Trust, 2010).

Kapstein, N. (ed.), *Jubilee Book. Essays on Amateur Film* (Charleroi: Association européenne inédits, 1997).

Katelle, A. D., *Home Movies. A History of the American Industry, 1897–1979* (Nashau, NH: Transition Publishing, 2000).

——., 'The Amateur Cinema League and its films', *Film History*, 15:2 (2003), 230–51.

Kedward, J., 'On Péter Forgács', www.forgacpeter.hu/prev_version/eng/main/press/articles/jessica_kedward.html, accessed on 7 February 2012.

Kidd, A. and Nicholls, D. (eds), *Gender, Civic Culture and Consumerism* (Manchester: Manchester University Press, 1999).

——., *The Making of the British Middle Classes? Studies of Regional and Cultural Diversity since the Eighteenth Century* (Stroud: Sutton Publishing, 1998).

King, D. S., *In the Name of Liberalism: Illiberal Social Policy in the USA and Britain* (Oxford: Oxford University Press, 1999).

Kirkham, R. S., 'Filming for victory', *Home Movies and Home Talkies*, 9:1 (1940), 5–6.

Kmec, S. and Thill, V. (eds), *Private Eyes and the Public Graze. The Manipulation and Valorization of Amateur Images* (Trier: Kliomedia, 2009).

Koenker, D. P., 'Travel to work, travel to play: on Russian tourism, travel and leisure', *Slavic Review*, 62:4 (2003), 657–65.
Korda, A., 'Readers' thoughts', *Amateur Cine World*, 1:2 (1934), 7.
Kuhn, A., *Family Secrets: Acts of Memory and Imagination* (London: Verso, 2002).
Kuhn, A. and Emiko McAllister, K., 'Locating memory – photographic acts – an introduction', in A. Kuhn and K. Emiko McAllister (eds), *Locating Memory. Photographic Acts* (Oxford: Berghahn Books, 2006), pp. 1–20.
Kynaston, D., *Family Britain, 1951–1957. Tales of a New Jerusalem* (London: Bloomsbury Publishing, 2009). Review by Simon Garfield, *Observer*, 1 November 2009, 21.
Landzelius, M., 'The body', in J. S. Duncan, N. C. Johnson and R. H. Schein, *A Companion to Cultural Geography* (Oxford: Blackwell, 2004), pp. 279–97.
Langhamer, C., *Women's Leisure in England, 1920–60* (Manchester: Manchester University Press, 2000).
Langlands, T., *Popular Cinematography* (London: W. & G. Foyles, 1926).
——., 'Profitable everyday cine subjects', *Amateur Photographer and Cinematographer*, 64:2033 (1927), 148.
Lascot, F., 'My very first film', *Amateur Films*, 1:5 (1928), 75.
Law. J. M., 'Introduction: cultural memory. The past and the static of the present', *Acta Orientalia Vilnensia*, 7:1–2 (2006), 7–12.
Le Neve Foster, P., 'Money or brains', *Amateur Photographer and Cinematographer*, 64:2034 (1927), 33.
——., 'Music for films', *Amateur Photographer and Cinematographer* 64:2037 (1927), 526.
——., 'A movie maker in Moscow. A presentation at the Photographic Society's kinematograph meeting', *Amateur Cine World*, 1:1 (1934), 31.
——., 'Manchester Film Society news', *Amateur Cine World*, 1:1 (1934), 40.
——., 'Every cine enthusiast must aim at originality', *Amateur Cine World*, 1:1 (1934), 27.
League of Nations Child Welfare Committee, *Recreational Aspects of Cinematography* (Geneva: League of Nations, 1936).
Leigh and District Cine Society, '*Our Town*', *Amateur Cine World*, 16:10 (1953), 676.
LeMahieu, D. L., *A Culture for Democracy* (Oxford: Oxford University Press, 1988).
Lewis, J., *Women in England 1870–1950* (Brighton: Harvester Wheatsheaf, 1984).
Lomax, H., 'Plan a scenario for filming the family', *Amateur Cine World*, 1:1 (1934), 7.
Lotts, A., 'Price rises', *Movie Maker*, 11:12 (1977), 1006.
Lovell Burgess, M. A., *A Popular Account of the Amateur Cine Movement in Great Britain* (London: Sampson Low, Marston & Co., 1932).
Low, R., *The History of the British Film, 1918–1929* (London: Routledge, 1997).
——., *The History of the British Film, 1929–1939: Documentary and Educational Films of the 1930s* (London: Allen & Unwin, 1979).
——., *History of British Film: Films of Comment and Persuasion of the 1930s* (London: Routledge, 1997).
'Lynx', 'But why not try to be better than professionals?', *Amateur Cine World*, 19:6 (1955), 541–2.
Macdougall, D., 'Anthropology and the cinematic imagination', in C. Morton and E. Edwards (eds), *Photography, Anthropology and History. Expanding the Frame* (Farnham: Ashgate Publishing, 2009), pp. 55–65.

Mackenzie, J. M., *Propaganda and Empire: The Manipulation of British Public Opinion 1880–1960* (Manchester: Manchester University Press, 1984).

Macpherson, K., *Close Up*, Vols 1–10 (Territet: Pool, 1927–33).

Malholtra, R. and Puwar, N., 'Selections from Raj Malhotra's (Indian Workers' Association) cine collection', presented at *AHRC Cine, Space and Memory Workshop*, The Herbert, Coventry, 30 January 2007.

Malik, S., 'Beyond the cinema of duty?', in A. Higson (ed.), *Dissolving Views: Key Writings on British Cinema* (London: Cassell, 1996), pp. 202–15.

Malthouse, G., '21 years of amateur movies. ACW celebrates its majority', *Amateur Cine World*, 19:1 (1955), 36–9, 166–9.

——., 'ACW badge is on its way', *Amateur Cine World*, 15:3 (1951), 226.

——., 'Amateur status', *Amateur Cine World*, 11:11 (1948) [New Series, 4:2], 51.

——., 'Cinematography in wartime', *Amateur Cine World, Diary, 1941* (London, 1941).

——., 'Editorial', *Amateur Cine World*, 12:1 (1948), 137.

——., 'Editorial', *Amateur Cine World*, 11:10 [New Series 4:1] (1948), 11.

——., 'Editorial', *Amateur Cine World* (Double quarterly issue), December 1946, 23.

——., 'Editorial', *Amateur Cine World*, 6:7 (1939), 309.

——., 'Editorial', *Amateur Cine World*, 8 January 1961, 746.

——., 'Editorial', *Amateur Cine World*, 6:7 (1939), 309.

——., 'Editorial', *Amateur Cine World*, 11:12 [New Series 4:3] (1948), 93–4.

——., 'How the prize winning films were chosen', *Amateur Cine World*, 15:1 (1951), 31.

——., 'Introducing *Amateur Cine World* Weekly', *Amateur Cine World*, 24:8 (1961), 784.

——., 'Joy through strength', *Amateur Cine World*, 6:4 (1939), 161–2.

——., 'Leader strip', *Amateur Cine World*, 15:9 (1953), 894.

——., 'Letters' page – editor's note', *Amateur Cine World*, 7:12 (1940), 520.

——., 'Markets for your films', *Amateur Cine World*, 6:8 (1939), 345.

——., 'The 1948 "Ten Best"', *Amateur Cine World*, 11:10 (1948) [New Series, 4:1], 11.

——., 'The ACW badge is here', *Amateur Cine World*, 15:9 (1952), 889.

——., 'The ACW cine circles', *Amateur Cine World*, 15:3 (1953), 227.

——., 'The films that did not win', *Amateur Cine World*, 11:12 [New Series 4:3] (1948), 93–4.

——., 'The widening pattern of amateur filmmaking' *Amateur Cine World*, 24:7 (1960), 650.

——., 'TV beckons the amateur', *Amateur Cine World*, 19:5 (1955), 438.

——., 'What shall I film in wartime?' *Amateur Cine World*, 6:9 (1940), 412–13.

——., 'Why does the amateur filmmaker copy the prof?', *Amateur Cine World*, 19:2 (1955), 153.

——., 'Why the hose piping?', *Amateur Cine World*, 14:11 (1951), 1070.

Mangan, J. A. (ed.), *Reformers, Sport, Modernizers: Middle-Class Revolutionaries* (London: Frank Cass, 2002).

Marcus, L., *The Tenth Muse: Writing about Cinema in the Modernist Period* (Oxford: Oxford University Press, 2007).

Marr, A., *A History of Modern Britain* (London: Pan Books, 2007).

Marsh, P., 'Predictions', *Movie Maker*, 4:6 (1970), 324–5.

Martin, J., '*Man of the Road*. How the Ten Best Winners made their films', *Amateur Cine World*, 6:2 (1939), 77–8.

Matless, D., *Landscape and Englishness* (London: Reaktion, 1998).
Maynard Hackett, H., 'A successful amateur movie maker asks "Coming my way?"', *Amateur Cine World*, 11:11 [New Series, 4:2] (1948), 60–2.
McBain, J., 'And the winner is … A brief history of the Scottish Amateur Film Festival, 1933–86', in Kapstein (ed.), *Jubilee Book*, pp. 97–105.
McDonald, J., 'Filming a portrait from life', *Movie Maker*, 7:7 (1973), 458–60.
McDonald, S., *History of Picture Post Hulton Archive – History in Pictures*, 15 October 2004, http://corporate.gettyimages.com/masters2/conservation/articles/HAHistory.pdf, accessed on 14 January 2010.
McKee, G., *Half Century of Film Collecting* (Gerrards Cross: Privately published, 1993).
——., *The Home Cinema: Classic Home Movie Projectors, 1922–1940* (Gerrards Cross: Privately published, 1989).
McKernan, L., *Yesterday's News: The British Cinema Newsreel Reader* (London, BUFVC, 2002).
Merriman, P., 'Driving places: Marc Augé, non-places and the geographies of England's M1 motorway', in M. Featherstone, N. Thrift and J. Urry (eds), *Automobilities* (London and New Delhi: Sage) and *Theory, Culture & Society*, 21:4/5 (2004), 145–67.
Messel, R., *This Film Business* (London: Ernest Benn, 1928).
Miller, R., 'Letter', *Movie Maker*, 4:12 (1970), p. 782.
Ministry of Education, *The Youth Service in England and Wales*. Cmnd. 929 (HMSO, 1960).
Moir, S., 'New ideas in your holiday film', *Amateur Photographer and Cinematographer*, 84:2541 (1937), 91.
Moran, J. M., *There's No Place Like Home Video* (Minneapolis: University of Minnesota Press, 2002).
Mortimer, F. J., 'Amateur cinematography matters for social purposes', *Amateur Photographer and Cinematographer*, 84:2540 (1937), 53.
——., 'The coming boom in amateur cinematography', *Amateur Photographer and Cinematographer*, 64:2020 (1927), 77.
——., 'Spirit of the times', *Amateur Photographer and Cinematographer*, 64:2019 (1927), 45.
Morton, H. V., *In Search of England* (London: Methuen & Co., 1927).
Motrescu, A., 'British colonial identity in amateur films from India and Australia, 1920–1940s', Department of Drama, University of Bristol (unpublished thesis, 2007).
——., 'Private Australia: re-imagined nationhood in interwar colonial home-movies', *Journal of Australian Studies*, 34:3 (2010), 317–30.
——., 'Uncensored politics in British home-movies from 1920s–1950s', presented at *Saving Private Reels. On the Presentation, Appropriation and Re-contextualisation of the Amateur Moving Image*, University College Cork, Ireland, 17–19 September 2010.
Mowat, C. L., *Britain between the Wars: 1918–1940* (London: Methuen, 1968).
Muir, R. '"A Land" revisited: Jacquetta Hawkes and the landscape tradition', *Proceedings of the Dorset Natural History and Archaeological Society*, 119 (1997), 25–30.
——., *Approaches to Landscape* (Basingstoke: Macmillan, 1999).
Museums, Libraries and Archives Council, *Hidden Treasures: The U.K Audiovisual Archives Strategic Framework* (London: Film Archive Forum, 2004).

Nalbantian, S., *Memory in Literature: from Rousseau to Neuroscience* (London: Palgrave Macmillan, 2003).
Nicholls, R., *The Belle Vue Story* (Manchester: Neil Richardson, 1992).
Nichols, B., *The Memory of Loss: Péter Forgács's Saga of Family Life and Social Hell – in Dialogue with Péter Forgács* (2005), http://forgacspeter.hu/english/bibliography, accessed on 19 May 2010.
Nicholson, L. and McMullen, H. T., *History of the East Lancashire Regiment in the Great War 1914–1918* (Liverpool: Littlebury Bros, 1936).
Nicholson, S., *The Censorship of British Theatre, 1900–1968 Vol. 1 1900–1932* (Exeter: Exeter University Press, 2003).
'1914–18 of Gidea Park, Essex', 'Letters', *Home Movies and Home Talkies*, 8:7 (1939), 251.
Norris Gleason, M., *Scenario Writing and Producing for the Amateur* (Boston, American Photographic Publishing Co., 1929).
Norris Nicholson, H., 'Amateur film culture and practices: almost one hundred years of changing solitudes', presented at *Personal Film: From Home Movie to User-generated Content*, British Library, London, 24 November 2009.
——., 'At home and abroad with cine enthusiasts: regional amateur filmmaking and visualising the Mediterranean, c. 1928–1962', *Geo Journal*, 59:4 (2004), 323–33.
——., '"At Ilkley they sell lovely": regional memory and experience in amateur movies', in P. van Wijk (ed.), *'You Can't See What You Don't Know. Amateur Film as Evidence* (Amsterdam: Film Research Foundation SFW, second edition, 1996), pp. 26–31.
——., 'Authority, aesthetics and visions of the workplace in home movies', in K. L. Ishizuka and P. R. Zimmermann (eds), *Mining the Home Movie: Excavations in Histories and Memories* (Berkeley: University of California Press, 2008), pp. 214–30.
——., 'British holiday films of the Mediterranean. At home and abroad with home movies, c. 1925–36', *Film History*, 15:2 (2003), 102–16.
——., 'Cinemas of catastrophe and continuity: mapping out amateur practices of intentional history-making in North West England, c. 1927–1977', in B. Monahan, L. Rascardi and G. Young (eds), *Saving Private Reels. Presentation, Appropriation and Re-contextualisation of the Amateur Moving Image* (London: Continuum, forthcoming).
——., 'Cultural relations and comfortable curiosity: Manchester's Cold War tourism in archive film', in C. Danks (ed.)., *Manchester/St Petersburg Friendship Society 50th Anniversary* (Moscow: Europe Publishing House, 2012).
——., 'Floating hotels: cruise holidays and amateur filmmaking in the interwar period', in D. Clarke, M. Doel, and V. Crawford Pfannhauser (eds), *Moving Pictures / Stopping Places: Hotels & Motels on Film* (Lanham, ML: Rowman and Littlefield, 2009), pp. 49–71.
——., 'Framing the view: holiday recording and Britain's amateur film movement c. 1925–1950', in I. Craven (ed.), *Movies on Home Ground*, pp. 93–127.
——., 'Handle with care! Working with other people's memories', presented at *The Visual Archive: The Moving Image and Memory*. ESRC Centre for Research on Socio-Cultural Change, Open University, Milton Keynes, 28–9 May 2009.
——., 'In amateur hands: framing time and space in home movies', *History Workshop Journal*, 43 (1997), 198–212.

——., 'Journeys into seeing: amateur film and British tourism encounters in Russia, c. 1932', *New Readings*, 10 (2009), 57–71, www.cardiff.ac.uk/euros/resources/newreadings/, accessed on 1 May 2010.

——., 'Manchester's *Moving Memories: Tales from Moss Side and Hulme*: archive film and community history-making', in S. Kmec and V. Thill (eds), *Tourists and Nomads. Amateur Images of Migration* (Marburg: Jonas Verlag, 2012).

——., 'Moving bodies and the amateur gaze: A historical perspective', in Grethe Mitchell (ed.), *Theory, Art and Practice of Movement Capture, Analysis and Preservation* (Bristol: Intellect, 2012).

——., 'Moving pictures; moving memories: framing the interpretative gaze', in S. Kmec and V. Thill (eds) *Private Eyes and the Public Gaze. The Manipulation and Valorization of Amateur Images* (Trier: Kliomedia, 2009), pp. 69–78.

——., 'Old world traditions ... and modernity', in Cunard's transatlantic films, c. 1920–35: making connections between early promotional films and urban change', in R. Koeck and L. Roberts (eds), *The City and the Moving Image* (Basingstoke: Palgrave Macmillan, 2010), 63–9.

——., 'Purposeful pleasures: social awareness and amateur film practice in Britain', presented at *Ways of Watching*, North East Historic Film Archive, Maine, USA, 24–5 July 2009.

——., *Screening Culture: Constructing Image and Identity* (Lanham, ML.: Rowman and Littlefield / Lexington Books, 2003).

——., '"Seeing it how it was?": Childhood, memory and identity in home-movies', *Area*, 33:2 (2001), 128–40.

——., 'Shooting the Mediterranean: conflict, compassion and amateur filmmaking in the Mediterranean, c. 1925–1939', *Journal of Intercultural Studies*, 27:3 (2006), 313–30.

——., 'Sites of meaning: picturing Mediterranean and other landscapes in British home movies, c. 1928–1965', in M. Lefebvre (ed.), *Film and Landscape* (London: Routledge, 2006), pp. 167–88.

——., 'Telling travellers' tales: framing the world in home movies, c. 1935–67', in T. Cresswell and D. Dixon (eds), *Engaging Film: Geographies of Mobility and Identity* (Lanham, ML: Rowman and Littlefield, 2002), pp. 47–68.

——., 'Through the Balkan states: home movies as travel texts and tourism histories', *Tourist Studies*, 6:1 (2006), 13–36.

——., 'Two tales of a city: Salford in regional filmmaking, c. 1957–1973', *Manchester Review for Regional History*, 15 (2001), 41–53, www.mcrh.mmu.ac.uk/pubs/, accessed on 20 October 2009.

——., 'Virtuous or virtual histories? Changing ways of working with archival film footage', presented at *Future Histories of the Moving Image*, University of Sunderland, 16–18 November 2007.

——. 'Women and amateur filmmaking' (forthcoming).

Notcutt, L. A., 'Ideas for documentary films', *Amateur Cine World*, 6:1 (1939), 9–11.

Odin, R. (ed.), *Le Film de famille: usage privé, usage public* (Paris: Méridiens-Klincksieck, 1995).

——. 'Le film de famille dans l'institution familiale', in R. Odin (ed), *Le Film de famille: usage privé, usage public*, pp. 35–7.

Osterling, J. and Dawson, G., 'Early recognition of children with autism: a study of first birthday home videotapes', *Journal of Autism and Developmental Disorders*, 23:3 (1994), 247–57.

Palmer, A., *Recording Britain* (Oxford: Oxford University Press / The Pilgrim's Trust, 1946–49).

Peterson, J. L., *Making the World Exotic: Travelogue and Silent Non-fiction Film*, (Durham: Duke University Press, 2004).

Phillips, C., 'Your comments', *Movie Maker*, 4:7 (1970), 390.

Pople, K. A. S., 'TV commericals: a model for the amateur', *Amateur Cine World*, 23:8 (1960), 797–8.

Porter, J. M., *The Fishing Industry at Fleetwood* (Fleetwood Maritime Heritage Trust: Fleetwood Fishing History, 2008), www.fleetwood-fishing-industry.co.uk/fleetwood-fishing-history/, accessed on 8 October 2009.

Powell, D., 'A considerable advance', *Amateur Cine World*, 14:1 (1950), 33.

'Professor Gumm Boyle', 'A new invention', *Amateur Films*, 1:3 (1928), 36.

'Provincial', 'Postscript to a festival visit', *Amateur Cine World*, 15:3 (1951), 239–40.

Pudovkin, V. R., *National Convention of Amateur Cinematograph Societies of Great Britain and Ireland*, 22–6 October 1929 (brochure).

Puwar, N., 'Social cinema scenes', *Space and Culture*, 10 (2007), 253–67, http://sac.sagepub.com/cgi/content/abstract/10/2/253, accessed on 6 May 2010.

Rabinbach, A., *The Human Motor: Energy, Fatigue, and the Origins of Modernity*, Berkeley and Los Angeles: University of California Press, 1992).

Reich, S. and Korot, B., *Three Tales* (2002), www.shapesoftime.net/pages/viewpage.asp?uniqid=990, accessed on 19 May 2010.

Reid, A., 'Exploring the magic of places', *Movie Maker*, 4:8 (1970), 480.

Rendell, D., *Photographers in the Altrincham area* (self-published: Altrincham, 2006).

Rhu, L. F., 'Home movies and personal documentaries. An interview with Ross McElwee', *Cineaste*, 29.3 (2004), 6–12.

Richards, J., 'Cinema-going in Worktown: regional film audiences in 1930s Britain', *Historical Journal of Film, Radio and Television*, 14:2 (1994), 147–66.

——., *Film and British National Identity* (Manchester: Manchester University Press, 1997).

Ricoeur, P., *Memory, History, Forgetting* (Chicago: University of Chicago Press, 2004).

Rodgers, L., 'Editorial – Is it my imagination or are members of cine clubs getting older and older?', *IAC News*, June 1973. Cited in M. and J. Coad, *The IAC*, p. 90–1.

Rodgers, P., 'So much for the clubs', *Movie Maker*, 1:1 (1967), 9.

Roepke, M., 'Analysing acts of acting in amateur films', presented at *Small-gauge Storytelling: The Amateur Fiction Film*, University of Liverpool, 9 June 2010.

——., *Privat-Vorstellung. Heimkino in Deutschland vor 1945. (Private Screening: Home Cinema in Germany before 1945)* (Hildesheim, Zürich and New York: Olms, 2006).

Rojek, C. and Urry, J. (eds), *Touring Cultures: Transformations of Travel and Theory* (London: Routledge, 1997).

Rose, G., 'Practising photography: an archive, a study, some photographs and a researcher', *Journal of Historical Geography*, 26:4 (2000), 555–71.

Rose, T., 'A family for adventure', *Movie Maker*, 4:4 (1970), 220–2.

——., 'A movie holiday to remember', *Movie Maker*, 4:1 (1970), 32.

——., 'Comment', *Movie Maker* 7:6 (1973), 362–3.

——., 'Comment', *Movie Maker*, 4: 11 (1970), 685–7.
——., 'Editorial', *Movie Maker*, 1:1 (1967), 8.
——., 'Editorial', *Movie Maker*, 9:1 (1975), 11.
——., 'Editorial', *Movie Maker*, 4:9 (1970), 527–8.
——., 'Making the whole world kin', *Movie Maker*, 7:9 (1973), 578.
——., 'Memo to the BBC', *Movie Maker*, 7:9 (1973), 578.
——., 'Other peoples films', *Movie Maker*, 7:9 (1973), 594–6.
——., 'Other peoples pictures', *Movie Maker*, 4:4 (1970), 208–9.
——., 'Other peoples pictures', *Movie Maker*, 4:9 (1970), 546–8.
——., 'Running, jumping and never standing still', *Movie Maker*, 3:6 (1967), 260–3.
——., 'Russian visits Grasshoppers', *Movie Maker*, 1:1 (1967), 12.
——., 'Surprises galore at San Feliu', *Movie Maker*, 1:2 (1967), 136–7.
——., 'The night home movies were seen by more than a million', *Movie Maker*, 1:6 (1967), 423–33.
——., 'Why we are launching *Movie Maker* and what's in it for you?', *Amateur Cine World*, 19 January 1967, 68–9.
Rose, T. and Cleave, A., 'Super 8 wins Ten Best trophy for first time', *Movie Maker*, 4:6 (1970), 345.
Russell, C., *Experimental Ethnography: The Work of Film in the Age of Video* (Durham, NC: Duke University Press, 1999).
Russell, D., *Looking North. Northern England and the National Imagination* (Manchester: Manchester University Press, 2004).
——., 'Sporting Manchester: from 1800 to the present. An introduction', *Sport in Manchester* (themed issue), *Manchester Region History Review*, 20 (2009), 1–23.
——., 'The football films', in S. Popple, P. Russell and V. Toulmin (eds), *The Lost World of Mitchell and Kenyon: Edwardian Britain on Film* (London: British Film Institute, 2004) pp. 169–80.
Ryan, J. R., *Picturing Empire. Photography and the Visualisation of the British Empire* (Chicago: University of Chicago Press, 1997).
Salford Cine Society, 'All are welcome', *Amateur Cine World*, 1:1 (1934), 40.
Salkeld, L., 'Named and shamed: the mother, gran and aunts who forced toddlers to fight like dogs', *The Daily Mail* (*MailOnline*, 21 April 2007), www.dailymail.co.uk/news/article-449714/, accessed on 10 November 2009.
Sampson, A., *Who Runs This Place? The Anatomy of Britain in the 21st Century* (London: John Murray, 2004).
Samuel, R., *Theatres of Memory* (London: Verso, 1994).
Sandbrook, D., *Never Had It So Good 1956–1963. A History of Britain from Suez to the Beatles* (London: Abacus, 2006).
——., *White Heat. A History of Britain in the Swinging 1960s* (London: Abacus, 2006).
Sandles, A., '100 years of recorded sound. Looking into the future', *The Financial Times*, 20 October 1977, 42.
Schivelbusch, W., *The Railway Journey. Trains and Travel in the Nineteenth Century* (Oxford: Blackwell, 1986).
Schneider, A., 'Home movie-making and the Swiss expatriate identities, in the 1920s and 1930s', *Film History*, 15:2 (2003), 166–76.
Schneider, T. D., 'The role of archived photographs in Native California archaeology', *Journal of Social Archaeology*, 7:1 (2007), 49–71.

Schwartz, J. M. and Cook, T., 'Archives, records and power. From (postmodernism) theory to archival performance', *Archival Science*, 2 (2002), 171–85.

———., 'Archives, records and power. The making of modern memory', *Archival Science*, 2 (2002), 1–19.

Schwartz, J. M. and Ryan, J. R., 'Photography and the geographical imagination', in Schwartz and Ryan (eds), *Picturing Place*, pp. 1–18.

———. (eds), *Picturing Place. Photography and the Geographical Imagination* (London: I. B. Tauris, 2003).

Sewell, G. H., 'Amateur cine-plays', *Amateur Photographer and Cinematographer*, 64:2021 (1927), 18–22.

———., *Commercial Cinematography for Business and Commerce using Sub-standard Film* (London: Pitman, 1933).

———. [?], 'Free services offered to readers', *Amateur Cine World*, 1:1 (1934), 23.

———., 'Here is advice on filming baby', *Amateur Cine World*, 1:2 (1934), 6.

———., 'Home movie-making is NOT expensive', *Amateur Cine World*, 1:2 (1934), 6.

———., 'London Film Festival', *IAC News*. Reprinted in M. and J. Coad. *The IAC*, p. 91.

———., 'Odd shots', *Amateur Cine World*, 14:1 (1950), 61.

———., 'Odd shots', *Amateur Cine World*, 15:3 (July 1951), 273–5.

———., 'On the set', *Amateur Films*, 1:12 (1929), 273.

———., 'Our cover picture', *Amateur Films*, 1:12 (1929), 294.

———., 'Rambling with a cine-camera', *Amateur Cine World*, 1:3 (1934), 162–3.

———., 'Talks to the tyro – I. What is it all about?', *Amateur Films*, 1:11 (1929), 252–3.

———., 'The editor to his readers', *Amateur Cine World*, 5:4 (1938), 226.

———., 'The ideal cine club', *Amateur Cine World*, 2:4 (1935), 163.

———., 'Tracing projector troubles under an African sun', *Amateur Cine World*, 11:11 [New Series, 4:2] (1948), 56, 62.

———., Untitled note, *Amateur Cine World*, 1:6 (1934), 245.

Shand, R., 'Amateur film re-located: localism in fact and fiction', in I. Craven, *Movies on Home Ground*, pp. 156–81.

Shand, R., 'Theorising amateur cinema: limitations and possibilities', *The Moving Image: The Journal of the Association of Moving Image Archivists* 8:2, (2008), 36–60, http://museweb01 pub.mse.jhu.edu/journals/the_moving_imagetoc/mov.8.2.html, accessed on 10 November 2010.

Shapely, P., 'The press and the system built developments of inner-city Manchester', *Manchester Region History Review*, 16 (2002–3), 30–9.

Shoard, M., *This Land Is Our Land. The Struggle for Britain's Countryside* (London: Paladin and Grafton, 1987).

Smith, J., 'A new wave of non-professionals', *Amateur Cine World*, 24:1 (1960), 46–7.

Smith, R. C., 'Analytic strategies for oral history interviews', in J. F. Gubrium and J. A. Holstein (eds), *Postmodern Interviewing* (London: Sage Publications, 2003), pp. 203–24.

Sowerby, A. L. M., 'Stereo cinematography', *Amateur Photographer*, 97:3075 (15 October 1947), 700.

Spence, J. and Holland P. (eds), *Family Snaps: the Meanings of Domestic Photography* (London: Virago, 1991).

Spencer, T., *Huddersfield Video and Cine Club Presents 75 Years of The Way We Were, 1932–2007* (Anniversary Club Programme, November 2007).

Spender, H., *Worktown People: Photographs from Northern England 1937–38* (Bristol: Falling Wall Press, 1995).

Spillman, R., 'Holiday cruise', *Movie Maker*, 5:3 (1971), 228–9.

'Sprocket's New Gate', 'Short ends', *Home Movies and Home Talkies*, 9:4 (1940), 94.

(Staff reporter), 'Home movies will help BBC to recreate 1930s', *The Times*, 21 September 1977, 16.

Stallybrass, P., and White, A., 'Bourgeois hysteria and the carnivalesque', in S. During (ed.), *The Cultural Studies Reader* (London: Routledge, 1993), pp. 291–2.

Stanley, J., 'Man goes to Moss Side: Caribbean migration to Manchester in the 1950s and 1960s', *Manchester Region History Review*, 16 (2002–3), 40–50.

Stebbins, R., *Serious Leisure. A Perspective for Our Time* (New Brunswick, NJ: Transaction Publishers, 2007), pp. 1–37.

Steedman, C., *Dust* (Manchester: Manchester University Press, 2001).

Stewart, J., 'South Side history in locals' home movies', *University of Chicago Magazine*, 99:4 (2007), http://magazine.uchicago.edu/0734/features/stewart.shtml, accessed on 18 November 2010.

Stockport and District Cine Club, 'Club news', *Amateur Cine World*, 1:7 (1934), 325.

Stone, M. and Streible, D., 'Introduction: small gauge and amateur film', *Film History*, 15:2 (2003), 123–5.

Straker, J., '*Man of Aran*: a lesson for amateurs', *Amateur Cine World*, 1:3 (1934), 175–6.

Strasser, A., *Amateur Films. Planning, Directing, Cutting* [trans. P. C. Smethurst] (London: Link House Publications, 1936).

——., 'Auntie and the blackout: a little comedy to show how our own life is affected by war', *Amateur Cine World*, 6:11 (1940), 475.

——., 'A war, a dog and a bone – a script for food rationing and a dog', *Amateur Cine World*, 7:12 (1940), 503–5.

——., 'Wartime plots for filming', *Amateur Cine World*, 6:10 (1940), 433–4, 444.

Struna, N. L., 'Historical research in physical activity', in J. R. Thomas and J. K. Nelson (eds), *Research Methods in Physical Activity* (Champaign: Human Kinetics, 2001), pp. 203–17.

Szczelkun, S., 'The value of home movies', *Oral History*, 28:2 (2000), 94–5.

Tait, G. B., 'Audiences are so contrary', *Amateur Cine World*, 20:2 (1956), 659, 678.

Talbot, F. A., *Practical Cinematography and its Applications* (London: W. Heinemann, 1913).

Tarrant, P., 'Planet usher: an interactive home movie', *Proceedings of the 12th Annual ACM International Conference on Multimedia, International Multimedia* (New York, 2004) pp. 987–8, http://portal.acm.org/citation, accessed on 10 November 2009.

Taylor, J., *A Dream of England. Landscape, Photography and the Tourist's Imagination* (Manchester: Manchester University Press, 1994).

Taylor, J., 'Seeing and sustainability', presented at *The Visual Archive: The Moving Image and Memory*, The ESRC Centre for Research on Socio-Cultural Change, Open University, Milton Keynes, 28–9 May 2009.

Tebbutt, M., 'Rambling and manly identity in Derbyshire's Dark Peak, 1880s–1920s', *Historical Journal*, 49:4 (2006), 1125–53.

——., *Being Boys: Youth, Leisure and Identity in the Interwar Years* (Manchester: Manchester University Press, 2011).

Tenkanen, S., 'Children as amateur filmmakers', presented at *Making Visual Histories: Critical Perspectives on Amateur Film Practice*, Manchester Centre for Regional History, Manchester Metropolitan University, 17 September 2008.

——., 'Searching for a 9.5mm family. Aspects on the privacy of home movies', *Ethnologi Fennica*, 33 (2006), 24–31.

'The Walrus', 'Piffle – a satirical column', *Amateur Photographer and Cinematographer*, 64:2021 (1927), 129.

Timmins, G., *Made in Lancashire: A History of Regional Industrialisation* (Manchester: Manchester University Press, 1998).

Titus, W. L., 'Extended family films from the Dutch East Indies'. *The 6th Orphan Film Symposium*, comments posted on 28 March 2008, http://blogs.nyu.edu/blogs/mlj260/orphans6/2008/03, accessed on 20 May 2010.

Todd, S., *Young Women, Work and Family in England, 1918–50* (Oxford: Oxford University Press, 2005).

Tomlinson, J., 'Welfare and the economy: The economic impact of the Welfare State, 1945–1951', *Twentieth Century British History*, 6:2 (1995), 194–219.

Toulmin, V., Russell, P. and Popple, S., *The Lost World of Mitchell and Kenyon: Edwardian Britain on Film* (London: British Film Institute, 2004).

Towner, J., *An Historical Geography of Recreation and Tourism, 1540–1940* (Chichester: John Wiley, 1996).

Trainor, R., 'Neither metropolitan nor provincial: the interwar middle class', in A. Kidd and D. Nicholls (eds), *The Making of the British Middle Class. Studies of Regional and Cultural Diversity since the Eighteenth Century* (Stroud: Sutton Publishing, 1998), pp. 203–13.

Urry, J., 'Globalising the tourist gaze. On tourist and tourism', *Barcelona Metropolis*, www.barcelonametropolis.cat/en/, accessed on 20 October 2009.

——., 'The place of emotions within place', in J. Davidson, L. Bondi and M. Smith (eds), *Emotional Geographies* (Aldershot: Ashgate, 2005), pp. 77–86.

——., *Sociology Beyond Societies: Mobilities for the Twenty-first Century* (London: Routledge, 2000).

van Alphen, E., *Towards a New Historiography: Péter Forgács and the Aesthetics of Temporality (2004)*, http://forgacspeter.hu/english/bibliography, accessed on 19 May 2010.

van Wijk, P. (ed.), *You Can't See What You Don't Know: Colloquium Reader of the Association Européean Inédits* (Charleroi: AEI / Amsterdam: Stichting Film en Wetenschap, 1994 [reprinted 1996]).

Victoria and Albert Museum, *Recording Britain*, www.vam.ac.uk/collections/paintings/stories/recording/index.html, accessed om 6 October 2009.

Volkert, G. R., 'A cine travel society', *Amateur Cine World*, 13:1 (1949), 36.

Wade, J., *Cine Cameras* (Princess, Risborough: Shire Publications, 2004).

Wadley, N. J., 'To the editor', *Amateur Cine World*, 5.2 (1938), 109.

Wahrman, D., *Imagining the Middle Class: The Political Representation of Class in Britain* (Cambridge: Cambridge University Press, 1995).

Wain, G., 'Hyde Cine Society', *Amateur Cine World*, 2.2 (1935), 20.

——., 'Notes on educational matters', *Home Movies and Home Talkies*, 8:9 (1940), 324.

Wallasey Amateur Cine Club, 'Club news', *Amateur Cine World*, 6:4 (1939), 185.

Walton, J. K., *The British Seaside Holidays and Resorts in the Twentieth Century* (Manchester: Manchester University Press, 2000).

Washbrook, R., 'Innovation on a shoe string: the films and filmmakers of the Scottish Amateur Film Festival', in I. Craven, *Movies on Home Ground*, pp. 36–64.

Watson, I., 'Audiences and 8mm', *Amateur Cine World*, 24:1 (1960), 73.

——., 'Comment', *Movie Maker*, 4:7 (1970), 401.

——., 'Meet the winners', *Movie Maker*, 5:6 (1971), 374.

——., 'No need to say goodbye', *Amateur Cine World*, 13:4 (26 January 1967), 104–5.

——., 'Super 8. Never heard of it!', *Movie Maker*, 4:6, (1970), 332.

——., 'The home movie industry is not too healthy', *Movie Maker*, 4:1 (1970), 83.

——., 'The Ten Best', *Movie Maker*, 7:6 (1973), 386.

——., 'Throw away the guidebooks!', *Movie Maker*, 4:3 (1970), 141–2.

——., 'Time for amateur movies to grow up', *Movie Maker*, 9:2 (1975), 94–5.

——., 'Too big for our bootlaces', *Movie Maker*, 11:11 (1977), 919.

Webb, D., 'Bahktin at the seaside: Utopia, modernity and the carnivalesque', *Theory, Culture and Society*, 22:3 (2005), 121–38.

West, O., 'This thing called montage', *Amateur Films*, 2:4 (1929), 93.

Whitfield, G., 'Nine five in Super 8 cameras', *Movie Maker*, 7:6 (1973), 417.

Wilkinson, M., and Mchain, L., 'When oriental clichés hide western ways', *The Financial Times*, 16 December 1977, 21.

Williams, P. M. and D. L., *Hooray for Jollywood: The Life of John E. Blakeley and the Mancunian Film Corporation* (Manchester: History on Your Doorstep, 2001).

Willumson, G., 'Making meaning. Displaced materiality in the library and art museum', in E. Edwards and J. Hart (eds), *Photographs Objects Histories*, pp. 65–84.

Winston, B., *Technologies of Seeing* (London: British Film Institute, 1996).

Winter, M. and Spurr, N. F., *Filmmaking on a Low Budget: The UNESCO-UNRWA Pilot Project* (Paris: UNESCO, 1960).

Witmore, C., 'Between media archaeology and memory practices: two recent excavations', *Archaeography Photoblog*, posted 6 December 2007, http://traumwerk.stanford.edu/archaeolog/2007/12, accessed on 10 September 2010.

Wood, L. 'At your cinema – remarkable thrills', *Amateur Cine World*, 16:8 (1952), 786.

——., 'At your cinema: wanted – Cine suffragettes', *Amateur Cine World*, 14:10 (1951), 993–6.

Wright, B., 'It began like this', *Amateur Cine World*, 5:1 (1938), 7–9.

Wright, J., 'Club commentary', *Movie Maker*, 1:2 (1967), 117.

——., 'Club commentary', *Movie Maker*, 4:6 (1970), 368.

——., 'Club commentary', *Movie Maker*, 4:10 (1970), 651.

——., 'Club commentary', *Movie Maker*, 5:2 (1971), 111–12.

——., 'Club commentary', *Movie Maker*, 7:5 (1973), 339–42.

——., 'Club commentary', *Movie Maker*, 7:11 (1973), 780.

——., 'Club commentary', *Movie Maker*, 11:7 (1977), 585.

——., 'Memberships melting', *Movie Maker*, 4:8 (1970), 508–9.

——., 'P. H. Cappello, *Life in a Movie Club* (New York: Vantage Press, 1970). A book review', *Movie Maker*, 4:8 (1970), 505.

——., 'Travellers' tale', *Movie Maker*, 11:10 (1977), 857.

Wylly, H. C., The *Loyal North Lancashire Regiment 1914–1919* (National Army Museum, London: The Naval and Military Press, 2007 [original pub.1933]).

Zimmermann, P., *Reel Families. A Social History of Family Film* (Bloomington and Indianapolis: Indiana University Press, 1995).

——., 'Speculations on home movies: thirty axioms for navigating historiography and psychic vectors', in S. Kmec and V. Thill (eds), *Private Eyes and the Public Gaze: The Manipulation and Valorization of Amateur Images* (Trier: Kliomedia, 2009), pp. 13–23.

Index

abroad 11, 28-39, 63, 75-6, 98-104, 118, 127-30, 167-200 *passim*, 220, 229-30
Acres, Birt 3
actors 1, 33
actuality 112, 118, 135, 152, 226
    see also topical
adolescent 66, 101, 160, 211, 227–8
    see also teenager; youth; youth culture
adoption 12, 209
advertising 3–5 *passim*, 64–9, 74, 126, 200
advisory press 36, 64, 67–8
    see also hobby press; specialist press
aesthetic 6, 16, 40–53 *passim*; 64–72 *passim*, 78, 95, 103–11 *passim*, 118–20, 147–54 *passim*, 162, 166, 198, 226, 242, 248
air travel 186–7, 195–9
    see also holiday films; holidays; leisure
album 93, 94, 109, 177, 243, 246
    see also snapshot; still photography
Alexander, Marjorie 97
alienation 100, 129, 159
Altrincham Cine Society (Altrincham Cine Club, Altrincham Video Society) 45, 51, 81, 93, 223
    see also Smith, Arthur
Amateur Cine World (ACW) 1–2, 30–9 *passim*, 62–87, 153–4, 182, 210, 214–15, 226, 238–9
    see also hobby press
Amateur Films 29, 62

amateur/professional relations 1–10 *passim*, 18, 32–55, 65–70, 74–9, 85–7
Anderson, Lindsay 120
animals 70, 96, 107, 145, 159, 179–82, 192, 194
animation 14, 31, 48–54 *passim*, 65, 76, 107, 179, 241, 243
anthropology 146, 244–5
archaeology 243–5
archival contexts 9, 16, 18, 30, 77, 109–112, 177, 185, 229–44
    digitisation and 247–9
    under representation and 12, 112, 166–8
    see also broadcasting; digital
art 7, 13, 32, 33
audience 1, 3, 5, 7, 12, 18, 28–30, 40–51 *passim*, 76–7
authority 73, 85, 104, 111, 120, 126, 161–76 *passim*, 201, 226–31
    see also local authority
avant-garde film 13, 14, 40, 55, 118
    see also experimental
award 31–2, 36–8, 44–51 *passim*, 64–5, 70, 80, 95, 106, 175, 199
    see also competition

Ball, Ashby 46–7, 213
    see also Southport Movie Makers
Barker Scarr John 187, 194–5
belonging 12, 20, 34, 55, 73, 121–3, 218, 239, 243

see also identity

Bickerstaffe, Arthur 50–1

birthday 2, 9–10, 13, 93–4, 102–3, 244

Black 12, 13, 43, 131, 148, 167–8, 227
    see also diversity; ethnicity; migration

blackout 35, 71, 73, 220

Bolton Amateur Cine Association (Bolton Cine Society) 30, 33, 70, 99
    see also Higginson, George

Boulting, John and Roy 1

British Broadcasting Corporation (BBC) 1, 35, 45–55 *passim*, 77, 83–4, 134, 218, 222–3

British Film Institute (BFI) 54, 74, 153–4, 156

broadcasting 7, 21, 77, 222, 228

Brookes, Ralph 99, 101–2, 129–32, 185

Brownlow, Kevin 67, 78, 222

Bury Cine Society 48–50

camera work 39, 77, 93, 107–8, 144, 154, 159, 177, 187, 197, 216–17, 228–9, 239

carnival 13, 123, 124–6, 130, 178, 180, 209, 209

car ownership 11, 30, 107, 132–5, 164–86 *passim*, 196–7

cataloguing 21, 22, 110, 154, 165, 167

celebrations 42–3, 51, 120–6 *passim*, 164

censorship 5, 8, 112, 153

charity 41, 48, 181, 209, 214
    see also welfare

childhood 2–3, 50, 92–117 *passim*, 132

children 2, 7, 12, 20, 30–1, 66, 80–1, 92–117, 121–35 *passim*, 154–5, 158–9, 179, 182, 185–6, 192–9, 211, 214, 220, 223

Chislett, Charles 45, 92, 104, 106, 126, 145, 152, 178, 188, 216–17

Christmas 4, 71, 94, 100, 212, 216

Church 68, 103, 108, 131–2, 178, 188, 194, 213, 227

cine camera design 4, 6, 9–17 *passim*, 29, 48–53, 68, 96, 109, 146–63 *passim*, 238

cine club 2, 6, 9–18, 28–61, 64–86, 106–7, 133–60, 187, 198, 212–16, 221–7, 238–43, 247
    see also club members; club production

class attitudes 5, 55, 129–31, 153, 163–6, 216–18, 223, 228
    middle class 6–10 *passim*, 14–15, 28, 35, 40, 50, 93–7, 104–7, 112, 143, 179, 183, 192–5
    working class 6, 14, 130, 151, 159, 164

club members 5, 6, 13–17, 28–61, 71, 74, 79–99 *passim*, 123, 134, 183, 239

club production 11, 14, 16, 29–61, 70, 79–81, 133–7, 212–16, 223–4

coal industry 135, 150–2, 159

Cold War 7, 64, 183, 188, 195, 221–2

colonial 15, 19, 64, 103–4, 113, 125, 148, 168, 192–5, 228–31

colour film 8, 44, 65, 92–101 *passim*, 133–4, 179–88 *passim*, 213–17, 226

comedy 44, 134, 178
    see also humour

commemoration 10, 105, 123, 224

commercial cinema 1, 5, 30, 36, 40, 55, 68, 75, 146, 224
    see also amateur/professional relations

community 10–21 *passim*, 42, 86, 122–3, 130–1, 215–16, 247

competition 14, 28, 40–54 *passim*, 65–86 passim, 134, 137, 177, 188, 223–41 *passim*
    see also award

composition 40, 64, 67

Copestake, Peter and Dee 50–1

copyright 16, 53, 111, 248

Coronation 11, 42, 46, 76, 121–2
    see also royalty

Coulter, Alan 51, 93, 223

countryside 83, 136, 157, 182–3

craft films 153–162 *passim*, 165

Croydon Cine Club 29

cruise holidays 119, 147, 177, 188, 191–3, 197

daily life 120, 129, 146, 246
  see also everyday life
Davies, Terence 16
Davison, Bill 80–1
Day, Laurie and Stuart 31
death 10, 50, 75, 83, 104–5, 109, 221, 224
  see also funeral
design *see* cine camera design
diary 72, 103, 178, 191–2
digital 18, 22, 48, 56, 198–200, 241–9 *passim*
  see also archival contexts
disability 112, 211, 216
diversity 12, 16, 21, 211, 131, 135, 167
  see also Black; ethnicity; migration
documentary 12–19 *passim*, 42–3, 65, 83, 152–4, 213, 225–9, 241
documentary movement 14, 15, 71, 77, 135, 145–7, 209–10, 216
domesticity 10, 15, 33, 93, 106–8, 197
  see also gender
dream sequences 40–1
drugs 80, 214

editing 2, 11, 13, 21–2, 32–3, 42, 50
education 8, 28, 52–4, 69, 81–6, 108, 134–6, 164–5, 209–10, 228–30
Eisenstein, Sergei 14, 146
elderly people 101–2, 122–9 *passim*, 154, 159, 169, 217
empire 7, 36, 104, 131, 147, 191–2, 229–30
  see also imperial
ethical issues 21, 111, 113, 244, 248
ethnicity 113, 126, 131, 176
  see also Black; diversity; migration
ethnographic 19, 105–7, 113, 135, 146, 162, 189, 192–4, 230
evacuation 72, 73
Evans, Rob *see* Warrington Cine Society
everyday life 7, 136, 146, 165, 200
  see also daily life
excursion 135, 162, 164, 175, 181–3, 216
experimental 1, 12, 16, 32, 68, 98, 106, 120, 185, 225, 227–31 *passim*

Fairbank, Lucy 126–9, 199
faith communities 104, 105, 131, 143, 227, 230
family 40–55 *passim*, 72–84 *passim*, 92–116, 118–23, 128–33, 145–66, 176–201 *passim*
  audience and 7, 12, 28, 76
fantasy 31, 40, 65, 131
fashion 55, 84, 126, 127, 132, 159, 160, 164–5
Federation of Cinematograph Societies (FCS) 28, 31
Festival of Britain 11, 45, 76, 122
fiction 6–7, 8 *passim*, 19–20, 39–42, 54, 134, 181, 207–10 *passim*, 221–7 *passim*, 241, 243
  see also story film
film gauge
  9.5mm 4, 8, 11, 28–38 *passim*, 43–8 *passim*, 95–9, 103, 154
  16mm 1, 4, 7–11 *passim*, 30, 38, 40–8 *passim*, 97–103 *passim*, 127, 147, 213, 218, 224–5
  17.5mm 3
  35mm 3, 4, 8, 46, 179, 209, 213
  Standard 8mm 4, 8, 38, 46, 78, 82, 101–3, 129, 133, 158, 179, 224
  Super 8 8, 48, 78
film studies 16, 242
First World War 66, 86, 122, 129, 201
fishing 136, 152, 160–2, 197
Flaherty, Robert 70
flashback 213
focal length 40, 123, 146–8, 190
Forgács, Péter 16, 98
found footage 13
free cinema 225, 238
funding 214, 240, 247
funeral 105, 220
  see also death

gadgets 33, 49, 51, 85, 107, 187
gender 13–19 *passim*, 97–8, 129–33, 144, 149, 165–6, 199, 209–11, 230, 243
  see also domesticity
genre 42, 63, 66, 105, 120, 191, 231, 241

Goodger, Mike 126, 217–19
Gough, Linda and Michael 198
Grasshopper Group 54, 82
Grierson, John 71, 77, 209–10

Hanna, Sam 97–101, 145, 154–7, 165, 167–8, 213
Haworth, Dorothy and Geoffrey 188, 195, 223
Higginson, George 33, 99–100, 107, 148, 177, 194
　see also Bolton Amateur Cine Association
Hindley, John 98, 191, 192
hobby press 17, 38, 56, 62–91, 136, 175–7, 187–8, 208–10, 229, 238
　see also advisory press; specialist press
holiday films 9, 11, 14, 49–54, 64, 76, 80–3, 166, 175–207, 209, 217, 222–3, 229
　see also cruise holidays
holidays 34, 37, 47–8, 122, 128, 150, 175–207
　see also excursion; leisure; seaside
Hollywood 32
Home Movies and Home Talkies (*HMHT*) 62, 63, 69–72 *passim*
Hoylake Cine and Video Club (Hoylake Movie Makers) 47
humour 62, 68, 107, 144, 177, 183, 211, 216, 230
　see also comedy
Hyde Cine Society 31–5 *passim*

identity 7, 12, 30, 34, 110–11, 126, 175–6, 228, 243
　see also belonging
imperial 104, 125, 192, 195
　see also empire
Indian Workers's Association 12
insider/outsider relations 113, 129–32, 147–9, 189, 215, 218, 231, 247
Institute of Amateur Cinematographers (IAC) 2, 28, 35–9, 62–3, 69–70, 75, 94, 188
intertitle 124, 132, 149, 150, 154, 191–2, 220, 245

interview 15, 34, 52, 84, 92, 168, 213

Kodak 3, 4, 6, 8, 11, 29, 54, 79, 246

Labour 7, 14, 49
　see also Left
landscape 118, 127–8, 157–9, 175–86 *passim*, 243, 245
lantern slide 31
Lascot, Frances 32
Leek Amateur Cine Society 35, 43, 216
Le Neve Foster 29, 31, 37, 63, 67, 181
　see also Manchester Film Society
Left 7, 14, 38, 40, 143, 153, 195
　see also Labour
leisure 3–17 *passim*, 33, 53–4, 63–86, 126–32, 145, 174–207, 240
lip sync 52
local authority 19, 21, 54, 214, 217–18
Lumière, Auguste 5
Lumière brothers 29
Lumière, Louis 38

Malhotra, Raj 12
Malthouse, Gordon 35, 74, 136, 229, 230
Manchester Film Society 29, 63, 71
　see also Le Neve Foster
manual 3, 66, 119, 175
Martin, John 31, 35, 95, 216
Mass Observation 146, 183
materiality 18, 22, 93, 94, 243, 244
Maxwell, Keith 47–8
　see also Hoylake Cine and Video Club
Mee, Gerald 43, 44, 95
Mekas, Jonas 16
melodrama 32, 40, 191, 209
memories 5, 10, 18–20, 96–8, 105–8, 122–3, 162, 169, 200, 242–6 *passim*
Mercury Movie Makers 84
Merseyside Workers' Film Society 7
metadata 21, 22, 77, 110
Mid-Cheshire Amateur Cinematography Society 40–1
migration 7, 108, 198, 213
　see also Black; diversity

military 8, 9, 72, 82, 178, 195, 209, 220, 223–5
 see also Second World War; wartime
missionary 103, 186, 230–1
Mitchell and Kenyon 42
mobile phone 2, 111, 215, 245
modernity 3, 55, 136, 144, 157–8, 175, 189–90, 198–200, 217, 245
montage 40, 67, 84, 133, 159, 177, 180
Mosque 192
Movie Maker (*MM*) 38, 62, 78–86, 157, 193, 222–4
music 43, 53, 68, 124–8, 131, 134, 160, 193, 217–19, 228

National Service 43–5, 133
Newcastle Amateur Cine Association (Newcastle ACA Film and Video Makers) 29–30, 32, 40, 84
 see also Gough, Linda and Michael
new media 83, 246
newspapers 3, 6, 66, 80, 119
newsreel 3, 5, 9, 42, 45, 49, 119–22 *passim*, 143, 152, 188, 223–8 *passim*
nuclear 183, 221–3
nursery 100, 113, 148, 179, 212

Olivier, Sir Laurence 1
online 21–2, 113, 247–8
overseas 7–15 passim, 38–47 *passim*, 103–4, 147–8, 176–98, 212–13, 228–9

Pathé 3, 4, 6, 8, 29, 31, 47, 96, 223, 246
patronage 49, 67, 70, 166
peacetime 10, 55, 102–3, 123, 124, 163, 187, 191, 220
Pendle Film Society (Pendle Movie Makers) 50, 134, 226
personal films 12, 67
photography *see* still photography
pictorial 72, 136, 183
police 13, 123, 124, 195, 213, 221, 223–4, 226, 227
Powell, Dilys 1
Preston and District Cine Society (Preston Cine Club, Preston Movie Makers) 50, 60
Preston, Harold and Sidney 97, 119–20, 123, 149, 177, 179, 195, 211
projector 3–13 *passim*, 33, 46–7, 63, 66, 69, 96, 108, 168, 188, 200, 246
promotional film 145–7, 150, 162–5 *passim*, 191, 210–11, 219
propaganda film 71
provincial 31, 35, 121, 240
psychosis 64, 225
public health 54, 168, 185, 211, 213
Pudovkin, Victor 67, 94

Ramsden, Betty and Cyril 93, 100–1
rationing 9, 43–4, 71–3, 95, 100, 102, 122, 184
 see also Second World War; wartime
realism 39, 67, 72, 136, 147, 210, 218, 225–6
recruitment
 club members and 33, 52, 227
 employment 147, 150
 overseas 165, 167–8, 212–13
Red Cross 43, 209, 213, 214
redevelopment 51, 64, 101, 131–2, 218
repatriation 19, 113, 242, 247
road safety 10, 45, 51, 74
Rose, Tony 78, 81, 83, 84, 177, 224
Rotha, Paul 1, 38, 70, 71, 153, 210
royalty 10, 42–3, 120–1, 212, 214, 230
 see also Coronation
rural 65, 118, 128, 132, 145–7, 153–7, 162, 183, 224
Russell, Ken 222
Russia 14, 38, 188, 195, 215
 see also Soviet

Salford Cine Society 30, 40
school 3–11 passim, 28, 33, 43–54 *passim*, 97–101, 127, 154–5, 183, 214, 229, 239
science fiction 49
Scottish Amateur Film Festival (SAFF) 34, 37, 39, 106
script 73, 75, 92, 104, 107, 162, 217
scriptwriter 224

seaside 98, 102, 123–4, 150, 160–1, 179–84, 200, 223
second hand equipment 12, 47, 69, 75, 184
Second World War 4, 9, 10, 37, 69, 82, 152, 188, 220–1, 224
  see also military; rationing; wartime
Sewell, George 32, 62, 68–9, 76, 146–7, 209, 230
Shabazz, Menelik 13
Smith, Arthur 44–5, 51, 101, 223–4
snapshot 12, 69, 99, 133, 177, 189
  see also album; still photography
Solo Films 44–6, 51
Southport Movie Makers 46–7, 213–14
  see also Ball, Ashby
sound 8, 33–43 *passim*, 47–8, 50–4 *passim*, 75, 134, 156, 214–19 *passim*, 227
Soviet 54, 67, 82, 146, 153, 223
  see also Russia
Spanish Civil War 8, 188, 215
specialist press 4, 37, 52, 62–91, 95, 133, 137, 146, 153, 215, 231, 241
  see also advisory press; hobby press
sponsorship 36–8, 66, 76, 147, 213–14, 225, 227
sport 77, 99, 120, 123, 178, 181, 227
still photography 6, 30, 44, 95, 215
  see also album; snap shot
Stoke on Trent Amateur Cine Club (Stoke Cine and Video Society) 31, 38, 43, 95, 216
Stockport Amateur Cine Players' Club 40
Stockport Cine Society 29, 37
story film 14, 29, 39, 93
  see also fiction film
students 6, 13, 52–3, 199, 213–14, 217–19 *passim*, 228
Swan Cine Club (Swan Movie Makers) 50
Synagogue 108, 186

tape slide sequence 53
Taylor, Horace Wilfred 188, 195–6, 214–15

teenager 46, 101, 133, 151, 160, 192, 227, 231
  see also adolescent; youth; youth culture
television 11–16 *passim*, 34, 55, 74–87 *passim*, 110–11, 120, 134, 226, 242
  see also British Broadcasting Corporation; broadcasting
Ten Best 38, 39, 45, 54, 75, 80–1, 212–14, 223, 226, 227
Tilston, Angus 29
topical 62, 66, 70, 258
  see also actuality
Townley, Bill 224
trade union 7, 14, 150
trauma 20, 109, 136, 243
travelogue 45, 47, 145, 177, 188, 229, 241
trick filming 31, 40, 101, 144
trophy 91
  see also award

unemployment 69, 79, 121, 130, 143, 150, 209–10, 216, 219
Union international du cinema d'amateur (UNICA) 38–9, 74, 77, 82
university 6, 13, 29, 43, 46, 217

veterans 49, 122–3
video 2, 13, 16, 31, 47, 69, 95, 109, 199, 243–7 *passim*
visibility 21, 97, 164, 195, 213, 243, 247
voice 50, 156, 219, 228
voice-over 156, 219
voyeurism 113, 189

Wain, George 34, 35, 106
Wallasey Amateur Cine Club (Wallasey Cine Group) 30, 52
Warrington Cine Society (Warrington Cine and Video Society) 28–31, 43–52 *passim*, 84
wartime 10, 34–5, 63–4, 102–3, 144, 153–5, 162, 192, 216, 220

see also military; rationing; Second World War
Watkins, Peter 67, 78, 222, 224, 225
wedding 10, 102, 104, 108, 112, 130
welfare 132, 150–1, 164, 211, 228–31
Wirral Movie Makers 52
women
   cine clubs and 5, 30, 32–3, 53
   filmmakers 6, 11, 19, 32–3, 37, 53
workhouse 210, 216
working lives 38, 137, 143–74, 201

Wright, Basil 71, 209
Wright, John 38, 81

youth 150, 151, 159–60, 226–8
   see also adolescent; teenager; youth culture
youth culture 132, 227
   see also adolescent; teenager; youth

Zapruder, Abraham 83
zoos 17, 34–5, 92–3, 122, 156–7, 183